ID0850846

SAME SEX LOVE AND DESIRE AMONG WOMEN IN THE MIDDLE AGES

THE NEW MIDDLE AGES

BONNIE WHEELER, *Series Editor*

The New Middle Ages presents transdisciplinary studies of medieval cultures. It includes both scholarly monographs and essay collections.

PUBLISHED BY PALGRAVE:

SAME SEX LOVE
AND DESIRE AMONG
WOMEN IN THE MIDDLE AGES

edited by
Francesca Canadé Sautman
and Pamela Sheingorn

palgrave

"Pleasure Garden," *Roman de la rose,* 387, fol. 7v. Reproduced by
permission of Valencia, Bibliotecha universitaría.

Adam and Eve, Lucas Cranach the Elder, reproduced with permission of
the Graphische Sammlung, Albertina, Wien.

First published 2001 by PALGRAVE™
175 Fifth Avenue, New York, N.Y. 10010 and
Houndmills, Basingstoke, Hampshire, England RG21 6XS.
Companies and representatives throughout the world.

PALGRAVE is the new global publishing imprint of St. Martin's Press
LLC Scholarly and Reference Division and Palgrave Publishers Ltd.
(formerly Macmillan Press Ltd.).

ISBN 0–312–21056–6

Library of Congress Cataloging-in-Publication Data
Same sex love and desire among women in the Middle Ages / edited by
Francesca
Canadé Sautman and Pamela Sheingorn,
    p.   cm.—(New Middle Ages series)
  Includes index.
  ISBN 0–312–21056–6
    1. Lesbians—History.   2. Lesbianism in literature.   3. Literature,
Medieval.   I. Canadé Sautman, Francesca.   II Sheingorn, Pamela.   III.
Series.
HQ75.5.S25   2001
305.48'9664'0902—dc21   2001031312

A catalogue record for this book is available from the British Library.

Design by Letra Libre, Inc.

First edition: September 2001
10   9   8   7   6   5   4   3   2   1
Printed in the United States of America.

CONTENTS

SERIES EDITOR'S FOREWORD

The New Middle Ages contributes to lively transdisciplinary conversations in medieval cultural studies through its scholarly monographs and essay collections. This series provides focused research in a contemporary idiom about specific but diverse practices, expressions, and ideologies in the Middle Ages; it aims especially to recuperate the histories of medieval women. *Same Sex Love and Desire Among Women in the Middle Ages,* a focused collection of essays edited by Francesca Canadé Sautman and Pamela Sheingorn, is the twenty-first volume in this series. How did medieval women experience and perform same-sex affection and desire? How are the lives and relationships of women who loved women recorded and encoded? This important cross-cultural set of case studies maps and makes visible a range of behaviors that, in the editors' words, "infringe upon and challenge normative expectations as they were lived in the Middle Ages." One effect of this work is to challenge the hegemonic "Othering" and ignorant belittling of the Middle Ages so often found in contemporary cultural theory. But this work primarily challenges us to understand how Eve's daughters, living in and shadowed by her guilt, saw each other as subjects and objects of desire.

Bonnie Wheeler
Southern Methodist University

1.1 *Adam and Eve,* Lucas Cranach. Reproduced with permission of the Graphische Sammlung Albertina, Wien.

CHAPTER ONE

INTRODUCTION: CHARTING THE FIELD

Francesca Canadé Sautman and Pamela Sheingorn

> *Framing the essays in the volume, the editors examine current critical thinking on medieval women, gender, and same-sex desire, provide new interpretations, and propose avenues for further research.*

Prologue: What Is Visible

Written sources for the Middle Ages preserve no language, no affective grammar through which medieval women might have expressed their emotions of love and desire for other women. In every legal case involving women's same-sex desire, the abjectifying, ill-fitting vocabulary of the court is drawn over them like a shroud; in every literary manifestation, the expression of such desires is contrived through a muddling syntax of silence. In every instance in which women discovered and acted on such inclinations toward each other, they groped for words capable of whispering the interpellation of the beloved while concealing the nature of their emotions from guardians, patrons, and confessors. And possibly, in the inchoate workings of a transgression not fully matured to become the act of naming, they whispered it even to themselves. Thus, we cannot expect to find such emotions made evident, let alone easily recognizable and immediately readable hundreds of years later. Relationships characterized by same-sex love may have been nameless, but we need not read them as powerless, for we must seriously consider the possibility that people did not feel the need to name themselves, to enter self-imposed categories; rather, as the evidence shows, they fought—in deeds, if not in words—against the categories imposed on them, as did the fifteenth-century Eleno whose transgendered history Israel Burshatin has uncovered.[1] And we should perhaps remind ourselves that there is no reason to expect people to construct categories to fit their experiences and emotions just because heteronormative power centers do so in order to exercise control. In effect, remaining nameless can signify not only powerlessness but also, paradoxically, power reclaimed through resistance to externally imposed categories with their implicit negative assessments and marginalizations. Further, it is possible to be visible, and perhaps even to find power in visibility, without being named. Given the intensely visual nature of medieval culture,[2] we might understand the visual as one of those "gaps" through which we catch glimpses of what remained unnamed. That is, we catch such glimpses if we attend to what we see. As Diane Wolfthal has noted, "The scarcity of gay studies of medieval art might suggest a lack of imagery, but the real problem is that such images have been ignored."[3] One such image can serve as a visual metaphor for our project in this book: to render visible without insisting upon categorizing or naming.

In the *Romance of the Rose,* one of the most widely circulated and frequently illustrated of all medieval secular texts, the author of the first section, Guillaume de Lorris, describes a pleasure garden seen through the eyes of a would-be lover (Figure 1.2). Filled with songbirds and herb-scented air, the garden functions as a site where "fair folk" take their pleasures. A manuscript of the *Romance of the Rose* made in Paris early in the fifteenth century provides a pictorial representation of the vividly described acrobats, singers, dancers, and musicians in the pleasure garden.[4] We note a round dance at the far left, and a female figure throwing her tambourine up in the air at the far right. Just to the left of the center, which is marked by an acrobat walking on her hands, is a couple described as follows:

Two very charming maidens with their hair in a single braid and dressed only in their tunics were led into the dance by Pleasure, who

1.2 "Pleasure Garden," *Roman de la rose,* Valencia, Biblioteca universitaría 387, fol. 7v

bore himself most nobly; but I need not say how beautifully they danced: one would approach the other very elegantly, and when they were close together, their lips would touch in such a way that you might have thought they were kissing one another's faces. They knew well how to sway in the dance. I cannot describe it to you, but as long as I could have seen those people thus exerting themselves in the rounds and dances, I would never have wanted to move.[5]

The artist has attended carefully to most aspects of the text, though the two "maidens" perform in a space separated from the round dance, whereas the text indicates that they were brought into the round. The two dancers are rendered at the precise moment described: the dancer to the left, hands on hips, is approached by the other dancer, who extends an arm across the back of her partner to grasp her shoulder and bring them close together. At that moment they turn their heads toward each other and their lips touch. The exaggerated curves of their lower bodies encode swaying motion. But where language leaves a gap, refusing to name—"I need not say"; "you might have thought"; "I cannot describe"—the artist's visual interpretation fills it. The shoulder grasp is an embrace, one in which power differential is signaled as the embracer claims the embracee, the lover claims the beloved.[6] The touch of lips is a kiss, and the curves of the swaying bodies meld the two forms into one ovoid shape, with the characteristic contour of the mandorla—the highly sexualized almond, the ambiguous and disruptive diamond—gaping between their arms:[7] in all of these features, the representation visualizes the eroticism of same-sex desire.

Similarly we aim, in this book, to make same-sex love and desire among medieval women visible to our readers, neither by forcing contemporary categories onto texts and experiences, nor by compelling resilient medieval cultural practices to divest themselves of their complexities, but by bringing together a number of case studies in each of which the author has interrogated a deceitful normativity. We are not charting out a definitional continuum of lesbian identity but rather a history of the range of same-sex behaviors between women that infringe upon and challenge normative expectations as they were lived in the Middle Ages.

The essays that follow look at the powerful consequences of same-sex affectivity, especially when strong erotic tension is present, with the understanding that not all such relations need develop into full-fledged intercourse to warrant our attention. In particular, we look at those relationships between women that make all others in their lives secondary. We also pay careful attention to instances, historical or fictional, in which a breakdown of gender norms and reconfigurations of the performance of gender enable a reconsideration of affective relations between women. In short, we concern ourselves with the ways a multitude of factors, doctrinal, social, legal, political, and personal, shaped the sexual landscape of medieval women and the means they may have found to make their affective and erotic voices heard.

Theoretical Spectrum

Any investigation of sexualities in the distant past is compelled, at the onset, to contend with theories of sexual identity forged by postmodernists, most notably Michel Foucault, or rather by certain readings of Foucault that have spawned a by-now firmly entrenched critical tradition. Further, the long-standing debate between essentialism and constructionism has taken a new turn, having moved through the phase in which the term "essentialist" was reduced to an insulting epithet. This new turn is not a reversal, for it does not mean that essentialism is the most desirable or the only possible response to some of constructionism's extreme positions. The discussion might better be framed as one that avoids the dicta of extreme constructionism, the position that insists on considering homosexuality (regardless of sex or gender of participants) strictly as an emergent sexuality of the late nineteenth century, crafted by people like Hirschfeld, Havelock Ellis, or Krafft-Ebing and their disciples; this position holds to the assertion that there were simply no lesbians before 1900. In this school of thought, the historical production of "homosexuality" is inseparable from the term "identity," which is itself laden with undisclosed problems and seems to justify the exile of sexual patterns of the distant past and their attendant affirmations of same-sex consciousness to a neverland peopled by crazed essentialists. George Chauncey pointed out these flaws in a 1983 essay in which he contested the assumption that "doctors created and defined the identities of 'inverts' and 'homosexuals' at the turn of the century," for "[s]uch assumptions attribute inordinate power to ideology as an autonomous social force; they oversimplify the complex dialectic between social conditions, ideology, and consciousness which produced gay identities, and they belie the evidence of preexisting subcultures and identities contained in the literature itself."[8] Foucault's revolutionary thinking on the production of knowledge within society and on the mechanisms by which discourses constitute power, and his attack on the social undergirdings of intellectual authority have paradoxically been subsumed at times into a hasty reading of the history of sexuality, then made into canon and dogma. Resistance to such a dogma is strongly expressed in the essays in this volume by Edith Benkov and Ruth Vanita.

We might more fruitfully start from the understanding articulated by Diana Fuss in *Essentially Speaking* that the two positions of essentialism and constructionism have a great deal more in common than is usually thought. Fuss argued that essentialism can be "*essential* to social constructionism, a point that powerfully throws into question the stability and impermeability of the essentialist/constructionist binarism."[9] She pointed out that constructionism often displaces essentialism rather than countering it, using such "maneuvers" as pluralizing terms rather than answering the question of what "motivates or dictates the continued semantic use" of certain terms, like "women" or "histories." In fact, she added, "it is difficult to see how constructionism can be constructionism without a fundamental dependency upon essentialism."[10]

Among scholars, medievalists may be especially sensitive to the necessity of carefully documenting the historical conditions of text production, whether of a literary work or a record of public behavior, thereby avoiding the essentialist temptation. Karma Lochrie, for example, has recently questioned the "cluster of truths about premodern sexualities" that medievalists have derived from their readings of Foucault: "that they were organized around acts rather than identities, that they were discursively produced, and that this discursive production in turn came to characterize a whole regime of knowledge and power in the twentieth-century."[11] She charges that "the Christian Middle Ages . . . functions as the historical 'other' in Foucault's history of sexuality, as that time when discourse about sexuality was 'markedly unitary.'" She concludes, "Neither his Middle Ages nor his view of medieval sexuality . . . will aid in the kind of cultural genealogies that Foucault's work so admirably fostered."[12]

It is indeed true that Foucault was neither a medievalist nor, for that matter, a classicist. Yet different readings of pertinent texts of the classical Greek period by dissenters from the "sex before sexuality" position, like the French lesbian philosopher Geneviève Pastre in her *Athènes et le "Péril saphique,"*[13] have been ignored. Further, medievalist John Boswell's work has come under such fierce attack that the challenge he posed to our thinking as historians of sexuality goes unnoticed by many. It is now known, however, that Foucault was impressed and troubled by Boswell's work, and had planned to write his last volumes of the *History of Sexuality* in response to it. In a 1983 interview, for instance, Foucault clearly expressed his interest in Boswell's formulation of a medieval episteme of sexual genealogy.[14]

Possibly it is these very genealogies, eloquently forged by Foucault in *The Order of Things,* that suggest valuable tools for understanding the place of that sometimes vague and conceptually fraught entity, the Middle Ages, in relation to other periods in which the discursive dimensions of sex and sexuality were being actively elaborated. And possibly, Foucault's brilliant excursus on Velazquez's *Las Meninas,* which opens *The Order of Things,* should be seen as one of the most incisive texts written on the ambiguous and mutually informing relationship between visibility and invisibility.

Foucault did not separate the Middle Ages from what he defined as a "pre-classical" period, in which resemblance predominated in the organization of knowledge, and although his genealogies of knowledge may not always stand up to detailed historical verification in the medieval period, their broad outlines can remain suggestive. This discussion begins with a forceful anchoring of representation in the concept of resemblance: "Up to the end of the sixteenth century, resemblance played a constructive role in the knowledge of Western culture. It was resemblance that largely guided exegesis and the interpretation of texts; it was resemblance that organized the play of symbols, made possible knowledge of things visible and invisible, and controlled the art of representing them."[15]

Of the four concepts on which Foucault based his sixteenth-century episteme, three in particular—*convenentia, aemulatio,* and sympathy—allow a reading of scientific discourse in which discourses on sexuality have a place. In these, the Middle Ages do not appear so much as the "other" of the modern period, but as the cultural and historical site in a long-term continuum on which precise epistemes were located and a certain type of heuristics was put into practice. These knowledge categories identified by Foucault raise questions about medieval perceptions of sexual differentiation and the ways gender differences were connected to the world at large, reflected that world, and were readable within it. In such a system, the "resemblances" between male and female bodies can be seen as border zones in which female encroachment remains possible and the fundamentals of difference can be erased. According to the Hippocratic-Galenic system, the female body remains a less complete version of the male but shares some of its reproductive characteristics, a theory that Guillaume de Conches, who taught in Paris until about 1120, would extend to make female sperm an active ingredient in procreation. Louise Fradenburg, writing on Thomas Aquinas's *Commentary on the Nicomachean Ethics,* noticed a parallel relationship in Aquinas's discussion of gender characteristics: "While Aquinas distinguishes men with good habits from women and imperfect men, these categories are not secure. Women are not the same as men, but they resemble men (the kind with bad habits) closely; as ethical subjects this resemblance to perfect men is flawed ('qualified') but unmistakable. This figure of flawed but evident similarity formulates an intimate or proximate other, a distanced but still recognizable (self-)image, an imaginary support for the perfect ethical subject."[16]

Jo Ann McNamara has underscored the historicity of gender construction in the medieval period, speaking of a "crisis of masculinity" or "Herrenfrage" between the mid-eleventh and early twelfth century.[17] Medieval models of gender and the sexual body were at variance with Aristotle's more frankly male-centered and male-dominated model because they maintain maleness as the core of the human person and see femaleness as an accidental deviation. McNamara reminds us that such models could allow women to return to that "natural maleness" by divesting themselves of all "womanly" functions, namely sex with men and procreation. Renunciation of their inferior status as women enabled them to be recognized, within the limits of particular communities, as equal to men. This possibility was, of course, short-lived and confined to very particular monastic movements, such as that of Robert of Arbrissel, who responded to the virulent attempts on the part of the monastic clergy to separate men and women completely with a doctrine of ministering to women and incorporating them in communities in which they could even become leaders. In the context of the gender crisis identified by McNamara, such movements were rapidly labeled heretical and suppressed, but they revealed the clearly fragile nature of the medieval gender order, its instabilities and potential ruptures.

Another witness to this fragility can be found in the many medieval depictions, both historical and fictional, of women who cross-dressed.[18] The medieval gender order, or rather, as Joan Cadden puts it, "a cluster of gender-related notions, sometimes competing, sometimes mutually reinforcing; sometimes permissive, sometimes constraining; sometimes consistent, sometimes, ad hoc,"[19] stands in stark contrast to the regimented and all-encompassing sexual order of the modern period that Foucault retraced, and also problematizes the trend in medieval feminist scholarship that sees in the "one-sex" theory merely an example of the male specularity sharply criticized by Luce Irigaray.[20] The renouncing of one's sex, which in some secular contexts took the form of the "sworn virgin" custom,[21] is a telling difference between Western medieval and modern sexualities, one whose import cannot be ignored.

The system of resemblance that Foucault thought essential to the pre-classical period, up to the early seventeenth century, is not merely useful in deciphering the archaeology of knowledge. It can profitably be read against those medieval canons that provided neat articulations of entire sets of anatomical questions and sexual behaviors, which they appeared to organize into categories structured by the uncontested belief in binary sexuality. Thomas Laqueur, however, has argued that a one-sex system of differentiation dominated in the West until the eighteenth century.[22] This theory has been refuted, notably by Katherine Park and Robert A. Nye, who maintain that the difference between sex and gender makes it impossible to posit a Middle Ages in which a one-sex system prevailed.[23]

Outside of theological and scientific discourse, medieval textual practice and medieval historical experience provide different solutions to the quandaries of gender. When historical figures like Joan of Arc or Jeanne des Armoises seriously trouble the gender order while surreptitiously trying to invade and infiltrate it, binary sexual ideology is put under severe strains. For instance, Joan's short hair, wearing of armor, and role as a leader of troops in battle may have been counterbalanced by the appellation "la pucelle" (the maiden), which reestablishes the questionable status of women's sexual bodies and legal condition.[24] Indeed, the concept of the "maiden," shored up by folk belief[25] and non-Christian traditions, occupies a middle ground. It is less threatening than the category "woman" when propelled into gender-inappropriate domains, apparently because the maiden body is devoid of—or represented as devoid of—the mark of sex. Works of fiction offer other sets of solutions. Where sexual binaries seem to reign supreme, alternative forms of embodiment are proposed in which surrogate identities can be read as displacing the strict, overarching power of the binary. Thus, the functions of zoomorphism, expressed through full or partial transformations such as the doe in Marie de France or Melusine's disturbing tail,[26] provide rich areas for investigating the profound anxieties that may have resided at the heart of Western medieval perceptions of gender. Until recently medievalists have analyzed these embodiments primarily in relation to their potential sources in distinct ethnic and cultural traditions. A different understanding would question their assimilation into binary divisions of gender and seek formulations of a third or more gender categories through the medium of the fantasmic. Further, such interpretations are encouraged by the timing of a shift in attitude toward bestiality in the Middle Ages. As Joyce Salisbury points out, although "the early church fathers recognized similarities between human and animal bodies," they also identified "irreconcilable differences that kept them apart." As a result, early penitentials rated bestiality fairly low in lists of sins and imposed only a mild penance.[27] With time and the influence of the Eastern Church, attitudes shifted so that animals were considered to be partners in sin. By the turn of the millennium, bestiality and homosexuality often received the same penance. Differences were articulated, with the aim of punishing while maintaining the distance stipulated by doctrine. By the twelfth and thirteenth centuries, scholastics were ranking bestiality as the worst of sexual sins and legislating to create firmer boundaries. It is this uneasiness, this anxiety over separation and the proximity to the sin of homosexuality, that suggests new ways of reading narratives of animal or monstrous spouses.[28]

In spite of the many advances made in theorizing about sexualities, lesbians have little chance of seeing their history written if "homosexuality"—as a combination of practices, behaviors, networks, and sociabilities building up to an "identity"—was created by modern sexologists as a pathological condition linked to mental illness and criminality. When identity is seen to emerge both as a means of survival through subculture reinforcement and as an internalization of identity models formed and imposed by the medical academy, lesbians become merely an appendage to a version of the more visible grand narrative of homosexual identity. In this narrative, women, especially during the Western Middle Ages, are commonly assumed to be devoid of any sexual history not shaped by men. Diana Fuss has pointed out that the quasi exclusion of lesbians from the definitional field of homosexuality has reinforced an apparent lesbian investment in "essentialism"; at the same time, this exclusion raises questions about the validity of such all-encompassing theories.[29]

Well before nineteenth-century identity formation, however, terms denoting lesbians and lesbianism were in use, as has been demonstrated by Bernadette Brooten in her work on late antique and early Christian expressions of love between women.[30] As Marie-Jo Bonnet notes, the term itself begins to acquire modern acceptance in the time of Brantôme, who employed the word "Lesbos" knowingly.[31] Emma Donoghue for the seventeenth century,[32] Randolph Trumbach and others for the eighteenth,[33] and Francesca Canadé Sautman for the last decades of the nineteenth[34] have all criticized the demotion of lesbian identities to a post-homosexual epistemology. Work on the history of women loving women should be seen as inseparably linked to the history of all women's struggles to assert independent livelihoods and ways of life over the centuries. One path has been laid out by historian Judith Bennett: "To approach the social history of lesbianisms in the Middle Ages, I suggest that we try broadening our perspective to include women whom I have chosen to call 'lesbian-like': women whose lives might have particularly offered opportunities for same-sex love; women who resisted norms of feminine behavior based on heterosexual marriage; women who lived in circumstances that allowed them to nurture and support other women. . . . 'Lesbian-like' can allow us to imagine in plausible ways the opportunities for same-sex love that actual women once encountered."[35]

As Bennett points out, women's history "has resolutely defined 'women' as 'heterosexual women.'"[36] Yet identity is foremost a reaction to marginalization and ostracism; it has little to do with the individual and everything with society, and thus differs from consciousness and self-perception. To deny the latter, we would have to surmise a medieval model of homosexuality whereby persons who were keenly aware of their same-sex sexual proclivities—regardless of what they called them, or whether they called them anything at all—would never have met those who shared like feelings except purely by accident, and would not have sought out or known how to seek out ways to find such persons in order to fulfill their desires. Scholarship on medieval homosexualities and on queering medieval sexualities has revealed a much more complex situation among men with same-sex affectivities.[37] Although more work in this direction with respect to women is certainly needed, it is unwarranted to assume that same-sex affective choices were unknown to medieval women or that women were too acculturated in the oblivion of their sexual desires to resist the imposition of heterosexual life upon them. Foucault himself made a careful distinction between identity and consciousness, one that contemporary readings have tended to overlook:

> . . . I would say that homosexual consciousness certainly goes beyond one's individual experience and includes an awareness of being a member of a particular social group. This is an undeniable fact that dates back to ancient times. Of course, this aspect of their collective consciousness changes over time and varies from place to place. It has, for instance, taken the form of membership in a kind of secret society, membership in a cursed race, membership in a segment of humanity at once privileged and persecuted, all kinds of different modes of collective consciousness.[38]

In addressing questions of the distant past and the need to historicize it, we have to rethink the ways in which the category "identity" has been made to operate in the early history of sexuality. We certainly do not assume that medieval women expressed a clearly defined and public "identity." But that is something quite different from assuming that they had no consciousness or self-perception at all. This seems to us to be the false dichotomy implied, for example, in D. M. Hadley's introduction to the collection *Masculinity in Medieval Europe:*

> It is important to note that although homosexual activity might be condemned there had not yet developed a concept of the homosexual figure. The "stigmatization of homosexuals as an aberrant cate-

gory of men set apart from the 'normal' is a modern phenomenon; to medieval authors the euphemistic 'sins *contra naturam*' were possibilities open to all men, in contrast to 'modern notions of "innate homosexuality,"'" as Balzaretti puts it. Proper sexual restraint was what was expected and those who failed to exercise it were liable to criticism; ultimately it did not matter whether the failing was adultery, sex *contra naturam* or clerical marriage.[39]

It has been assumed that the study of same-sex affectivity in the distant past could yield merely fantasmic visions (of inquisitors, for instance) or "isolated sexual acts." But how does the sum of these "isolated acts" add up in the lifetime of an individual who negotiates the system of patriarchal gender enforcement in ways consonant with the particularities of her time and culture—experiencing a complex range of prohibitions, dangers, rejections, and tolerance? This "sum" of cultural experiences and tensions strikes us as an important site for the exploration of early same-sex sensibilities and for the retracing of their discursive practices. Yet as long as we are bound to the concept of "identity," we will be blinded to the rich array of possibilities for resistant or dissident sexual expression that people of the distant past may have explored.

The presupposition of lack of same-sex consciousness has to be interrogated in relation to another, more foundational assumption, namely that matters of sexuality were unknown to the pre-modern individual. Although scholars have recently unearthed considerable amounts of documentation on sexual behavior in the Middle Ages,[40] that position remains firmly entrenched. In general terms, as Jacqueline Murray pointed out in her landmark essay, "Twice Marginal and Twice Invisible," "It is contrary to evidence to suppose that the Middle Ages were devoid of the erotic expression of sexual desire or, for that matter, individual sexual preference."[41] The terms of the debate thus need to be drastically altered. It is highly problematic to assume that sexuality begins to exist only when discourse says it does, either by explicitly naming it (as in the modern period) or by speaking authoritatively of it (as in the medieval period).

The attention given to enormously varied sexual matters in the French fabliaux presents one instance of a site of intense preoccupation with defining gender and sexuality. This corpus has consistently been read as an affirmation of the workability of the heterosexual project, but can be understood just as profitably as the expression of unchecked anxieties about it. A steady stream of interpretation of the fabliaux has only recently broken away from strictly normative models. Reading against the "naturalizing" tendency of traditional criticism, Howard Bloch refocused the reading of fabliaux on their "scandalous" content, albeit with the uncritical presupposition that "desire" can effectively be located in women's bodies without any agency of their own;[42] E. Jane Burns's feminist analysis in *Bodytalk* was an early attempt to identify an autonomous language of women's bodies as a form of rebellion against the specularity of male visions of the body and social order;[43] and John Baldwin's review of fabliaux literature insisted on the constructed nature of sexuality.[44] These readings of the fabliaux have not, however, taken into account the strong homoeroticism and the intensive border raids against gender norms found in several of the most prominent fabliaux. Much more needs to be done in particular in the direction of queer readings of numerous fabliaux (in addition to the well-known "Berenger au long cul") marked by gender and erotic ambiguities. Edith Benkov, for instance, has offered a queer reading of the most apparently heteronormative motifs, like those found in the fabliau of the "Souhaits Saint Martin."[45]

Further, any attempt to unearth expressions of same-sex love among medieval women must give ample consideration to the factor of sex itself, meaning here the practice of sexual acts. When medieval sexualities existed in a Christian cultural environment, they were marked by the ecclesiastical condemnation of sex and by intense self-reflection on its pitfalls and dangers among the clerical class and in religious groups. In this climate, celibacy was not merely the result of Church-inspired repression and terror exercised against the body, but it played an important societal role as well. At the nexus of several sharp crises in gender enforcement,[46] celibacy could have negative value in lay society, as has been shown with respect to aristocratic and patrician marriage.[47] Furthermore, we must guard against the tendency to read the musings of clerics as the full expression of a society's views. In popular contexts, in which, for instance, issues such as the protection of honor and reputation far supersede nostalgia for an Edenic pre-sexual world, sex is an entirely different matter.[48]

Sex as a defining factor in establishing same-sex identity also needs to be revisited. For instance, pornography, a focus of debates and alternative readings today, has its own history. Lynn Hunt points out that although early modern pornographers "were not intentionally feminists *avant la lettre,* . . . their portrayal of women, at least until the 1790s, often valorized female sexual activity and determination much more than did the prevailing medical texts."[49] What we call pornography today, Andrew Taylor has suggested, is a thing of modern, technologically sophisticated capitalism, with the means to make the representation of explicit sexual acts both mass-produced and eminently visible; the Middle Ages, on the other hand, would only have "dirty bits" available.[50] And last, but by no means least, we cannot continue to assume, even in speaking of the position of sex in Western medieval societies, the culturally and religiously monolithic nature of these societies, and to write as if they were completely defined and silenced by a Christian majority. Although dominant in the West, the medieval Christian community was not immune to contact with other communities that forged their own systems for regulating sex and gender. In this volume, Sahar Amer's essay demonstrates that the vocabulary for describing female same-sex activity was much more developed in Arabic literature and could be adopted by Western medieval writers, and Fedwa Malti-Douglas's essay addresses the regulation of sex and gender with respect to women in the Arabic tradition as well as providing an overview of current work on male homosexuality in the Arabic Middle Ages. Discussion of medieval Jewish life has, to date, concerned the construction of male sexualities,[51] and there remains an urgent need for work that explores the sexual worlds of medieval Jewish women.[52] And in this volume as well, Ruth Vanita's analysis of Indian devotional material questions Western assumptions about defining early lesbian history.

In addition to gender, we also need to pay attention to the other dimension of sex, that "factic," biological basis for gender construction against whose apparently unproblematic simplicity Judith Butler has warned us. Butler suggests that "biological" sex is too hastily viewed as the solid, unquestionable ground on which the more fantasmatic gender is constructed; rather, she argues, sex itself is constituted in discourse as a form of knowledge.[53] Claire Fanger artfully summarizes Butler's position: "[Sex] derives its cultural power from an assumed reality of being that is supposed to underlie it and to be separable from the cultural knowledge that overlays it, but in fact is not."[54] In effect, interrogating the discursive control mechanisms, representational systems, and potential for instabilities and deviations in medieval women's sexual bodies is a crucial aspect of deconstructing medieval heteronormativity. The doxa on the nature of women's sexual bodies is central to it, yet constantly threatening, because that threat is inscribed in the theoretical foundations of medieval biology. If woman is indeed an imperfect male, one can expect her to aspire to perfection, which would mean making herself thoroughly male, or at least moving in that direction, as has been argued with respect to medieval women saints.[55] Such a contradiction elicited response; for example, the letter to Heloise in which Abelard establishes the genealogy of the nun's condition argues for and defends the preeminence of women, but also attempts to reinscribe their inferior status as weaker beings, as Alcuin Blamires has elucidated.[56] Understanding women's sexual bodies has to account for the coexistence of the binaries underscored by patristic as well as secular literature—man is the head, woman the body; man the flesh, woman the skin; manliness is virtue and strength, womanliness is frailty and weakness. For an Early Christian writer like Tertullian, all manners of deviations from socially acceptable and strictly gendered dress were crimes against the natural order and were associated with the wantonness of the *fricatrices*. Clement of Alexandria also condemned homoeroticism among men and women and called for strict gender differentiation; for Clement, in fact, the natural order demands that males be active and females passive, so that female-female marriages, apparently known to him in his time, seemed an unspeakable practice both for the women "taking the active role in marrying" and for those assuming the role of bride.[57]

As Kathleen Biddick suggested in her now-classic essay on "visual technologies," embodiment is a crucial structure of gender in medieval cultures; both the violence of gender and the contentious, disruptive nature of sexual being and sexual acts are tattooed on women's bodies.[58] Western medieval culture had a relationship to "body parts" altogether different from our own. Not only was special public status conferred on some (honor was to be rendered to the head as its seat) but discrete parts of the body were thought of as the locus of all sorts of emotions and qualities: masculinity and male honor in the beard,[59] truth and rage in the tooth,[60] and courage in the stomach. In the language of love, the privileged conduits of emotions and desire were the eyes and mouth.

The essays in this volume bring together the insights of feminist scholarship, gender studies, and queer studies to reconfigure the presence and voice of women who desired or loved other women—and at times fully and dangerously consummated their love for them. In so doing, these essays reconsider the very ways pre-modern sexualities are discursively deployed: many view terms such as heterosexuality and homosexuality not merely as linguistic anachronisms but as categories intrinsically unable to serve the complex array of self-perceptions, legal definitions, and visual and literary representations that chart the busy map of medieval sexualities.

The impact of queer studies and gender studies on this type of historiography has been huge, greater than some of its detractors have been willing to acknowledge. Recently, Allan Frantzen has sought to take queer theory to task for its inconsequent rhetoric; he proposes an alternative model, focused on "shadowing."[61] Although it is true that one cannot indiscriminately embrace any and all writing that comes to us wrapped in the flag of "queer theory"—a term that Lauren Berlant and Michael Warner suggested in 1995 might itself need unpacking and would be felicitously replaced by "queering"[62]—it seems to us that Frantzen's stance of suspicion toward queer studies neither renders justice to actual work in that direction by other medievalists nor necessarily clarifies the matter. "Shadows" and "shadowing" can be useful concepts in dealing with the distant past.[63] However, the terms also have an uncomfortable textual and cultural history in gay and lesbian experience, one inescapably linked to echoes of the "love-that-dares-not-speak-its-name" period, and to representations of homosexuals and lesbians skulking in the dark, marginalized and rejected, a view that current work on

lesbian and gay cultures in the modern age makes increasingly un-
tenable. It might possibly be more useful for all scholars interested
in problematizing the presumptive heteronormativity of the distant
past to agree, regardless of terminology, that much needs to be done
and can be fruitfully accomplished with an obdurate will to interrogate silences, to bring out the unsaid, to expose fractures and
complexities. This is certainly the perspective taken by the essays in
this volume.

"Queering," a heuristic tool devised originally by scholars like
Eve Sedgwick and Judith Butler, has made it possible to understand the function of the (homo)social and (homo)erotic versus
the fully sexual or the sexual in the purely genital sense, both
within cultural performances and in opaque, resilient texts.[64] It
has, in particular, fostered a new kind of reading for the questions
of "friendships," passion, and sex. Foundational studies in relation
to medieval texts have been Carolyn Dinshaw's work on Middle
English literature,[65] which was followed by an impressive series of
incisive essays that engage multiple layers of medieval cultural expression and representation.[66]

However, a central problem has become increasingly clear: queer
studies has paid insufficient attention to the specific roles played by
desire among women, although gender studies has been pointing to
such affectional and romantic instabilities as fundamental discursive
sites. These fields must be brought together in a review of women's
roles in medieval sexualities. As Bruce Holsinger has pointed out:

> . . . it is important to realize the extent to which modern readings
> of medieval devotional texts have failed to take into account the
> centrality of homoerotic desire to women's religious experience and
> expression. Much of the secondary literature on women's religious
> discourse uses phrases such as "unashamedly erotic" or "even sexual
> at times" when describing female devotion to God or Jesus Christ,
> but when a woman expresses an intense longing for and devotion to
> the Virgin Mary or other female figures, the language is described in
> [Barbara] Newman's words as "asexual eros."[67]

We need to look more closely at what gender transgression really
means for both fictional and actual medieval women, what these

models tell us of the possibilities ascribed to women (what is expected and what is tolerated from a woman constructed as manly?), the limitations that certain religious paradigms placed on transgression. Particularly relevant are the models found in saints' lives, in which cross-dressed female saints or mannishly gendered saints such as Thecla are breezily reincorporated and inscribed into normative religious discourse.[68] In this volume, both Susan Schibanoff and Lisa Weston read female saints against the grain of heteronormativity. We need more work seeking out the homosocial in medieval women's lives[69] and its particular links to play, eroticism, and bending the gender order.[70] And we need to acknowledge the complicating factor that not all representations of women in the Middle Ages are negative,[71] that some can therefore offer other models for identity and consciousness of self to women inclined to seek out a woman-defined world. It is in the thin cracks of these narratives that we might find some deviations from unthreatening appropriations of gender-transgressive behaviors among women that may lead to traces of same-sex sensibilities.

The essays in this volume compel us to consider same-sex desire among women as a writable and important historical category that enables us to interrogate assumptions of heteronormativity in the medieval world and to complicate the presumed absence of same-sex identities.

The "Problem" of Sodomy

Mark Jordan's reevaluation of sodomy's genealogy in medieval culture,[72] followed by Karma Lochrie's discussion of sodomy as a "female deviance,"[73] invites a reconsideration of its place in same-sex love among medieval women. Is sodomy out of place in a consideration of same-sex love among women? We suggest here that on the contrary, the invention of sodomy can be understood as a crucial hinge in the history of women's same-sex affectivity. Given that binary thinking about sexual practices and sexuality does not apply well to the Middle Ages, we might do well to rethink the "problem" of sodomy in relation to women. It will then appear that sodomy inflects a whole set of unnamed and even unarticulated practices and emotions around same-sex affectivity, straining against the realm of the discursive, the public, and the condemned. In effect, the invention of sodomy may have had a major impact on the sexual horizons of medieval women, specifically on the restrictions they would be taught to envision.

Jordan's careful analysis of the semantic and ideological underpinnings of the medieval concept of sodomy identified its precise functions in the historical marginalization and repression of persons choosing erotic and affective partners of the same sex. It might seem that these developments had little or no impact on the construction of women's sexualities and that sodomy followed a parallel course, relevant to women because the sodomite was characterized as an effeminate male. But what of the relevance to women of his pendant, the predatory, aggressive male who hid more successfully behind apparent heteronormativity but was nevertheless identified and held up to opprobrium, for instance in the French vernacular, which lists "sodomites" and "*fout-en-cul*" separately?[74]

It behooves us first to contextualize the discussion, acknowledging that early Western cultures do not appear to have been permissive toward same-sex love and that this negative position became more rigid after the invention of sodomy, or, as John Boswell suggested, at a specific moment in the mid-medieval period.[75] The classical world did not afford women the same economic and political potential as men to live a double life that combined proper marriage and family with fulfillment of same-sex erotic desires. Acculturation into heterosexuality was not identical for men and women: to the latter not only was procreation prescribed as a sacred task and duty, but heterosexuality assigned as well the obligation to provide vast amounts of unpaid labor within the household. Thus, there was no question of allowing women to pursue freely same-sex affinities: passions and strong emotions directed at other women would be as dangerous as unauthorized sexual practices, because they would compete with and displace women's allegiance to marriage and their obligation to serve men and the family unit.

According to Jordan, the invention of sodomy occurred in a precise historical context, between Peter Damian's virulent pamphlet and Alain of Lille's eloquent naturalizing of heteronormativity.[76]

Further, at this time the intense struggles around the reconfigura-
tion and distribution of gender roles outlined by Jo Ann McNamara
were taking place in Western society. This process had grave consequences for women, mainly in two directions. A certain equilibrium
in the negative had been achieved in biblical discourse and apoc-
ryphal texts—that is, acts reprehensible between men were deemed
reprehensible as well among women.[77] Now, however, the balance
of perversity tipped distinctly, and males became primary perpetra-
tors of the "foul vice," not least because Peter Damian's overriding
concern was the control of clerics. Medieval theologians would
continue to refer to women engaging in same-sex love as
sodomites, but the construction of the sodomite as one who engages in sodomy as often and with as much impunity as circumstances permit had congealed around the persona of a male,
effeminate in his mores as a receptor, shameless and socially irre-
sponsible as a predator. This focus on male sexuality and its deviations meant that the enforcement of heterosexual coupling and
normative familial structures for women would intensify: if men
were now being evaluated with respect to their manliness, they had
to prove themselves virile by their ability to have sexual relations
with women, their public affirmation of the will to engage in heterosexual intercourse, and the begetting of heirs as confirmation
that they had done so. If effeminate men who refused or shirked
these duties became the center of a discourse of exclusion and punishment, then women were to be the means of that enforcing, the
sometimes passive, sometimes militant participants in that testing.
Any exploration or problematization of their own sexuality would
be consciously obliterated in favor of the added duty of providing
men and their social networks with the incontrovertible proof of
their proper mores. The invention of sodomy as an identifiable, cri-
sis-producing category thus had as its inescapable consequence increased expectations and enforcing of heterosexual performance
among women.

The second major consequence is that the invention of sodomy
marked the beginning of a discourse of minimization and inconse-
quence for female deviance. Since laws and proscriptions could not
eradicate sexual perversity, it was to be expected that men's "evil

ways" in the practice of homosex would persist. Condemnation did not make homosex disappear, so it would become a subject not only of regulation but of long-winded discourse, whether based on the category of sin, or later, of disease, or both.[78] But women who deviated from the heteronorm became, through application of the term sodomy and the moral and legal categories it presupposes, merely an appendix to the deviant sexuality of men. This state of affairs has prevailed into the modern age, when an adequate vocabulary for women's same-sex affections has not been created, and linguistic approximations such as "female homosexuality" persist. From the thirteenth century to the present, the sodomite practicing sodomy, by his very centrality and the male-defined nature of his deviance, in effect relegates the same-sex sexuality of women to the margins of the unnamed, the unconceivable, the unfathomable.

This second consequence, in turn, raises some unexpected problems. There is no physical reason for women to be excluded from a definition that bases itself heavily on the practice of one specific, forbidden sexual act between men, anal penetration; nor for that matter, of practices equivalent to those identified by Damian, such as grabbing parts and friction *inter femoras.*[79] Yet, in effect, only the third, rubbing, was retained in the early vocabulary of female deviance. A heavy mantle of silence falls on the very possibility that women could put their hands to use or engage in the act of anal penetration. The awareness that women did not accept limited options and resorted to "diabolical machines" to reappropriate penetration (see the essays by Benkov, Clark, and Amer) is interesting in and of itself but leaves a large question unresolved. Indeed, the social codes that regulate the representation of deviance refuse to comprehend a female sexuality separate from the vaginal and, in effect, oriented to penile-vaginal intercourse. What matters here is the existence of categories that require fitting the sexual practices of women, even when deviant, into something familiar and understandable within dominant gender scripts. Thus, the perversity of men can take any number of forms, the most despised purportedly that which makes a male into a "female" receptor; but the much-advertised perversity of women is still conceived of as linked to reception, in illegitimate but not same-sex contexts—adultery, multiple lovers, bestiality. In that sense, the transgression of women who "play the male role" and use dildos evokes horror and repression, although is not unfathomable. The category sodomy thus at once erases women from same-sex deviance—it is assumed that they cannot perform sodomy with each other—or erases the array of techniques they may use to attain pleasure: women are just a subcategory of sodomites, and thus what they do is not important. The actual practices of women loving other women thus became shrouded in an unspoken mystery that modern misogynist discourse has interpreted as the relative safety of lesbians. Because women's practices don't matter, this discourse suggests, they are left unmolested.[80] Calling this safety—that is, suggesting that there is a positive and desirable social view toward lesbians as opposed to male homosexuals—effectively precludes any effort to reach the understanding that it is the very conceptualization of sex in their own bodies that has been refused to women. Danielle Regnier-Bohler has pointed out that for the European Middle Ages, speaking of sex or articulating any of its components was not permissible in women's speech. Transgression of this social code could not go unnoticed whether in literature or actual speech.[81] A fortiori, the articulation of women's desires for other women would avoid mention of any explicit tools other than those attributed to women who engaged in same-sex activity, whether such an attribution was correct or not.

At stake then is the question of pleasure in women's sexual lives and, to an extent, the question of pleasure itself regardless of object choice or sex of its performers. Sodomy has been treated thus far as a problem of transgression against affirmed social norms, those that consecrate penetration as the lot of the subjected female position and male deviations from such an order as humiliating, debasing, and ostracizing. As a practice, however, sodomy has been recognized in early penitentials as separate from object choice, revealing that the initial prohibition had to do with things other than gender roles.[82] The most obvious is not necessarily the only answer: if such techniques exclude procreation, nothing prevents partners from adding them to a menu that includes procreative acts. Somewhere in the interstices of belligerent, self-confident discourse on sex in

the later Middle Ages lies the inchoate refusal to discuss those dark,
hidden zones of pleasure that risk the sowing of upheaval and disorder in the social fabric. Here again, consideration is needed of
ethnic and cultural factors that make the discourse of sex relative
even within the narrow parameters of Western Christianity. In plain
terms, in much of the Mediterranean region, women who must
safeguard the physical mark of their virginity (the unbroken hymen)
in order to marry might engage in anal sex with a male partner. Although this transgresses official codes, it is not necessarily frowned
upon by a large section of the population. We are still in a sense at
the beginnings of uncovering medieval discourses on sex; how
much remains to be understood with respect to the gaps between
doctrinal pronouncements and actual practice? And in secular discourse, how much still needs to be found that is not derisive or
satirical around the forbidden act of anal penetration?[83] French medieval literature, for instance, provides a fairly wide array of textual
sites where fear of and fascination with buggery and the bugger surface.[84] Only later texts begin to bring out the varieties and practices, including anal intercourse, that made up "actual people's"
sexual lives. For women, suspect as a group of engaging in illicit
pleasure and of setting out to destroy the social fabric through their
immoderate pursuit of it, the imperative of keeping certain sexual
secrets locked up is even stronger. In the sixteenth century the doc-
tor Joubert was threatened and harassed for having discussed openly,
in the vernacular, the need for women to enjoy marital sex more.[85]
While such matters cannot be seen as "revolutionary," there is cause
to question and scrutinize the vocabulary of sex inscribed on
women's bodies, a vocabulary that, for instance, in the *chanson de
geste,* contrasts the many aggressive women who demand and speak
of lovemaking, and the act consummated with women in a subject
position ("il fist son bon / elle souffrit tout" [he had his will / she
suffered all]).[86]

Thus, if the invention of sodomy held grave consequences for the
ways male sexuality was to be regulated and circumscribed, it held as
many for the construction of sexuality as a network of ideologies,
practices, and discourses. And it held momentous consequences for
the construction of women's sexuality, regardless of the object choices

in their lives, for it strengthened women's role in the maintenance of the heteronorm and rendered their search for alternative positions and modes of pleasure more obscure, hidden, forbidden, and hence dangerous.

Looking for the "Lesbian"

The late John Boswell stated that little could be said about female same-sex unions not only because of a paucity of documents but also because male authors, living in societies that considered women to be property and sexual instruments devoid of sexual agency, displayed little interest in their transgressions.[87] However, more recent scholarship suggests that what we lack is not so much documents as the theoretical and methodological tools to read them, the instruments that would allow us to see, as we proposed in our opening remarks on visual culture.

Until very recently, scholarship devoted little attention to early modern same-sex pleasure among women, and none to the medieval period. As Valerie Traub remarks, "With the exception of recent work by Katherine Park and Lorraine Daston, little historical, theoretical or literary investigation has been attempted on early modern female same-gender pleasure. Lillian Faderman's encyclopedic historical overview of love between women devotes only two short chapters to the period prior to the eighteenth century, focusing mainly on Brantôme's Lives of Fair Gallants and Ladies." Judith Brown's work on the life of Benedetta Carlini comes even later and, suggests Traub, "in many ways is more revealing of religious than erotic practices."[88] Nevertheless, the same-sex affectivity of women in the medieval period has been the focus of several crucial essays: first, E. Ann Matter's "My Sister, My Spouse,"[89] and more recently, Jacqueline Murray's previously mentioned essay, in which she offers us a blueprint for further investigation:

> The study of attitudes and ideas about lesbians in the Middle Ages is neither as anachronistic as some theorists might believe nor as futile as traditional historians might think. The flexible understanding of female sexuality offered by contemporary theory meshes nicely with the complex interweaving of the psychological, spiritual, physical, and

emotional that characterizes medieval culture. New theoretical and methodological techniques, combined with interdisciplinary approaches, promise a more sophisticated examination of human sexuality in the past, an examination that will extend far beyond a litany of prohibitions and condemnations, that will read from silence and absence, and that, freed from the limitations of genital sexuality, will see medieval women's relationships in their richness, complexity, and diversity.[90]

In this search for traces of same-sex affectivity between women, we certainly cannot afford to overlook the impact of patriarchy on women's lives. By patriarchy, we mean a set of institutions, laws, and sanctioned practices, public and private, that maintain the minorization and dependent status of women. The historical specificity of patriarchy and the ways it shaped the sexual beings of women are crucial elements in researching same-sex affectivity among women. For the Middle Ages, the patriarchal investment in the subjection of women (socially, politically, legally) was bolstered by a construction of sexual hierarchy believed to be divinely ordained and therefore part of the "natural order" that was not to be disrupted. Furthermore, the idea that the hierarchy of the sexes was "natural" resulted in the unchallenged availability of free labor, whose importance can be measured both in historical terms (as shown by studies on women in the medieval economy),[91] and in cultural ones, reflected, for instance in the ways that this compliance was seen as perpetually contested, a social tension illustrated by railings against women in comic bourgeois literature that takes as its subject marriage and the domestic flaws of women.

Very helpful here is Judith Bennett's concept of "patriarchal equilibrium," which suggests that rather than positing an invariant and unassailable patriarchy, we should historicize its specific manifestations, keeping in mind "the possibility that patriarchal institutions can shift and change without much altering the force of patriarchal power."[92] Bennett sees a new women's history as "a history of *change without transformation,* a history of the many changes in women's lives that have occurred without usually transforming in significant ways the imbalance of power between the sexes. This does not mean that there is no history to be written. Rather, it means that there are new histories to be written, histories that trace changes in women's lives without resorting to narratives of transformation, histories that seek to problematize continuity, and histories that grapple with the challenge of understanding patriarchy."[93]

Thus, our task in this volume is not to document the transformation of female same-sex desire into "lesbianism" as it is understood in modern terms, but to unearth the expressions and history of that desire in the face of hostile patriarchal power. The impact of queer studies on the work of medievalists and the increasing consensus that binary divisions are useless, as well as the practical difficulties in documenting same-sex medieval affectivity, particularly among women, have generated a collective conversation around the need for a different sort of vocabulary, at once more flexible and more accurate in its ability to accommodate nuances, and around the relationship of homoaffectivity and same-sex love. In this context, a reevaluation of Adrienne Rich's famous "lesbian continuum" and homoaffectivity's role within it has taken place.[94] We are indeed no more justified in assuming that women could not replace or displace the imperatives of heterosexuality with homoaffective bonds of varying intensities, than in assuming that they were indifferent to the pursuit of sexual pleasure that was not limited to but did include genital sex, and its enactment through a variety of techniques available, then as now, to women who loved other women. These questions, in various ways, have been discussed in the essays by Amer, Benkov, Clark, Malti-Douglas, and Sautman.

One of the most difficult problems in this type of cultural archaeology in the medieval period remains one we alluded to in our prologue to this introduction: our fraught relationship to available sources that would allow us to retrace the subjectivity of women who embraced same-sex affectivity. Too often, scholars have to take the easier path where women do not speak but are spoken about, are subsumed under a male gaze, represented according to norms and tropes alien to their social experience, and stripped of agency in interpreting the world they lived in. This dismal state of affairs has nevertheless begin to crack under the patient tapping of feminist scholarship, focusing on women as actual and implied readers, on communities of readers, on women as patrons of the arts and authoritative voices in the production of texts.[95] In a larger sense, we need to question the assumption that "gender-heretical" texts and images were flat and meaningless to medieval people, and only acquire meaning for modern readers. There is a possibility of opening a wide window in this area by giving special attention to the lives of medieval women saints and the cults they generated, to their relation to legendary sites, and to evidence that these saints became the object of homoaffective desire. While rules of monastic life provide glimpses of what was considered licit and illicit and, therefore, of what types of behavior might occur to warrant such regulation, other aspects of women's interactions in monasteries call for attention. The vitas of beguines give such prominent place to the body and its manifestations that they can be privileged sites for queer readings of homoerotic expression in the bodily and fantasmic lives of women living among other women. They can, in particular, direct the gaze to more intimate spaces than those effectively controlled by the rules, such as sleeping quarters. The narrators of vitas, invested in producing face-value accounts of events that confirm the miraculous powers of a saintly woman and thus the holiness of a place, cannot be expected to acknowledge their fault lines, but the contemporary reader can. For instance, the life of Ida of Louvain includes a "marvelous" example of the body expanding beyond its natural confines; when Ida is sharing a bed with a younger beguine and is filled with "lingering thoughts of the Savior's infancy," she feels her entire body swell, gaining so much girth and weight that one of her feet bursts and her companion is crowded to the edge of the bed. The passage is quite detailed, and while it focuses on Ida's bodily transformation, marked tensions resignify the way both women occupy the bed space and demand greater attention to the workings of sexual fantasy and of the homoerotic effects of bodily contact and physical proximity between women.[96]

Vitas of medieval saints who are clearly inscribed in a local or regional context often invite queer readings of narratives otherwise glossed over as strictly heteronormative. For instance, the thirteenth-century saint Douceline of Digne's relationship to "others" (her nuns, the worshipers of her town and region) has been

read as the expression of a deep-seated neurosis in which Douceline replaces the mother and mediates the presence of the father,
controlling her daughters and letting herself be assaulted and controlled by others on the outside. The love and solicitude of Douceline's "daughters" toward her, especially in her ecstatic trances,
appear at first glance to be those shown to a mother. Analysis of the
circumstances and manner of intervention in the 25 mostly local
miracles attributed to Douceline during her life and after her death
confirms, according to Claude Carozzi, the female nature of the
cult.[97] But a closer reading may bring out homosocial and powerful homoaffective aspects of these interactions, particularly when
Douceline creates special bonds with some, such as a young beguine
who wanted to have the assurance of her love every single day. And
the fierce retribution exacted by an otherwise gentle and kind
Douceline against the nuns if they deviated in the slightest way
from their vocation as brides of Christ may be more than simply
acting as guardian of the "Father's" possessions. Douceline indeed
forbade her nuns to look at men, to speak to them, or even to speak
of them, punishing them brutally when they did not obey; she
whipped a very young girl bloody for having watched some work-
men on the job, telling the girl she would "sacrifice her to God."
The exclusive nature of her rapport with the nuns and the jealous
anger she displayed to keep men away from their very thoughts are
strong indications that such relationships might gain from more
complicated readings.

There is an entire field of medieval mysticism that demands to be
queered, as Karma Lochrie has urged, in particular late medieval female mysticism.[98] Complicating the usual binaries that have
presided over readings of female devotion, Lochrie asks such trou-
bling questions as, "What does it signify when a female mystic desires and adores the feminized body of Christ?"[99] She points out
that "The queering of Christ's body and of mystical desire is more
common in female mystical discourse than has yet been considered
by medieval scholarship."[100] For Lochrie, the instability of the heterosexual paradigm of mystical desire requires constant vigilance
and correction on the part of the scholar to maintain it and to oc-
clude the queer tendencies. When the devotee is male, he desires

(but never identifies with) the feminized body, while the female devotee identifies with the feminized body, ever reminding herself in her more erotic transports that Christ is male. The wound, *vulnus,* leads to an analogy with vulva, a pun on wound joined to wound, *"vulnus vulneri copulatur."* Christ's wound becomes the site of the "garden enclosed," usually occupied by the intact vagina of the feminine lover, and thus become queer. This leads Lochrie to a fresh look at late medieval devotional imagery.

In correspondence and love poetry as well, carefully coded homoerotic texts allow us to see glimpses of same-sex attraction and lived emotion among women (essays by Schibanoff and Eisenbichler in this volume). When women wrote coded poetry to other women, the convention's very existence is worth noting, for it verifies that poetic discourse has a form for the expression of marginalized or forbidden sexualities and, in general, of emotions and feelings "unspeakable" in the discourse of social, political, or legal life, and dangerous in autobiographical texts.

In an early analysis of the famed and only poem by the trobairitz Bieiris de Romans, Angelica Rieger asserted that the poet could not possibly have been a lesbian, arguing that that negative view of homosexuality in some poems of the troubadour corpus made it impossible that any poet would have endorsed it publicly. Therefore, to find same-sex love in Bieiris's poem is to misread a text that resembles other poems in which "colloquial" language between women is used, with a tone of intimacy unfamiliar to us, hence our propensity to find "lesbians" where proper heterosexual ladies simply indulge—for intellectual reasons—in the delights of highly erotic language among themselves.[101] This reductive interpretation elicits a number of objections. For instance, if the poem is "coded" in frequently used, intimate, but not overtly sexual language, why should that make it any less a poem written by a "lesbian" to a woman she desires? Enough examples of such language exist in modern times so that one should not find the medieval precautions so hard to understand. The essay supposes that a "true lesbian" could only write a poem in which she revealed her sexual identity and spelled out the form and object of her love, even though to write so overtly would contravene all the rules of pre-modern poetry, as well as the daily practice of sexual marginalization. We cannot ignore the fine-tuning of secret communication between marginal, subsumed people and in particular the overwhelming historical evidence of such careful coding among lesbians. Without further details about this poet and other women of her group, it is impossible to know whether she was a "lesbian" or not; secondly, while that might be an interesting historical question, it has no bearing on recognizing the expression of same-sex love in this particular poem. What remains important is that an entire style of poetry in the early Middle Ages entertained numerous ambiguities about the sex of the recipient, that women writing to each other dared to appropriate that language for themselves, and that this poetry afforded the possibility for women who had same-sex inclinations to read it freely in that way for themselves. Such possibilities disappear when narrow, binary readings, in which only a lesbian/heterosexual opposition is envisaged, take over the text. The result is to claim that same-sex affectivity did not exist simply because social disapproval was unambiguous.

Other areas that call for careful scrutiny in the search for same-sex affectivity between women and might yield to queering include penitentials, female monasteries, fears of same-sex passion expressed by ecclesiastical authorities, and the lives of desert mothers, mystics, and saints in which bodily rapture can be read as sexual in same-sex contexts. Finally, a rich domain of investigation remains the application of queer theory to the lives of historical figures, such as Radegund, Hildegard, Wallada Bint Musakfi,[102] or even Christine de Pizan, and as Gregory Hutcheson and Konrad Eisenbichler do in this volume, to the noblewomen Leonor López de Cordoba, Margaret of Austria, and Laudomia Forteguerri. For example, Bruce Holsinger has explored in Hildegard's work a fissure between her writing, which usually conveys her "obedience to patriarchal authority," and her devotional music, which recuperates female embodiment. Holsinger shows that "both musically and textually . . . homoerotic desire is integral to the discursive strategies through which Hildegard expressed her devotional sensibility."[103] According to Holsinger, "Hildegard reacted through music to the constraints of the male-dominated Church—the Church to which she was devoted but whose leaders she criticized over and over in her visions and letters—by constructing powerful alternatives to patriarchal traditions, alternatives centered around the female body, sensuality, and homoerotic desire."[104]

Coda: Revising the Script

The woodcut *Adam and Eve* by Lucas Cranach the Elder returns us to the subject of visualizing female same-sex desire that we explored in the opening of this introduction (see figure 1.1). The illustration to the *Roman de la Rose* represented this desire in the setting of a secular pleasure garden, but Cranach's woodcut takes as its setting *the* garden, the paradise that, according to the Book of Genesis, the Creator-God made for innocent humanity.

Cranach's woodcut visualizes a central subject in medieval art that is usually called the Fall of Man: the first woman, Eve, tempted by the devil in the form of a serpent, eats the fruit of the one tree that God had proscribed and convinces Adam to do likewise. As a result, God's messenger, an angel, evicts Adam and Eve from Paradise. Cranach employed a well-known medieval convention of representing the serpent from whom Eve receives the fruit of the tree of knowledge as part human female.[105] The two female bodies in the center of Cranach's woodcut focus attention on two exchanges, that between the serpent and Eve and that between Eve and Adam. Portrayed as if rushing in from the left, a way of indicating subsequent action, a military angel angrily points out the consequences of these exchanges.

Even in a black-and-white woodcut, the viewer is struck by Cranach's endeavor to represent Eve and the serpent as mirror images; in bodily proportions, hairstyles, and poses, one very curvaceous, nude female body reflects back the other. Less blatant but surely significant is the resemblance between the angel and Adam; the angel's armor, muscular calf, and short hair leave little doubt that this angel encodes masculinity; Adam's curly hair and facial type repeat those of the angel, and his stocky body is of the same type. These resemblances reinforced exegetical interpretation of the story that held a foundational position in Christian salvation history. The serpent tempted Eve, who succumbed, and Eve tempted Adam, who succumbed. As the tempting party in each interaction, the serpent and Eve resembled one another. Overwhelmingly viewed as responsible for humankind's expulsion from Paradise, Eve was also seen as an active participant, as opposed to Adam's passivity, signaled in Cranach's woodcut by his upraised left hand, palm open. Adam's resemblance to the angel reminds the viewer that man was made in God's image. In crude terms, human females resemble the devil and human males resemble God.

On this unequal distribution of blame Saint Paul built the edifice of male dominance within Christianity, for he insisted that men ruled over women in deserved and just punishment for Eve's action. Saint Augustine amplified the import of Paul's pronouncement when he introduced the idea that what entered the world with the eating of the forbidden fruit was sex.[106] By tempting Adam to eat the fruit, Eve became a sexual temptress. From Augustine's male perspective, his desired state of chastity was made difficult by the sexual allure of the female. Christian attitudes toward sex formed around this pattern of the female temptress and the male victim of her predatory desire. Western patriarchy takes its strength from this,[107] and its deep embeddedness in Christian discourse has made it difficult to uproot. Feminist biblical scholars have begun, however, to argue that the interpretation of medieval exegetes represents only one possible reading of this story, and a self-interested reading at that. Inspired by scholars such as Phyllis Trible, Elaine Pagels, and Mieke Bal, we offer here another reading.

Cranach's woodcut might be telling quite another story—the story of female same-sex desire. Not only resembling one another but also facing each other—like the two dancers in the *Rose* illustration—as if totally engaged with one another, Eve and the serpent form a closed unit, a unit that rejects any possibility of male penetration; they are a self-sufficient pair whose physical closeness signals erotic engagement. Since the procreational imperative had not yet come into existence, their preference for one another cannot represent a rejection of all that has since been associated with heterosexuality; perhaps it represents instead Eve's full appreciation of the female beauty mirrored back at her. Perhaps Eve hands the apple to Adam as a sign that he should also search for his mirror likeness.[108] Perhaps what the angel comes to condemn and punish is the first desire, which males fear and therefore prohibit—female same-sex desire.

Writing about female same-sex desire in the Middle Ages requires acts of interpretation as radical as our reading of Cranach's woodcut. It means, to use a formula of Judith Butler's, to occupy and resignify the name.[109] A dominant discourse that taught Eve's guilt and punished all women with subordination had no language for the female as subject of same-sex desire but gaps in that discourse that can be found through deconstructive readings render that desire visible. As we proceed, we must also recognize the complexity of this task and thus ask in what forms and according to what positions along the spectrum of affectional and erotic expression we might find female same-sex desire in the Middle Ages. There is even now no dearth of documents allowing us to chart the traces of women engaged in various levels of homoerotic—gynoerotic—affection. We can explore the tensions that (homo)social and (homo)affective situations create within heteronormative institutions and ideological constructs, the disruptions they introduce, by listening carefully, not only to the voices but also to the silences in the texts—be they legal documents or saints' lives[110]—by considering an inclusive configuration of sexual and gender transgressions in their interconnectedness; such perspectives allow us to demonstrate the ultimate fragility of the heterosexual gender and sexual order in its project of controlling medieval women.

Notes

1. Israel Burshatin, "Elena alias Eleno: Gender, Sexualities, and 'Race' in the Mirror of Natural History in 16th-Century Spain," in *Gender Reversals and Gender Cultures: Anthropological and Historical Perspectives,* ed. Sabrina P. Ramet (New York: Routledge, 1996), pp. 105–22.

2. For discussion of the visual nature of medieval culture, see Michael Camille, *The Gothic Idol: Ideology and Image-making in Medieval Art* (Cambridge: Cambridge University Press, 1989); Michael Camille, "Seeing and Reading: Some Visual Implications of Medieval Literacy and Illiteracy," *Art History* 8.1 (March 1985): 26–47.

3. Diane Wolfthal, "An Art Historical Response to 'Gay Studies and Feminism: A Medievalist's Perspective,'" *Medieval Feminist Newsletter,* no. 14 (fall 1992): 17.

4. The miniature is on fol. 7v of Valencia, Biblioteca universitaría 387, which was illustrated during the first decade of the fifteenth century. It should be noted that these illustrations are unusual, though not unique, among illustrations in *Rose* manuscripts for the explicit nature of their eroticism. A complete catalogue of *Rose* illustration is being prepared by Meradith T. McMunn.

5. Guillaume de Lorris and Jean de Meun, *The Romance of the Rose,* trans., intro., and notes by Frances Horgan (Oxford: Oxford University Press, 1994), p. 13. For the French original see Guillaume de Lorris and Jean de Meun, *Le Roman de la Rose,* ed. Félix Lecoy (Classiques Français du Moyen Age 92, 95, and 98) 3 vols. (Paris: Champion, 1965–70; reprinted in 1973–75 and 1985), 1: lines 757–74.

6. See Pamela Sheingorn, "The Bodily Embrace Or Embracing the Body: Gesture and Gender in Late Medieval Drama and Art," in *The Stage as Mirror: Civic Theatre in Late Medieval Europe,* ed. Alan E. Knight (Cambridge, Eng.: D. S. Brewer, 1997), pp. 51–89.

7. See Karma Lochrie's interpretation of the wound of Christ as lesbian emblem: "Mystical Acts, Queer Tendencies," in *Constructing Medieval Sexuality,* ed. Karma Lochrie, Peggy McCracken, and James S. Schultz (Minneapolis: University of Minnesota Press, 1997), pp. 180–200. Francesca Canadé Sautman's unpublished work on the ambiguous diamond shape, "Espaces symboliques du temps," explores connections to sexuality as well as to death and magic.

8. George Chauncey, Jr., "From Sexual Inversion to Homosexuality: Medicine and the Changing Conceptualization of Female Deviance," *Salmagundi* 58–59, "Homosexuality: Sacrilege, Vision, Politics" (fall 1982-winter 1983): 115.

9. Diana Fuss, *Essentially Speaking: Feminism, Nature and Difference* (New York: Routledge, 1989), pp. 1–2.

10. Fuss, *Essentially Speaking,* p. 4.

11. Karma Lochrie, "Desiring Foucault," *Journal of Medieval and Early Modern Studies* 27 (winter 1997):4; Lochrie has taken up a similar critique of Foucault and his uses in medieval studies in her *Covert Operations: The Medieval Uses of Secrecy* (Philadelphia: University of Pennsylvania Press, 1999), pp. 14–24.

12. Lochrie, "Desiring Foucault," 9.

13. Geneviève Pastre, *Athènes et le "Péril saphique": Homosexualité fémi-nine en Grèce ancienne* (Paris: Librairie "Les Mots à la bouche," 1987).

14. James O'Higgins, "Sexual Choice, Sexual Act: An Interview with Michel Foucault," trans. James O'Higgins, *Salmagundi* 58–59 (fall 1982-winter 1983): 10–24; this point was developed again in a ple-nary address delivered by Carolyn Dinshaw at the Queer Middle Ages Conference, New York City, November 5–7, 1999, an ex-panded version of which appeared as the first chapter in her *Get-ting Medieval: Sexualities and Communities, Pre- and Postmodern* (Durham: Duke University Press, 1999), pp. 1–54.

15. Michel Foucault, *The Order of Things: An Archaeology of the Human Sciences* (1971; New York: Vintage, 1994), p. 17.

16. Louise Fradenburg, "The Love of Thy Neighbor," in *Constructing Medieval Sexuality,* p. 136.

17. Jo Ann McNamara, "The *Herrenfrage*: The Restructuring of the Gender System, 1050–1150," in *Medieval Masculinities: Regarding Men in the Middle Ages,* ed. Clare Lees (Minneapolis: University of Minnesota Press, 1994), pp. 3–29.

18. As Valerie R. Hotchkiss argues with regard to medieval women who cross-dressed as men, "women in male dress are noteworthy precisely because they are unlike other women; their freedom to participate in a variety of activities contrasts with the constraints on the lives of ordinary women and offers a variety of models that challenge previous understandings of medieval definitions of gen-der" (*Clothes Make the Man: Female Cross Dressing in Medieval Eu-rope* [New York: Garland, 1996], p. 12).

19. Joan Cadden, *Meanings of Sex Difference in the Middle Ages: Medicine, Science, and Culture* (Cambridge: Cambridge University Press, 1993), pp. 9–10.

20. For an application of Irigaray's views to a body of medieval litera-ture within a feminist perspective, see E. Jane Burns, *Bodytalk: When Women Speak in Old French Literature* (Philadelphia: University of Pennsylvania Press, 1993).

21. On the "sworn virgin," see Carol J. Clover, "Maiden Warriors and Other Sons," in *Marginal Women in Medieval Society,* ed. Robert R. Edwards and Vickie Ziegler (Rochester, NY: Boydell Press, 1995), pp. 75–87; and Antonia Young, *Women Who Become Men: Albanian Sworn Virgins* (Oxford: Berg, 2000).

22. Thomas Laqueur, *Making Sex: Body and Gender from the Greeks to Freud* (Cambridge, MA: Harvard University Press, 1990), pp. 19–20: "Here the boundaries between male and female are primarily po-

litical; rhetorical rather than biological claims regarding sexual difference and sexual desire are primary. It is about a body whose fluids—blood, semen, milk, and the various excrements—are fungible in that they turn into one another and whose processes—digestive and genetive, menstruation and other bleeding—are not so easily distinguished or so easily assignable to one sex or another as they become after the eighteenth century. This 'one flesh,' the construction of a single-sexual body with its different versions attributed to at least two genders, was framed in antiquity to valorize the extraordinary cultural assertion of patriarchy"; also passim, pp. 26–62, 63–113. Further, for Laqueur, "the body is like an actor on stage, reading the book on the roles assigned it by culture. In my account sex too, and not only gender, is understood to be staged"(61).

23. "Aristotle, in fact, together with the Aristotelian theorists who dominated European thinking on sexuality between 1250 and 1550, expounded a two-sex model more sharply delineated than any modern theory" (Katherine Park and Robert A. Nye, "Destiny is Anatomy," *New Republic,* February 18, 1991: 54). See also Danielle Jacquart and Claude Thomasset, *Sexuality and Medicine in the Middle Ages,* trans. Matthew Adamson (Princeton: Princeton University Press, 1988).

24. Susan Crane, "Clothing and Gender Definition: Joan of Arc," *Journal of Medieval and Early Modern Studies* 26.2 (spring 1996):297–319; see also Bonnie Wheeler and Charles T. Wood, eds. *Fresh Verdicts on Joan of Arc* (New York: Garland, 1996).

25. This is sometimes referred to as the complex of Brynhilde; see Theodore M. Andersson, *The Legend of Brynhild,* Islandica 43 (Ithaca: Cornell University Press, 1980).

26. Claude Gaignebet's work had a pioneering impact on the interpretations of Melusine's body; see his *Art profane et religion populaire* (Paris: Presses Universitaires de France, 1985). It was followed by studies in a similar direction, such as Françoise Clier-Colombani, *La fée Mélusine au Moyen Age: Images, mythes et symboles* (Paris: Le Léopard d'Or, 1991). Other studies have taken as their point of departure Jacques Le Goff's famous essay, "Melusina: Mother and Pioneer," in *Time, Work, and Culture in the Middle Ages,* trans. Arthur Goldhammer (Chicago and London: University of Chicago Press, 1980), pp. 205–222, which was previously published as *Pour un autre Moyen Age: Temps, travail et culture en occident* (Paris: Editions Gallimard, 1977). See in particular Gabrielle M. Spiegel, "Maternity and Monstrosity: Reproductive Biology in the Roman de Mélusine," in *Melusine of Lusignan: Founding Fiction in Late Medieval France,* ed.

Donald Maddox and Sara Sturm-Maddox (Athens, GA: University of Georgia Press, 1996), pp. 100–24.

27. Joyce E. Salisbury, "Bestiality in the Middle Ages," in *Sex in the Middle Ages: A Book of Essays,* ed. Joyce E. Salisbury (New York: Garland, 1991), pp. 175; 177.

28. For the argument that Christine de Pizan's revisions of Ovidian myths of bestiality in her *Epistre Othea* employ outlaw theory to "contradict the standard disciplinary gestures of medieval mythography that attempt to shape and control female sexuality," see Marilynn Desmond and Pamela Sheingorn, "Queering Ovidian Myth: Bestiality and Desire in Christine de Pizan's *Epistre Othea,*" in *Queering the Middle Ages,* ed. Glenn Burger and Steven F. Kruger (Minneapolis: University of Minnesota Press, 2001), pp. 3–27.

29. Fuss, *Essentially Speaking,* pp. 97–111, esp. 98–99.

30. Bernadette Brooten, *Love Between Women: Early Christian Responses to Female Homoeroticism* (Chicago: University of Chicago Press, 1996), pp. 4–7; interpretation of Romans 1.18–32, pp. 201–14.

31. Marie-Jo Bonnet, "Sappho, or the Importance of Culture in the Language of Love: Tribade, Lesbienne, Homosexuelle," in *Queerly Phrased: Language, Gender and Sexuality,* ed. Anna Livia and Kira Hall (New York: Oxford University Press, 1997), pp. 147–66.

32. Emma Donoghue, *Passions Between Women: British Lesbian Culture 1668–1801* (New York: HarperCollins, 1993), esp. introduction, pp. 1–24.

33. Randolph Trumbach, *Sex and the Gender Revolution, Volume I: Heterosexuality and the Third Gender in Enlightenment London* (Chicago: University of Chicago Press, 1998).

34. Francesca Canadé Sautman, "Invisible Women: Lesbian Working-Class Culture in France, 1880–1930," in *Homosexuality in Modern France,* ed. Jeffrey Merrick and Bryan T. Ragan Jr. (New York: Oxford University Press, 1996), pp. 177–201, and "Invisible Women: Retracing the Lives of French Working-Class Lesbians, 1880–1930," in *A Queer World: The Center for Lesbian and Gay Studies Reader,* ed. Martin Duberman (New York: NYU Press, 1997), pp. 236–47.

35. Judith M. Bennett, "'Lesbian-Like' and the Social History of Lesbianisms," *Journal of the History of Sexuality* 9.1–2 (January/April 2000): 9; 22.

36. Bennett, "'Lesbian-Like,'" 24.

37. See, for instance, James A. Brundage, "Politics of Sodomy: Rex v. Pons Hugh de Ampurias (1311)," in *Sex in the Middle Ages,* pp. 239–46; Linda Lomperis, "Bodies That Matter in the Court of Late

Medieval England and in Chaucer's 'Miller's Tale,'" *Romanic Review*
86.2 (March 1995): 243–64; Ad Putter, "Transvestite Knights in Medieval Life and History," in *Becoming Male in the Middle Ages,* ed. Jeffrey Jerome Cohen and Bonnie Wheeler (New York: Garland, 1997),
pp. 279–302; Garrett P. J. Epp, "The Vicious Guise: Effeminacy,
Sodomy, and *Mankind,*" ibid, pp. 303–20; and essays by Claire Spon-
sler, Gregory S. Hutcheson, Peggy McCracken, Francesca Canadé
Sautman in *Queering the Middle Ages,* ed. Glenn Burger and Steven F.
Kruger (Minneapolis: University of Minnesota Press, 2001).
38. Foucault, "Interview," 11–12.
39. D. M. Hadley, "Introduction: Medieval Masculinities," in *Masculinity in Medieval Europe,* ed. D. M. Hadley (London: Longman, 1999),
p. 17. The first internal quotation is from J. Tosh, "What Should
Historians Do with Masculinity?" *History Workshop Journal* 38
(1994): 191; the second internal quotation is from R. Balzaretti,
"Men and Sex in Tenth-century Italy," in *Masculinity in Medieval
Europe.*
40. On medieval sexuality see, for instance, John W. Baldwin, *The Language of Sex: Five Voices from Northern France around 1200* (Chicago:
University of Chicago Press, 1994); Kathryn Gravdal, ed., *Romanic
Review* 86.2 (March 1995), Special issue: The Production of
Knowledge: Institutionalizing Sex, Gender, and Sexuality in Me-
dieval Discourse; Jacqueline Murray and Konrad Eisenbichler, eds.,
Desire and Discipline: Sex and Sexuality in the Premodern West
(Toronto: University of Toronto Press, 1996). Among individual essays of particular import, we might cite Marilynn Desmond's
"*Dominus/Ancilla:* Rhetorical Subjectivity and Sexual Violence in
the Letters of Heloise," in *The Tongue of the Fathers: Gender and Ideology in Twelfth-Century Latin,* ed. David Townsend and Andrew
Taylor (Philadelphia: University of Pennsylvania Press, 1998), pp.
35–54.
41. Jacqueline Murray, "Twice Marginal," p. 191.
42. R. Howard Bloch, *The Scandal of the Fabliaux* (Chicago: University
of Chicago Press, 1986), pp. 5–10. See responses to his essay "Medieval Misogyny" (*Representations* 20 [1987]: 1–24) in "Commentary," *Medieval Feminist Newsletter* 6 (December 1988): 2–15.
43. Burns, *Bodytalk,* pp. 31–70.
44. Baldwin, *Language of Sex,* pp. 108–15.
45. A version of a well-known folk narrative, the "Souhaits Saint Martin," tells of a wife who rashly misuses three magic gifts. She wishes
her husband to be covered with penises and is countered by the
wish that she be similarly covered with vaginas. The whole business

is annulled with the third wish, leaving the couple in their initial state. Edith Benkov presented a queer analysis of this text in her "Prickly Questions, Queer Judgments in the Old French Fabliaux," a paper delivered at the Queer Middle Ages Conference, New York City, November 5–7, 1998.

46. See Jo Ann McNamara, "The *Herrenfrage*."

47. Essays by Jacqueline Murray, Shannon McSheffrey, Frederik Pederson, and Margaret H. Kerr in *Women, Marriage, and Family in Medieval Christendom: Essays in Memory of Michael M. Sheehan,* ed. Constance M. Rousseau and Joel T. Rosenthal (Kalamazoo, MI: Medieval Institute Publications, 1998); Georges Duby, *The Knight, the Lady and the Priest: The Making of Modern Marriage in Medieval France,* trans. Barbara Bray (New York: Pantheon, 1983); see also Eleanor S. Riemer, "Women, Dowries, and Capital Investment in 13th-Century Siena," in *The Marriage Bargain: Women and Dowries in European History,* ed. Marion A. Kaplan (New York: Institute for Research in History, Haworth Press, 1985), pp. 59–79. On the intersection of celibacy and marriage, see Dyan Elliott, *Spiritual Marriage: Sexual Abstinence in Medieval Wedlock* (Princeton: Princeton University Press, 1993).

48. Jean S. Peristiany, ed., *Honour and Shame: The Values of Mediterranean Society* (1966; Chicago: University of Chicago Press, 1974). David D. Gilmore, ed., *Honor and Shame and the Unity of the Mediterranean* (Washington, DC: American Anthropological Association, 1987).

49. Lynn Hunt, "Introduction," in *The Invention of Pornography: Obscenity and the Origins of Modernity, 1500–1800,* ed. Lynn Hunt (New York: Zone, 1993), p. 144. See also Manuela Mourao, "The Representation of Female Desire in Early Modern Pornographic Texts, 1660–1745," *Signs: Journal of Women in Culture and Society* 24 (1999): 573–602.

50. Andrew Taylor, "Reading the Dirty Bits," in *Desire and Discipline,* pp. 280–95.

51. See also Norman Roth, "Fawn of my Delights: Boy-Love in Hebrew and Arabic Verse," in *Sex in the Middle Ages,* pp. 157–72; Steven F. Kruger, "Conversion and Medieval Sexual, Religious, and Racial Categories," in *Constructing Medieval Sexuality,* pp. 158–79, and "Becoming Christian, Becoming Male?" in *Becoming Male,* pp. 21–41.

52. A dissertation in progress by Rosa Attali entitled "Women of Valor: Social Roles and Gender Patterns Among Jewish Women in Northern France (12th–13th centuries)" (The Graduate Center, CUNY) examines homosocial networks among medieval Jewish women.

53. Judith Butler, *Gender Trouble: Feminism and the Subversion of Identity* (New York: Routledge, 1990), p. 146.

54. Claire Fanger, "The Formative Feminine and the Immobility of God: Gender and Cosmogony in Bernard Silvestris's *Cosmographia*," in *Tongue of the Fathers*, p. 82.

55. John Kitchen, *Saint's Lives and the Rhetoric of Gender: Male and Female in Merovingian Hagiography* (New York: Oxford University Press, 1998), esp. pp. 101–33.

56. Alcuin Blamires, "*Caput a femina, membra a viris:* Gender Polemic in Abelard's Letter 'On the Authority and Dignity of the Nun's Profession,'" in *Tongue of the Fathers*, pp. 55–79.

57. Brooten, *Love Between Women*, pp. 313–16, 320, 323.

58. Kathleen Biddick, "Gender, Bodies, Borders: Technologies of the Visible," *Speculum* 68.2 (April 1993): 389–413.

59. The beard was linked to virility, male sexual performance, and male honor in numerous medieval sources. For France, one might quote a passage in Lambert of Ardres in which the beardless man is effeminate: " . . . quod tunc temporis qui prolixam barbam non haberet, effeminatus diceretur et in derisum et despectum haberetur" (Lambert d'Ardres, *Chroniques de Guines et d'Ardres par Lambert, Curé d'Ardres, 918–1203. Textes latin et français en regard*, ed. De Godefroy de Menilglaise [Paris: Jules Renouard, 1855]). The Middle French translation for "effeminatus" is, curiously, "coeurs failliz" or "faint hearts." See also the fabliau of the "Sentier batu," in which a knight who lacks interest in a woman is chidingly described as "having no beard."

60. On the tooth, see Francesca Canadé Sautman, "A Troubled History: Folklore and Competing Texts in *Baudouin de Sebourc*, a Fourteenth-Century *Chanson de Geste*," in *Telling Tales: Medieval Narratives and The Folk Tradition*, ed. Francesca Canadé Sautman, Diana Conchado, and Giuseppe Carlo Di Scipio (New York: St. Martin's Press, 1998), p. 233.

61. Allen Frantzen, "Introduction: Straightforward," *Before the Closet*, pp. 1–29, esp. pp. 13–26.

62. Lauren Berlant and Michael Warner, "What Does Queer Theory Teach Us about X?" *PMLA* 110.3 (May 1995): 343–49.

63. For the application of these terms to the relation between folklore and canonical medieval literature, see Canadé Sautman, Conchado, and Di Scipio, *Telling Tales*, esp. "Texts and Shadows: Traces, Narratives and Folklore," pp. 1–17.

64. Judith Butler, "Against Proper Objects," *differences* 6.2–3 (1994): 1–26; "Imitation and Gender Subordination," in *Inside/Out: Lesbian*

Theories, Gay Theories, ed. Diana Fuss (New York and London: Routledge, 1991), pp. 13–31; Eve Kosofsky Sedgwick, *Epistemology of the Closet* (Berkeley: University of California Press, 1990); "Queer and Now" in *Tendencies* (Durham, NC: Duke University Press, 1993).

65. Carolyn Dinshaw, *Chaucer's Sexual Poetics* (Madison: University of Wisconsin Press, 1989); Carolyn Dinshaw, "A Kiss is Just a Kiss: Heterosexuality and Its Consolation in Sir Gawain and the Green Knight," *Diacritics* 24.2–3 (1994): 205–26.

66. Mark D. Jordan, "Homosexuality, *Luxuria,* and Textual Abuse," in *Constructing Medieval Sexuality,* pp. 24–39; Joan Cadden, "Sciences/Silences: The Natures and Languages of 'Sodomy' in Peter of Abano's *Problemata* Commentary," ibid., pp. 40–47; E. Jane Burns, "Refashioning Courtly Love: Lancelot as Ladies' Man or Lady/Man?," ibid., pp. 111–34.

67. Bruce Wood Holsinger, "The Flesh of the Voice: Embodiment and the Homoerotics of Devotion in the Music of Hildegard of Bingen (1098–1179)," *Signs: Journal of Women in Culture and Society* 19.1 (1993): 119.

68. J. L. Welch, "Cross-Dressing and Cross-Purposes: Gender Possibilities in the Acts of Thecla," *Gender Reversals,* pp. 66–78.

69. On women's networks see, for instance, Mary Wack, "Women, Work, and Plays in an English Medieval Town," in *Maids and Mistresses, Cousins and Queens: Women's Alliances in Early Modern Europe,* ed. Susan Frye and Karen Robertson (New York: Oxford University Press, 1999), pp. 33–51. For essays on women in religious and local communities, see *Medieval Women in Their Communities,* ed. Diane Watt (Cardiff: University of Wales Press, 1997).

70. Joan Ferrante, "Public Postures and Private Maneuvers: Roles Medieval Women Play," in *Women and Power in the Middle Ages,* ed. Mary Erler and Maryanne Kowaleski (Athens, GA: University of Georgia Press, 1988), pp. 213–29.

71. Alcuin Blamires, *The Case for Women in Medieval Culture* (Oxford: Clarendon Press, 1997), esp. pp. 171–98.

72. Mark D. Jordan, *The Invention of Sodomy* (Chicago: University of Chicago Press, 1998).

73. Lochrie, *Covert Operations.*

74. The thirteenth-century satirical romance of Wistace le Moine makes that distinction: "herites, / Ne fout-en-cul ne sodomites" [neither heretics nor those who fuck in the ass nor sodomites] (*Le romans de Witasse le Moine, roman du treizième siècle, Édité d'après le manuscrit, fonds français 1553, de la Bibliothèque nationale, Paris, par*

Denis Joseph Conlon, North Carolina Studies in the Romance Languages and Literatures no. 126 [Chapel Hill: University of North Carolina Press, 1972], lines 1185–1281).

75. John Boswell, *Christianity, Social Tolerance and Homosexuality* (Chicago: University of Chicago Press, 1980) and *Same-Sex Unions in Pre-Modern Europe* (New York: Villard Books, 1992).

76. On Peter Damian, see Jordan, *Invention of Sodomy,* pp. 45–66, and on Alan of Lille, pp. 67–91.

77. Brooten, *Love Between Women,* pp. 313–14.

78. Jordan, *Invention of Sodomy,* p. 57 n. 54.

79. Jordan, *Invention of Sodomy,* p. 53.

80. This refers to what has been called the "myth of lesbian impunity." For an early discussion, see Louis Crompton, "The Myth of Lesbian Impunity: Capital Laws from 1270–1791," *Journal of Homosexuality* 6 (1980–81): 11–25. The question is taken up again in, for instance, Canadé Sautman, "Invisible Women" (1996 and 1997), and "Myth of Lesbian Impunity," in *Encyclopedia of Homosexualities,* 1: *Lesbian Histories and Cultures,* ed. Bonnie Zimmerman (New York: Garland, 1999), pp. 460–61.

81. Danielle Regnier-Bohler, "Literary and Mystical Voices," in *A History of Women in the West,* ed. Georges Duby and Michelle Perrot, 2: Silences of the Middle Ages, ed. Christiane Klapisch-Zuber (Cambridge, MA: Belknap/Harvard University Press, 1992), pp. 427–82; see especially the sections entitled "Naming Sex" (pp. 459–63) and "Saying the Unsayable" (pp. 463–66).

82. See Michael Goodich, "Sodomy in Ecclesiastical Law," *Journal of Homosexuality* 1.4 (1976): 427–34; Michael Goodich, *The Unmentionable Vice: Homosexuality in the Later Medieval Period* (Santa Barbara, CA: ABC-Clio, 1979); Pierre Payer, *Sex and the Penitentials: The Development of a Sexual Code, 550–1150* (Toronto: University of Toronto Press, 1984).

83. On the rites of the compagnons and anal penetration, see Claude Gaignebet, *Art profane et religion populaire au Moyen Age* (Paris: Presses Universitaires de France, 1985), pp. 29a, 222–23, 276c, 281.

84. See discussion of Lanval, Eneas, fabliaux, and other texts in Gerald Herman, "The 'Sin Against Nature' and Its Echoes in Medieval French Literature," *Annuale medievale* 17 (1976): 70–87. Also, women who are disguised and living as men can encounter the same fears, as does Silence.

85. See Nicole Belmont, "Corps populaire et corps savant dans l'oeuvre de Laurent Joubert, *Erreurs populaires au fait de la médecine et régime de santé (1578),*" in *100ᵉ Congrès national des sociétés savantes,*

Le corps humain: nature, culture surnaturel (Paris: CTHS, 1985), pp. 9–17; and Canadé Sautman, *La religion du quotidien: Rites et croyances populaires de la fin du Moyen Age* (Florence: Olschki, 1995), chap. 3, "Prévenir et soigner," pp. 133–34 and passim.

86. This formula and some variants are extremely frequent throughout the French epic and offer a curious contrast with scenes in which women act aggressively and independently to affirm desire. For a variant that retains the meaning of the formula, see *Tristan de Nanteuil,* ed. Keith Val Sinclair (Assen: VanGorcum, 1971), lines 13690–710: "Sy en fist son vouloir, car forment il l'ama / A lui print tel deduit que jamés n'y ara; / Et la baise et acolle, et elle l'endura / Come l'omme du monde que elle trop mieulx ama" [(Tristan) had his will of her, for he loved her deeply / From her took such pleasure that never he would have again; / And kisses and embraces her, and she endured it / from the man in the world she loved the most].

87. John Boswell, *Same-Sex Unions in Pre-Modern Europe* (New York: Villard Books, 1992).

88. Valerie Traub, "The (In)significance of 'Lesbian' Desire," in *Queering the Renaissance,* ed. Jonathan Goldberg (Durham, NC: Duke University Press, 1994), pp. 62–83 at 81 n. 5.

89. E. Ann Matter, "My Sister, My Spouse: Woman-Identified Women in Medieval Christianity," in *Weaving the Visions,* ed. Judith Plaskow and Carol P. Christ (San Francisco: Harper and Row, 1989), pp. 51–62.

90. Murray, "Twice Marginal," p. 208.

91. See, for example, Judith M. Bennett, *Ale, Beer, and Brewsters in England: Women's Work in a Changing World, 1300–1600* (New York: Oxford University Press, 1996); Martha C. Howell, *Women, Production, and Patriarchy in Late Medieval Cities* (Chicago: University of Chicago Press, 1986); David Herlihy, "Women's Work in the Towns of Traditional Europe," in *Women, Family and Society in Medieval Europe: Historical Essays, 1978–1991* (Providence: Berghahn Books, 1995), pp. 69–95; William Chester Jordan, *Women and Credit in Pre-Industrial and Developing Societies* (Philadelphia: University of Pennsylvania Press, 1993); and Marilyn Stone and Carmen Benito-Vessels, eds., *Women at Work in Spain from the Middle Ages to Early Modern Times* (New York: Peter Lang, 1998).

92. Judith M. Bennett, "Confronting Continuity," *Journal of Women's History* 9.3 (autumn 1997): 82.

93. Bennett, "Confronting Continuity," 88.

94. Adrienne Rich, "Compulsory Heterosexuality and Lesbian Existence," *Signs: Journal of Women in Culture and Society* 5.4 (summer 1980): 631–660. Judith Bennett, for example, writes, "The essence of Rich's continuum is 'primary intensity between and among women,' and intensity that involves both 'sharing of a rich inner life' and 'bonding against male tyranny.' Some behaviors that I would identify as lesbian-like—such as singleness—were not necessarily based in the female bonding at the center of Rich's analysis" ("'Lesbian-Like,'" 15).

95. On various aspects of women and books, see essays in the three volumes edited by Lesley Smith and Jane H. M. Taylor, *Women, the Book and the Godly* (Woodbridge: D. S. Brewer, 1995); *Women, the Book and the Worldly* (Woodbridge: D. S. Brewer, 1995); and *Women and the Book: Assessing the Visual Evidence* (London: The British Library, 1996). On women as readers see, for example, Anne Clark Bartlett, *Male Authors, Female Readers: Representation and Subjectivity in Middle English Devotional Literature* (Ithaca: Cornell University Press, 1995); David N. Bell, *What Nuns Read: Books and Libraries in Medieval English Nunneries* (Kalamazoo, MI: Cistercian Publications, 1995); and *Women and Literature in Britain, 1150–1500* (Cambridge: Cambridge University Press, 1993). On women as patrons see, for example, *The Cultural Patronage of Medieval Women,* ed. June Hall McCash (Athens, GA: University of Georgia Press, 1996).

96. Walter Simons, "Reading a Saint's Body: Rapture and Bodily Movement in the *vitae* of Thirteenth-Century Beguines," in *Framing Medieval Bodies,* ed. Sarah Kay and Miri Rubin (Manchester: Manchester University Press, 1994), pp. 10–23; quotation at p. 18.

97. Fifteen concern women directly, and four indirectly; six concern beguines, and one another local nun; four are cures of lay women from various illnesses, four are difficult births, and four are cures of small children brought by their mothers; see Claude Carozzi, "Douceline et les autres," in *Cahiers de Fanjeaux, 11. La religion populaire en Languedoc du XIIIe siècle à la moitié du XIVe siècle* (Toulouse: Privat, 1976), pp. 251–67; esp. 253–56 and 262–65.

98. Lochrie, "Mystical Acts, Queer Tendencies."

99. Lochrie, "Mystical Acts, Queer Tendencies," p. 186.

100. Lochrie, "Mystical Acts, Queer Tendencies," p. 194. For Lochrie, "female mystical discourse confounds gender and the heteronormative categories it inhabits, queering them, causing them to lapse, balk, and swerve." Further, "Such a possibility for queering exists in the feminizing of Christ's body, in the genitalizing of his wound in

representational art, and in the discursive expressions of feminine desire. This desire is potentially oppositional in that it seeks to disturb these same categories, and in the process, it exposes the heteronormative laws governing most mystical discourse. The transpositioning of vulva to Christ's wound, the partial feminizing of Christ's body, and Catherine's pleasure contest our own categories for understanding the cultural archives available to medieval mysticism—categories of feminine and masculine, typologies of love, sexualities, and desire" (p. 195).

101. Angelica Rieger, "Was Bieiris de Romans Lesbian? Women's Relations with Each Other in the World of the Troubadours," in *The Voice of the Trobairitz: Perspectives on the Women Troubadours,* ed. William D. Paden (Philadelphia: University of Pennsylvania Press, 1989), pp. 73–94.

102. Wallada Bint Mustakfi, daughter of the last Umayyad caliph of Cordoba (d. 1087 C.E.), was loved by the poet Ibn Zaydun (d. 1070), with whom she broke her ties by sending him obscene poems on the subject of his virility, and loved a woman named Mouhja ("Exigence d'aimer: Entretien avec Jamel Eddine Bencheikh," *Quantara,* Special Issue, *De l'amour et des Arabes,* 18 (January 1996): 20–24, at p. 24.

103. Holsinger, "The Flesh of the Voice," 120.

104. Holsinger, "The Flesh of the Voice," 116.

105. Henry Ansgar Kelly, "The Metamorphoses of the Eden Serpent during the Middle Ages and Renaissance," *Viator* 2 (1971): 301–27.

106. Jean M. Higgins, "The Myth of Eve: The Temptress," *Journal of the American Academy of Religion* 44 (1976): 639–47; Elaine Pagels, *Adam, Eve, and the Serpent* (New York: Random House, 1988), chap. 6, passim, discusses Augustinian and other early perspectives on the punishments of Adam and Eve, including that of "desire" (see esp. pp. 116–17).

107. It has been argued that Muslim patriarchy has interpreted the myth of Eve in a slightly different manner, which led to a different type of negativization of women. See Azizah Al Hibri, "Eve: Islamic Image of Woman," in *Women and Islam* (Oxford [Oxfordshire], New York: Pergamon Press, 1982), pp. 135–44; published as a special issue of the journal *Women's Studies International Forum* (5.2).

108. Paul Rudnick's play, *The Most Fabulous Story Ever Told,* which was produced in New York during the 1998–99 season, explores exactly this possibility through a revisionist retelling of the Genesis narrative in which the first humans are two same-sex couples: Adam and Steve, Jane and Mabel. For the play text, see Paul Rud-

nick, *The Most Fabulous Story Ever Told* (New York: Dramatists Play Service Inc., 1999).

109. Judith Butler, "Gender is Burning: Questions of Appropriation and Subversion," in *Bodies That Matter: On the Discursive Limits of "Sex"* (New York: Routledge, 1993), p. 122.

110. Murray, "Twice Marginal," esp. pp. 195–98; 201–203; 207.

CHAPTER TWO

HILDEGARD OF BINGEN
AND RICHARDIS OF STADE:
THE DISCOURSE OF DESIRE

Susan Schibanoff

> *Rooted in Canticles, poetic devotional discourse made it possible for*
> *the twelfth-century German abbess, Hildegard of Bingen, to imagine*
> *and express a same-sex desire for Richardis of Stade that medieval*
> *moral, legal, and scientific discourse was bent on making either un-*
> *speakable or impossible.*

> I so loved the nobility of your character, your wisdom, your chastity,
> your spirit, and indeed every aspect of your life that many people
> have said to me: What are you doing?
>
> *—Hildegard, letter to Richardis, ca. 1152*★

Hildegard (later of Bingen) was born in 1098 in Bermersheim,
a town near the cathedral city of Mainz.[1] At the age of eight,
her parents, members of the nobility, dedicated her to the service of
God as a tithe. This dedication took the form of Hildegard's enclosure in the cell of the anchoress Jutta of Spanheim, whose hermitage
was affiliated with the Benedictine monastery at Disibodenberg.
Daughter of a local count, the educated Jutta provided Hildegard

with rudimentary instruction in Latin and saw to her further tutoring by Volmar, a monk from the nearby monastery. Other aristocratic families soon began to send daughters to Jutta's cell, which expanded into the equivalent of a small Benedictine convent attached (and subordinate) to Disibodenberg. One of the newcomers to the convent was a cousin of Jutta's, the young Richardis (born ca. 1123), member of a wealthy and influential family in Stade. Subsequently, Richardis's young niece, Adelheid, also joined the community. In 1136, Hildegard became *magistra* of the convent.

At Disibodenberg, Hildegard and Richardis developed a close personal relationship that continued for upward of ten years. They lived and worked together until Richardis was elected abbess of a convent in northern Germany and left Hildegard to assume her new post. The exact nature of their relationship is never explicitly defined in the extant references to it, but it became both controversial and, near the end, conflict-ridden. Its various enigmas continue to intrigue modern readers. Editors, biographers, and other scholars of Hildegard grapple with the question of the nature of Hildegard's attraction to Richardis.[2]

Hildegard's relationship with Richardis also intrigued some of their contemporaries, and the principal task of this essay is an analysis of the ways in which Hildegard herself and those around her read her "loving friendship"[3] with Richardis. The major documents I use to interpret Hildegard's attachment to Richardis are letters that Hildegard wrote to various ecclesiastical authorities protesting Richardis's departure to Bassum (and responses to those letters) as well as Hildegard's sole extant letter to Richardis.[4] Although literate, Richardis wrote nothing back, at least nothing that has survived. At the end of this essay, I shall argue that Hildegard's musical poems illuminate her letter to Richardis, which is *sui generis* among the correspondence. But I begin with Hildegard's earlier and unsuccessful attempt to block her beloved Richardis's departure.

The Letter Wars

When Jutta died in 1136, the nuns elected Hildegard *magistra* of the convent,[5] which, by 1150, Hildegard managed to detach from the

Disibodenberg monastery and reestablish independently at the Rupertsberg, on the Rhine near Bingen. During this period, Hildegard also began to record the visions that she had experienced since childhood. This text, the *Scivias,* a summa of Hildegard's theological doctrines, took some ten years (1141–51) to complete, due in part to Hildegard's intermittent illness and her time-consuming struggles to overcome opposition to her move to the Rupertsberg. According to Hildegard, her "deeply cherished" Richardis began to play a central role in her life at this time: "[Richardis] had bound herself to me in loving friendship in every way, and showed compassion for my illnesses, till I had finished the [*Scivias*]."[6] It is possible that Richardis provided technical as well as emotional support for Hildegard's literary endeavors, serving, along with Volmar, as her amanuensis and secretary from time to time,[7] and that Richardis also assisted Hildegard in founding the Rupertsberg convent. Whatever the nature and scope of her aid, Richardis had become one whom Hildegard described as her "dearest daughter" by the end of the 1140s.[8]

Just as Hildegard finished the *Scivias* in 1151, Richardis was elected abbess of a prestigious convent at Bassum near Bremen, and her niece, Adelheid, was appointed abbess at Gandersheim. Both Richardis's mother, the marchioness of Stade, and her brother, Archbishop Hartwig of Bremen, approved—indeed, had arranged—Richardis's removal to Bassum, and, as Hildegard would later believe, Richardis also "hankered after" the appointment.[9] Hildegard did little to hinder Adelheid's departure, but she strongly opposed Richardis's move and as *magistra* refused to release Richardis from the Rupertsberg convent. Hildegard first wrote to Richardis's mother, who had earlier helped her in her struggle to move to the Rupertsburg, and begged the marchioness not to "disturb my soul and draw bitter tears from my eyes and fill my heart with bitter wounds" by allowing "our dearest daughter Richardis" to leave.[10]

This time the marchioness paid no apparent heed to Hildegard's distress. In due course, Heinrich, Archbishop of Mainz, sent messengers to escort Richardis to Bassum. Clearly anticipating difficulty in extricating Richardis, Heinrich also sent Hildegard an accompanying letter in which he warned her that if she failed to follow his command to release the "sister who is a nun in your monastery" immediately to those who "seek and desire her," Heinrich would issue the edict again "in even stronger terms" and pursue the matter until Hildegard acquiesced.[11] Hildegard's response to Heinrich was rhetorically bold. In what Baird and Ehrman call a "missile" of a letter,[12] Hildegard assumed the first-person voice of the Living Light, the Bright Fountain—metaphors for the spirit of God that Hildegard had used in her recently completed *Scivias*—and claimed an authority over "this girl" (Richardis) superior to the archbishop's. As Hildegard saw it, "I," the Spirit of God, "neither initiated nor wanted" Richardis's election, which, Hildegard charged, was motivated by "opportunities for money" and the "foolishness of wicked men who do not fear God." The duty of the faithful, Hildegard further implied, was to recognize that God wished Richardis to remain at Hildegard's side.[13]

Although Hildegard ended her letter to Heinrich by refusing to heed or obey his "malicious curses and threatening words," Richardis's departure evidently occurred forthwith, for Hildegard soon wrote to Richardis's brother, Archbishop Hartwig, to secure the return of her "dearest daughter."[14] Since Richardis's new post at Bassum lay within Hartwig's ecclesiastical domain, he indeed had the power to return his sister to Hildegard, and so Hildegard begged Hartwig not to "cast off" her plea, as had Richardis's mother, Count Hermann, and Richardis herself.[15] In this letter, Hildegard implied that a desire for power had motivated Abbot Kuno of Disibod (who earlier had blocked Hildegard's move to the Rupertsberg) to "rashly drag our beloved daughter Richardis out of our cloister,"[16] and therefore, as were Heinrich, Hermann, and others, Kuno was guilty of simony, the buying and selling of ecclesiastical office. He was further guilty of encouraging "great temerity" in Richardis.[17]

Like all the others who favored Richardis's abbacy, Hartwig stood fast, and Hildegard took the final step of appealing to Pope Eugenius III to retrieve her most beloved nun. The letter that Hildegard wrote to Eugenius has not survived, but its existence may be inferred from Eugenius's oblique reference to her petition—"that matter you wished to consult us about"—and to Richardis—"that sister"—at the close of his answering epistle:

"Finally, we have delegated that matter you wished to consult us about to our brother Heinrich, archbishop of Mainz. His task will be to make sure that the Rule is strictly observed in that monastery entrusted to that sister (the nun that you delivered up to him)—either that or send her back to your supervision."[18]

Sabina Flanagan reads Eugenius's final proviso about the observation of the Benedictine rule at Bassum as a "mere face-saving device" that allowed the pope to send the matter back to the archbishop's court rather than a serious contemplation of returning Richardis.[19] And Dronke correctly sees in Eugenius's selection of Heinrich to judge whether or not Bassum was monastically suitable for Richardis a confirmation of Heinrich's earlier opposition to Hildegard.[20] Heinrich never found Bassum wanting.

Authorization and Discourse

Flanagan observes that in the controversy over Richardis, "the facts of the matter seem fairly uncomplicated; the emotions engendered by them less so."[21] That is, the influential von Stade family evidently sought to consolidate and extend its power in northern Germany by Richardis's election to Bassum and used its connections to secure her position, whereas Hildegard alone opposed the election. The factual basis of her opposition varied somewhat, but in essence Hildegard alleged that Richardis's elevation was an act of simony, or trafficking in ecclesiastical office. The buying and selling of bishoprics and abbacies, with the attendant installation of unqualified clerics, was an especial problem for the secularized church of the late eleventh century, and it became a major target of the reform pope, Gregory VII, who took office in 1073.[22] In blocking Richardis's abbacy, Hildegard took the public stance that she was helping to reform the clergy and saving the Church from egregious error.

But these "facts" quickly lead to the implication that Hildegard had a strong and complex bond with Richardis that encompassed affectional and physical ties as well as spiritual ones. The central issue here is not simply that Hildegard attempted to prevent Richardis's departure from Bingen, for she simultaneously opposed Adelheid's move to Gandersheim. It was only Richardis, however, whom Hildegard campaigned to have removed from her new appointment and returned to Bingen, evidently against Richardis's will. To modern sensibilities, at least, this is disturbing. Hildegard's repeated efforts to keep Richardis at her side, and later to return her there, occasion extreme language from Dronke, who characterizes them as "savage" and "overbearing" acts of "arrogant possessiveness" that contain a "frightening hint of megalomania."[23]

Although the grounds for Hildegard's attempt to end Richardis's new career were her allegations of simony, simony implied the installation of unqualified clerics with "bought votes."[24] This charge might possibly apply to the young Adelheid, who was probably not old enough to have taken vows when she became abbess at Gandersheim. But Richardis was both professed and in her late twenties. And elsewhere, Hildegard acknowledged that Richardis was an "exemplary nun," well-suited to the office of *abbatissa,* and thus not herself guilty of simony.[25]

A more revealing motivation for Hildegard's effort to retrieve Richardis lies in Hildegard's other claim that she was inspired by the Living Light to proclaim that God had willed Richardis to remain content where she was—that is, to stay physically at Hildegard's side in Bingen. If Richardis's appointment was made in violation of the monastic vow of stability, Hildegard never argued that the welfare or continuity of her institution required Richardis's presence. Instead, Hildegard implied that her personal well-being required it. She reiterated the simple claim that God meant for Richardis to be in Bingen with her, which intimates that Hildegard could not accept a distanced relationship with Richardis, spiritual or otherwise, and that her attempt to bring Richardis back was driven more by her need to have Richardis with her than by anything else. Whether or not Hildegard's possessiveness was arrogant and overbearing, as well as ill-considered and potentially detrimental to Richardis, it was most surely the result of a desperate and physical loneliness.

Other emotions—anger, feelings of betrayal, jealousy—perhaps colored Hildegard's pursuit of Richardis, yet they would all seem to stem from Hildegard's profound need for Richardis's corporeal presence. The statement attributed to Hildegard in her *Vita* that, while Hildegard was writing her *Scivias,* Richardis "had bound [*coniunxerat*] herself to [Hildegard] in loving friendship in every way,"[26] chooses a telling metaphor of physical contact (*conjungo*) between the two women, a contiguity ruptured by Richardis's removal to Bassum.

Her possessive desire to regain physical contact with her *conjunx* not only led Hildegard into opposing her beloved nun's abbacy but also into devising new ways of negotiating her relationship to the Church. Hildegard had resisted ecclesiastical authorities before, most recently in overcoming Abbot Kuno's disinclination to allow her move to the Rupertsberg, but typically she was careful to cultivate powerful allies in such confrontations. For instance, when Hildegard later persisted in her refusal to disinter a formerly excommunicated man she had buried at her convent, she had on her side an influential ecclesiastical ally, Archbishop Philip of Cologne.[27]

Indeed, Hildegard's pattern of gaining approval from prominent churchmen for her unconventional activities is evident from the beginning of her public life. As Hildegard composed the *Scivias,* which recorded for the first time the visions she had experienced since childhood, she carefully garnered a number of male ecclesiastical allies, beginning with her secretary, Volmar, who brought her work to the attention of Abbot Kuno, who notified Archbishop Heinrich of it, who alerted Pope Eugenius, in Germany at the time for the synod of Trier (1147–48). Hildegard also wrote to Bernard of Clairvaux in 1146–47 to seek his advice about whether she should make her visions public. Bernard not only approved Hildegard's visionary gift and encouraged her writing,[28] but he too promoted it to Eugenius. After reading portions of the *Scivias* aloud to the synod, Eugenius sent Hildegard a letter granting her apostolic license to continue her writing. In short, Hildegard took great care to have her writing mentored at every turn, from her male secretary to the pope. Hildegard's other most unusual activity, public preaching, was similarly approved by powerful male ecclesiastical figures. For instance, the future archbishop of Cologne, Philip of Heinsberg, wrote to Hildegard in 1163 to request a copy of a sermon she had preached at Cologne, sanctioning a preacher of Hildegard's humble and "fragile" sex on the scriptural grounds (John 3.8) that "the spirit breatheth where he will."[29]

The salient point about Hildegard's modus operandi is not that she was politically shrewd enough to cultivate male ecclesiastical favor, but that this support often materialized in textual form, characteristically a letter, that provided a justificatory discourse with which Hildegard might authorize her unusual activities. For Hildegard's writing and preaching, authorization issued from the rhetoric of female humility, which forms the basis of the early epistolary exchange between Hildegard and Bernard of Clairvaux and the later correspondence with Philip of Heinsberg quoted above.[30] In the terms of this exchange, Hildegard formulaically submits to her male superiors, abasing herself as "a poor little woman," and they in turn accept her obeisance and offer their support to her as a member of the "frail sex." Regardless of Hildegard's untraditional pursuits, her use of the rhetoric of humility provided her protection in the form of membership in a discourse community that repeatedly shielded and supported her.

In the matter of Richardis, however, no powerful ecclesiastical or lay figures backed Hildegard, except, she claimed, God. Hildegard's lack of validation from her usual quarter is apparent in her claim that it was not her "desire and will" alone to retain Richardis, "but also my sisters' and friends.'"[31] Hildegard never named these like-minded sisters and friends, and, if they actually existed, they left no epistolary traces of their support for her. Yet Hildegard persevered in her attempt to keep Richardis with her, taking the issue all the way to the pope, and one must wonder upon what rationale or precedent Hildegard based her action. Specifically, what discourse authorized Hildegard in her pursuit of Richardis?

Paralipsis and the *Peccatum Mutum*

That different modes of discourse inform contemporary understanding of Richardis and Hildegard's relationship is evident in the correspondence quoted above, and Hildegard herself spoke in different "languages" about the relationship. The first linguistic code I examine here is the paradoxical diction of Eugenius's letter to Hildegard, which names but does not name Hildegard's desire and the focus of that desire, Richardis.[32] Eugenius's veiled reference to

Hildegard's plea to keep Richardis with her—"that matter you wished to consult us about" [de cetero super hoc quod a nobis requirere uoluisti]—is balanced by his avoidance of naming "that sister" whom Hildegard had relinquished [illius sororis, que a te fuit ei concessa].[33] To be sure, unlike modern letters, medieval letters were public, not private, documents, and their writers took care not to reveal secrets in them; confidential or sensitive material was delivered orally by the letter carrier to its recipient.[34] Yet this facet of medieval correspondence offers no logical reason for Eugenius to mask his references to what, thanks to Hildegard, had already become a well-publicized controversy. Nor does the pope's probable wish, in Flanagan's words, to "distance himself as far as possible from the dispute"[35] account for his oblique diction, for Eugenius might have removed himself even further from the dispute by not writing about it at all. Instead, his mode of expression has a specific effect: it at once acknowledges and silences Hildegard's desire, denying her any textual basis, any discourse or common language, on which to authorize her petition to keep Richardis at her side.

The larger domain to which Eugenius's diction belongs is medieval moral discourse that speaks in apparent euphemisms about what it wishes to condemn. The most common examples of such moral discourse occur in the confessor's *summa,* which would begin to appear in increasing numbers after the Fourth Lateran Council of 1215 decreed annual performance of the sacrament of penance an obligatory act for the faithful. Designed to instruct priests in the art of interrogating the penitent, the confessor's manual enjoined priests to adopt a matter-of-fact tone in the confessional and to practice especial discretion in the discussion of *luxuria,* or sexual sin. The confessor should never, for instance, ask the name of the penitent's sexual partner, nor should the penitent volunteer the name of that person. Furthermore, the confessor was required to walk a fine line between a thorough and an overly detailed examination of *luxuria.* If the confessor were too explicit in naming and describing these vices, the *summas* warned, he ran the risk of teaching the faithful how to sin in new ways.[36] At the same time, however, the manuals exhorted the confessor to be as complete as possible in his interrogation, to uncover every possible sexual infraction and analyze it fully. As an aid

to achieve a full examination, the manuals offered confessors formulaic lists of questions to pose: *quis, quid, ubi* (who, what, where). If he
were to fulfill these somewhat contradictory goals of discretion and
thoroughness, it was incumbent upon the priest to master the discourse of paralipsis, diction that simultaneously named but did not
name, invoked but contained the sexual sin in question.[37]

The sexual vice most consistently handled in this paraliptical fashion was the so-called unnatural sin, which variously included sodomy
(homosexual or heterosexual), bestiality, onanism, and other sexual
practices and specific acts deemed *contra naturam* (that is, non-
procreative).[38] By the high Middle Ages, and lasting into the twentieth century, the moral discourse of Christianity rendered homosexual
sodomy synonomous with the "unspeakable sin,"[39] and in succeeding
centuries, Judith C. Brown argues, female sodomy would be silenced
even more rigorously than male sodomy:

> In the sixteenth century, Gregorio Lopez had called [sodomy be-
> tween females] "the silent sin, *peccatum mutum*," and earlier [in a con-
> fessor's manual] Jean Gerson had called it a sin against nature in
> which "women have each other by detestable and horrible means
> which should not be named or written."[40] For this reason the fa-
> mous jurist Germain Colladon (16th c.) advised the Genevan au-
> thorities, who had no prior experience with lesbian crimes, that the
> death sentence should be read publicly, as it normally was in cases of
> male homosexuality, but that the customary description of the crime
> committed should be left out. . . . [B]ecause women were thought
> to have weaker natures, it was feared that they were more suscepti-
> ble to suggestion.[41]

In his letter to Hildegard, Eugenius nowhere explicitly charges
her with sexual impropriety in her relationship to Richardis, yet his
neutral tone, his oblique reference to "that matter," and his disinclination to name Richardis evoke the paraliptical discourse of the
confessor conducting an examination of sexual sins, specifically the
sin against nature. The pope's rhetoric at least implies that his refusal
of Hildegard's request is based upon moral reservations about the
nature of the physical relationship between the two women. In
moving the matter into this court, Eugenius may have meant to

force Hildegard into complicity with him, for in a portion of Hildegard's recently completed *Scivias* that Eugenius could personally have read at Trier, she not only names the "unnameable" sin, but condemns "devilish" female homosexuality as "most vile." While medieval moral discourse commonly kept homosexuality in the public eye yet unable to speak for itself, as in the topos of *peccatum mutum* of the increasingly vernacular confessor's manual, in certain other rhetorical and linguistic circumstances—beyond the hearing of susceptible audiences—moralists were more than willing to speak for sodomy, that is, to define it and defame it,[42] and in the persona of the Living Light in the *Scivias,* Hildegard herself indicated her contempt for women who act sexually as men: "And a woman who takes up devilish ways and plays a male role in coupling with another woman is most vile . . . and so is she who subjects herself to such a one in this evil deed. For they should have been ashamed of their passion, and instead they impudently usurped a right that was not theirs. And, having put themselves into alien ways, they are to Me transformed and contemptible."[43]

As Murray observes, this passage in the *Scivias* "reinforce[s] traditional understanding of lesbians."[44] Hildegard takes here a conventionally phallocentric view of female homosexuality, the view that occasioned the most serious overt moral opposition to women who loved women in the Middle Ages. She condemns women who play male roles in coition because these women usurp a "right" that is not theirs, taking up "alien" masculine ways. When she calls this impudence "devilish," she echoes earlier moralists such as Hincmar of Reims, who labeled dildos and other sexual devices used (or thought to be used) by women "instruments of diabolical operation" (*machinas diabolicae operationis*).[45] It is possible that Hildegard circumscribed her censure of sexual activity between women to "alien ways," the use of instruments.[46] Murray explains that "women's use of 'instruments' such as dildos was considered far more serious than simple rubbing or mutual masturbation" because it usurped male prerogative and thus challenged "the hierarchy natural to sexual relations." Similarly, she continues, "sexual activity between women that did not attempt to replace the male organ with an artifical penis was regarded as a less serious crime than activity that sought to usurp male prerogative by the use of dildos. Ultimately, female sexuality was not taken seriously except insofar as it threatened male privilege or the natural hierarchy of the genders."[47]

This phallocentric attitude to female sexuality dominated conventional thinking long after Hildegard's era. Indeed, Brown argues, as late as the eighteenth century, "*lesbian* sexuality did not exist. For that matter, neither did *lesbians.*" What most commonly did exist was the belief in a "demonic" sexuality between women that imitated heterosexual practices, simultaneously privileging and threatening them. Beyond that, Brown concludes, there was a "fundamental ignorance about women's sexual practices and how they fit into established sexual categories and sexual crimes."[48]

Whether or not Pope Eugenius shared that ignorance, the fastidious diction of his letter to Hildegard invokes the traditional phallocentric concept of female sexuality, which seems to have had a blunt effect on Hildegard, for with one exception, it halted her known attempts to block Richardis's departure or to arrange her return. In moving the "matter" of Richardis into the realm of moral discourse, with its obsessive concern to distinguish proper and improper sexual acts and to safeguard male prerogative, Eugenius signalled Hildegard that her continued pursuit of Richardis could be interpreted as "alien," as masculine. Once in that domain, the "matter" was all but foreclosed. Yet Hildegard did make one last recorded attempt to retrieve her beloved Richardis, and in the remainder of this essay I shall suggest that her authority for doing so resided in a different discourse based upon a different understanding of sexuality between women than the phallocentric moral view Hildegard articulated in the *Scivias.*

A Different Discourse:
Maternity and Matrimony

In 1151–52, Hildegard's last known attempt to retrieve Richardis occurs in the letter she wrote to Richardis's brother, Hartwig. As archbishop of Bremen, Hartwig held authority over Richardis's convent at Bassum and thus could have ordered his sister's return to Hildegard, and that is precisely what Hildegard requested of him: "I be-

seech you. . . . to send my dearest daughter back to me."[49] Her letter is significant here for the testimony it offers of Hildegard's use of
a different type of rhetoric about Richardis than the moral one I
have just discussed, and this last quotation suggests the distance between the two discourses. No longer alluding to Richardis as "this
girl," in effect closeting her, Hildegard both names her beloved friend
and indicates the superlative nature of her feeling for her—"my
dearest daughter." In this letter, I suggest, we may hear traces, albeit
faint ones, of the discourse with which Hildegard authorized her
emotional—and (homo)erotic—attraction to Richardis. This discourse will sound familiar to readers today for, as does some modern
lesbian writing, it merges the mother-daughter affectional expectations and responses with same-sex love between two women.

   In her letter to Hartwig, Hildegard again indicts Kuno for simony in the appointment of Richardis to her abbacy.[50] Also again,
Hildegard suggests that it is God's will for Richardis to remain with
her and implies that what she does is for the salvation of Richardis's
soul. These charges and tactics are largely familiar from Hildegard's
earlier letter to Heinrich. What differs in the letter to Hartwig is not
only the personalized references to Richardis, but Hildegard's decision to speak in her own persona as *magistra* of the convent
Richardis had left rather than in the divine persona of the Living
Light.[51] In her human guise, Hildegard presents herself as a mother
mourning the loss of her most beloved daughter. "Hear me," begs
Hildegard, who is "cast down" and "miserably weeping" at
Hartwig's feet, "my spirit is exceedingly sad, because a certain horrible man has trampled underfoot my desire and will (and not mine
alone, but also my sisters' and friends'), and has rashly dragged our
beloved daughter Richardis out of our cloister."[52]

   Hildegard's presentation of Richardis as her spiritual daughter
is both conventional and accurate,[53] yet in creating even this traditional metaphorical filiation, Hildegard introduced the possibility of entertaining more intimate relationships between herself
and Richardis. One of these imaginatively closer relationships occurs in a letter (ca. 1151–52) Hildegard wrote to Richardis after
she had gone to Bassum, the only extant correspondence between
the two and their last known communication.[54] No longer trying

to persuade Richardis to return, Hildegard wrote to her of her grief over their separation. Speaking in her own persona, Hildegard addresses her lament directly to Richardis: "Now, again, I say: Woe is me, mother, woe is me, daughter, 'Why have you forsaken me' like an orphan?" [Nunc iterum dico: Heu me, mater, heu me, filia, *quare me dereliquisti* sicut orphanam].[55] Employing a discourse here akin to poetry, Hildegard moves out of her maternal role ("Woe is me, mother") and momentarily merges herself into Richardis, crossing over the boundary between them into Richardis's role as daughter ("Woe is me, daughter"); the two female figures then separate as Richardis is transformed into the mother who has forsaken her daughter, the orphan Hildegard who yearns for reunion. Although Hildegard ultimately represents herself and Richardis as exchanging their conventional roles of mother and daughter, for one brief moment she positions herself and Richardis on an equal footing and in the same poetic space.[56]

A final imaginative transformation of the two women's relationship occurs near the end of Hildegard's plaintive letter to Richardis. Hildegard (homo)eroticizes her role of mourner, the orphaned daughter who echoes Christ's words, "why hast thou forsaken me?" (Matthew 27.46, Mark 15.34, John 13.18). While Hildegard's use of Christ's lament suggests—audaciously, for some[57]—the magnitude of her grief at the loss of Richardis, Hildegard continued to search for a mournful female figure with which to identify and found it at letter's end. Hildegard's concluding lament ("Now, let all who have a sorrow like my sorrow mourn with me . . ." [Nunc plangant mecum omnes qui habent dolorem similem dolori meo])[58] echoes the words of Jeremiah's female figure, Jerusalem, who sorrows over her desolation and destruction and the captivity of her people ("O all ye that pass by the way, attend, and see if there be any sorrow like to my sorrow . . . ," Lamentations 1.12). In Jeremiah's words (Lamentations 1.1), Jerusalem, mistress of the Gentiles (*domina gentium*), has become as a widow (*quasi vidua*) through the loss of her people. In appropriating Jerusalem's lament, Hildegard becomes, like her imaginative model, not the mother who mourns for her daughter (or vice versa) but the widow who laments the loss of her spouse.

"Lesbian Love Letters"
and the Song of Songs

Of the possible discourses on which Hildegard might have modeled her allusive transformation from mournful mother to widowed spouse, that of "spiritual friendship" (*spiritualis amicitia*) comes first to mind. As Flanagan notes, the twelfth century witnessed an about-face on the issue of monastic same-sex friendship. Before then, she elaborates, "what writing there was on the subject had been largely admonitory" and concentrated on the necessity of avoiding "the possible dangers of such friendship."[59] In the twelfth century, however, Cistercians in particular began to encourage monastic friendship as a way toward God. Inspired by an early reading of Cicero's *De amicitia,* Aelred of Rievaulx, for instance, wrote his *De spirituali amicitia* to promote human friendship as a means of attaining divine love.

Whether Aelred promoted "entirely chaste and disinterested" relationships devoid of mutual passion among monks, as Flanagan writes about his *De spirituali amicitia,*[60] or whether, as Boswell sees it, Aelred's "idealization of love between men was a dramatic break with the traditions of monasticism" which heretofore had discouraged "particular friendships of any sort—especially passionate ones"[61] is an arguable question on several counts.[62] However, Boswell's larger point is that, at the very least, Aelred evidences a period (ca. 1050–1150) during which the "development of theological argument among those hostile to gay sexuality came to a standstill."[63] If one accepts Boswell's putative "golden age" (or century), which overlaps Hildegard's dates (1098–1179), it is possible to speculate that the temporary hiatus in the development of Christian homophobia encouraged Hildegard in her public attempt to keep Richardis with her.[64]

Yet Hildegard's discourse of desire shows no affinity with at least one significant aspect of the Ciceronian rhetoric of spiritual friendship found in Aelred's work and elsewhere. As Flanagan notes, Aelred's argument, based on Cicero, that true friends do not fear physical separation, for "even when friends are absent they are present to one another," runs counter to Hildegard's emphasis on her need to have Richardis physically present.[65] And as I have suggested

above, one of Hildegard's most prominent discursive topoi is her intense yearning for physical reunion with Richardis. She displays no
inclination to accomodate herself to such separations through Ciceronian oxymorons of "absent presence" or on any other grounds.

If the Ciceronian branch of spiritual friendship, with its ethic of
disinterest, its stoical acceptance of physical distance, offered Hildegard no rhetorical model, another possible textual precedent for her
discourse of desire lies in the more openly homosexual poetry of
the high Middle Ages, Hildegard's opposition to homosexuality in
the *Scivias* notwithstanding. But there is virtually no trace of the
dominant stylistic characteristic of medieval homosexual poetry in
Hildegard's letters or elsewhere.

As Thomas Stehling describes it,[66] the large majority of such
verse is by and about men, and typically it looks back to classical literature and mythology to find its themes and subjects, invoking
Apollo's love for Hyacinth, Jupiter's for Ganymede, and the like. In
part, this orientation toward Greece and Rome reflects the classical
education of its male authors, the kind of instruction that a child
oblate like Hildegard would not be likely to receive from a Jutta or
a Volmar. Outside of her medical and scientific writings, in which
Hildegard cites Pliny, Galen, Soranus, and others, she rarely quotes
classical authors, and if she knew the homosexual poetry of her
male contemporaries, her work shows little influence of it.

Stehling further notes that few medieval love poems written
from one woman to another exist; his anthology includes but two
examples, both anonymous and from a German manuscript of the
twelfth or thirteenth century, which he entitles "lesbian love letters."[67] Other medieval female homoerotic poems remain extant,[68]
although the total comprises a small proportion of all medieval homosexual poetry. Yet what Stehling detects as the characteristics of
his small sample bears repeating, for it resonates with Hildegard's
discourse of desire: "these two lesbian poems differ from the love
poems written by men. Whereas male love poems tend to reach
back to classical literature and mythology for their literary sources,
these poems draw on the sensual language of the Song of Songs."[69]
Not only do Stehling's two female love letters draw specific and
erotic imagery from Canticles, but their overall rhetorical stance de-

rives from that text as well. The speakers of both letters characterize themselves as separated from their beloved. In one the speaker
languishes, as does the turtledove who sits forever on the barren
twig after it has lost its spouse; in the other, the speaker avers that
the "worst misery" is to be far from one's beloved, as she is. Like the
spouse of Canticles before Christ calls her, the speakers of these
poems long for union with the beloved. Hildegard's spousal imagery
in her letter to Richardis does not derive from Canticles[70] but from
Lamentations, yet striking here is the common imaginative conversion of the image of heterosexual matrimony into homoerotic
trope, and I wish to explore the mechanism of this transformation
further, for I believe at its source lies the authorization upon which
Hildegard based her public pursuit of Richardis.

Regendering Canticles

The obvious difference between Stehling's female love poems and
the Song of Songs lies in the biological gender of the lover and the
beloved. Canticles genders the beloved spouse or bride, typically interpreted to be Ecclesia (the Church),[71] a feminine noun in Latin,
as female, the lover Christ as male, whereas the female love letters
gender both the speaker and the subject of the speaker's desire as female. In essence, the question becomes, on what grounds, or authority, was the Song of Songs regendered (or, as Stehling might
phrase it, "lesbianized")? The answer in part, I believe, lies in the
treatment of gender in medieval religious thought and devotion, a
subject extensively explored in recent scholarship. Unlike the rigid
classification of gender in medieval moral discourse, gender was an
unstable category in medieval religious discourse. Especially fluid
was the category of male: Christ, as well as the male clergy devoted
to him,[72] was often feminized in behavior and body, figured, for instance, as the tender mother giving suck to a child.[73] Less elastic was
the category of female in religious discourse. While religious
women were encouraged to aspire to "honorary maleness" of spirit,
they were not fully troped as biologically male.[74] And increasingly
toward the end of the Middle Ages, the Virgin's especial virtue ac-
crued from her female trait of excessive humility rather than from

conventionally masculine attributes such as reason, learning, strength, and the like.[75]

Whether the feminization of Christ pays homage to women or whether it simply heterosexualizes the paradigm of male devotion by figuring Christ as a female recipient of men's adoration is a question outside the scope of this essay. What is germane here is the clue that the latitude—indeed, play—within gender categories in medieval religious discourse, specifically the feminization of Christ, offers to the question of how the Song of Songs was regendered to accommodate female homoeroticism. If medieval Christians were accustomed to the regendering of Christ elsewhere—that is, to concentrating upon his so-called feminine qualities, even to entertaining images of Christ as biologically female—is it impossible that at least some Christians might regender him female within an erotic context such as the Song of Songs? Or substitute another female figure for Christ that becomes the subject of the bride's (Ecclesia's) homoerotic longing and desire? For evidence of the latter possibility, I return to Hildegard herself, not to her letters and *vita* discussed above, but to the religious poetry she wrote and set to music.

Hildegard included fourteen poetic songs (minus musical notation) honoring the Virgin, the angels, and saints at the end of the *Scivias*. Although the textual history is obscure, Hildegard evidently continued writing these liturgical songs through the 1150s, resulting in the work known as *Symphonia armonie celestium revelationum* (Symphony of the Harmony of the Revelations), which exists in two manuscript versions, the longer a cycle of 75 lyrics (with musical notation). Barbara Newman believes that Hildegard intended her music to be used during Mass and the Divine Office at her monastery, although some may have been written on commission for other religious establishments.[76] In any event, Marian songs form the largest thematic category in the *Symphonia:* Hildegard wrote sixteen lyrics on Mother and Son, compared to seven on Father and Son and five on the Holy Spirit.

Of especial interest among Hildegard's Marian songs is her hymn to the Virgin, *Ave, generosa* (no. 17), upon which Bruce Wood Holsinger bases much of his analysis of the "homoerotics of devotion" in the music of Hildegard.[77] His attention is particularly

drawn to the seventh and final stanza of the hymn, in which Hildegard describes the female figure, Ecclesia (the beloved bride-of-
Christ figure of Canticles): "Now let all Ecclesia blush in joy and /
sound in *symphonia* for the sweetest / virgin and praiseworthy Mary,
/ mother of God."[78] As Holsinger reads this stanza, it unites two female figures, Ecclesia and the Virgin, in mutual pleasure: "the body
of Ecclesia resonates with the same sounds that filled the Virgin's
womb two [stanzas] earlier. Sharing the same, sonorous experience,
the bodies of the Virgin and Ecclesia are linked through the sensual,
corporeal bonds of music and melodious pleasure."[79]

Holsinger concludes that *Ave, generosa* conjoins two female terms
(Ecclesia and the Virgin, and by extension, Hildegard and her nuns)
not only in space but in "sensual, corporeal bonds as well" and that
Hildegard foregoes the customary medieval metaphors of heterosexual intercourse in describing communion with the divine to employ what she found much more central to her concerns, female
homoerotic images.[80] To consider it in terms of the material from
Canticles I have discussed above, Hildegard replaced Ecclesia's male
subject of desire—Christ—with a female one—the Virgin. As I
have suggested earlier, the instability of Christ's gender identity in
medieval devotional discourse, specifically his feminization, may
have allowed Hildegard and others sufficient latitude to envision
Ecclesia's relationship with an altogether female figure, the Virgin.[81]

Gynocentrism and the Irrelevance
of the Male Phallus

Hildegard's homoerotic discourse resonates with the alternative, gynocentric view of female sexuality disclosed in her scientific writing. Rather than viewing female sexuality only in phallocentric
terms as dependent on the male phallus, necessitating the substitu-
tion of "devilish" instruments for the absent penis, Hildegard also
described a sexual pleasure for women that is not contingent upon
the male organ. This gynocentric concept may be glimpsed in
Hildegard's *Causes and Cures* (ca. 1151–58), also titled *The Book of
Compound Medicine,* a descriptive and therapeutic work. Empirical
in nature, *Causes and Cures* strikes modern scholars as innovative in

its treatment of human sexuality. Flanagan notes that the work contains "an unexpected account of the nature of sexual pleasure" from the female rather than male point of view and recognizes "other forms of sexual expression and behavior" than marital sex.[82] Joan Cadden judges Hildegard's discussion of sexuality in *Causes and Cures* "both wide-ranging and undogmatic" compared to what her contemporaries had to say.[83]

In this work, Hildegard attributes differences in the nature of male and female sexual desire to the uncomplementary physical constitutions of men and women. Unlike many medieval scientific writers, Hildegard did not regard female genitalia as the anatomical inversion of male genitalia. Or, as Cadden says, Hildegard did not consider woman to be a "pale imitation" of man. In *Causes and Cures,* women "merit separate consideration and are characterized on their own terms."[84] These terms are both literal and explicit: Hildegard explains in detail how male sexual anatomy occasions one kind of sexual desire and pleasure, intensely concentrated in the loins, while female anatomy gives rise to another type, diffused throughout the entire body.[85]

When Hildegard went on to offer her gynocentric view of female sexuality in *Causes and Cures,* however, she supplemented literal description with poetic discourse, reaching again for the language in which I have argued that she regendered Canticles to express her homoeroticism. Hildegard stated directly, if succinctly, in *Causes and Cures* that woman "may be moved to pleasure without the touch of a man."[86] But her more extended gynocentric description of female sexual arousal in *Causes and Cures* employs a trope to represent the irrelevance of the penetrative phallus to female desire. As Hildegard figures it, woman's pleasure [*delectatio*] is comparable to the sun, which gently, lightly, and continuously [*blande et leniter et assidue*] perfuses the earth with its heat.[87] Although the sun and its quality of heat are masculine in conventional medieval thought, Hildegard poetically regenders them feminine and shines their warming power onto the female body, earth. Like Ecclesia and the Virgin, the sun and earth in Hildegard's *Causes and Cures* represent a female sexual pleasure not centered on the male phallus or its absence.

Flanagan remarks that Hildegard's "mixture of metaphorical and direct language" in her discussion of sexual desire in *Causes and Cures* "at times defies translation."[88] More to the point here is the observation that Hildegard's "poeticization" of science was perhaps necessary to articulate a gynocentric concept that her culture generally found impossible or rendered trivial, hence invisible: the idea of sexual pleasure between women that occurred without the male phallus or its "demonic" substitute. That Hildegard's homoerotic discourse is more poetic than prosaic is not surprising. As Bruce R. Smith argues, the expression of homosexual desire, impossible in early moral, legal, and medical discourse, is often possible in poetic discourse, for the latter requires neither logic nor consistency and "is uniquely fitted to address the contradictions that must be covered up to make ordinary life possible."[89]

This is not to argue that Hildegard's homoerotic attachment to Richardis was a fiction, a mere figure of speech, even though one need not necessarily "genitalize" it in phallocentric terms, but to acknowledge that a poetic devotional discourse, rooted in Canticles, made it possible for her to imagine and express what medieval moral discourse was bent on making "unspeakable." Nor is it to suggest that Hildegard held a resolved and unified vision of female sexuality. Indeed, to modern eyes, her homoeroticism appears fissured with self-contradiction and denial, even hypocrisy, and shrouded in obscurity. But such a judgment holds Hildegard hostage to the relatively recent reconciliation of various expressions of lesbian affection into one whole that proceeds in part from a viable same-sex identity based on community.[90] As the conclusion to this essay, I shall suggest that Hildegard came to recognize the fractures in what we would now call her same-sex identity. That understanding alone pays tribute to Hildegard's insight and courage.

"What are you doing?":
Moral vs. Poetic Discourse

Hildegard's understanding manifests itself in her recognition of the extent to which medieval poetic and moral discourse were at odds on the subject of homoeroticism. In the course of her attempt to retrieve

Richardis, Hildegard spoke both languages. With the pope and the archbishops, who regarded lesbianism as a threat to male authority, Hildegard employed the language of phallocentric moral discourse; in her music and even in her science, Hildegard voiced the gynocentric language of poetry. But in her final letter to Richardis, in the passage quoted as the opening epitaph to this essay, Hildegard juxtaposed these two languages to display her awareness of the way in which poetic discourse was all too often called into account by moral discourse, with its obsessive need to interrogate and silence sex and love. In the hyperbolic language of love poetry, Hildegard told Richardis that she had loved every aspect of her life and being, to the point that it drew scrutiny from others, who only wanted to hear her answer to the moral-phallocentric question of "what"—*quid*—she was doing.[91]

Such moral inquisition did not altogether silence Hildegard, although her poetic discourse about Richardis largely ceased, if only because Richardis died soon after Hildegard wrote to her. A final flash of poetic discourse appears in Hildegard's letter to Hartwig of 1152, as Hildegard acknowledged Hartwig's sad news that his sister had died and had been unable to fulfill her own desire to return to Hildegard, albeit for a short visit. As a gesture of farewell to Richardis, Hildegard triangulated desire and ceded her favorite nun to God: "So my soul has great confidence in her, though the world loved her beautiful looks and her prudence, while she lived in the body. But God loved her more. Thus God did not wish to give his beloved to a rival lover, that is, to the world."[92]

If this essay employs what Nancy F. Partner calls "gingerly paraphrase"—the replacement of the blunt word "sex" by the politely distant "erotic"[93]—it does so because Hildegard herself coded her sexual feelings in poetic scriptural language. Such coding does not equal denial, however. Poetic paraphrase differs from moral paralipsis; the former opens up the possibility of expressing various types of human sexual feeling in language, while the latter renders all but one type unspeakable. In a culture whose official (moral) language policed the sexual act, Hildegard was fortunate to have access to another discourse that could accommodate and authorize her desire. Whether or not one wishes to "out" medieval devotion, as Holsinger urges, it is indeed worth our effort to reconstruct its polymorphous potential.[94] It is equally important, I believe, to hear in Hildegard's final words to Richardis an intimation of the ensuing struggle lesbian and gay people have undertaken to achieve a unified same-sex identity and consciousness.

Notes

* Hildegard of Bingen, *The Letters of Hildegard of Bingen,* trans. Joseph L. Baird and Radd K. Ehrman (New York and Oxford: Oxford University Press, 1994), 1:144.

1. Compare Peter Dronke's translation of the passage in the epitaph: "I loved the nobility of your conduct, your wisdom and chastity, your soul and the whole of your life, so much that many said: What are you doing?" (*Women Writers of the Middle Ages: A Critical Study of Texts from Perpetua (d. 203) to Marguerite Porete (d. 1310)* [Cambridge: Cambridge University Press, 1984], p. 157).

   The most comprehensive biography of Hildegard is Sabina Flanagan, *Hildegard of Bingen, 1098–1179: A Visionary Life* (London: Routledge, 1989). Shorter accounts of Hildegard's life may be found in Kent Kraft, "The German Visionary: Hildegard of Bingen," in *Medieval Women Writers,* ed. Katharina M. Wilson (Athens, GA: University of Georgia Press, 1984), pp. 109–23, and Marcelle Thiébaux, trans. and intro., *The Writings of Medieval Women: An Anthology,* 2d ed. (New York: Garland, 1994), pp. 315–21.

2. For instance, Flanagan, *Hildegard,* pp. 180–84; Kraft, "German Visionary," pp. 111–12; Hildegard of Bingen, *The Letters of Hildegard of Bingen,* 1, trans. Joseph L. Baird and Radd K. Ehrman (New York and Oxford: Oxford University Press, 1994), p. 18; hereafter cited as B&E with page number[s]; Dronke, *Women Writers,* pp. 150–59; Thiébaux, *Writings of Medieval Women,* pp. 317–18. See also Frances Beer, *Women and Mystical Experience in the Middle Ages* (Rochester, NY: Boydell and Brewer, 1992), p. 25; Ulrike Wiethaus, "In Search of Medieval Women's Friendships: Hildegard of Bingen's Letters to Her Female Contemporaries," in *Maps of Flesh and Light: The Religious Experience of Medieval Women Mystics,* ed. Ulrike Wiethaus (Syracuse: Syracuse University Press, 1993), pp. 105–10; Barbara Newman, *Sister of Wisdom: St. Hildegard's Theology of the Feminine* (Berkeley: University of California Press, 1987), pp. 222–23; Fiona Bowie and Oliver Davies, eds. and intro., *Hildegard of Bingen: Mystical Writings* (New York: Crossroad, 1990), pp. 35–37; and Marianna Schrader and Adelgundis Fuhrkotter, *Die Echtheit des Schriftums der*

heiligen Hildegard von Bingen (Cologne and Graz: Bohlau, 1956), pp. 131–41.

3. The phrase is attributed to Hildegard by Gottfried of Saint Disibod and Theodoric of Echternach, the biographers who composed her *vita* between 1177 and 1181, which may be found in *Sanctae Hildegardis Abbatissae opera omnia,* PL 197. This excerpt, in which Hildegard discusses her former relationship with Richardis, is translated by Dronke in *Women Writers,* p. 151.

4. Beyond the correspondence, Hildegard's first-person statements about Richardis appear in her *vita* (see note 3). Although I occasionally quote the *vita* in this essay, I have not relied heavily upon it for several reasons, including the likelihood that it more heavily edits (or shapes) Hildegard's sentiments than do the early compilers of her letters, who assembled her correspondence with less attention to the events of her life than to the status of her correspondents. Although the hierarchical arrangement of the correspondence requires one to rearrange letters in order to trace the flow of events in Hildegard's life, it may also suggest that the compiler was less interested in editing those events than were the *vita* authors, who must already have had an eye out for Hildegard's canonization. Canonization proceedings began in 1233, although they ended inconclusively, and Hildegard was not commemorated as a local saint in Germany until 1940. (See Flanagan, *Hildegard,* pp. 12–13, and Newman, *Sister of Wisdom,* p. 15.)

   Gillian T. W. Ahlgren, "Visions and Rhetorical Strategy in the Letters of Hildegard of Bingen," in *Dear Sister: Medieval Women and the Epistolary Genre,* ed. Karen Cherewatuk and Ulrike Wiethaus (Philadelphia: University of Pennsylvania Press, 1993), pp. 46–63, analyzes the overall corpus of Hildegard's extant correspondence, 284 letters, and also discusses how the earliest edition of Hildegard's letters, the Wiesbaden Riesencodex of 1180–90, paired Hildegard's epistles with those from others that supposedly elicited her response. This creates the impression that Hildegard was "more passive than she was." B&E, pp. 16–18, discuss further problems in the textual history of Hildegard's letters.

5. Although commonly titled "abbess" in modern scholarship, Hildegard was more usually addressed with the lesser titles of *magistra* and *praeposita* ('mistress' or 'superior') or *prioressa* ('prioress') in contemporary correspondence. See B&E, p. 22.

6. This statement is attributed to Hildegard in her posthumous *vita* (trans. Dronke, *Women Writers,* p. 151).

7. Flanagan, *Hildegard,* p. 180, notes that Hildegard does not specify the actual nature of Richardis's aid. Typically, however, modern readers find a visual allusion to Richardis in a work Hildegard wrote after Richardis died in 1152: in the opening illumination to Hildegard's *De operatione dei* (1163–73), a nun stands behind Hildegard as she receives and records her vision. This illumination, from an early thirteenth-century manuscript of *De operatione dei* (Lucca, Biblioteca Statale, Cod. lat. 1942, fol. 1v), is reproduced as the frontispiece in Newman, *Sister of Wisdom.* Newman (p. 6) suggests that the nun in this picture is Richardis von Stade.

8. B&E, p. 49.

9. A statement attributed to Hildegard in her posthumous *vita* (trans. Dronke, *Women Writers,* p. 151).

10. B&E, pp. 69–70.

11. Ibid., p. 70.

12. Ibid., p. 48.

13. Ibid., p. 70.

14. Ibid., pp. 48–49.

15. Count Hermann is Hermann of Stahlek, Count of the Rhine Palatinate, who along with his wife Gertrude, a member of the high nobility, had also earlier aided Hildegard in her struggles to move to the Rupertsberg. (Hildegard later returned the favor to Gertude, who, after she was widowed, entered a Cistercian convent; in 1157, Hildegard successfully petitioned the Bishop of Bamberg to find hospitable surroundings for Gertrude and her nuns. See B&E, pp. 93–94.)

16. B&E, p. 48.

17. Ibid., p. 49.

18. Ibid., p. 35. "De cetero super hoc quod a nobis requirere uoluisti, uenerabili fratri nostro H<enrico>, archiepiscopo Maguntino, mandauimus, quatenus uel illius sororis, que a te fuit concessa, regulam faciat in loco ei commisso firmiter obseruari, uel eam ad magisterium tue discipline remittat" (vol. 91, p. 11).

    In cases where the original wording is critical to my argument, I cite in my notes the Latin passage from Lieven Van Acker, ed., *Hildegardis Bingensis epistolarium,* Corpus Christianorum: continuatio medievalis, vols. 91 and 91 A (Turnhout, Belgium: Brepols, 1991–93).

19. Flanagan, *Hildegard,* p. 182.

20. Dronke, *Women Writers,* p. 156. See also B&E, p. 36 n. 3.

21. Flanagan, *Hildegard,* p. 180.

22. See B&E, p. 11.

23. Dronke, *Women Writers,* pp. 154–56.

24. Flanagan, *Hildegard,* p. 181, although Flanagan also argues that Hildegard's definition of simony is "any ecclesiastical action against the manifest will of God," which "renders its participants suspect of trafficking in the offices of the church."

25. Hildegard intimated in a letter to Hartwig of Bremen, discussed below, that she would favor Richardis's abbacy at a later date (B&E, p. 49), and elsewhere in her correspondence she praised Richardis's purity, integrity, and nobility (e.g., B&E, p. 51). Dronke, *Women Writers,* p. 159, remarks upon the "touching incongruity" in Hildegard's later negative reflections upon Richardis in her *Vita.* This essay will suggest why one need not be troubled by Hildegard's apparent inconsistency on Richardis. (Furthermore, as I have also noted above, Hildegard's *vita* was probably edited more heavily than her letters, perhaps advertently or inadvertently suppressing evidence of her positive feelings for Richardis.)

26. Dronke gives the Latin text of the *Vita* in *Women Writers,* p. 234. The verb *conjungo,* 'to bind together,' could apply to the union of both married partners and of friends.

27. Flanagan, *Hildegard,* p. 184 ff., discusses this episode more fully.

28. B&E, pp. 31–33.

29. Ibid., p. 54.

30. On female modesty topoi, see Susan Schibanoff, "Botticelli's *Madonna del Magnificat:* Constructing the Woman Writer in Early Humanist Italy," *PMLA* 109 (1994): 190–206, and Alison Weber, *Teresa of Avila and the Rhetoric of Femininity* (Princeton: Princeton University Press, 1990), pp. 42 ff.

31. B&E, p. 48.

32. Eve Kosofsky Sedgwick, *Between Men: English Literature and Male Homosocial Desire* (New York: Columbia University Press, 1985), p. 2, defines this kind of desire as "the affective or social force, the glue . . . that shapes an important relationship" and has erotic dimensions.

33. Eugenius was not the first to suppress Richardis's name. Earlier, as I have noted above, Heinrich alluded to Richardis as "that sister" [soror illa] (Van Acker, vol. 91, p. 53), and Hildegard had responded in kind, referring to Richardis as "this girl" [huius puelle] (Van Acker, vol. 91, p. 54).

34. Giles Constable, *Letters and Letter-Collections* (Turnholt, Belgium: Brepols, 1976), p. 11, doubts whether there were any "private" medieval letters in the modern sense of the term.

35. Flanagan, *Hildegard,* p. 182.

36. Thomas N. Tentler, *Sin and Confession on the Eve of the Reformation* (Princeton: Princeton University Press, 1977), p. 104 ff., discusses

the requirements of the good and complete confession. The translation of Latin confessor's manuals into the vernacular further mandated discretion in the naming of sexual sins. Michel Foucault (in *The History of Sexuality, Volume I: An Introduction,* trans. Robert Hurley [New York: Random House, 1978], p. 18) dates the "veiling" of sexual discourse in Catholic pastoral literature after the Council of Trent, although its beginnings are evident considerably earlier.

37. Related to the verbal figures of *occupatio, occultatio,* and *praeteritio, paralipsis* is defined in the *Oxford English Dictionary* as "a rhetorical figure in which the speaker emphasizes something by affecting to pass it by without notice." Medieval rhetoricians commonly discuss the figure under the heading of *occupatio.* See, for instance, Margaret F. Nims, trans., *Poetria Nova of Geoffrey of Vinsauf* (Toronto: Pontifical Institute of Mediaeval Studies, 1967), pp. 58 and 105, and Traugott Lawler, ed. and trans., *The "Parisiana Poetria" of John of Garland* (New Haven: Yale University Press, 1974), p. 123. In *Ad Herennium* 4.27, pseudo-Cicero uses the term *paralipsis,* however, a device the author recommends for creating suspicion without running the risk of a direct reference that is tedious or "undignified." As pseudo-Cicero implies, paralipsis is indeed a "tricky" or oxymoronic device. Related to ellipsis, which removes words, paralipsis simultaneously removes words and recalls them. Later, the figure will be referred to as *negatio;* see Gregory W. Bredbeck, *Sodomy and Interpretation: Marlowe to Milton* (Ithaca: Cornell University Press, 1991), p. 20.

38. Vern L. Bullough, "The Sin Against Nature and Homosexuality," in *Sexual Practices and the Medieval Church,* ed. Vern L. Bullough and James Brundage (Buffalo, NY: Prometheus Books, 1982), p. 57, remarks that the "appeal to nature" was a pedagogical device not based upon actual empirical observation. John W. Baldwin, *The Language of Sex: Five Voices from Northern France around 1200* (Chicago: University of Chicago Press, 1994), pp. 43–47, notes that homophobia is the common denominator of different medieval discourses about sex.

39. Michael Goodich, *The Unmentionable Vice: Homosexuality in the Later Medieval Period* (Santa Barbara, CA: Ross-Erikson, 1979), p. 62, traces the long pedigree such writers as William of Auvergne (ca. 1180–1249) claimed for the "unspeakable sin." In his *Summa de poenitentia,* William connects the muteness of the original Sodomites before God with the necessity for contemporary preachers to silence the "sin against nature" through paralipsis: "This sin is so heinous . . . that preachers dare not name it, referring instead to the 'unmentionable vice'; for, as Gregory the Great notes, the air itself is corrupted

by its mention, and the Devil himself is embarrassed. In Ezekiel 16.27, it is noted that even the shameless Philistines were shamed by such 'whoredoms.' God himself was so outraged that he refused to recognize the Sodomites as men, raining fire and brimstone on them; and the men of Sodom became mute in their confessions before God." Bullough, "Sin Against Nature," pp. 66–67, cites several medieval instances of the "unspeakable sin" topos that give one or more of William's reasons to justify paralipsis. Elsewhere, I am currently exploring the connections between the *peccatum mutum* of the Middle Ages, the modern "closet" or "open secret" as defined, for instance, by Eve Kosofsky Sedgwick, *Epistemology of the Closet* (Berkeley: University of California Press, 1990), and "the love that dare not speak its name."

40. However, some moralists would define and name women's "horrible and detestable means" as involving the "demonic" use of "instruments" (for example, dildos) to imitate heterosexual intercourse. See my discussion immediately below.

41. Judith C. Brown, "Lesbian Sexuality in Medieval and Early Modern Europe," in *Hidden from History: Reclaiming the Gay and Lesbian Past,* ed. Martin Duberman, Martha Vicinus, and George Chauncey, Jr. (New York: Meridian, 1990), p. 75. See also Judith C. Brown, *Immodest Acts: The Life of a Lesbian Nun in Renaissance Italy* (New York: Oxford University Press, 1986), pp. 17–18, on the silencing of female sodomy. Jacqueline Murray ("Twice Marginal and Twice Invisible: Lesbians in the Middle Ages," *Handbook of Medieval Sexuality,* ed. Vern L. Bullough and James A. Brundage [New York: Garland, 1996], pp. 191–222), documents her claim that "of all groups within medieval society lesbians are the most marginalized and least visible." Bernadette J. Brooten, *Love Between Women: Early Christian Responses to Female Homoeroticism* (Chicago: University of Chicago Press, 1996), pp. 356–57, concludes that "a number of early Christian writers knew about and condemned sexual love between women" and that "one can no longer claim that sexual love between women was unknown in the early church." Brown's point and mine are somewhat different and concern how female sodomy was "silenced," not unknown. E. Ann Matter ("My Sister, My Spouse: Woman-Identified Women in Medieval Christianity," in *Weaving the Visions: New Patterns in Feminist Spirituality,* eds. Judith Plaskow and Carol P. Christ [San Francisco: Harper & Row, 1989], p. 53) discusses the relatively "few comments about lesbian acts" compared to the "obsessive detail" about male sodomy in earlier penitentials (sixth to twelfth centuries).

Warren Johannson and William A. Percy ("Homosexuality," *Handbook,* ed. Bullough and Brundage, p. 171) observe that Christianity not only prohibited homosexual behavior but banished "the subject from the realm of polite discourse," although I would argue that the subject was not so much exiled as kept accessible yet silenced through the topos of "unspeakability." The rhetorical device of paralipsis simultaneously stresses and suppresses its subject. See Jonathan Goldberg, ed., *Reclaiming Sodom* (New York: Routledge, 1994), p. 5, who observes that "not to name [sodomy] is a way to allow it," and Larry Scanlon, "Unspeakable Pleasures: Alain de Lille, Sexual Regulation and the Priesthood of Genius," *Romanic Review* 86 (1995): 219, who explores the way in which Alain makes unspeakability a "linguistic category" before it becomes a moral one.

42. Pierre J. Payer, *Sex and the Penitentials: The Development of a Sexual Code, 550–1150* (Toronto: University of Toronto Press, 1984), pp. 40–44 and 135–39, discusses the specificity of canons against homosexuality in the earlier, largely nonvernacular manuals.

43. Mother Columba Hart and Jane Bishop, trans., *Hildegard of Bingen: "Scivias"* (New York: Paulist Press, 1990), p. 279 (Book 2. 6. 78). In her *Book of the Rewards of Life* 3.79–80, Hildegard also implicates homosexuality as devilish in origin. See Bruce W. Hozeski, trans., *Hildegard of Bingen, The Book of the Rewards of Life (Liber Vitae Meritorum)* (New York: Garland, 1994), pp. 166–67.

44. Murray, "Twice Marginal," p. 199.

45. Quoted by John Boswell, *Christianity, Social Tolerance, and Homosexuality: Gay People in Western Europe from the Beginning of the Christian Era to the Fourteenth Century* (Chicago: University of Chicago Press, 1980), p. 204.

46. Whether Hildegard considered all male sodomy as requiring the role reversal—one man sinning with another "in a feminine manner"—she condemns in women's use of instruments is unclear.

For discussion of Hildegard's concern about sexual role reversal in the context of her times, see Joan Cadden, *Meanings of Sex Difference in the Middle Ages: Medicine, Science, and Culture* (Cambridge: Cambridge University Press, 1993), pp. 218–27.

47. Murray, "Twice Marginal," p. 199.

48. Brown, "Lesbian Sexuality," p. 73.

49. B&E, p. 49.

50. Hildegard morally condemns Kuno through indirection: in the letter she does not refer to him by name but calls him "a certain horrible man" [quidam horribilis homo] (B&E, p. 48; Van Acker, vol. 91, p. 27).

51. Flanagan, *Hildegard,* p. 180, notes that many of Hildegard's letters on subjects other than Richardis are written in the persona of God or the Living Light. Hildegard's first letter on Richardis to the marchioness uses the same personal voice as does the one to Hartwig.

52. B&E, p. 48.

53. In her letter to the marchioness, Hildegard had also called Adelheid her "dearest daughter" (quoted in Flanagan, *Hildegard,* p. 180.

54. Richardis died October 29, 1152.

55. B&E, p. 144 (Van Acker, vol. 91, p. 147).

56. Sabina Flanagan, ("Spiritualis Amicitia in a twelfth-century Convent? Hildegard of Bingen and Richardis of Stade," *Parergon* 29 [1981]: 19) puzzles over this "confusing" passage: "The idea of Hildegard's considering herself as Richardis's daughter is arresting, but can be paralleled in contemporary writings. The Cistercians especially were fond of playing about with relationships. . . . St Bernard even went so far as to appropriate for himself the maternal relationship proper to nuns." Wiethaus ("Friendships," p. 107) finds it "puzzling to note that Hildegard saw herself paradoxically both as mother and as dependent daughter in her relationship to the younger Richardis." Although Dronke (*Women Writers,* pp. 156–57) quotes and translates the passage, he ignores it when he asserts that Hildegard does "not address Richardis as an equal"; "[Richardis] is still 'the maiden', the spiritual daughter, who must listen to her mother." None of these critics reads the passage as a poetic moment of Hildegard's merger with Richardis.

57. For example, Dronke, *Women Writers,* p. 158; B&E, p. 144.

58. B&E, p. 144; Van Acker, vol. 91, p. 147.

59. Flanagan, "Spiritualis Amicitia," p. 15.

60. Flanagan, "Spiritualis Amicitia," p. 16.

61. Boswell, *Christianity, Social Tolerance, and Homosexuality,* p. 225.

62. Critical opinion on Aelred and, by extension, spiritual friendship, ranges along a spectrum from finding monastic *amicitia* altogether disinterested to seeing it as more openly entertaining the possibility of a sexual component. For instance, Jean LeClercq (*The Love of Learning and the Desire for God: A Study of Monastic Culture* [New York: Fordham University Press, 1961], pp. 225–27) sees monastic *amicitia* of the type Aelred promoted as disinterested, whereas Brian Patrick McGuire ("Love, Friendship and Sex in the Eleventh Century: The Experience of Anselm," *Studia Theologica* 28 [1974]: 111–52) more readily acknowledges that unlike Anselm, Aelred confronted the possibility that emotional love between monks

could turn into physical love, for Aelred himself most likely had had youthful homosexual experiences.

63. Boswell, *Christianity, Social Tolerance, and Homosexuality,* p. 226.

64. Prudence Allen (*The Concept of Woman: The Aristotelian Revolution, 750 BC - AD 1250* [Montreal: Eden Press, 1985], p. 315) situates Hildegard in a different "golden age," that period just before the reintroduction of Aristotle's works, which devalued women, and the development of the University of Paris, which excluded women from formal study.

65. Flanagan, "Spiritualis Amicitia," p. 19. See *Aelred of Rievaulx: Spiritual Friendship,* tr. Mary Eugenia Laker (Kalamazoo, MI: Cistercian Publications, 1977), pp. 72–73: "'Wherefore, friends,' says Tullius, 'though absent are present . . . '"

66. Thomas Stehling, trans., *Medieval Latin Poems of Male Love and Friendship* (New York: Garland, 1984), pp. xx–xxii. Stehling also notes that the line between poems of "friendship" and poems of "love" is often a fine one, and that the traditions of male friendship "allowed men to write with great emotional coloring about men they loved, and to imagine intimate physical union with them." My definition of "homosexual" poetry here includes poems that express "imagined" physical union.

67. Stehling, *Medieval Latin Poems,* pp. xxv. Boswell (*Christianity, Social Tolerance, and Homosexuality,* p. 220) calls one of these poems ("To G.") "perhaps the most outstanding example of medieval lesbian literature," whereas Peter Dronke (*Medieval Latin and the Rise of the European Love-Lyric,* 2 vols. [Oxford: Clarendon Press, 1968], 2:482) states the matter more cautiously: the poem to G. "seems to presuppose a passionate physical relationship."

68. See Susan Schibanoff, "Chaucer's Lesbians: Drawing Blanks?," *Medieval Feminist Newsletter* 13 (1992): 14 n. 9, for further bibliographical citations.

69. Stehling, *Medieval Latin Poems,* p. xxv. Matter ("My Sister, My Spouse," p. 53) links the literature of spiritual friendship with the Song of Songs, a connection I would not deny, even if, for instance, Aelred's *De spirituali amicitia* avoids the Song of Songs (see Douglass Roby, "Sources of the *Spiritual Friendship,*" in *Aelred,* ed. Lasker, p. 33). But there is a branch of writing on spiritual friendship that mines the Song of Songs, for example, the commentary of Bernard of Clairvaux. As I shall argue below, it is the Song of Songs, whether appropriated for female love letters or treatises on monastic friendship, that authorizes Hildegard's discourse of desire.

70. Elsewhere, however, Hildegard does mine the Song of Songs for her poetic imagery; see Peter Dronke, *The Medieval Lyric* (New York: Harper & Row, 1968), pp. 75–78, and Newman, *Sister of Wisdom,* s.v. "Song of Songs."

71. Both Ann W. Astell, *The Song of Songs in the Middle Ages* (Ithaca: Cornell University Press, 1990), and E. Ann Matter, *The Voice of My Beloved: The Song of Songs in Western Medieval Christianity* (Philadelphia: University of Pennsylvania Press, 1990), address the central problem this frankly erotic biblical text posed to medieval readers and the various solutions—or allegorical interpretations—medieval readers devised.

72. For example, Saint Bernard (see note 56 above).

73. See, especially, Caroline Walker Bynum, *Jesus as Mother: Studies in the Spirituality of the High Middle Ages* (Berkeley: University of California Press, 1982) and "' . . . And Woman His Humanity': Female Imagery in the Religious Writing of the Later Middle Ages," in *Fragmentation and Redemption: Essays on Gender and the Human Body in Medieval Religion* (New York: Zone, 1991).

74. It was primarily through suppression of (hetero)sexuality, or virginity, that religious women achieved honorary maleness; see Barbara Newman, *From Virile Woman to WomanChrist: Studies in Medieval Religion and Literature* (Philadelphia: University of Pennsylvania Press, 1995), pp. 4–7.

   Grace Jantzen *(Power, Gender and Christian Mysticism* [Cambridge: Cambridge University Press, 1995], pp. 26–58) discusses the way in which early Christian women "internalized the concept that spirituality is the province of males," which, she argues, accounts for women's cross-dressing and "passing" as men. Yet it is important to note that medieval narratives of female transvestite saints do not, in fact, allow women to "pass"—that is, as their denouement these cautionary tales reveal the female saint's biological gender and restore her external appearance to the conventions of that gender. See my "True Lies: Transvestism and Idolatry in the Trial of Joan of Arc," in *Fresh Verdicts on Joan of Arc,* Bonnie Wheeler and Charles T. Wood, eds. (New York: Garland, 1996), pp. 31 ff. Gillian Cloke, *"This Female Man of God": Women and Spiritual Power in the Patristic Age, AD 350–450* (New York: Routledge, 1995), pp. 214–19, observes that women escaped their culturally disparaged femaleness through the "masculine" means of struggling for virtue or the "feminine" means of absolute negation of self. But those women who chose "masculine" struggle were carefully marked as biologically female, as was Olympias, about whom Palladius remarked that she was "a manly creature, a man in everything but body." Women might be given an individual masculine attribute—a beard, for instance—but otherwise they remained recognizably female.

75. The "dumbing down" (or "feminization") of the Virgin is especially apparent if one compares early legends of Mary's education in the temple and her coolly rational inquisition of Gabriel in early versions of the Annunciation with later medieval representations of the Virgin's childhood and her instant submission to God.

76. Barbara Newman, intro., trans., and commentary, *Saint Hildegard of Bingen, Symphonia: A Critical Edition of the "Symphonia armonie celestium revelationum" [Symphony of the Harmony of Celestial Revelations]* (Ithaca: Cornell University Press, 1988), pp. 12–13.

77. "The Flesh of the Voice: Embodiment and the Homoerotics of Devotion in the Music of Hildegard of Bingen," *Signs* 19 (1993): 92–125. Holsinger discusses both the music and lyrics of Hildegard's songs, although I refer only to his observations on her text. For an interesting corollary study of the thematization of music as homosocial desire, see Judith A. Peraino, "Courtly Obsessions: Music and Masculine Identity in Gottfried von Strassburg's *Tristan,*" *repercussions* 4 (1995): 59–85.

78. I quote Holsinger's translation here from his "Flesh of the Voice," p. 101. Compare Newman's literal rendering of the stanza in *Symphonia,* p. 125: "7. Now let the whole Church flush with joy / and resound in harmony / for the sake of the most tender Virgin / and praiseworthy Mary, / the bearer of God. / Amen."

79. "Flesh of the Voice," p. 102.

80. Holsinger discusses a second lyric by Hildegard as well in "Flesh of the Voice," the song *O viridissima virga,* which, he argues, represents the "radical irrelevance of the phallus" (111).

 (In her *Causes and Cures* 2.96, Hildegard asserted that a woman's sexual pleasure did not depend upon the "touch of a man.")

81. On Ecclesia's importance in Hildegard's "theology of the feminine," see Newman, *Sister of Wisdom,* chap. 6, and Newman, *Symphonia,* p. 57. Newman further discusses Hildegard's feminine theology in "Divine Power Made Perfect in Weakness: St. Hildegard on the Frail Sex," in *Medieval Religious Women II: Peaceweavers,* Lillian Thomas Shank and John A. Nichols, eds., Cistercian Studies Series, no. 72 (Kalamazoo, MI: Cistercian Publications, 1987), pp. 103–22.

82. Newman, *Hildegard,* pp. 99–101.

83. Joan Cadden, "It Takes All Kinds: Sexuality and Gender Differences in Hildegard of Bingen's 'Book of Compound Medicine'," *Traditio* 40 (1984): 149–50.

84. Cadden, "It Takes All Kinds," 166.

85. Joyce E. Salisbury, "Gendered Sexuality," in Bullough and Brundage, *Handbook,* pp. 93–94, observes that Hildegard's view that women were less lustful than men departs from the traditional medieval view and anticipates modern analysis.

86. *Hildegardis Causae et curae,* ed. Paul Kaiser (Leipzig: Teubner, 1903), p. 77: " . . . sine tactu viri in delectationem movetur." See Cadden, "It Takes All Kinds," 168.

87. Kaiser, *Causae et curae,* p. 76. Hildegard goes on to note that the even and constant nature of woman's desire serves the functional purpose of facilitating reproduction.

88. Flanagan, *Hildegard,* p. 100.

89. Bruce R. Smith, *Homosexual Desire in Shakespeare's England: A Cultural Poetics* (Chicago: University of Chicago Press, 1991), p. 17.
    On Hildegard's talent as a poet (and dramatist) see Peter Dronke, *Poetic Individuality in the Middle Ages: New Departures in Poetry, 1000–1150* (Oxford: Clarendon Press, 1970), pp. 150–79. As I suggest here, Hildegard used her poetic ability to code her desire for Richardis. Cf. B&E, p. 10: "What one does not find [in Hildegard's letters], at least not to speak of, is any kind of emotional self-revelation, even, for example, in those letters that deal with what we know was a great personal loss to Hildegard, the departure of her favorite nun, Richardis. This is the twelfth, not the nineteenth century."

90. Indeed, that Hildegard related in non-erotic fashion to a community of women is considered noteworthy. See, for instance, Joan M. Ferrante, *To The Glory of Her Sex: Women's Roles in the Composition of Medieval Texts* (Bloomington: Indiana University Press, 1997), pp. 173–74.

91. The original Latin of this passage, translated above in full in the epitaph, reads: "Amaui nobilitatem morum tuorum, et sapientiam et castitatem, et tuam animam et omnem uitam tuam, ita quod multi dixerunt: Quid facis?" (Van Acker, vol. 91, p. 147.)

92. Trans. Dronke, *Women Writers,* p. 159. Patricia A. Kazarow, "Text and Context in Hildegard of Bingen's *Ordo Virtutum,*" in *Maps of Flesh and Light,* ed. Wiethaus, p. 134, speculates that Hildegard may have written an epitaph of sorts for Richardis in her play on the virtues. If so, the epitaph also cedes Richardis, in the role of Chastity, to the King's embrace. See also Gunilla Iversen, "*O Virginitas, in regali thalamo stas;* New Light on the *Ordo Virtutum*: Hildegard, Richardis, and the Order of the Virtues," *The Early Drama, Art, and Music Review* 20 (1997): 1–16; and Pamela Sheingorn, "The Virtues of

Hildegard's *Ordo Virtutum;* or, It *Was* a Woman's World," in *The Ordo Virtutum of Hildegard of Bingen: Critical Studies,* ed. Audrey Davidson (Kalamazoo, MI: Medieval Institute Publications, 1992), pp. 43–62.

93. Partner, "Did Mystics Have Sex?" in *Desire and Discipline: Sex and Sexuality in the Premodern West,* ed. Jacqueline Murray and Konrad Eisenbichler (Toronto: University of Toronto Press, 1996), p. 302.

94. This effort is underway. In addition to Holsinger, see, for example, Murray, "Twice Marginal," pp. 206–207, and Mary Anne Campbell, "Redefining Holy Maidenhood: Virginity and Lesbianism in Late Medieval England," *Medieval Feminist Newsletter* 13 (1992): 14–15.

CHAPTER THREE

ELEGIAC DESIRE AND FEMALE COMMUNITY
IN BAUDONIVIA'S *LIFE OF SAINT RADEGUND*

Lisa Weston

> *In Baudonivia's* Life of Saint Radegund, *foundress of a convent at Poitiers, the writer constructs the saint as both model and object of devotional longing. Baudonivia's text redefines female desire and redirects it into homosocial union and community.*

Shortly before Radegund of Poitiers died (ca. 587), as her hagiographer Baudonivia relates, the saint experienced a vision in which she was greeted by a most beautiful and charming young man. That she repels his advances puzzles him; why, then, he asks, had she been wooing him for so long? "Why, burning with desire, have you sought me with so many tears?" [Quid me desiderio accensa cum tantis lacrimis rogas?].[1] "Undoubtedly," Baudonivia concludes rhetorically, this visitor was Christ the Bridegroom revealing to the saint her impending union with him in heaven. But there is doubt: despite—or perhaps because of—the surety with which Baudonivia constructs this unequivocally allegorical reading, the scene reveals itself as the site of textual anxiety. Certainly this vision depicts Radegund as if inscribed into the narrative of the Song of Songs, courted by Christ, the heretofore absent Bridegroom she has been seeking in her prayers. At the same time, however, the saint's rejection of an apparent male suitor—described initially as a typical young nobleman, an intruder in the convent—continues to trouble any neat literalization of Bride and Bridegroom. Though this vignette seems to stage Radegund's embrace of and by the Bridegroom, it might be read initially as a scene of marriage resistance, and, further, the Bridegroom's address, his questions, and his depiction of her desire go unanswered.

Moreover, if his present suit echoes her previous desire, the incident stages not so much this Bride's marriage as her elision with the Bridegroom as equally desiring (and unrequited) lover. The incident delineates a discourse of unconsummated, elegiac desire, a discourse deployed within this text less frequently between Radegund and Christ than it is between Radegund and the female congregation she gathered around her at Poitiers, a congregation given voice by Baudonivia.[2] In fact, Radegund's most zealous expressions of desire, earlier in this *vita,* address the female community she founded: "You, daughters, I chose; you, my light, you, my life, you, my rest and all my joy" [Vos elegi filias, vos, mea lumina, vos, mea vita, vos, mea requies totaque felicitas].[3] Her affection is emulated and returned throughout Baudonivia's text, most explicitly in the elegiac passages lamenting the saint's death that frame this vision account. No wonder, then, that the Bridegroom is so problematically threatening: Christ's summons may seal the marriage of the Bride and Bridegroom, may consummate Radegund's sanctity, but it also disrupts and imperils a desiring female community.

Such contradictions play throughout Baudonivia's *vita* of Saint Radegund, written by the nun specifically for the women of the saint's community at Poitiers, the community within which she was raised and educated. And such anxiety makes this text an especially interesting narrative of what Jo Ann McNamara has called "the ordeal of community."[4] If the establishment of female monastic communities in the early Middle Ages required, as extant rules and hagiographical narratives both suggest, a radical redefinition of self contingent on the renunciation of position and family, such redefinition of self within a female homosocial community such as Radegund's is also contingent upon the reorganization and disciplining of desire. Self-identification as the Bride of Christ—and thus identity with all other Brides—is, of course, one very common form by

which desire can be organized, if one that can paradoxically perpetuate even as it renounces the heteronormativity of prevailing
sex/gender systems. Another and potentially more radical strategy
entails the channeling of desire into veneration for a saint, especially
a foundress, who can serve in written *vita* and in cult as both a
model desiring subject and an object of a focused communal homoaffectivity. As Bruce Holsinger suggests in regard to various
hymns and sequences of Hildegard of Bingen—similarly products
of female monastic culture—the latter strategy especially enacts
what Terry Castle has theorized as a model for female homosocial
desire. The "canonical" male-female-male triangle supportive of
male bonding and patriarchal desire is subverted to some extent
even in deployment of a "parallel" female-male-female triangle—as
when the women of a community are united through the mediating figure of Christ the Bridegroom. The elimination of the middle term, or its elision with one of the female terms—as when the
female saint becomes the focus of devotion in place of or in conjunction with Christ—effects what Castle calls "the most radical
transformation of female bonding."[5]

Female bonding, or at least the maintenance of community, was
particularly a concern at Poitiers. In 589 two of Radegund's royal
step-granddaughters, Basinia and Clotild, led an insurrection within
the abbey walls. Following the looting of the monastery by their
hired thugs and their attempted assassination of the new abbess,
Leubovera (the first abbess, Agnes, having died soon after her close
companion and spiritual mother), the revolt was finally put down
by an episcopal tribunal convened to restore discipline and order.[6]
Within a generation after Radegund's death, two hagiographers,
Venantius Fortunatus and Baudonivia, both intimates of the saint
during her lifetime, textualized the memory of the saint so as to address the disciplining of individual desire, to make her a model
Christian subject and a focus for the continued communal veneration that can create and sustain community.

Supportive of Radegund's cult as productive of political and religious unity throughout Francia as well as within the confines of
her monastic house, the *vita* authored by Venantius Fortunatus addresses its readers from the position of ecclesiastical authority

charged with administrative oversight of the saint's convent. Her
destiny as a royal bride making her mediatrix between the violent
Clothar and his turbulent realm on the one hand and God on the
other, Radegund proves doubly a wife—and thus doubly contained
and defined, however contrary to her will, by a heteronormative
sex/gender system—married to an earthly prince and yet never
separated from the heavenly one, for whose love she will eventually
renounce wealth and power. As Suzanne Wittern observes, this first
vita focuses upon conversion and renunciation, the exchange of
worldly for divine status.[7] As exemplified by Venantius Fortunatus,
Radegund's transformation is contingent upon her total abandon-
ment of subjectivity, will, and desire.

In one dramatic scene Radegund leaves her (earthly) husband's
bed to prostrate herself in prayer upon the cold floor of the privy
until chilled almost to death. This abjection, the moment of her almost total denial of her flesh—and certainly of her marital sexuality—coincides paradoxically with her self-naming: indifferent to
bodily suffering, she focuses on the paradise she hopes to gain, a
moment the text celebrates by punning in Latin on the meaning of
her Germanic name, "mind intent," *mens intenta*.[8]

Upon her withdrawal from marriage and her claustration at
Poitiers after Clothar's death, the Radegund of Fortunatus's text is
continually solitary and sundered even from the female community
she founds. This Radegund does not maintain contacts outside the
cloister; she does not send embassies to Byzantium for relics to support and strengthen both her community and Christian faith in
Francia—even though Venantius Fortunatus was himself the author
of several poetic orations on this subject and of hymns in celebration
of the piece of the Holy Cross after which Radegund's monastery
was named. This *vita* provides neither any indication of Radegund's
own poetic skills nor notion of her deep friendship with Agnes,
whom she installed as first abbess of her foundation, even though this
occasion was celebrated by Fortunatus's *De Virginitate*. The text is,
rather, surprisingly silent on precisely those aspects of her life at
Poitiers with which Venantius Fortunatus had the most connection.
These omissions are the more surprising since a large number of
short, personal poems testify to the role correspondence with both

women played in the male poet's own emotional life. The Radegund of this *vita* is instead abstemiously immune to all earthly beauties and distanced from all human connections.

Though ever willing to contribute both menial labor (the more humiliating the better) and miracle to the life of the community, this Radegund renounces all self, all desire. Not content with fasting and wearing hair shirts, she binds her neck and arms with iron chains so tightly that the flesh swells around them, and she brands herself with a cruciform brass plate. Her self-mutilation occurs always in private, before no human audience; her sanctity similarly manifests itself in miracles that occur away from human eyes. And although a miraculous vision implicitly proclaims the hour of her death while she is explicitly accomplishing a cure, for Venantius Fortunatus, Radegund is the object of the vision, not the visionary as she is in Baudonivia's *vita*. The role of visionary falls instead to the man in whose dream Radegund invokes God's cure for his disease after first indicating the site on which he should build an oratory for Saint Martin and petitioning him for the release of prisoners. In this vision, as in the extremities of her self-martyrdom, Radegund thus embodies and mediates a spiritual power hers not intrinsically, but paradoxically, through renunciation. In so representing Radegund the text constitutes her an earthly vessel purified of flesh and filled with heavenly treasure, as its prologue (citing 2 Corinthians 4.7) proclaims all Christians, including the women of Poitiers, should aspire to be.

In her own prologue, Baudonivia explicitly announces her intention to undertake a paratextual continuation of the earlier text that will speak only of what the bishop considered unworthy of inclusion. In the event, however, writing within the gaps and interstices of his narrative, Baudonivia rewrites Radegund more fully as a model desiring subject as well as the object of communal desire and veneration, the foundress of a space within which and from which women like both Radegund and Baudonivia can construct and speak their desire for other women and for female community.

Addressing her *vita* explicitly "to the holy ladies and the entire glorious congregation of the Lady Radegund" [Dominabus sanctis . . . vel omni congregationi glorisi dominae Radegundis],[9] Baudonivia

positions herself and her text within a self-defining female homosocial world. The community's corporate attention and prayer must, in
fact, aid in generating the text's celebration, its reembodiment of their
foundress, thereby completing and fulfilling the saint's foundation.
The author's foregrounding of the relationships, the ties of identity as
well as love among the saint, Baudonivia herself as hagiographer, and
her audience suggests, moreover, an all-but-exclusively-female community. This emphasis on relationships presupposes a communal reading of the text, most likely on the saint's feast day, whether (as was the
common reading context in early medieval monastic houses) as a
complete piece in refectory or chapter house, or in sections excerpted
as lections through the cycle of the day's devotions.

The importance of texts—including this one—in the construction
and discipline of community is also implied in the dense network of
intertextualities within which Baudonivia writes her Radegund. As
Suzanne Wemple has noted, far from a figure of renunciation and denial, Baudonivia's Radegund actively involves herself in affairs of
church and state, both before and after her claustration.[10] The saint's
first miracle, for example, is her heroic destruction of a pagan temple.
The action, very much in the style of Saint Martin, whose *vita* by
Sulpicius Severus Baudonivia appropriates here, places the scene
within a female homosocial frame, Radegund's visit to a woman
friend named Ausifrid. Borrowing the very words of other previous
hagiographical narratives, seeming at times indeed more crestomathy
than original composition, the text draws upon other works by
Venantius Fortunatus, particularly his *Life of Saint Hilary* and his
hymns: in praise of the Cross, upon the *Inventio Sanctae Crucis,* and,
most significantly and extensively, upon the *vita* of Caesarius of Arles.
As E. Gordon Whatley observes, all these have connections to the
monastery's existence and integrity: in a letter to various bishops (included in Gregory of Tours's *History of the Franks*), Radegund invokes
both Saints Hilary and Martin, along with the Virgin Mary and the
power of the Cross, in order to safeguard her foundation after her
death.[11] The model for this letter was the *Testamentum* of Caesarius of
Arles, whose *Rule for Nuns* was observed at Poitiers.

As deployed by Baudonivia, however, such intertextuality does
more than testify to the community's history and literacy, its partic-

ipation in a sophisticated monastic culture. The male-authored texts cited and appropriated are positioned so as to support and sustain the bonds between Baudonivia and her female audience. More significantly, perhaps, the text's adaptation of male lives to a female subject, accomplished not only by necessary grammatical shifts, but also (as in the first miracle) by the setting within specifically female community, renders Radegund's sanctity ambiguously androgynous as Baudonivia's saint constitutes herself the creator of her own model of behavior, a model "which she herself might wish to emulate" [Quod ipsa desideraret imitari].[12]

Baudonivia's text crystallizes this curiously circular model in its use of Venantius Fortunatus's pun on the saint's name. Repeatedly identifying Radegund as "mind intent on Christ," Baudonivia's text makes it a marker not of self-renunciation but rather of active desire and will. Its assertion of her self-definition as well as the fervor of her intimacy with God particularly marks her creation of the female homosocial space. Rejecting the false honors of this world, "mind intent on Christ," she builds herself a monastery beautified by "ornaments of perfection, a great congregation of virgins for the Eternal Bridegroom." As Radegund's conversion begins to "flower in the humble behavior, abundant love, and bright chastity" of her community, the consummation of her identity as Bride of Christ is embodied not only in her own transformation but in the formation of the congregation that she, following and imitating the Bridegroom and calling to his Brides, gathers around her ["Mens intenta ad Christum . . . monasterium sibi . . . construxit . . . ubi perfectionis ornament conquireret et magnam congretaionem puellarum Christo numquam morituro sponso. Mox etiam eius sancta conversatio coepit fervere in humitatis conversatione, in caritatis ubertate, in castitatis lumine, in ieiunorum pinguedine, et ita toto amore caelesti tradidit Sponso"].[13] In fact, within Baudonivia's text, being Bride seems to entail Radegund's elision with the Bridegroom: in constructing the convent at Poitiers, she enacts his wooing of Brides, and in her turn becomes with him a focus for the congregation's veneration and desire. Accordingly, as the earthly embodiment of the Bride (or perhaps Bride/groom), Radegund sees her "joyful" and triumphant process toward freedom and community "flower" in both her own acts of sanctity and the devotion of her congregation of fellow Brides.

Thus it is appropriate that further repetitions of the "mind intent" name-pun introduce Radegund's exemplary embodiment of monastic unity and discipline: within the community Radegund serves as a living gloss on the Rule that binds the women. As Susanne Wittern notes, Baudonivia's narrative distinguishes itself from that of Venantius Fortunatus especially in its focus on the saint's life within the cloister and the struggles inherent in day-to-day cloistered life, rather than the process of ascetic withdrawal.[14] Alluding only briefly to the fasts, privations, and self-tortures of which Venantius Fortunatus provides such graphic detail, for example, Baudonivia describes Radegund as a model less of self-martyrdom than of devotion to prayers and especially to the reading of Scripture and to the intertextuality her text exemplifies. "Mind intent on Christ" Radegund has the Scriptures read to her even as she sleeps, and should her reader cease even for moment, "just as if she were to say, 'I sleep, but my heart wakes,' she would ask, 'why are you silent? Read. Do not stop'" ["Mens intenta ad Christum, tamquam si diceret: Ego dormio, et cor meum vigilat, aibat, 'Quare taces? Lege, ne cesses'"].[15] Radegund's behavior here marks her literal inscription of the Song of Songs 5.2, but a similar embodiment of Scripture should be the goal of each member of the community.

Constant study as well as unceasing devotion and praise—communal rather than individual—shapes a congregation as intent on God as its foundress and enables the unity of the convent, the creation of community as a chosen family: "I chose you [to be] daughters" [Vos eligi filias].[16] Radegund further admonishes her congregation. Where the Radegund of Venantius Fortunatus denies family, marriage, and kinship, this Radegund's words—and Baudonivia includes many more examples of Radegund as speaking subject than Venantius Fortunatus—actively refigure kinship and marriage bonds. Just as Radegund's identity and her desire for God coincide with and are embodied in her desire for her flock, so the identity of her chosen daughters coheres with their reading of Scripture, their constitution as readers who hear and understand, as members of a textual community who actively pursue their own salvation. Thus, Baudonivia's Radegund counsels her community that if they do not understand what they read, they should seek for understanding "in the mirror of [their] souls" ["Si non intellegitis quod legitur, quid est, quod non sollicite reuiritis speculum animarum vestrarum?"].[17] If, as Baudonivia admits, Radegund's preaching perhaps trespasses on male ecclesiastical privilege, it also witnesses a subtle redefinition of gender in the cloister that depends upon and enables the circulation of texts within a female homosocial circle.

The foundation of this self-defining textual community also links both materially and metaphorically to her acquisition of relics: at Poitiers Brides of Christ join with a multitude of saints present metonymically in the bones housed in gem-encrusted reliquaries. The convent stands symbolically at the center of the universe, a place in which—"as the East testifies, and the North, South, and West bear witness"—Radegund gathered a heavenly, paradisial treasure of "precious jewels" [hoc oriens testatur, aquilo, auster vel occidens profitetur, quid undique preciosas gemmas caeloque reconditas, et quas paradysus habet, ipsa devota tam muneribus quam precibus sibi habere obtinuit].[18] It becomes a liminal space where difference between worlds does not exist, where past and present coexist, and where relics are indistinguishable from the saints they represent. There, Brides of Christ and saintly "gems" join in unending praise of God.

The most precious jewel among these relics, of course, is the piece of the Holy Cross from which the convent would take its name. In bringing it to Poitiers, Radegund shows herself a second Saint Helen. In the process of likening Radegund to Helen, moreover, and in echoing very closely the text of the *Inventio Sanctae Crucis,* Baudonivia obscures the role of the male Judas Cyriacus by transferring his words and actions to the mother of Constantine.[19] This is one more instance in a pattern of textual elision between male and female models that simultaneously destabilizes established heteronormative gender and redirects veneration within a strictly female homosocial world.

More tellingly, in her acquisition of relics for her community, Radegund becomes explicitly a Good Shepherdess: "a best provider, a good ruler, [who] would not abandon her sheep" [Provisatrix optima, guvernatrix bona, ut oves non usquequaque relinqueret].[20] The acquisition of relics has, of course, its practical utility. A monastic community, especially one of women bound by a rule of strict enclosure such as Radegund laid down for her daughters, frequently ran into difficulties maintaining its autonomy and financial viability.[21] But what this second Saint Helen, this Good Shepherdess has provided for her flock has within this text primarily an allegorical significance: Radegund builds outside the walls of Poitiers an image of the New Jerusalem, full of saints present in their relics and a congregation of living virgins, joined in communion around the Cross of Christ. Heaven on earth, the product of the foundress's visionary power, it is a place of perfect, constant, and ever-fulfilled desire constructive of a community.

Considering the way that subsequent historical events had belied this image of the ideal community, Baudonivia's text bespeaks a nostalgic longing for a lost ideal unity. In it Radegund becomes a utopian figure, the focus of a second, particularly elegiac desire predicated on the impossibility of either immediate fulfillment or even adequate expression—predicated, that is, on the loss, rupture, and even failure of female community. Frequent repetitions of an inability to express (often in close and ironic conjunction with a use of the "mind intent" pun that implies Radegund's self-expressive ability) betray a gap between the absent ideal and the present real. Radegund thus both represents a model subject within an ideal textual community and prompts its emulation by a community all but incapable even of expressing her virtues. Her self-referential perfection provides an object for a desiring veneration that must continually fall short of perfect expression. Again and again Baudonivia questions the possibility of full expression: "Who could ever imitate" the saint's great love? "Who is able to say in words" the pains she endured to bring peace to her country? "Who is able to enumerate" those she healed? "Who can seek to tell" the riches she brought to Poitiers? "Who might be able to express how greatly she loved her flock?" [Caritatis autem eius ardorem . . . quis umquam poterit imitari? . . . Se vero in quantum cruciatum affligebat, quis hoc verbis explere valeat? . . . Quanti infirmi ad eius invocationem sunt sani redditi, quis enumerare valeat? . . . Quis queat dicere, quantum et quale donum huic urbi beata contulit? . . . Quantum suam congregationem dilexerit, quis effari valet?].[22] Yet it is, paradoxically, precisely this inability to express the saint completely, this unfulfilled elegiac desire, that sustains her veneration in this text. Baudonivia's inability to express Radegund fully is tied directly with the saint's death, an event that robs her community of her physical presence while at the same moment confirming her sanctity and establishing her as an appropriate focus of communal desire and veneration.

It is in this regard that Radegund's pre-mortem vision of the Bridegroom, cited at the beginning of this essay, becomes the more problematic. It heralds Radegund's long desired union with the Bridegroom, a union figured as inevitable in the name pun and in the way Radegund functions as Bride/groom calling to Brides and as Good Shepherd/ess providing for the flock; yet summoning her to his side, the Bridegroom intrudes upon the ideal female homosocial space of the community. The language attributed to Christ— "Oh my precious gem, you must know that you are the first jewel in the crown on my head"—echoes language descriptive of the convent's foundation, even as the Bridegroom's characterization of his Bride's previous fervor—"Why then have you sought me, with burning desire, with so many tears?"—establishes an appropriate discourse of desire. Consequently, in the fulfillment of her union with Christ, Radegund herself becomes with him the object of communal language, as Baudonivia's text deploys the language of her desire for the Bridegroom (and of his for his Bride) within her lament.

Radegund's own prophetic words, warning her community of its future loss, equated here with the Last Judgment, provide Baudonivia's example: her mind intent (as ever) on Christ, meditating in her sleep on the future judgment and the eternal reward, she would preach, saying, "gather, gather, the harvest of the Lord, for truly I say to you, it will not be long that you may gather it. Mark what I say; gather it, for you will seek this time and long to have it again." And, laments Baudonivia, "in us the prophecy is fulfilled: I shall send you a famine in the land, a famine not of bread and water but of hearing the words of God." Radegund's remembered warning echoes the biblical prophecy (Amos 8.11) also preached in this

text by Baudonivia. Such echoes implicitly correlate the Lord and
his saint. This passage, in fact, ends with a double invocation of both
God and Radegund in a compound image of shepherd and flock:
"Oh, most pious lady, may you obtain from the Lord in Heaven that
you may drive before you the sheep you have collected and that
you, following the Good Shepherd, may herd your flock to the
Lord" [Colligite, colligite triticum dominicum, quia vere dico vobis,
non diu erit, ut colligatis. Videte quod dico: colligite, quia quaesitur
a e estis istud tempus; vere, vere, quaesitur a e estis dies istos et valde
desideratur a e . . . Illud profeticum in nobis implementum est. Mit-
tam vobis famem in terra, famem, inquit, non panis et aqua, sed au-
diendi verbum dei . . . O piissima domina, obtinuisses cum caeli
Domino, ut ante te oves quas congregaveras direxisses; tu pastorem
bonum sequens, gregem Domino tradidisses!].[23]

The separation that the Shepherdess's flock feels is occasioned by
its sin, and occasions in turn its copious and, in this text, copiously
described lamentation. Their sin is explicitly their inattention to
Radegund's preaching. But their failure as a textual community,
their failure to hear and attend the saint's embodied proclamation
(and embodiment) of the Word of God, would be all the more
grievously final only if they were silent: "the less we speak of her
faithful devotion, the more we sin" [Si de eius fideli devotione
minus dicimus, plus peccamus].[24] Speech thus serves as their repa-
ration; after Radegund's desiring and desirable voice is silenced, it
falls to her community to raise theirs in elegy. Surrounding the bed
of the dying saint, they lament and beat their breasts. The metaphor
for their loss, which first arises out of their inarticulate lamentation—"Lord, you are taking our light. Why do you leave us in darkness?" [Domine, . . . lumen nostrum recipis, nos cur in tenebris
relinquis?]—echoes, of course, Radegund's description of her community at its foundation, "you are my light" [Vos, mea lumina].[25]

However incomplete in expression, their elegy implicitly extends
into their participation in Baudonivia's text. Accordingly, the hagiographer's voice in the narrative present continues the prior
lament directed now jointly toward the saint herself and the community that has lost her. In crying out in shared grief and longing,
the women of the congregation become in their turn Brides, seek-

ing, as in the Song of Songs, the Bride/groom. At this point the women depicted within the text, the Baudonivia who recalls their cries, and her audience a generation later are all united in uttering their elegiac desire for the absent beloved.

The text provides a final expression of this desire by appropriating the words (and in that way claiming the intertextual mediation) of Gregory of Tours in his *Glory of the Confessors*. Called upon to conduct the funeral rites, Baudonivia relates, the bishop saw "in [Radegund's] human form an angelic countenance, a face glowing with roses and lilies" [In specie hominis vultum angelicum . . . facies illius velut rosa et lilium fulgebat] and was as awestruck as if he stood before the Lord's Blessed Mother.[26] Her body is, appropriately enough, interred alongside those of all the dead of the community, in a chapel dedicated to the Blessed Virgin Mary. Within this last female homosocial space, that body becomes itself a relic like those she had previously gathered to found and sustain the community. Like those saint-relics, Radegund is both present and absent. Like them, her physical body still overflowing with sanctity and power and her soul now united (and elided) with Christ their Lord and his Virgin Mother, she continues to work miracles and thus to sustain the community. The resolution of loss within this text thus entails the awareness that if the women of Poitiers have lost their foundress in this world, they have her in the Kingdom of God.

In union with Christ and his mother, Radegund provides a place, a model, and, upon her death, an occasion for her spiritual daughters to define themselves. Thus, at least, Baudonivia, writing within the gaps and silences of Venantius Fortunatus's *vita,* rewrites Radegund. Within the female homosocial world of the monastery of the Holy Cross at Poitiers, the saint's textualized example transforms powerless, inarticulate grief into a complex dynamic of veneration as homoaffective elegiac desire that produces and is produced by both community and text.

Notes

1. Baudonivia of Poitiers, *De vita Sanctae Radegundis* 2.20, lines 4–5, ed. Bruno Krusch, *Monumenta Germaniae Historia Scriptorum Rerum*

Merovingicarum 2 (Hanover: Hahn, 1888), p. 391; for the entire text see pp. 377–95. Translations are mine; for a translation of the entire text, see Jo Ann McNamara and John Halborg with E. Gordon Whatley, eds. and trans., *Sainted Women of the Dark Ages* (Durham: Duke University Press, 1992), pp. 86–105.

2. As E. Ann Matter has argued in "My Sister, My Spouse: Women-identified Women in Medieval Christianity" (reprinted in *Weaving the Visions,* ed. Judith Plaskow and Carol P. Christ [San Francisco: Harper and Row, 1989], pp. 51–62), the theme of longing for an absent beloved, influenced by the imagery of the Song of Songs, echoes widely in medieval monastic texts and especially in frequently passionate expressions of spiritual friendship. Matter cites among her examples two female homoerotic poems preserved in a twelfth-century German manuscript, poems also discussed by Jacqueline Murray in "Twice Marginal and Twice Invisible: Lesbians in the Middle Ages," in *Handbook of Medieval Sexuality,* ed. Vern L. Bullough and James A. Brundage (New York: Garland, 1996), pp. 191–222. It is perhaps interesting that one manuscript containing a fragmentary copy of Baudonivia's text also includes a near-contemporary letter celebrating the spiritual friendship of two anonymous monastic women. For a translation see Marcelle Thiébaux, trans., *The Writings of Medieval Women,* 2d ed. (New York: Garland, 1994), pp. 125–33.

3. Baudonivia, *De Vita Sanctae Radegundis* 2.8, lines 26–27, p. 383.

4. Jo Ann McNamara, "The Ordeal of Community: Hagiography and Discipline in Merovingian Convents," *Vox Benedicta* 34 (1986): 293–326.

5. Terry Castle, *The Apparitional Lesbian: Female Homosexuality and Modern Culture* (New York: Columbia University Press, 1993), p. 73; Bruce Holsinger, "The Flesh of the Voice: Embodiment and the Homoerotics of Devotion in the Music of Hildegard of Bingen," *Signs* 19 (1993): 92–125.

6. See Gregory of Tours, *History of the Franks* 10.15 and 16, trans. Lewis Thorpe (London: Penguin, 1974).

7. Susanne Wittern, "Frauen zwischen asketischem Ideal und weltlichem Leben," in *Frauen in der Geschichte* 7, ed. Werner Affeldt and Annette Kuhn (Düsseldorf: Schwann, 1986), pp. 272–94. See also Janet Nelson, "Queens as Jezebels: The Careers of Brunhild and Balthild in Merovingian History," in *Medieval Women,* ed. Derek Baker (Oxford: Blackwell, 1978), pp. 31–78; and Suzanne Wemple, *Women in Frankish Society: Marriage and the Cloister 500–900* (Philadelphia: University of Pennsylvania Press, 1981).

8. Venantius Fortunatus, *De vita Sanctae Radegundis* 1.5.1–5, ed. Bruno Krusch, *Monumenta Germaniae Historia Scriptorum Rerum Merovingicarum 2* (Hanover: Hahn, 1888), pp. 366–67.
9. Baudonivia, *De vita Sanctae Radegundis* 2. Prologus, lines 1–3, p. 377.
10. Wemple, *Women in Frankish Society,* esp. pp. 183–84.
11. E. Gordon Whatley, "An Early Literary Quotation from the *Inventio S. Crucis:* A Note on Baudonivia's *Vita S. Radegundis* (BHL 7049)," *Analecta Bollandiana* 111 (1993): 81–91. On the appropriation of earlier texts, see also Krusch, *De vita Sanctae Radegundis Libri Duo,* esp. p. 360; William E. Klingshirn, "Caesarius' Monastery for Women in Arles and the Composition and Function of the *Vita Caesarii," Revue Benedictine* 100 (1990): 441–81; and Thomas J. Heffernan, *Sacred Biography: Saints and Their Biographers in the Middle Ages* (New York: Oxford University Press, 1988).
12. Baudonivia, *De vita Sanctae Radegundis* 2.1, line 7, p. 380.
13. Baudonivia, *De vita Sanctae Radegundis* 2.5, lines 1–13, pp. 381–82.
14. Wittern, "Frauen zwischen asketischem Ideal und weltlichem Leben."
15. Baudonivia, *De vita Sanctae Radegundis,* 2.9, lines 15–16, p. 384.
16. Baudonivia, *De vita Sanctae Radegundis,* 2.8, line 26, p. 383.
17. Baudonivia, *De vita Sanctae Radegundis,* 2.9, lines 7–8, p. 383.
18. Baudonivia, *De vita Sanctae Radegundis* 2.14, lines 2–4, p. 386.
19. Whatley, "An Early Literary Quotation," 88–89.
20. Baudonivia, *De vita Sanctae Radegundis* 2.16, line 47, p. 389.
21. See Isabel Moreira, "Provisatrix Optima: St. Radegund of Poitiers' Relic Petitions to the East," *Journal of Medieval History* 19 (1993): 285–305; and Jane Tibbetts Schulenburg, "Strict Active Enclosure and Its Effects on the Female Monastic Experience (500–1100)," in *Medieval Religious Women 1: Distant Echoes,* ed. John A. Nichols and Lillian Thomas Shank (Kalamazoo: Cistercian Publications, 1984), pp. 51–86.
22. Baudonivia, *De vita Sanctae Radegundis* 2.9.21, line 22, p. 384; 2.10, lines 16–17, p. 387; 2.15, line 13, p. 389; 2.16, lines 53–54; 2.17, line 23, p. 390.
23. Baudonivia, *De vita Sanctae Radegundis* 2.19, lines 15–17 and 19–20; 2.2, lines 35–37, pp. 391–92.
24. Baudonivia, *De vita Sanctae Radegundis* 2.21, lines 3–4, p. 392.
25. Baudonivia, *De vita Sanctae Radegundis* 2.21.9–10 and 2.8.26.
26. Baudonivia, *De vita Sanctae Radegundis* 2.23, lines 6–7, p. 393.

CHAPTER FOUR

THE ERASED LESBIAN:
SODOMY AND THE LEGAL TRADITION
IN MEDIEVAL EUROPE

Edith Benkov

> *Legal prosecutions for lesbian relations were rare. What is at stake in*
> *the prosecution of lesbians is less the sexual act than the usurping of*
> *the male role by a woman.*

> The fourth aspect of the sin against nature is when men have rela-
> tions with each other in the rear or elsewhere. Or women with each
> other by detestable and horrible means which should not be named
> or written about, or men with women in places that are not natural
> [La quarte partie du pechié contre nature est avoir les ungs hommes
> compaignée les ungs des autres ès fondemens ou ailleurs. Ou les
> femmes des autres par detestable et horribles façons qui ne se doib-
> vent ne nommer ne escripre, ou les hommes des femmes es lieu non
> naturelz].

> —*Jean Gerson*★

Nearly two decades ago, Louis Crompton noted, "little has been
written about lesbianism and the law from a historical point
of view."[1] Although Crompton's essay and others in the same issue

of the *Journal of Homosexuality* were intended as a corrective to that lack, his observation is still valid at the beginning of this century, especially if we consider the medieval period. Crompton compiled what remains the most extensive overview of prosecutions in Europe before the French Revolution for sexual relations between women in order to dispel the "myth" that female homoerotic acts went unpunished in the medieval and early modern periods. He maintains: "in such countries as France, Spain, Italy, Germany, and Switzerland, lesbian acts were regarded as legally equivalent to acts of male sodomy and were, like them, punishable by the death penalty. On occasion, executions of women were carried out."[2]

Yet what is most striking about Crompton's findings is not that women were brought to court for such acts but rather how few recorded cases Crompton cites in comparison to the numbers of prosecutions for sodomy between men.[3] Crompton mentions fewer than ten cases, including those instances subject to Church investigations that were not subsequently remanded to the secular courts. Even when one adds to these the investigation of Benedetta Carlini, Judith Brown's "lesbian" nun, the statistics hardly change.[4] Indeed, Brown remarks upon the scarcity of prosecutions for female homoeroticism and posits that it stems from the overarching dismissal of sexual relations between women as insignificant: "Europeans had long found it difficult to accept that women could actually be attracted to one another. Their view of human sexuality was phallocentric . . . there was nothing in a woman that could long sustain the sexual desires of another woman."[5] That noted, I suggest a more fruitful approach would be an exploration of the dialectics of those texts that locate female homoerotic relations in the domain of sinful and criminal sexual practices. In so doing, my essay questions ways to consider what may have constituted lesbian identity—or identities—in medieval Europe.[6]

To use the term "lesbian" implies certain presumptions about how sexuality functions within a given society. If we accept the social constructionist views popularized by the late philosopher Michel Foucault, the concept of homosexuality, as indeed the concept of sexuality, was absent in medieval and early modern Europe. Historians of sexuality would argue that "lesbianism" is a product of Freudian theory and of late-nineteenth- and early-twentieth-century sexologists. More recently, critics have countered that we must first confront the problem of how to define sexuality in the early modern period, and second, attempt to fit lesbian sexuality—and lesbian identity— into that context. I should like, however, to suggest yet another approach to their dilemma, a path around the critical space of the constructionist debate on sexuality. I shall use the term "lesbian" as a type of shorthand and *dehistoricize* the term. Lesbian will carry its most banal meaning: a woman who engages in or desires homoerotic sexual relations. Although focusing on sexual relations imposes certain limits on the concept of "identity," it does offer a common thread for dealing with the disparate documents from medieval Europe. I shall, then, examine the ways in which same-sex desire is constructed by medieval secular and ecclesiastic justice, with the full moral weight these discourses exercised and continue to exercise in society and contrast these to instances in which women were tried for "criminal" sexual behavior. The keys to understanding these prosecutions lie, I believe, in the attempts to articulate definitions of sexual infractions, definitions that by their language tend to erase any presence of the lesbian as a distinct category, that assimilate her to the homosexual male and to a model of male sexual practices, and that account for the apparent dearth of records of accusations brought against women for sexual crimes.

The Church Leads the Way

As arbiter of morality for the vast majority of the population of Western Europe during the Middle Ages, the Catholic Church is the single most dominant voice in the discourse on sexuality, and that voice is heard most distinctly in penitential literature. As Pierre J. Payer has shown, the authors of the penitentials display a great interest in sexual practices that we would group under the broad category of homoerotic. The emphasis on enumeration, on definable acts or practices found in these collections, stems from their specific design as guidebooks for confessors, dealing with a range of behaviors that went contrary to Christian moral teachings.[7] Indeed, Payer points out that "all of the Penitentials have at least one

canon concerning homosexuality and many have a relatively extensive treatment of the subject."[8] When these texts refer to acts
subsumed under the term sodomy, two parallel, sometimes con-
current, sometimes separate, definitions of what can be considered
unnatural sexual practices occur with some regularity: "using a
member not granted for this," as Ivo, bishop of Chartres, would
have it or spilling seed outside the proper "vessel."[9] These broad
definitions implicitly follow a paradigm of phallic primacy (wasted
seed) and form the basis for what Valerie Traub has called the "in-
significance" of lesbian desire.[10]

Not surprisingly then, penitential literature does not consistently
impose equal penalties for all unnatural practices. While male
sodomites were frequently assigned seven years of penance, three
years appears as a typical term of penance for female sodomites.
Thus, Theodore of Tarsus (archbishop of Canterbury, 668–90) includes in his penitential under the category of fornication the recommendation that "a woman [practicing] vice with another woman
do penance for three years" [Si mulier cum mulier fornicaverit, III
annos poenitat].[11] Theodore, however, makes no attempt to explain
the details of that vice, and through this omission his text is typical
of the majority of the penitentials. This marked lack of elaboration
contrasts with the variety of acts constituting proscribed male sexual practices and the range of penance prescribed according to the
gravity of the sin. In practical terms, the grouping of female homoerotic practices with other forms of proscribed sexual acts found in
the majority of the penitentials and the tendency to avoid any elaboration of what these acts might be clearly do not facilitate a confessor's dealings with a female penitent.[12] What is more important
in historical terms is that these elisions and silences perpetuate a
phallic model of sexuality that denies agency to women.

For that reason, perhaps the most significant of the early penitential literature's treatment of lesbian sexual practices may be found
in Hincmar of Rheims: "They do not put flesh to flesh as in the
fleshly genital member of one into the body of the other, since nature precludes this, but they do transform the use of that part of
their body into an unnatural one: it is said that they use *instruments*
of *diabolical operations* to excite desire" [Quae carnem ad carnem,

non autem genitale carnis membrum intra carnem alterius, factura prohibente naturae, mittunt, sed naturalem hujusce partis corporae usum in eum usum qui est contra naturam communtant: quae dicantur quasdam machinas diabolicae operationis nihilominus ad exaestuandam libidem operari].[13] Hincmar's text, with its emphasis on "instruments," neatly exposes the problematic nature of lesbian sex within the Christian tradition. Bernadette J. Brooten demonstrates conclusively that early Christian thought, in a manner that paralleled the non-Christian traditions of the Roman world, often constructed sexual acts in terms of penetration: "thus the Apocalypse of Peter apparently shares the widespread ancient view that homoerotic women imitate men: just as men penetrate either females or males, so too do homoerotic women penetrate other women."[14] Although Hincmar may then be read as a continuation of this long-standing tradition, his particular formulation merits closer attention. Where earlier writers frequently grounded female same-sex desire, at least on the part of the active partner, in physiology, Hincmar does not construct a "naturally" phallic woman—"natural" in that an elongated or enlarged clitoris would be a physical state, albeit one that could easily be construed as pathological and therefore treated along with other deformations. He excludes the possibility of clitoral penetration, a permutation frequently mentioned in ancient and medieval medical texts.[15]

Rather, Hincmar seems to be recasting the ancient notion of the fricatice into a phallic model. Female genitalia, in his formulation, do not allow for lesbian relations; so Hincmar posits these sexual relations as being effected through artificial means, diabolically inspired. In essence, the standard of proof for lesbian sexual practices is established as the presence of material "instruments."[16] Further, where ancient writers maintained the binary logic of a strictly active/passive coupling within a static, predetermined relation between the partners, Hincmar appears to leave a space for either partner (or both?) to be "active" within a less rigid sexual relationship.[17] Although Hincmar's destabilizing construction of alternatively active/passive modes within a lesbian sexual relationship does not become the dominant view in medieval culture,[18] his insistence on the nonexistence of female homoerotic relations

without an instrument can facilitate our understanding of later juristic interpretations of lesbian sexuality.

Perhaps, however, what is most important about our consideration of penitential literature is the privileged discourse in which it
comes into use—privileged in that it offers a forum for the unbur-
dening of "sin" and thus may be seen as non-threatening. Moreover,
it implies a voluntary act on the part of the penitent. In that sense,
revelations made in confession may well have been able to make
their way back into penitential literature. Even the broad definitions
of sodomy found in the majority of penitentials could be sufficient
to elicit admissions of sexual misconduct from the penitent and
allow the confessor to impose an appropriate penance. The nature
of the confessional mode maintained an effective yet discreet control of individual conduct. When matters of sexuality move beyond
the confines of confession, when we enter the arena of criminal sexuality, we are also confronted by the methods through which sexuality is regulated and controlled in the public domain. We are led to
question why certain types of conduct would be considered a threat
to the social order and what relationship exists between this threatening conduct and "normal"—that is, non-criminal—behavior, lo-
cating the lesbian at the site where notions of possible sexualities
intersect with social and political structures.

From Private Piety to Public Control

While the confessional offered a means of private spiritual cleans-
ing, a more public ritual could be equally beneficial in demonstrat-
ing the moral leadership of the Church. James Brundage comments
in "Playing by the Rules" that the thirteenth century saw a movement by the Church "to create procedures specifically designed to
deal with special problems that deviant sexual conduct presented."[19]
Brundage reminds us of the special status of sexual crimes: "Within
the universe of crimes, sexual crimes presented particularly difficult
juristic problems. Since sex offences characteristically occurred in
private, so that the only witnesses were usually the parties themselves, these crimes were exceptionally difficult to prove unless the
participants confessed to them."[20] Thus, the adoption by the Fourth

Lateran Council in 1215 of "a new process for initiating criminal actions, the procedure *per denunciationem,* in which no public accuser was required,"[21] clearly facilitated prosecution for sexual crimes. A second procedure allowed an ecclesiastical judge "to initiate an *ex officio* inquiry on his own authority when common belief or report (*fama*)" led him to believe his inquiry was justified.[22] A concomitant change in the law of evidence lowered the standard of proof required for conviction. If, then, individuals could be accused without witnesses to corroborate (at least in principle) the veracity of the accusation, or an inquiry could be based on supposition and rumor, allowing a judge to proceed *per inquisitionem* and have more leeway in evaluating evidence, Brundage's assertion that the impact of these changes "was in fact far greater in the field of sexual behavior than anywhere else" appears justified.[23]

The conflicting and contradictory status of female homoerotic relations within these new structures may help to explain why Hincmar's standard of proof did not immediately become the benchmark in the expanded ecclesiastic judiciary. According to Mark Jordan, "sodomy" as a "category for classifying—for uniting and explaining—desires, dispositions, and acts that had earlier been classified differently and separately" first appears in the eleventh century—that is, the abstract category *sodomia* is a concept that derives from Peter Damian's *Liber Gomorrhianis.*[24] Whereas Damian understands *sodomia* only as a particularly male vice and inveighs against its spread among clerics, the significance of his text in the articulation of a paradigm for female same-sex desire in the Middle Ages is manifest. Through its exclusion of women, the *Liber Gomorrhianis* nearly erases the lesbian from the mainstream of medieval theological discourse: Damian thrusts transgressive sexuality back into the domain of the male. In so doing, he reinforces the dominant construction of phallocentric sexuality and by extension, the valorization of a normative heterosexuality. Moreover, if, as Jordan maintains, Damian's notion of *sodomia* creates the beginnings of a notion of homosexual identity—that is, an identity linked to sexuality—then women are excluded from this developing sexual identity. Simply put, by scripting a male-dominated view of sexual identity, Damian effects a secondary type of erasure.

Yet however far-reaching the influence of Damian's text, it did not entirely expunge lesbians from ecclesiastic discourse. Nonetheless, while the term sodomy continued to encompass sexual relations between women in the writings of some theologians, the description of those relations remains a field of discursive ambiguity. Thus when Peter Abelard in his *Commentary on Saint Paul* underscores the importance of relations between women through his gloss on the Pauline concept of "against nature," "against nature, that is, against the order of nature, which created women's genitals for the use of men and not so women could co-habit with women" [Contra naturam, hos est contra naturae institutionem, quae genitalia feminarum usui virorum praeparavit . . . non ut feminae feminis cohabiterent],[25] he does not detail what type of unnatural use he construes. His silence in this respect locates him in the mainstream of clerical commentators. In the thirteenth century, both Albertus Magnus and his pupil Thomas Aquinas continue the formulation that delineates sodomy as sin against nature inclusive of men with men and women with women. Jordan suggests that unlike many penitential authors, Albertus Magnus offers relatively few descriptions of male sexual acts, perhaps out of fear of promoting them.[26] His omission of female homoerotic practices cloaks them in an even greater obscurity. Although Aquinas in his *Summa theologica* (1267–1273) broadens the categories of acts against nature, he too elides female homoerotic acts and groups them broadly with sodomy.

In the thirteenth century, transgressive sexuality became associated with heretical religious practices, especially in southern France.[27] The rejection of the flesh and procreative sexuality among the priest class of the Cathars, the Perfects, led incontrovertibly to same-sex relationships, or so concluded the Dominican Guibert de Nogent in his autobiography.[28] The bull of Pope Gregory IX against the Cathars imaginatively describes orgies in which Cathari men and women engage in same-sex relations. It is worth noting, however, that to date the records of the Cathar inquisition have revealed no instances of charges of lesbianism and only one charge of male sodomy.[29] Regardless of the sparse evidence, the connection between homoerotic sexual practices and heresy remains strong throughout the ensuing centuries.[30] One aspect of this slippage from sexual transgression to religious transgression may well be that through the association of homoerotic practices with heresy, the penalties became more severe: heretics could be remanded to secular authorities for execution. And the term *bougrerie* (heresy) became conflated with sodomy: "when someone is said to be a *bougre* (sodomite/heretic) . . . and if he must be burned . . . secular justice will burn him."[31]

Lay Justice Follows

It is not surprising, given the cross-fertilization of moral and legal ideals, that secular law exhibits many of the same inconsistencies and tendencies as ecclesiastic justice. Jacqueline Murray sums up the position of the lesbian in secular legal discourse: "The relative neglect of lesbians by ecclesiastical . . . writers is paralleled in secular law."[32] Formulations found in customaries reflect this elision.[33] While the section of Philippe de Beaumanoir's *Coutumes de Beauvaisis* (1283) that details different crimes and their punishments includes the typical formulation that links heresy and sodomy—"Whoever goes against the faith so that through disbelief he does not come to see the way of the truth or who commits sodomy, he shall be burned and forfeit all his possessions" [Qui erre contre la foi en mescreance de laquele il ne veut venir a voie de verité, ou qui fet sodometerie il doit estre ars et forfet tout le sien comme il est dit devant]—Beaumanoir does not elaborate on what constitutes sodomy or who can commit it.[34] Similar statutes can be found in other French customaries, such as the *Etablissements de Saint Louis,* that stipulate for *sodomie* or *bougrerie* without any specific mention of women.

In this sense the *Livre de jostice et de Plet,* a customary from the Orleanais district in France compiled about 1270, stands out as somewhat of an anomaly among secular juridical texts of the thirteenth through fifteenth centuries. The *Livre de Jostice et de Plet* marks out a space for lesbian relations distinct from male homosexual relations. The formulation of the punishments for criminal sexual activities epitomizes difficulties encountered by legal discourses, be they secular or ecclesiastical, when faced with female homoerotic practices. Paragraph twenty-two prescribes the penalties for male sodomites: "Those who are proved to be sodomites shall lose their [testicles]. And if he should do it a second time, he will lose his member. And if he should do it a third time, he must be burned." (Three strikes, you're out is apparently not a new concept.) Following the section treating male sodomites, paragraph twenty-three lists the penalties for women offenders: dismemberment (*perdre membre*) for the first two convictions and burning for the third.[35] As nearly every modern scholar commenting on this text has noted, the terms of this statute when applied to women make very little sense. While it is possible to consider that statute twenty-two presents a (somewhat) logical progression in severity when dealing with a male sodomite (testicles-penis-death), the rather startling repetition of "lose a member" [*perdre membre*] in statute twenty-three leads us to a number of possible scenarios, none of which is particularly convincing.[36] By relying on a construction of female homoeroticism derived from the male body, the *Livre de Jostice et de Plet* prescribes punishments that appear both arbitrary and unclear. Perhaps we have no prosecutions for lesbianism from the Orleanais because the statute itself proved difficult to enforce.

Secular legal discourse of the period, then, was struggling to find a way to define a non-phallic sexuality. That a woman could engage in some sorts of sexual acts with another woman was not in dispute, but what posed a problem was the articulation of these acts in a coherent form of legal discourse. The resolution of this dilemma seems to focus on an elaboration on what constitutes transgressive behavior. That is, by opting for a version of the "lesbian" that follows a passive/active and therefore female/male paradigm, an avenue of prosecution can be found. The Italian legist Cino da Pistoia, for example, in a gloss on the *lex foedissimam,* interprets it as including "women who exercise their lust on other women and pursue them like men."[37] By 1400, Bartolomeus of Saliceto, in another gloss on the *lex foedissimam,* prescribes the death penalty for the defilement of a woman by another woman. Both Cino and Bartolomeus specifically emphasize the "active" or "male" partner in the lesbian relationship and single her out as especially culpable.

Although commentaries such as Cino's and Bartolomeus's were not official, this type of pronouncement, when made by noted legal scholars, often carried the weight of law and could exert an influence in the drafting of legal codes. Through the assimilation of female homoerotic practices to male practices, the death penalty for lesbian relations appears to become the norm in continental Europe by the end of the Middle Ages.[38] Article forty-one of the *Constitutio criminalis* of Bamberg (1507), for example, decrees that women "who have lain with other women" be burnt at the stake. Significantly, the Bamberg statute becomes, through its inclusion in the *Constitutio criminalis carolina* (1532, the criminal code of Emperor Charles V), the penalty for lesbians throughout the Holy Roman Empire during the sixteenth century.[39] Secular judicial discourse places lesbian sexual relations on an equal footing with other forms of sodomy and heresy: such a crime is not merely illegal, it is a capital offense.

Yet herein lies the contradiction: despite the existence of statutes condemning female homoerotic practices, actual prosecutions for lesbianism are, as we have already seen, exceedingly rare in the Middle Ages. Why then do so few investigations for lesbianism appear in the secular and ecclesiastic records of the Middle Ages? Guido Ruggiero concludes that in Venice during the fourteenth and fifteenth centuries "lesbianism . . . was not prosecuted" for "it was a form of sexuality that did not threaten the family with the birth of illegitimate children or with dissolution," rendering it, in essence a "non-crime."[40] Ruggiero bases his analysis on the lack of records of prosecution, and what he posits as the Venetian attitude toward lesbianism might appear easily applicable to any region in Europe.

Lesbians Have Their Day in Court

Joan Cadden partially concurs with Ruggiero when she explains that "the passive sexual and reproductive roles attributed to women and the lesser value placed on the feminine are likely to have led to a relative lack of concern about women betraying their gender roles within the domain of sexual relations." However, she goes on to affirm: "But women making love to women were sometimes seen as behaving 'like men' and were prosecuted."[41] As an example, Cadden cites an excerpt from a letter of pardon in a

1405 French royal register that appears as part of an entry in Du Cange's *Glossarium mediae et infimae Latinitatis.*[42] That letter deals with the sexual relationship between Jehanne and Laurence, two married women. As Cadden reads Du Cange's version of the text, as a result of their repeated sexual encounters both women faced prosecution, but Laurence based her appeal on her role as passive woman while Jehanne "climbed on her as a man does on a woman." Thus Cadden reasons that the defense presented by Laurence hinges on the upholding of gender roles of passive/active. Although the performing of the male role by one of the partners (Jehanne) threatens the stability of the imposed gender roles, the acting out of the female role by the other partner (Laurence) reinforces it and disculpates the woman who did not cross gender boundaries. By casting Jehanne as the aggressor, Laurence seeks to establish her innocence by affirming that she had not strayed from accepted gender roles. To read the appeal in this way, we assume that friends who organized Laurence's appeal were able to find a savvy lawyer who knew of the distinction in punishment made between the active and the passive partner in Saliceto's gloss on the *lex foedissimam.*[43]

The case in question, which does not figure in Crompton's tally, may be the earliest attested trial for lesbianism we have. As such it merits close attention. Cadden's analysis of the text, drawn as it is from Du Cange's partial transcription of the letter of pardon, does not fully take into account the "facts" of the case. While her reading is consistent with one construction of lesbian sexuality in juridical discourse, we cannot ignore the fact that in the first hearing of this case, Laurence's "role" in the couple had little impact on the judgment.[44] The lower court's ruling placed Laurence in prison, "where she will soon finish her days." If her transgression is not a matter of dispute, why then does her appeal succeed? An examination of the complete letter of pardon yields a wealth of details of the relationship that shed light not only on how the young women involved acted toward each other but also on what appear to be the mitigating circumstances that led to Laurence's release from prison. The retelling of the tale that gained Laurence her freedom reflects a narrative carefully elaborated to convince the king to show her clemency.[45] When Jehanne asks

Laurence to be her "girlfriend/sweetheart" [*mie*], Laurence agrees because she "thought there was nothing evil in it" [*ne pensoit a nul mal*].
After Laurence overcomes her initial surprise at Jehanne's sexual advances, the two meet repeatedly, with Jehanne doing "what man does
to a woman." One night, when Jehanne has gained entrance to Laurence's house, Laurence tells Jehanne that she no longer desires her.
Jehanne reacts by attacking her with a knife.

The acknowledgment of her sexual relationship with another
woman makes Laurence guilty of sodomy, whatever her role might
have been.[46] The appeal goes beyond the fact Laurence played the
female-gendered role in this couple. Laurence's ultimate rejection of
Jehanne's attentions coupled with the assault that occurs as a result
of that refusal are, I believe, the factors that prevailed in the appeal.
In a sense, Laurence's appeal is not a defense of her actions nor is it
a claim of innocence. That Laurence had been a willing partner becomes an important element in the narrative, which is constructed
to portray her as a sinner who has left the path of evil. In this scenario, the king's role mimics that of the confessor who assigns a
penance: Laurence will remain in prison until she has served a total
of six months. Afterwards her name will be cleared and her good
reputation restored. Thus, Laurence's transgressive behavior is seen
as a limited aberration; she's been "cured."

This letter of pardon, however, raises more questions than it can
possibly answer. It is the final piece of a puzzle. Unfortunately, all
the others—if they still exist—are yet to be discovered. We have no
idea what first brought the two women to the attention of the
courts. Was it the *fama* of the affair? Was it the assault? Both Jehanne
and Laurence are married. Did that make them less culpable—that
is, could they be reintegrated into "normal" sexual relationships?
Did their husbands know of this affair and dismiss its importance?
We must consider, too, the social situation of the couple and their
knowledge of the law. Although theologians and jurists debated the
fine points of sodomy, was either of these young peasant women
aware of the possible consequences of their actions? When Laurence states that she "thought there was no evil in it," does that
mean that she had no concept of sex between women as "sinful"
and illegal?[47] Nowhere does the letter of pardon explicitly state that

she acknowledged the sinfulness or criminality of her conduct.[48] Rather, it is only her refusal to have sex with Jehanne that implies Laurence's realization of the "evil." What of Jehanne? We learn quite a bit about Jehanne's character (albeit through the biased filter of the appeal). She acts upon her attraction to Laurence; she exhibits resourcefulness in arranging to spend time alone with her; she speaks to Laurence as a lover would; she does not take rejection lightly. We also have a fair inkling of her fashioning of her "male" role: she does not cross-dress, nor does she use a "diabolical instrument" in her sexual relations with Laurence. If we apply the logic that the active partner should be put to death (Saliceto), we might assume that Jehanne met with this fate. However, all we really "know" from Laurence's version is that after the assault Jehanne left without closing the door behind her.

Despite the fragmentary nature of our knowledge of this case, it foregrounds several important issues. In terms of the juridical implications, we find a confessed lesbian receiving a relatively light sentence through royal clemency. However, if we think back to Hincmar's standard of proof, even though Jehanne may have been the active partner, she did not use a dildo. Lacking this material object, the relationship between Laurence and Jehanne would, when defined in terms of the phallic model of sexuality, have appeared less threatening to the social order. Sexual relations by *echaufoison* [chaffing] do not carry the same weight as those in which the female "lack" is supplemented by a simulacrum.

Du Cange cited these proceedings in his dictionary entry discussing the legal implication of "*hermaphroditus.*" Du Cange uses the excerpt from the letter of pardon to illustrate who is or is not a hermaphrodite. Through Jehanne's example, the reader should learn that a woman who pursues another woman is not necessarily a hermaphrodite, implying that gender is not necessarily linked to the physiological. Du Cange's nineteenth-century discussion of the term "hermaphrodite" would be of less interest were it not for a similar discussion in a passage from a late medieval German chronicle. Around 1514, a serving girl in Mösskirch "loved young daughters, went after them . . . and she also used all the bearings and manners, as if she had a masculine affect." The chronicler continues that although Greta was often thought to be a hermaphrodite, when examined she was found to be "a true, proper woman." He adds that "among the learned and well-read one finds this thing is often encountered among Greeks and Romans" [hat sie die jungen döchter geliept, denen nachgangen . . . auch alle geperden und maieren, ob sie als ain mannlichen affect hat . . . ain wahr, rechts weib gesehen worden . . . bei gelernten und belesen find man, [dass] dergleichen vil bei Graecis und Remern begegnet].[49] Lyndal Roper comments on this anecdote, noting that this "matter-of-fact tone" reveals that the "idea of 'unnatural' acts between women did not lie outside [the chronicler's] mental map."[50] Despite Greta's overt homoerotic desires, she does not seem to cause concern among the townsfolk of Mösskirch. She clearly plays the man's role but remains a "true woman"—that is, however masculine her actions, she was neither a hermaphrodite nor was she hiding a dildo under her skirt. I would speculate that Jehanne and Laurence's case may be located in that same space of "safe sex." The "masculine" women need not have a physiological source for their attractions. Moreover, if they do not mimic phallic sex, they are consequently less likely to face stiff prosecutions.

There could be no better proof of the distinction between the "safe" lesbian and the "dangerous" lesbian than the trial of Katherina Hetzeldorferin of Nuremberg in the town of Speyer in 1477. The salient features in this case were the presence of an "instrument" and the identification of Katherina as a man. Katherina admits to having fabricated a dildo out of leather, stuffed with cotton and made erect by means of piece of wood, which she tied on with cord and used in her sexual relations with other women. Both the witnesses and the drafter of the trial transcript repeatedly describe Katherina in terms of her masculinity: "*manlichkeit,*" "*buberÿ*"; or as being like a man: "eyn man sin soll"; or as acting like a man: "als eynn mann . . . getann hat." Her partners claim not to have realized that she was not a man: "She knew naught but that she [Katherina] was a man."[51] In effect, Katherina passed as a man disguised as a woman. Her alleged deception could succeed since it reproduced the heterosexual model. But of course, she was really a woman passing sexually as a man. Katherina's refusal of predefined gender roles is disruptive, and her self-construction as a "man" accords her the agency that she is otherwise denied.

For having engaged in sexual relations with other women, including one she claimed was her sister, Katherina was drowned. Katherina's partners were banished from the city for their actions. Following this binary construction of gender roles, the woman who had acted like a man merited the most severe punishment. The distinction between the "guilty" manlike woman and the "innocent" female partners exposes the underpinnings of the management of lesbian relations and its link to the exercise of power. It serves at once to condemn the woman who usurps male authority and privilege and to reenact the notion of woman as "lack" by hurriedly inserting her into the knowable constructs of heterosexual hierarchies. And as similar scenarios are played out in later trials of the modern period,[52] it becomes evident that this construction of lesbian sexuality is both facile and reassuring.

Mulier cum mulieribus

What I hope to have suggested in this study are two contradictory positions/positionings of the lesbian. First, for all intents and purposes lesbians did not "exist" as a legal category in medieval Europe (hence the term "lesbian impunity"). Since the definition of sexuality was phallic, criminal lesbian sexuality could only be phallic, which led ultimately to the definition of a lesbian act punishable by death (that is, the same penalty as "male" sodomy) as one in which a woman has sexual relations with another woman by means of "any material instrument." It is not surprising that this legal construction of female sexuality led to a more general social erasure of lesbian sexuality and identity in early modern Europe. However, this very erasure—that is, the elision of lesbian into sodomite and the emphasis on a "material instrument"—may well have been the mechanism that allowed female homoaffective/homoerotic relationships to flourish within broadly delimited situations. Certain privileged places, such as convents, or discourses, such as poetry, were often spared legal attack; the infamous and yet "innocent" poem of Bieiris de Romans successfully slipped between those discursive lines.

In the end, it was the very patriarchal, Catholic underpinnings of that society that rendered any non-binary construction of the lesbian impossible to conceive without risking its own logical ontological destabilization. On the other hand, subsumed under that "natural" male/female Christian model, deprived of the homoerotic agency emerging for men, she was given the role of manageable though rarely seen transgressor. Foucault recognizes that "sexuality is not the most intractable element in power relations, but rather one of those endowed with the greatest instrumentality: useful for the greatest number of maneuvers, and capable of serving as a point of support, as a linchpin, for the most varied strategies."[53] Though a medieval legal lesbian identity proved to be the unnamable, it was ironically in that very failure of the word that the lesbian found a strategy to rise above the laws meant to erase her.[54]

Notes

* Passage taken from the chapter on the sin of luxury, *Confessional . . .* (BnF, Rés D 11579), cited in Jean-Louis Flandrin, *Le Sexe et l'occident: Evolution des attitudes et des comportements* (Paris: Seuil, 1981), p. 256.

1. Louis Crompton, "The Myth of Lesbian Impunity: Capital Laws from 1270–1791," *Journal of Homosexuality* 6 (fall/winter 1980/81): 13–25. This same issue includes Brigitte Eriksson's "A Lesbian Execution in Germany, 1721," 27–40, and William E. Monter's "Sodomy and Heresy in Early Modern Switzerland," 41–55, both of which provide invaluable insights into the attitudes of secular justice towards homosexual relationships.

2. Crompton, "Myth of Lesbian Impunity," 11.

3. If we take Monter's data as an example, we find that some 75 individuals were tried for sodomy between 1444 and 1789 in Geneva. Of these, only one was a woman.

4. Judith C. Brown, *Immodest Acts: The Life of a Lesbian Nun in Renaissance Italy* (Oxford: Oxford University Press, 1986), p. 6. In *Les relations amoureuses entre femmes* (Paris: Odile Jacob, 1995), Marie-Jo Bonnet refers to the execution of two women indicted for sorcery in Peronne. Condemned to the stake by the Inquisitor Robert le Bougre, these women had "worn men's clothing." Bonnet does not give the complete reference for this trial, although she leads us to

believe that this and other proceedings about which a colleague of hers gave this basic information can indeed be found: "If we go back to the Middle Ages, we find examples of numerous death sentences pronounced by the tribunals of the Inquisition for the following causes: 'wearing men's clothing,' 'hiding one's status as women,' 'taking on men's status'" (pp. 32–33). Without having made a thorough analysis of the transcripts, I hesitate to posit that the women indicted in these cases were lesbians as well as cross-dressers. Nonetheless, such cases hint at the complex relationships among gender, cross-dressing, "sorcery," and homoeroticism and at their relation to the construction of female sexuality in the Middle Ages.

5. Brown, *Immodest Acts,* p. 6. Among the most frequently cited "authorities" for this view is Pierre de Bordellos, the sixteenth-century French abbot whose *Dames galantes* discussed lesbian relations in the context of adultery.

6. Any discussion of sexual identity in this period must begin by acknowledging John Boswell's contribution to the field in his *Christianity, Social Tolerance, and Homosexuality* (Chicago: University of Chicago Press, 1980). I note, as have others, that Boswell's "gay people in Western Europe" are primarily male homosexuals. In the two decades since the publication of this study, scholarship on lesbians from the same period has only begun to emerge. For a comprehensive and intelligent evaluation of the current status of scholarship on lesbians, see Jacqueline Murray, "Twice Marginal and Twice Invisible: Lesbians in the Middle Ages," in *Handbook of Medieval Sexuality,* ed. Vern L. Bullough and James A. Brundage (New York and London: Garland Press, 1996), pp. 191–222.

7. See Mark Jordan for a fuller discussion of penitential literature in *The Invention of Sodomy in Christian Theology* (Chicago: University of Chicago Press, 1997). In *Sex and the Penitentials* (Toronto: University of Toronto Press, 1984), p. 40, Pierre J. Payer recognizes, as does Jordan, that the term *sodomitae* of the penitentials cannot be simply translated as homosexuals.

8. Payer, *Sex and the Penitentials,* p. 135. Terms such as *luxuria, vitium sodomiticum, peccatum (vitium) contra naturam*—a diverse group of "non-normative" sexual practices that included non-procreative heterosexual acts, same-sex relations, and bestiality—appear with great frequency in these handbooks.

9. Vern L. Bullough, "The Sin against Nature," in *Sexual Practices and the Medieval Church,* ed. Vern L. Bullough and James A. Brundage (Buffalo, NY: Prometheus Books, 1982), p. 61.

10. Valerie Traub, "The (In)Significance of 'Lesbian' Desire in Early Modern England," in *Queering the Renaissance,* ed. Jonathan Goldberg (Durham: Duke University Press, 1994), pp. 62–83.

11. Cited in Brigitte Spreitzer, *Die stumme Sünde. Homosexualität in Mittelalter* (Göttingen: Kümmerle Verlag, 1988), p. 22.

12. See, for example, the eleventh-century decretals of Burchard, Bishop of Worms, and other texts cited in Bullough, "The Sin against Nature."

13. Emphasis added; Hincmar of Rheims, *De divortio Lotharii et Tetbergae,* interrogatio XII PL 125: 692–93, cited in Boswell, *Christianity, Social Tolerance, and Homosexuality,* p. 204 n. 132.

14. Bernadette J. Brooten, *Love Between Women: Early Christian Responses to Female Homoeroticism* (Chicago: University of Chicago Press, 1996), p. 307.

15. Although most historians (for example, Bonnet, *Relations amoureuses,* and Brooten, *Love Between Women*) maintain that clitorectomy appears with insistent regularity in medical texts from ancient times through the late nineteenth century as a "cure" for lesbianism, Danielle Jacquart and Claude Thomasset, *Sexuality and Medicine in the Middle Ages,* trans. Matthew Adamson (Princeton: Princeton University Press, 1988), first published as *Sexualité et savoir médical au Moyen-Age,* (Paris: PUF, 1985), offer a different view.

16. Hincmar is not alone in his knowledge of instruments. The Penitential of Bede recommends a penance of seven years for nuns who use instruments, and Burchard of Worms also signals "devices in the manner of a virile member" (Murray, "Twice Marginalized," p. 198).

17. Indeed, the sixteenth-century jurist Antonio Gomez mentions a capital case involving two nuns using an instrument (cited in Crompton, "Myth of Lesbian Impunity," p. 19).

18. One need only call to mind Etienne de Fougère's countervision: "one's the cock, the other's the hen / and each has her rôle" [l'un fet coc et l'autre polle / et chascune joue son rolle], lines 1123–24, *Le livre de manières,* ed. R. Anthony Lodge, (Geneva: Droz, 1979). On Etienne's poem, see the essays by Robert Clark and Sahar Amer in this volume.

19. James A. Brundage, "Playing by the Rules," in *Desire and Discipline: Sex and Sexuality in the Premodern West,* ed. Jacqueline Murray and Konrad Eisenbichler (Toronto: University of Toronto Press, 1996), p. 26.

20. Brundage, "Playing by the Rules," p. 27.

21. Ibid.

22. Brundage, "Playing by the Rules," p. 28.

23. Ibid.

24. Mark Jordan, *The Invention of Sodomy in Christian Theology* (Chicago: University of Chicago Press, 1997), pp. 1, 40–44.

25. Abelard, *Expositio in epistolam Pauli ad Romanos* I PL 178:806, cited in Boswell, *Christianity, Social Tolerance, and Homosexuality,* p. 313 n. 40; my translation.

26. Jordan, *Invention of Sodomy,* p. 165.

27. Brundage points out as well that the development of these procedures has commonly been linked to the inquisitorial role in thirteenth-century heresy prosecutions ("Playing by the Rules," p. 31).

28. *De vita sua,* 17: "viri cum viros, foeminae cum foeminis cubitare noscantur" (cited in Spreitzer, *Die stumme Sünde,* p. 153).

29. In Jacques Fournier's records of inquisitions, only Arnauldus de Vernhole, in a case dating from 1323, is accused of being guilty of sodomy as well as heresy. See Jean Duvernoy, *Le registre d'inquisition de Jacques Fournier, Evêque de Pamiers* (Toulouse: Privat, 1965) for a full account of this and other investigations from the Cathar inquisition.

30. See Derrick Bailey, *Homosexuality and the Western Christian Tradition* (Hamden: Archon Books, 1975), pp. 135–44, and Vern L. Bullough, "Postscript: Heresy, Witchcraft, and Sexuality," in *Sexual Practices and the Medieval Church,* ed. Bullough and Brundage, pp. 206–17.

31. Art. 142, *La très ancienne coûtume de Bretagne,* ed. Marcel Planiol (Paris-Geneva: Champion-Slatkine, 1984). Bailey shows that English laws of the same period link heresy and sorcery: "The same sentence shall be passed upon sorcerers, sorceresses, renegades, sodomists, and heretics publicly convicted" (*Homosexuality,* p. 146).

32. Murray, "Twice Marginalized," p. 200.

33. In his "Sodomy and Medieval Secular Law," *Journal of Homosexuality* 1(1976): 295–302, Michael Goodich briefly surveys many of these statutes.

34. Philippe de Beaumanoir, *Coutumes de Beauvaisis* (Paris: Picard, 1970) 1:431.

35. "Feme qui le fet doit a chescune foiz perdre membre et la tierce doit estre arsse" (*Li livre de jostice et de plet,* ed. Pierre Rapetti [Paris: Didot Frères, 1850], pp. 279–80).

36. One can posit a number of sequences, including various forms of mutilation: hand-hand-death; hand-clitoris-death; tongue-hand-death, etc.

37. See Crompton, "Myth of Lesbian Impunity," 15.

38. Boswell notes a marked shift occurring between 1250 and 1300 in the prevailing attitudes of secular justice: "homosexual activity passed from being completely legal in most of Europe to incurring the death penalty in all but a few contemporary legal compilations" (*Christianity, Social Tolerance, and Homosexuality*, p. 293). Although "completely legal" may be a bit of an overstatement, it is true that as secular statutes were drawn up, execution became the standard punishment for convicted sodomites. This imposition of this penalty may be linked to the association of heresy with sodomy and the development of the inquisitorial process in the early thirteenth century.

39. Cited in Spreitzer, *Die Stumme Sünde*, p. 22.

40. Guido Ruggiero, *The Boundaries of Eros: Sex Crime and Sexuality in Renaissance Venice* (New York: Oxford University Press, 1985), p. 189 n.21. This evaluation echoes the evidence of statutes concerning sodomy and the types of sexual practices prosecuted in medieval Italy that make up the bulk of the examples given by Michael Goodich's essay on secular law (cited above).

41. Joan Cadden, *Meanings of Sex Differences in the Middle Ages: Medicine, Science and Culture* (Cambridge: Cambridge University Press, 1993), p. 224.

42. Charles Du Fresne Du Cange, *Glossarium mediae et infimae Latinitatis* (Niort: L. Favre, 1885), 4: 202. The complete text of this letter can be found in the Archives Nationales de France, JJ 160: 112.

43. Saliceto's gloss dates from 1400.

44. I hesitate to say no impact, since Laurence had not been summarily put to death.

45. For an enlightening discussion of the "literary" aspects of appeals, see Natalie Z. Davis, *Fiction in the Archives: Pardon Tales and their Tellers* (Stanford: Stanford University Press, 1987).

46. At least that is presumably her crime, since the term appears nowhere in her letter of pardon. Perhaps, following the lead of Gerson, the crime is not named.

47. A Genevan woman executed for sodomy, fornication, and blasphemy in 1568, stated that although she knew heterosexual relations with a married man were sinful, she did not know that sexual relations with another woman were (Archives d'Etat de Genève, Procès Criminels I: 1465). For an analysis of this trial in relation to the medieval cases, see my unpublished article, "Je vien a toy parler d'amourete: Lesbians on Trial in Early Modern Europe."

48. A statement to that effect may well appear in the original trial transcripts. Nonetheless, it was not deemed necessary for the appeal.

49. Hansmartin Decker-Hauff, *Die Chronik des Grafen von Zimmern* (Stuttgart: Jan Thorbecke, 1967), 2, p. 212.

50. Lyndal Roper, *The Holy Household: Women and Morals in Reformation Augsburg* (Oxford: Clarendon Press, 1989), p. 257. I use Roper's translation of this passage of the *Chronik*.

51. I would like to thank Helmut Puff for his generous sharing of this text with me. For a more detailed reading, consult his forthcoming article, "The Rhetoric of the (Un)speakable: Female Sodomy around 1500."

52. The case of Catherina Margaretha Linck and Catherina Margaretha Muehlhahn presented in Birgitte Eriksson's article cited above is typical in this sense. See also Rudolf M. Dekker and Lotte C. van de Pol, *The Tradition of Female Transvestism in Early Modern Europe* (Basingstoke: Macmillan Press, 1989) and Crompton for other cases that follow this paradigm.

53. Michel Foucault, *The History of Sexuality: An Introduction* (New York: Vintage, 1980), p. 103.

54. Research for this study was funded in part by a Diversity Initiatives Grant from the College of Arts and Letters at San Diego State University.

CHAPTER FIVE

TRIBADISM/LESBIANISM AND
THE SEXUALIZED BODY IN
MEDIEVAL ARABO-ISLAMIC NARRATIVES

Fedwa Malti-Douglas

> *This study investigates one set of discourses surrounding same-sex de-
> sire among women in the medieval Arabo-Islamic period, in a work
> by al-Tîfâshî.*

In an impassioned dialogue with her male medical superior in the
asylum in which she is a worker, Nirjis, a female character in
Nawal El Saadawi's *Jannât wa-Iblîs,* challenges the patriarchal system
of which she has been a part by boldly declaring her sexual preference. In a moment of great courage, when the male director orders
her to prepare snacks for his later visit in the evening, she stares him
in the eye and announces that she is walking out on him. He immediately thinks that there is another man in her life. But she
quickly disabuses him, and when he asks her if she loves women, she
answers simply: "Yes." He declares that she will go to Hell with the
People of Lot, and to this statement she responds simply, "No." His
reply?: "Lesbianism is forbidden (*harâm*)." But the female hero answers: "No, Sir! It is not mentioned in the Book of God."[1]

Female same-sex desire and love is, indeed, not mentioned in
the Muslim Book of God, the *Qur'ân,* but fortunately for us it is

mentioned elsewhere. We shall investigate one set of discourses surrounding same-sex desire among women in the medieval Arabo-Islamic period, an investigation that will also deal with woman's body and its representation as a sexualized object.[2]

The opening interchange between the two characters in the contemporary novel by the Arab world's leading feminist is quite revealing. In six pithy lines, the narrator in El Saadawi's novel has spelled out the situation of same-sex relations in Islam. Female homosexual desire is seen in contrast to heterosexuality, here a clearly exploitative form of male-female relations. Nirjis's declaration of her sexual preference leads the director to comment on homosexuality in the Islamic tradition. The People of Lot is a reference to male homosexuals. Oddly enough, the director uses the phrase "the people of Lot" (*qawm Lût*) and not the more common *lûtî* (pl. *liwât*). Nevertheless, the Arabic reader is quite aware of the meaning of his words. When, on the other hand, he condemns love between women, he employs the word *sihâq*. We shall deal with this term momentarily.

No matter how they are referred to, same-sex relations between men are ubiquitous in the medieval Arabo-Islamic textual universe. Perhaps because of this ubiquity, male homosexuality has received a bit more attention than its female counterpart. This is not to say that the study of homosexuality in the Islamic tradition is a flourishing scholarly genre—far from it. Rather, lifting the veil from homosexuality has been a slow process, and many of the existing studies are still not well integrated into the larger humanistic discourses of queer studies.[3] Studies of the larger domain of sexuality in Islam, by contrast, have long formed part of the Western scholarly tradition on the Middle East, be these works written by Easterners or Westerners.[4]

The word used in El Saadawi's novel for love between women (this is, after all, the phenomenon described in this contemporary text) is *sihâq*. *Sahq, sihâq, musâhaqa*: these are all terms derived from the Arabic triliteral verbal root, *s-h-q,* meaning to pound, bruise, efface, render something soft.[5] Some have translated this as "rubbing."[6] From this term emanate the words that refer either to female masturbation or to homosexual activity between women. Given the lexicographical fluidity of this term, it is much more fitting to render

the Arabic words that refer to medieval Arabo-Islamic female homoeroticism with "tribadism." Indeed, to speak of *sahq* and *musâhaqa*
is to speak of more than just same-sex female activity. At the same
time, however, some of the textual materials, as we shall see, speak
eloquently to the existence of a an actual lesbian character.[7]

The absence of the subject of tribadism in the *Qur'ân*[8] must be
countered by the presence of same-sex corporal relations between
women in the medieval Arabo-Islamic textual universe. Our guide
here will be a medieval anecdotal collection, the *Nuzhat al-Albâb
fîmâ lâ Yûjad fî Kitâb* (loosely translated, The Diversion of the Hearts
by What Is Not to Be Found in Any Book) by the prominent author and jurist, Shihâb al-Dîn Ahmad al-Tîfâshî (d. 561 A.H./1253
A.D.).[9] Born in Tunisia, al-Tîfâshî was the son of a jurisconsult, an
occupation he would himself practice. Like other medieval Muslim
scholars, al-Tîfâshî traveled extensively and studied in Cairo and
Damascus. He held juridical appointments both in his native Tunisia
and in Egypt, dying in Cairo. Al-Tîfâshî's intellectual interests were
very broad, and he authored a number of books, including some on
geography, precious stones, and medicine.[10]

The *Nuzhat al-Albâb* is not conceived as an erotic manual but
rather as a collection of entertaining material centered on the areas
of sexuality and sexual practices. As such, it forms part of the more
anecdotal genre of *adab,* a medieval literary genre designed to be at
once edifying and entertaining. Erotic manuals, of course, flourished
in the Arabo-Islamic textual tradition and are replete with sexual
information, including recipes for aphrodisiacs, promoting potency,
etc. The overlap in materials that might exist between an erotic
manual and a more clearly defined anecdotal collection should not
mislead us into amalgamating these two quite distinctive types of
texts. If one looks for example, at the work of the fourteenth-century al-Nafzâwî, *Al-Rawd al-ʿAtir fî Nuzhat al-Khâtir* (popularly
known as *The Perfumed Garden*),[11] the difference between that and
al-Tîfâshî's work becomes evident.[12]

Adab discourse was an intertextually rich discourse that freely
mixed Qur'ânic verses with poetry, *hadîths* (the sayings and actions of
the Prophet), and philological and other materials to create a literary
ensemble of great sophistication. The *adab* writer had to display wide

mastery over the centuries-long textual tradition as he (for they were invariably male) wove his text.[13]

Al-Tîfâshî is no exception here. He is careful to imbricate himself in this tradition by citing in the opening of his introduction material that testifies to the fact that the Prophet liked to laugh and joke with people. The opening *hadîths* include one that is pertinent here, since it deals with women. One day, the Prophet said to an old woman, "Old women do not enter Paradise." So she cried. He then said, "They will be transformed into young women."[14] Whatever the humor in this particular incident, especially for a female reader, its presence is not so much as a commentary on women (though it is that as well) as it is a testimony and a validation for the work that is to follow.

And what a work is Al-Tîfâshî's! It covers a wide range of sexually related materials. Discussing subjects from male homosexuality to anal penetration of women, our medieval jurist mixes prose with poetry to educate his reader with verbal entertainment and wit.[15] Does that mean that al-Al-Tîfâshî's work is simply a collection of materials dealing with sexuality but without any seeming organization? Far from it.

When we look at the *Nuzhat al-Albâb* as an *adab* work, its organization becomes both more evident and more significant. *Adab* works ranged from the monographic, dealing with one topic, to the encyclopedic, dealing with numerous topics. Between the monographic and the encyclopedic lay the intermediate *adab* work, whose focus was one subject refracted through a variety of individuals or classes of people. As I have shown elsewhere, the organization of subjects in both the intermediate and the encyclopedic *adab* works reflected a descending social hierarchy, with the more important subjects coming first. Not surprisingly, women, children, and animals normally bring up the rear. In addition, a syntagmatic relationship existed between *adab* categories in all the types of *adab* works, the literary neighbors defining and recasting one another.[16] Sexuality and sexual deviants are the topic of al-Tîfâshî's work. And not surprisingly, lesbianism is dealt with toward the end of the work, preceded by anal sex with women and followed by the male effeminates, who close the book.[17]

That al-Tîfâshî is tapping fundamentally into an *adab* mental structure is further evidenced by the orientation of his materials, even within the subsections. The segment on tribadism is an excellent example of this, comprising a fairly large chapter with two subsections. The entirety of the materials is entitled: "Fî Adab al-Sahq wal-Musâhaqât wa-Nawâdir Akhbârihinna wa-Mulah al-Ash^câr fîhinna"(loosely translated: On the *Adab* [here, closer to etiquette] of Tribadism and the Tribades and the Rare Stories and Poetry about Them). Then follows a subsection on "Fî Madh al-Sahq wal-Ihtijâj lahu"(On Praise of Tribadism and Argumentation in Its Favor). This praise is followed by a subsection entitled: "Fî Dhamm al-Sahq" (On the Blame of Tribadism).

The unknowing reader might at first glance imagine that al-Tîfâshî is being indecisive or coy by first presenting materials that praise tribadism and then materials that censure it. In fact, al-Tîfâshî's method is part and parcel of a common *adab* orientation in which the same subject is at once praised and blamed. This structure is even more visible in those *adab* works that are dedicated to the praise and blame of various literary materials, and that often carry the words "al-mahâsin wal-masâwî" (or some variation, such as "al-mahâsin wal-addâd") in their titles.[18] Al-Tîfâshî's use of *madh* and *dhamm* is but a linguistic variant. This praise/blame orientation has the added benefit of integrating and mainstreaming female homoeroticism into the much larger *adab* spectrum.

Like other medieval *adab* prose works, the *Nuzhat al-Albâb* boasts a male writer. This means that all textual materials, whatever their ultimate origin, are in effect sifted through a male bias. A contemporary reader must not forget that even when a female is the main character of an anecdote or when a female narrator is responsible for a narrative unit, the male perspective always organizes and dominates the text.[19] Not surprisingly, female characters figure prominently under the watchful eye of the male writer in the section on tribadism. Medical lore mixes with anecdotes and poetry to draw a fascinating picture of woman's body and female same-sex desire. Yet one senses that lurking behind all the material is a strong heterosexist vision (both as point of view and as an activity of the male gaze, which is all-important in the Arabo-Islamic universe).[20]

I shall begin with the following anecdote: An important man said one day to an impudent[21] one, when the topic of tribadism came up: "By God, I want to know how women practice sex between them." The impudent man replied: "If you would like to know that, enter your house a bit at a time."[22]

This superficially simple anecdote, composed of a statement and its response, hides much that surfaces elsewhere in al–Tîfâshî's section on tribadism: voyeurism, heterosexuality, and, not least of all, female homosexual activity. The important man in this narrative unit is fascinated by women's sexuality. In his rhetorical question, he states his wish to learn more about tribadism. But he expresses this wish with an interesting term: *ashtahî*. This word hides a great deal, all of it subsumed in desire. It connotes yearning, craving, carnal appetite, and lust. For the Arabic reader, there is no question about the intensity of that desire. We shall meet this term again below.

When the male speaker asks about the act of tribadism, he employs the word *tatasâhaq*. Derived from the same root we have already discussed, *s-h-q,* this verbal form normally expresses reciprocity, a state in which the parties who are the subjects of the verbal action are performing the same action toward one another. What is being asked about here is an activity in which women are full-fledged sexual participants with one another—to wit, sexual performance between women.

To satisfy this intense desire, the other male populating the anecdote advises his colleague to enter his house a bit at a time. What are the implications of this simple response? The intense desire of the questioner is countered with a verb derived from the root meaning "love." By redirecting intense yearning to love, the impudent man redirects the question from the larger domain of unspecified women to the specified wife in the man's house. (Both male speakers could have used other terms, such as the ones derived from the verbal root *r-w-d,* whose use transmits a wish, but not one laden with yearning and love.) This terminology of love and desire imbues the anecdote with a sexual atmosphere.

But more importantly, the man is advised simply to enter his house gradually. The implications here are clear. The man's wife, the reader then understands, is most likely having sexual relations with other women, and if the husband should enter the house without warning, he would catch her in this activity. The verbal form *tatasâhaq* eliminates the possibility that the woman might be masturbating. What the husband is promised is a lesbian scene. His desire/lust/yearning to know about women's lovemaking will be satisfied. His activity will be largely voyeuristic, but no matter. It is the voyeurism that will teach our important man how women perform the sexual act between them. Lurking behind this anecdote is the possibility that all women are enjoying female same-sex activity in the privacy of their quarters. The curious husband need only observe the woman most easily accessible to him, his wife.

What about the lesbian herself in this anecdote? She may well be any man's wife, but she herself remains invisible. She is but the object of the discourse and, more importantly, of the voyeuristic gaze of the male. And of course, she is the object of male fantasy about woman's sexuality. At the same time, the entire narrative unit functions as a commentary on the instability of monogamous heterosexuality: when the husband is out of the house, his wife will find other sources of pleasure.

Heterosexuality is present behind many of al-Tîfâshî's anecdotal narratives on female homoeroticism. A certain Mazîd was told: "Your wife practices tribadism." He replied: "Yes, I ordered her to do that." He was then asked: "But why?" He replied: "Because it is softer on her labia, purer for the opening of her vulva, and more worthy when the penis approaches her that she know its superiority."[23] Once again, the anecdote stars a male, but this time his interlocutor is not mentioned: the verb is simply given in the passive form. This unknown speaker is making a statement about Mazîd's wife, which should discomfit him. But it does not. Instead, he posits that the entire idea of tribadism is his, an interesting perspective indeed. The male half of the heterosexual married couple does not seem threatened by this female corporal activity—perhaps because it is understood here as masturbation.

But much more interesting is Mazîd's answer to the "why" question posed to him: Why did he order his wife to practice tribadism? The answer is embedded in a corporal discourse that partakes of both male and female sexual parts. Tribadism, the male speaker argues, is more conducive to the female body. It is gentler on a woman's labia and vulva. So far so good. It is when the male organ enters the scene that the issue becomes complicated. Tribadism should make the woman understand the superiority of a man's penis when this sexual organ approaches her. Note that the penis becomes its own agent here, as the subject of the verb. The woman's body remains the passive object, receiving first one sort of pleasure and then another.

Mazîd's apparent concern for his wife's body hides a sexual discourse that tells a great deal about tribadism and heterosexuality. If tribadism is much more gentle—and the implication is that it is more comfortable for a woman's body—than the heterosexual act, why should the woman then need to recognize the superiority of the penis?

In fact, this corporal discourse is a commentary on the politics of sexuality. Heterosexuality is automatically superior, and, if tribadism is practiced, it is merely at the suggestion of the male. The man allows the woman to indulge in this activity in order to permit her to better appreciate his sexual organ. We are not very far here from some of the material Lillian Faderman discusses in her *Surpassing the Love of Men*. Faderman speaks of the importance of the attitude to "lesbian lovemaking" in other cultural contexts as "a prelude to heterosexual lovemaking."[24] In this particular anecdote, it is not clear what the nature of the tribadism is, but it does not matter. We know that it is but a passing phase that will end when the penis arrives on the scene. Not surprisingly this anecdote appears in the section on praise of tribadism. Other material on the praise of tribadism involves fear of pregnancy, an argument that is also adduced in favor of male homosexuality.[25]

Mazîd's attitude is reinforced in other anecdotes in al-Tîfâshî. A tribade who had gotten married was asked: "How was your night yesterday?" She said: "I have been yearning for meat for twenty years and I was only satiated with it yesterday."[26]

This anecdote surfaces in the section on the blame of tribadism. And how much more eloquent this censure can be when the words are put in the mouth of a female speaker! The structure of the anecdote is not too dissimilar from that of Mazîd. In both, the introductory materials set the background for the subsequent questions and responses. The context of this unit is fairly straightforward: a tribade gets married. How was her night? Her response is categorical: her twenty-year craving for meat has finally been satisfied. The retort of the unnamed woman, like Mazîd's answer, is imbued with corporality. Whereas his was overtly sexual (the labia, vulva, penis), hers, imbued with the alimentary, is equally sexual. The verb the female speaker employs to express yearning is the identical one used by the important man who wanted to know how women practiced tribadism: *ashtahî*. This woman's carnal appetite and desire are expressed in terms of "meat," a word that moves the reader between the universes of the alimentary and the sexual. Heterosexual relations have finally satisfied this craving. The woman's fulfillment is expressed with the word derived from the root *sh-b-ʿ*, a verb that most often connotes the satisfaction of corporal appetites.[27] Time is not insignificant here either. The twenty years of deprivation are vindicated by one night of satiation. Heterosexuality, the text tells us, is certainly worth waiting for. Food and sex in this anecdote also come together in a bisociation that is not unfamiliar in the medieval Arabo-Islamic textual tradition. Al-Tîfâshî himself exploits this bisociation elsewhere in his book.[28]

Once again, the reader understands that tribadism is but a passing phase meant to herald the onset of heterosexuality. Another unnamed woman testifies to this in the al-Tîfâshian collection. This particular tribade looks at a man with a large penis. She wonders how it is that with the likes of this pestle in the world she has been beating her own clothing with her hands. No, that will never do. So she gets married.

This unnamed woman is an eloquent spokesperson for heterosexual marriage. A triumphant heterosexuality that wins out over tribadism is generated by the sight of a man's large sexual organ. The subsequent marriage will obviously cure this woman of the need to practice her own kind of tribadism, here masturbation, which act is described as a beating of the clothing with the hands. This example, in its own way, confirms the true lexicographical meaning of the verbal root *s-h-q* as pounding or beating and not necessarily, as some have translated it, as rubbing. The verb the tribade uses in describing her act is *d-q-q*, one of the words used in the lexicographical tradition to explain *s-h-q*.[29] The vigor and quasi violence of the act are what is striking here. The tribade's use of what is really a synonym and a definition for her masturbatory act allows her to play with calling the man's penis a pestle, *midaqqa,* derived from the same verbal root of *d-q-q*. But most of all, this solitary woman populating the anecdote with but one male recognizes the superiority of his sexual organ. This is precisely what Mazîd was arguing for with his wife, although his argument made no mention of size.

Other issues are at play here, not the least of which is the entire game with sight. The important man and his impudent companion demonstrated the importance of the voyeuristic activity. By seeing his wife perform sex with other women, the man would learn about lesbianism. But the anecdote did not recount his actual visual experience. The fate of the woman who looks at the large penis is different. She also must see the object that will deliver the lesson, but for her, visuality is much more immediate.[30] Perhaps that is because the lesson that she must be taught, the superiority of heterosexuality and marriage, is more central to the culture in which she is operating. After all, did not the Prophet enjoin marriage?[31] To help her arrive at this juncture, man is transformed into nothing more than a large penis. The Arabic is instructive here. She looks at "a man large of penis." The "large of penis" defines the man, to the exclusion of any other attributes. In fact, we do not even know if this particular male will be the bridegroom. All we know is that the woman chooses to marry. Like her female colleague who had to forego her craving for meat for twenty years, the adventure of this woman is subsumed within the subsection on blame of tribadism.

From a practical point of view, one wonders how it is that this woman even had the occasion to observe this savior-penis. Were we to take even the most liberal interpretation of the various sanctions governing male-female relations in the medieval Arabo-Muslim literary universe, such access would be at best unlikely. Its existence reminds us, in case we have forgotten, that there is a large element of male fantasy in these texts. More importantly, we need to remember that we are dealing with a male writer manipulating and directing what his readers receive. But perhaps more is at stake here. Does the fact that the woman is a tribade place her in a different universe, one in which the normal societal and religious constraints that dictate male-female interaction can be modified? Possibly. Al-Tîfâshî will be the guide here.

In the opening section on tribadism, even before the reader has entered the praise/blame sections of the work, al-Tîfâshî presents different sorts of material, most of which comment, in one way or another, on the habits of tribades. Some of the most eloquent "facts" that our author presents concern what we might call lifestyle. Not only do these women use more perfume than necessary, but their clothes are cleaner than they need to be. In addition, the furniture, food, and objects at their disposal are the best and the most beautiful to be found at any time or place.[32]

The extravagances that al-Tîfâshî adduces testify to the consumption habits of tribades: perfume, clothing, furniture, food. Looking more closely at what the writer emphasizes about the material goods that make the woman reveals that excess is the key: more perfume than necessary, cleaner clothes, the best and most beautiful of furniture, foods, and objects. These goods point to another dimension, significant in the larger cultural context: the public and the private. If the consumption of furniture and foods could be said to operate in the world of the private, that is not necessarily the case for clothing or perfume. Both are, of course, used to cover (clothing) or adorn (perfume) the body. More importantly, their use by the tribades in al-Tîfâshî's textual universe is meant to call attention to the female body. After all, to determine that clothes are cleaner than the norm one must see them. And to determine that the use of perfume is outside the ordinary, one must smell it.

The body of the tribade, with its corporally related excesses, calls attention to itself, arousing the olfactory and visual senses of those near her. This exhibiting of the female body and its adornment operate outside the norm of the medieval Arabo-Muslim religio-moral universe (and, it could be added, outside the modern one as well). Numerous admonitions testify to the concerns with the limits and the excesses that relate to woman's body. Most often these prohibitions fall under the general rubric of *tabarruj,* loosely translated as adornment. Women have been and continue to be warned against *tabarruj.*[33]

In the vision of the *Nuzhat al-Albâb,* the medieval tribades are
able to skirt these limits and, in effect, to function outside this religio-moral universe. Al-Tîfâshî's work, at least in the introductory
materials, gives the impression that tribadism is not a temporary in-
terlude of female same-sex activity that will eventually lead to a heterosexual marriage. Rather, the tribades seem to form unions that
go beyond the transitory.

What better place to start than with a name? We learn, for example, that the women who practice tribadism refer to themselves
as "*zirâf,*" a word that means at once the witty, the elegant, the
graceful, the charming. "If they say so and so is a *zarîfa,* it is then
known among them that she is a tribade." This internal language
opens up a host of implications. In the culturally important medieval literary spectrum of *adab,* the *zirâf* (masc. sing.: *zarîf*) represent
an *adab* character category. Like other *adab* character types (such as
misers, uninvited guests, the intelligent), the *zirâf* had anecdotes devoted to them that would demonstrate their wit and verbal skills.
This means that they could become the subject of an intermediate
adab work, like that of Ibn al-Jawzî (d. 597/1200), the *Akhbâr al-
Zirâf wal-Mutamâjinîn* (loosely translated: The Stories of the Witty
and the Impertinent).[34] And not surprisingly, Ibn al-Jawzî devotes a
chapter to women in this work, a chapter in which sexual allusions
abound, though no references are made to tribadism.[35] Al-Tîfâshî
seems to be referring in this context to a specialized use of this term
within a specific social group—a term that links the group to a positive cultural category.

Al-Tîfâshî does not stop with language. He suggests to his reader
that he possesses great knowledge about the habits of the tribades. For
example, he mentions that they love each other like men do, in
fact more. They are also willing to spend a great deal of money on
one another, "like a man spends on his female beloved." Once again,
the specter of heterosexuality haunts the tribade. But this is not heterosexuality as the final stage of a process in which tribadism plays
a preparatory role. It is heterosexuality as an alternative that defines
tribadism as a parallel and potentially independent and rival activity. It is noteworthy here that our author then switches to the first
person singular to tell the story of a woman whom he saw in North

Africa spend extraordinary amounts on her "female beloved."[36] This first-person testimony adds the element of veracity, as al-Tîfâshî elaborates on the habits of the tribades.

The active/passive, top/bottom, lover/beloved role distribution in the structure is more apparent in the description of the physical positions two women take when involved in same-sex activity. Al-Tîfâshî places the female lover on top and her beloved below. Unless, he adds, the lover is slender and the beloved corpulent. In that case, the positions are reversed so that the rubbing (*hakk*) is more effective. This formula, if we may call it that, for woman-woman same-sex activity is corporally based. Woman's lovemaking is determined by the size of a woman's body. Lexicography plays a role here as well. The sexual activity between two women is described as *hakk,* rubbing, and not as *sahq* or *musâhaqa,* beating.

In fact, the "important man"—whom we first encountered when he was asking his impudent colleague about women's lovemaking— would have only to indulge himself in al-Tîfâshî's general materials on tribadism to satisfy his fantasies about woman's sexualized body. But for this male involved in a heterosexual relationship, tribadism would have been but an occasional activity on the part of his wife. This male-female couple is similar to that of Mazîd and his spouse. Mazîd was the one who encouraged his wife to practice tribadism. These two heterosexual couples may resemble each other insofar as the wives dabble in tribadism. They are quite different, however, from the female same-sex couple whom al-Tîfâshî saw in North Africa. The male first-person speaker testifies to the existence of this same-sex couple as an economic and emotional entity.

The contemporary female hero of El Saadawi's novel, *Jannât wa-Iblis,* would not be surprised by the tensions we encounter in al-Tîfâshî's materials between tribadism and heterosexuality. After all, was she not herself involved in this dilemma: infatuated with a woman but involved with a man? Whereas she is cursed for her love for a woman, this is not the case for any of al-Tîfâshî's tribades. We can go even further and say that, in fact, oddly missing from al-Tîfâshî's discussion of tribadism are the various materials condemning this practice in religious and moral terms, such as *hadîths* of the Prophet.[37] As our examples show, the "blame" of tribadism in the

Nuzhat al-Albâb is not a moral or ethical blame, but the expression of a negative aspect (often situated in a purely practical universe), of the sort that one finds commonly in the praise/blame sections of *adab* works. A learned jurist himself, al-Tîfâshî certainly knew that tribadism is forbidden in Islam. In his book, however, it is not *harâm,* as it was by contrast for the male director in El Saadawi's dialogue.

This absence of condemnation should perhaps not surprise us. True to their nature as characters in a medieval *adab* work, the tribades are free to be full participants in the ludic atmosphere that suffuses many an *adab* collection. As such they seem capable of escaping moral reprobation and thus, at the same time, of occupying and reshaping the traditional landscape of sexuality in medieval Islam.

Notes

1. Nawal El Saadawi, *Jannât wa-Iblîs* (Beirut: Dâr al-Adâb, 1992), pp. 134–35. This novel has been translated into English by Sherif Hetata as *The Innocence of the Devil* (Berkeley: University of California Press, 1994). For a discussion of this and other issues that relate to female homoeroticism in El Saadawi's corpus, see Fedwa Malti-Douglas, *Men, Women, and God(s): Nawal El Saadawi and Arab Feminist Poetics* (Berkeley: University of California Press, 1995). Although translations will be signaled when available, references in the notes will be to the Arabic originals of all the works. All translations are my own.

2. I am dealing with the larger cultural questions related to female same-sex desire in the Arabo-Islamic sphere in a book currently in preparation. This study will include a discussion of other literary and civilizational materials.

3. *Sexuality and Eroticism Among Males in Moslem Societies,* ed. Arno Schmitt and Jehoeda Sofer (New York: Harrington Park Press, 1992), is a collection of studies and personal testimonies. Once again, as the title indicates, the volume restricts itself to males and maintains a strong Eurocentric perspective. The collection edited by Stephen O. Murray and Will Roscoe, *Islamic Homosexualities: Culture, History, and Literature* (New York: New York University Press, 1997), is an important addition to the scant bibliography. As the plural in the title indicates, it is an ambitious attempt to go beyond male-male sexuality. However, the chapter by Stephen O. Murray, "Woman-Woman Love in Islamic Societies" (pp. 97–104)

is disappointing. The collection, *Homoeroticism in Classical Arabic Literature,* edited by J. W. Wright and Everett K. Rowson (New York: Columbia University Press, 1997) restricts itself to male homosexuality. In addition, a number of the chapters are innocent of the questions raised by the larger field of gay studies, not to mention gender studies in general. Nevertheless, some of the chapters in the volume are useful. See also Everett K. Rowson, "The Effeminates of Early Medina," *Journal of the American Oriental Society* 3 (1991): 671–693; Everett K. Rowson, "The Categorization of Gender and Sexual Irregularity in Medieval Arabic Vice Lists," in *Body Guards: The Cultural Politics of Gender Ambiguity,* ed. Julia Epstein and Kristina Straub (New York: Routledge, 1991), pp. 50–79. The lesbian receives passing mention here. Everett K. Rowson has a projected study on male homosexuality in Islam, which should contain much interesting material.

4. The following is not a bibliographical survey, but rather a series of markers along the road of sexuality studies and Islam. Abdelwahab Bouhdiba's *La sexualité en Islam* (Paris: Presses Universitaires de France, 1979), although a bit on the conservative side, is still an extremely valuable work. Another useful collection is that edited by Afaf Lutfi al-Sayyid-Marsot, *Society and the Sexes in Medieval Islam* (Malibu: Undena Publications, 1979). In the late 1990s, Malek Chebel began a series of works that in one way or another deal with sexuality. Most of these, however, remain fairly general and not extremely specific in their analysis. They function more as brief surveys for nonspecialists in the field. For a more historical treatment of the subject, see G. Hambly, ed., *Women in the Medieval Islamic World: Power, Patronage, and Piety* (New York: St. Martin's Press, 1998).

5. See, for example, al-Zabîdî, *Tâj al-ʿArûs* (Beirut: Dâr Sâdir, n.d.), 6:377–78; E. W. Lane, *Arabic-English Lexicon* (Cambridge, Eng.: Islamic Texts Society, 1984), 1:1318–19.

6. Rowson, "Medieval Arabic Vice Lists," p. 63.

7. I am aware of the pitfalls inherent in the use of the term "lesbian," especially in this context in which we are dealing not only with a non-Western culture but also with a pre-modern society. Questions of definition and terminology are discussed in Jacqueline Murray, "Twice Marginal and Twice Invisible: Lesbians in the Middle Ages," in *Handbook of Medieval Sexuality,* ed. Vern L. Bullough and James A. Brundage (New York and London: Garland, 1996), pp. 191–222. See also, for the modern period, the by-now-classic

essay by Adrienne Rich, "Compulsory Heterosexuality and Lesbian Existence," in *The Signs Reader: Women, Gender and Scholarship,* ed. Elizabeth Abel and Emily K. Abel (Chicago: University of Chicago Press, 1983), pp. 139–168; Bonnie Zimmerman, "What Has Never Been: An Overview of Lesbian Feminist Criticism," in *The New Feminist Criticism: Essays on Women, Literature, Theory,* ed. Elaine Showalter (New York: Pantheon, 1985), pp. 200–24, which I have found very useful here; Lillian Faderman, *Surpassing the Love of Men: Romantic Friendship and Love Between Women from the Renaissance to the Present* (New York: Quill, 1981); Eve Kosofsky Sedgwick, *Epistemology of the Closet* (Berkeley: University of California Press, 1990), especially pp. 1–63; Bonnie Zimmerman, ed., *Encyclopedia of Lesbian Cultures* (New York: Garland, 2000).

8. This absence is well known. See Malek Chebel, *Encyclopédie de l'Amour en Islam: Erotisme, beauté et sexualité dans le monde arabe, en Perse et en Turquie* (Paris: Editions Payot & Rivages, 1995), p. 314. Jamâl Jum^c a, in "al-Irûtîkiyya al-^c Arabiyya," in al-Tîfâshî, *Nuzhat al-Albâb fîmâ lâ Yûjad fî Kitâb,* ed. Jamâl Jum^c a (London and Cyprus: Riad El-Rayyes Books, 1992), p. 32, argues that sexual relations between women were alluded to in the *Qur'ân.* He adduces a verse from the "Sûrat al-Nisâ'" to buttress his argument: "Such of your women as commit indecency, call four of you to witness against them." (For the translation, I am using A. J. Arberry, *The Koran Interpreted* [New York: Macmillan, 1974], 1:102). The word in question in the Qur'ânic verse is "al-fâhisha," which is translated by Arberry as "indecency." Qur'ânic commentators are in agreement that "al-fâhisha" refers, in this case, to *zinâ,* or fornication. See, for example, al-Baydâwî, *Tafsîr al-Baydâwî—al-Musammâ Anwâr al-Tanzîl wa-Asrâr al-Ta'wîl* (Beirut: Dâr al-Kutub al-^c Ilmiyya, 1988), 1:205; Jalâl al-Dîn al-Mahallî and Jalâl al-Dîn al-Suyûtî, *Tafsîr al-Jalâlayn* (Cairo: Mustafâ al-Bâbî al-Halabî, 1966), 1:97; al-Qurtubî, *al-Jâmi^c li-Ahkâm al-Qur'ân* (Cairo: Dâr al-Kutub al-^c Arabiyya lil-Tibâ^c a wal-Nashr, 1967), 5:83.

9. Al-Tîfâshî, *Nuzhat al-Albâb.* The work has been translated into French in a non-scholarly format by René R. Khawam as Ahmad al-Tîfâchî, *Les Délices des coeurs ou ce que l'on ne trouve en aucun livre* (Paris: Phébus, 1981). The French translation is quite uneven. First, it does not contain all the material in the Arabic edition. Second, and just as important, this translation is not always correct and obscures the organization of al-Tîfâshî's materials on tribadism, an organization that is important for understanding the generic nature of the work. This French translation seems to have been the basis

for an English translation by Winston Leyland and Edward A. Lacey, *The Delight of Hearts, or, What You Will Not Find in Any Book* (San Francisco: Gay Sunshine Press, 1988).

10. For a biography of al-Tîfâshî see Jamâl Jumʿa's introduction to his edition of the *Nuzhât al-Albâb* ("al-Irûtîkiyya al-ʿArabiyya"), pp. 38–41.

11. Al-Nafzâwî, *Al-Rawd al-ʿAtir fî Nuzhat al-Khâtir,* ed. Jamâl Jumʿa (London and Cyprus: Riad El-Rayyes Books, 1990). This work has been widely translated. See Shaykh Nefzawi, *The Perfumed Garden,* trans. Richard F. Burton (Secaucus: Castle Books, 1964); Mouhammad al-Nafzâwî, *La Prairie parfumée où s'ébattent les plaisirs,* trans. René R. Khawam (Paris: Phébus, 1976). In his introduction to the Arabic edition, Jamâl Jumʿa discusses the numerous translations of this work, which enjoyed great popularity in the West.

12. See Charles Pellat, "Djins," in the *Encyclopaedia of Islam,* 2d ed. (Leiden: E. J. Brill, 1983) vol. 2, ed. Bernard Lewis et al., pp. 550–53. Pellat's survey is useful but does not really delve into the discourses of the *ars erotica* in Islam, which have still to be subjected to rigorous analysis. Unfortunately, nothing like the work of Michel Foucault, *Histoire de la sexualité,* 3 vols. (Paris: Gallimard, 1976–84) exists for the Islamic world. Nevertheless, many of Foucault's observations, especially those that deal with the ancient world, can be fruitful for an analysis of Arabo-Islamic materials.

13. For a discussion of *adab* and its discourses, see Fedwa Malti-Douglas, *Structures of Avarice: The Bukhalâ' in Medieval Arabic Literature* (Leiden: E. J. Brill, 1985), pp. 7–16; Fedwa Malti-Douglas, "Structure and Organization in a Monographic *Adab* Work: *al-Tatfîl* of al-Khatîb al-Baghdâdî," in *Arabic and Islamic Studies in Honor of Nabia Abbott,* special volume of the *Journal of Near Eastern Studies* 40 (1981):227–45; Fedwa Malti-Douglas "Classical Arabic Crime Narratives: Thieves and Thievery in *Adab* Literature," *Journal of Arabic Literature* 19 (1988):108–27. For a discussion of women in *adab* works, see Fedwa Malti-Douglas, *Woman's Body, Woman's Word: Gender and Discourse in Arabo-Islamic Writing* (Princeton: Princeton University Press, 1991), pp. 29–53.

14. Al-Tîfâshî, *Nuzhat al-Albâb,* p. 45.

15. I am uncomfortable with Rowson's classification of some of these meanings as "mujûn" (he translates "mujûn" as "profligacy," but this is only one of its meanings). He uses this term to apply both to "behavior, and particularly sexual behavior which flouted societal and religious norms" and to the "literary expression of such behavior." Such a classification isolates such "literary expression"

from its textual cousins and does not account for the complexity of the sexual—and nonsexual—discourses in the works themselves. See Rowson, "Medieval Arabic Vice Lists," p. 52.

16. See, for example, Malti-Douglas, *Structures of Avarice,* pp. 14–17; Malti-Douglas, *Woman's Body, Woman's Word,* p. 124.

17. On the effeminates, see Rowson, "The Effeminates."

18. Unlike Gériès, I do not consider these works to be an independent genre, but as I have argued elsewhere, their organization represents a possible orientation for the organization of *adab* materials. See, for example, Malti-Douglas, *Structures of Avarice,* p. 15. See also Ibrahim Gériès, *Un genre littéraire arabe: al-Mahâsin wa-l-Masâwî* (Paris: G.-P. Maisonneuve et Larose, 1977); I. Gériès, "al-Mahâsin wa-'l-Masâwî," in the *Encyclopaedia of Islam,* 2d ed. (Leiden: E. J. Brill, 1986), vol. 5, ed. C. E. Bosworth et al., pp. 1223–27.

19. Malti-Douglas, *Woman's Body, Woman's Word,* p. 29.

20. I have found very inspiring here the discussions by Judith Roof in her *A Lure of Knowledge: Lesbian Sexuality and Theory* (New York: Columbia University Press, 1991), especially pp. 15–89. Although she is dealing in that chapter primarily with cinema, her observations on the lesbian and the heterosexist gaze are quite pertinent. I have discussed the Arabo-Islamic scopic regime and its fascination with the gaze elsewhere. See, for example, Malti-Douglas, *Woman's Body, Woman's Word,* and Malti-Douglas, *Men, Women, and God(s),* which deals specifically with El Saadawi's subversion of this regime.

21. The word *majjân* actually combines impudence, impertinence, and a strong sense of play. It is, thus, very close in spirit to the American colloquial "wiseass."

22. Al-Tîfâshî, *Nuzhat al-Albâb,* p. 241.

23. Al-Tîfâshî, *Nuzhat al-Albâb,* p. 242.

24. Faderman, *Surpassing the Love of Men,* especially the chapter on "Lesbianism and the Libertines," pp. 23–30. The quotations are on p. 26.

25. Al-Tîfâshî, *Nuzhat al-Albâb,* p. 242. See also B. F. Musallam, *Sex and Society in Islam: Birth Control Before the Nineteenth Century* (Cambridge: Cambridge University Press, 1983), pp. 108, 154. I will be dealing with this material in depth in the book mentioned above (see n. 2).

26. Al-Tîfâshî, *Nuzhat al-Albâb,* p. 246.

27. The situation for these medieval women who are able to enjoy the pleasures of the body, and especially to satiate themselves, is completely different from that of contemporary female literary heroes. See, for example, Malti-Douglas, *Men, Women, and God(s),* pp.

52–55, 76ff., 200–201. Carol J. Adams, *The Sexual Politics of Meat: A Feminist-Vegetarian Critical Theory* (New York: Continuum, 1991) is a fascinating exploration of meat, gender, and corporality.

28. See, for example, al-Tîfâshî, *Nuzhat al-Albâb,* pp. 288–89.

29. See, for example, al-Zabîdî, *Tâj al-ʿArûs,* 6:377.

30. Al-Tîfâshî, of course, did not invent the gaze as a teacher in sexual matters. For a discussion of the importance of this element in other medieval Arabic sources, see Malti-Douglas, *Woman's Body, Woman's Word,* pp. 23 ff.

31. See, for example, Ahmad ibn Hanbal, *Musnad al-Imâm Ahmad ibn Hanbal* (Beirut: al-Maktab al-Islâmî lil-Tibâʿa wal-Nashr, n.d.), 5:163–64. For a discussion of this, see Malti-Douglas, *Woman's Body, Woman's Word,* p. 52.

32. Al-Tîfâshî, *Nuzhat al-Albâb,* p. 237.

33. There are innumerable sources, both medieval and modern, for the dangers of adornment. See, for example, Ibn al-Jawzî, *Ahkâm al-Nisâ'* (Beirut: Dâr al-Kutub al-ʿIlmiyya, 1985), p. 63. See also the extremely popular pamphlet by Niʿmat Sidqî, *al-Tabarruj* (Cairo: Dâr al-Iʿtisâm, 1975); Valerie J. Hoffman-Ladd, "Polemics on the Modesty and Segregation of Women in Contemporary Egypt," *International Journal of Middle East Studies,* 19 (1987): 29–42; Sanâ' al-Misrî, *Khalf al-Hijâb: Mawqif al-Jamâʿât al-Islâmiyya min Qadiyyat al-Mar'a* (Cairo: Sînâ lil-Nashr, 1989), p. 36; Fedwa Malti-Douglas, "Faces of Sin: Corporal Geographies in Contemporary Islamist Discourse," in *Religious Reflections on the Human Body,* ed. Jane Marie Law (Bloomington: Indiana University Press, 1995), pp. 67–75.

34. Ibn al-Jawzî, *Akhbâr al-Zirâf wal-Mutamâjinín,* ed. Muhammad Anîs Muharât (Beirut: Dâr al-Hikma, 1987).

35. Ibn al-Jawzî, *Akhbâr al-Zirâf,* pp. 215–31.

36. Al-Tîfâshî, *Nuzhat al-Albâb,* p. 237.

37. For some of these materials see, for example, Ibn al-Jawzî, *Ahkâm al-Nisâ',* p. 62.

CHAPTER SIX

JOUSTING WITHOUT A LANCE: THE CONDEMNATION OF FEMALE HOMOEROTICISM IN THE *LIVRE DES MANIÈRES*

Robert L. A. Clark

> *In assimilating* fin' amors *and female homoeroticism, Etienne de Fougères reveals them to be sites of male clerical anxiety in the attempt to control female sexuality through marriage.*

> The phallus is always present as prime mover in the lesbian discourse of male scriptors.
>
> —*Elaine Marks*★

The *Livre des manières* by Etienne de Fougères (d. 1178) is a remarkable work on any number of counts, not least of which is the oft-noted but seldom analyzed passage in which the author delivers a violent and scurrilous attack on sexual relations between women.[1] Etienne's is thus far the only known medieval text in French to refer explicitly to sex between women, and indeed, in this respect it seems to be unique among medieval vernacular texts.[2] This aspect alone would doubtless justify the text's interest for the study

of medieval gender, and the poet's rhetorical strategy, with its simul-
taneous representation and erasure of sexual relations between
women, is of particular import for the study of female homoeroticism, a topic that has remained largely unspoken and invisible in medieval textual culture. The intrinsic interest of the passage is,
moreover, greatly enhanced because it is embedded in an estates
poem, the earliest of its type in French, a poem that purports to represent Christian society in its different estates, or *manières* ("all manner of people"). The goal of this essay is to show how the highly
polemical condemnation of sex between women plays into the
larger ideological program of Etienne's text and, conversely, how the
text's ideological program, with its very specific preoccupations, must
necessarily inflect our understanding of what female homoeroticism
might have meant at this historical conjuncture, what it meant for
this author and his audience. In offering this reading, I shall not make
the a priori assumption, as other critics have done, that Etienne's is
an attack on "lesbians" or "lesbianism." In most cases, the use of these
terms has served only to obscure the cultural specificity of Etienne's
diatribe, and the identification of the proscribed behavior as "lesbian" has most often marked the end and not the beginning of critical evaluation of the passage.[3] In eschewing this terminology I do
not mean to suggest that the text does not have historical and political relevance for a modern readership—far from it. My reading of
Etienne's condemnation of female homoeroticism is motivated, first
of all, by a desire for a historical understanding of how it figures into
the larger polemical strategy of his poem and its representation of
Christian society in the second half of the twelfth century. That is
precisely because understanding the text on its own cultural terms is
the best way to make it politically relevant or useful for us as we read
today. In short, I am not assuming an identical cultural construction
or position shared by contemporary lesbianisms, in their many manifestations, and the practices evoked in Etienne's poem—except, perhaps, in the way that both may be circumscribed as the objects of a
discursive violence emanating from those who see themselves as the
defenders of a threatened patriarchal social order. My position is very
much in accord with Bernadette J. Brooten's in her recent book, *Love
Between Women: Early Christian Responses to Female Homoeroticism*. In

situating her work within the context of "Lesbian History," Brooten writes of the importance both of "open[ing] up the possibility of greater historical depth to current analyses of lesbian identity and of religious constructions of gender roles" and of "[giving] scholars of later periods of lesbian history a foundation for establishing discontinuities, turning points, and new—more appropriate—periodization."[4] In other words, positing historical continuities of gay or lesbian identity is not the only way to provide "historical depth" to current debates about gender; and indeed, a "Boswellian" approach tends to mask more than to illumine gender construction in the past.

Cultural Models and Model Societies

The *Livre des manières* has recourse to two models through which medieval clerical culture sought to define contemporary society: the triadic model of the three orders, and the estates model. The self-reflexive representation of social structures through cultural models is not, of course, simply a matter of "description." As the Soviet semiotician Iurii Lotman argues: "A [cultural] self-model represents a powerful means of 'self-adjustment' for a culture, since it bestows systematic unity, and determines from several aspects the qualities it will possess as an information-storage system."[5] As the term "self-adjustment" implies, a given cultural model will not produce an exact fit with the society to which it is applied. Nor are models static or unchanging, since the construction of culture is an ongoing and unending process. But the use of cultural models is, as Lotman suggests, a search for conceptual unity and an articulation of that unity into signifying structures. Through the cultural model, one seeks to make social reality intelligible, to interpret it and invest it with meaning, and ultimately to influence or control it.

In modern scholarship the triadic model of society has a rather more distinguished pedigree than the estates model. Georges Dumézil, through his studies of the Rig-Veda and of ancient Roman religion in particular, posits an ideological model of three functions— those of priests, warriors, and producers—as characteristic of Indo-European societies. In the field of medieval studies Georges Duby studies the history of the three orders (*oratores, bellatores, laboratores*) from the model's first elaboration in France shortly after the year 1000 to the early thirteenth century.[6] Duby places his study in the filiation of Dumézil's work but distinguishes between the latter's three functions and the three orders of feudal society. For Dumézil, the three functions are both a philosophical ideal and an analytical tool with which to interpret the forces that assure continuity in human culture, but they are not a class structure.[7] Duby, in a book that bears the significant subtitle *L'imaginaire du féodalisme,* traces the deployment of the triadic model in works that purport to represent social structure. His book, *The Three Orders,* bears the significant subtitle *Feudal Society Imagined.* Thus, the triadic model, like Dumézil's functions, is not in fact a social reality but an ideological construct, and the promotion of this ideal in society is an exercise of power wielded, first and foremost, through discourse.[8]

The division of society into estates is, by comparison, what might be termed the poor relation of the triadic model. Scholars have tended either not to distinguish between the two models, or, when they have made the distinction, to concentrate on the theory of the three orders with its theological and iconographic counterparts (the trinity, the triangle) while characterizing estates literature as being simply a rather arbitrary categorization of social groups.[9] The implicit assumption is that the triadic model lends itself more readily to theoretical and/or ideological interpretation. The opposition is that of theory versus lack of theory (or perhaps "strong" versus "weak" theory), highly defined structure versus loosely defined structure. All this is further complicated by the assumption that estates literature evolved from works expressing the three-orders concept. To quote Maria Corti: "There came a time when official culture realized that there had been a noticeable decline in the triadic model's information capacity."[10] The cause of this decline was, according to Corti, the rapid development of the towns with their new social and economic infrastructures, which she characterizes as horizontal, as opposed to the vertical orientation of the triadic model. In this view, after a phase of conflict and theoretical hybridism in the twelfth century, the new model came into its own in the thirteenth century, triumphing in such texts as the *De eruditione praedicatorum* by the Dominican Humbert of Romans, with its one hundred estates (*status*). I would like to take issue with Corti's theory on two points.

The two bishops in whose works the triadic model first appears in France, Gerard of Cambrai (d. 1051) and Adalbero of Laon (d. 1030), while perhaps drawing on somewhat earlier English uses of the triadic model, were above all writing to define clerical prerogatives and monarchical responsibility in the turbulent early years of the eleventh century.[11] They were reacting against the ravages and exactions of uncontrollable knights and against the growing importance of the Cluniac monks, who had begun exercising secular justice on their lands. The nightmare scenario for the bishops was that these two new power-hungry groups might join to form a new militant social force. Thus, as Claude Carozzi shows in his analysis of Adalbero's poem, *Carmen ad Robertum regem,* the author uses violent satire and burlesque epic to mock the ambitions of the knights and monks and to support his view that each group should remain subservient to the king as guarantor of civil peace.[12] Thus from the very beginning the triadic model was used in response to quite specific and urgent social concerns, in an attempt to impose order on a society being transformed by forces that were perceived as threatening any unifying control. It is therefore difficult to justify the assumption that the triadic model somehow fit feudal society better at an early stage, only to evolve into another model when social change had reduced its "information capacity."

A second problem with Corti's scheme is that well before the thirteenth century there were texts that provided a model for the genre known as estates literature, if not actual examples of the genre itself. These were the normative texts that guided the clergy in administering penance to the faithful, the penitentials. In the *Decretum* of Burchard of Worms (d. 1025), after books on the bishop, the priests, the deacons, the parish, and the sacraments, the author alternates books on specific sins (homicide, incest, fornication) and books devoted to particular social groups (monks, nuns, lay women).[13] The longest book in the work, which bears the title *Corrector et medicus,* constitutes the penitential proper, in which the appropriate penance is indicated for each sin, after which the work closes with a meditation on death. The *Corrector* shows a particular interest in the sins of women: according to Pierre Payer, "questions one to 152 are said to apply to men and women in general, and questions 153 to 194 especially to women."[14] Burchard's *Decretum,* according to Payer the most important penitential of the eleventh century, indicates the direction that much penitential and confessional literature would subsequently take: a double categorization, with particular sins ascribed to particular social groups.[15] It does not seem either useful or necessary, therefore, to interpret the apparent success of the estates model, as does Corti, to supposed dissatisfaction with the triadic model as an adequate representation of society. The two models were conceived in response to different social exigencies and constitute different and, in certain respects, complementary analytical tools. The triadic model, far from being replaced by the estates model, was to prove remarkably resilient, even as it showed in the twelfth century the strains and tensions of what Paul Edward Dutton has termed a "crisis in tripartite thinking." Dutton writes:

> By the twelfth century there was a profusion of overlapping and often confusing ways to divide society into social, anthropological, theological, and political twos and threes. When speaking of church and society some thinkers simply chose to repeat a number of classificatory schemes as though this would encompass them all. The abundance of ad status statements in the twelfth century represents in part only the persistence of past expressions, but it may also reflect a new awareness—this is particularly true of sermons—of audience, or rather audiences.[16]

Although he is writing about some of the more abstract, philosophical formulations of the tripartite scheme such as those to be found in glosses on the *Timaeus* and in the writings of the School of Chartres, Dutton's words apply equally well to the *Livre des manières.* Although its major organizing principle is the estates model, it also evokes the authority of the triadic model and uses both binary and ternary schemes of organization.[17] As Dutton suggests, the author's awareness of addressing several audiences is crucial for understanding the text, for Etienne as a bishop was keenly aware of his mission as preacher and minister to all "manner" of folk.[18] Indeed, his poem may be read as an extended sermon *ad status* that addresses the various estates through a model that is strikingly similar to Burchard's, down to the evocation of the Last Judgment at the poem's close.[19]

From Royal Scribe to Royal Scold

Etienne de Fougères was a cleric of obscure origins who rose to the position of royal scribe and chaplain in the chancery of Henry II Plantagenêt.[20] Acts in his hand show him with the court in England as early as 1157 and at Rouen in 1161, where Chancellor Thomas Becket, soon to become archbishop of Canterbury, figures among the witnesses.[21] Etienne was to be rewarded by the king for his services with important ecclesiastical offices, culminating with his appointment as bishop of Rennes in 1168. Even after becoming bishop, he appeared at court from time to time and took part in the deliberations of the king's council.[22] Etienne thus spent years at court where he could observe at first hand the workings of power and also the extraordinary literary and cultural flourishing promoted by Henry and Aliénor.[23] Like Peter Abelard, Etienne is said to have written songs in his youth, as well as prose works of a light-hearted nature, none of which has survived.[24] The *Livre des manières* makes what may be an oblique reference to those "youthful indiscretions" when, in his "confession" near the end of the poem, Etienne declares:

> Ma fole vie me espoente,
> quar grant poür me represente
> quant me sovient que ma jovente
> ai tote mise en fole entente. (1257–1260)[25]

> [My foolish life terrifies me, / for it shows me [cause for] great fear when I remember that my youth / I spent entirely in foolish pursuits.]

It is intriguing that Marbod (ca. 1035–1123), the well-known poet among whose works figure homoerotic verses, was one of Etienne's recent predecessors as bishop of Rennes, and while one can only speculate as to whether Etienne knew Marbod's homoerotic verse, Duby posits Marbod's *Liber decem capitulorum* as one of Etienne's sources in the *Livre des manières*.[26] Etienne was also familiar with Ovid's *Amores* and Juvenal's *Satires,* works that were standard fare in the teaching of Latin in the schools of his day and that served as a gold mine of misogynistic "wisdom" for generations of medieval clerics. It is moreover clear that his experience of court life informs the vision set forth in the *Livre des manières* and that he was well acquainted, as we shall see, with the commonplaces of courtly literature. But while recording these various influences, Etienne almost certainly conceived his poem at least in part as a response to the assassination in 1170 of his former associate in the royal chancery, Thomas Becket.[27] Etienne not only divides society into *manières* but is also anxious to define the bonds that should exist among these different social groups, bonds that he had seen strained beyond the breaking point with tragic results. Although dedicated to the Countess of Hereford (line 1205), the poem speaks quite bluntly in a number of passages to the moral failings of the royal court, even as it reminds bishops and archbishops that they must be prepared to suffer martyrdom in fulfilling their charge.[28]

Etienne divides society into six groupings: kings and other feudal lords; the clergy; knights; peasants; burghers; and finally (high-born) women. Etienne is careful not to designate all of these as *ordres,* for in his view only the clergy constitutes a true "order," a group that is *ordené,* 'ordained.' Etienne does apply the word *ordre* to the *chevalerie,* but the first time he does so, he pointedly uses past tense: "[H]aute ordre fut chevalerie, / mes or est ce trigalerie" [The knightly class was once a high order, / but now it is given to debauchery] (585–86).[29] We will see that the charge of moral turpitude, here limited to the male members of the knightly class, will be broadened in the poem's final section to include high-born women, among them those who prefer to have sex with each other. Of course, Etienne's representation of society is as interesting for what it excludes as for what it includes. For example, his discussion of the Church focuses on those who live in the world. Although the poem states that monks and nuns must be honored by the great lords, their status is not addressed in a separate section of the work. Other exclusions may be explained along similar lines. That is, Etienne is only interested in those groups that in his view may properly and profitably be integrated into Christian society. Hence, the poem makes no mention of Jews, paupers, lepers, and other "marginals." Nor do peasant women hold any interest for him.

It has long been noted that the poem's 336 quatrains fall into two equal parts. Exactly half the poem, or 168 stanzas, is devoted to the first three groups, the second half to the other three, plus the evocation of the Last Judgment and the litany that close the work. The major organizing principle, then, is binary, upper and lower. Further, each of the two major parts of the work presents a ternary arrangement, neither of which corresponds to the triadic model. The latter, however, is evoked precisely at the point of juncture between the two major divisions, in stanza 169:

> [L]i clerc deivent por toz orer,
> le chevalier sanz demorer
> deivent defendre et ennorer,
> et li païsant laborer. (673–76)

> [The clergy must pray for all, / the knights must be ready / to give protection and do honor, / and the peasants to plow]

The structure of Etienne's poem makes no attempt to adhere to this model, but it is invoked, perhaps somewhat nostalgically, as an ideal, a principle mediating between the high and the lowly, the powerful and the dependent—indeed, between order and disorder. And Etienne is quite specific about what he sees as the factors preventing the realization of the ideal Christian society. His program can be briefly summed up as the need to control three forces: the violence of the knights, to which, as already noted, he attributes the political disorders of his day; the growing economic power of the burghers; and finally sexuality, especially the sexuality of women. He is particularly anxious that lay sexuality be strictly controlled by the Church, primarily through the institution of marriage. Violence, money, and sex: these, then, are the forces that Etienne sees as threatening social order and the primacy of the Church.

Etienne follows the same general pattern for each of the groups and subgroups he treats. After making exceptions for those who live as they should—a poem consisting of these passages, it should be

noted, would be both short and dull—Etienne vigorously de-
nounces the vices of each group in violent and colorful language,
now satirizing and mocking, now cajoling or menacing. He is
hardly sparing in his review of the clergy, to whom he devotes by
far the longest section of the poem (eighty-seven stanzas, or roughly
one quarter). This section of the poem is divided into six subsections devoted to the lower clergy, deans and archdeacons, bishops,
archbishops, the pope, and the cardinals. Etienne shows himself to
be a proponent of Gregorian clerical reform by attacking the widespread clerical practice of maintaining concubines, as well as the
abuses of simony and nepotism.[30] These subsections show the same
binary structure that Etienne follows in each of the other major sections of the poem: moral obligations are first enumerated, then
moral failings pitilessly exposed. As we shall see, the only exception
is the final section on women, in which the pattern is reversed: the
foles come before the *bones fames.*[31] The responsibilities of each
group toward the Church are emphasized and the preeminence of
the clergy reinforced in each section, most of which conclude with
a brief exhortation in the form of a prayer and an evocation of the
Last Judgment. Etienne thus prepares for the fuller treatment of this
theme at the poem's end, where it is amply developed with a hor-
rific evocation of the contingent of snakes, toads, and tortoises that
will greet the unrepentant sinner. Before Christ's throne, of course,
all barriers and divisions will be erased, except for one: the separation of the saved from the damned. Etienne thus presents us with a
dance of death without the allegorical figure of Death to lead the
dance.[32] Death the leveler will ultimately undo the high/low dis-
position set forth in the poem. As Jacques Le Goff has pointed out,
the orientation of the estates model is ultimately horizontal.[33]

Etienne was not the first to use the triadic model in a text written in French, but the only earlier attested use occurs, interestingly
enough, in another text written for Henry II: Benoît de Sainte-
Maure had had recourse to the triadic model a few years before Etienne in the *Estoire des Ducs de Normandie,* the genealogical history
commissioned by Henry (genealogy being another orderly model
which can be imposed on a disorderly social reality). In his work,
Benoît had placed the prince securely at the head of the three or-

ders, albeit in close relationship with the clergy.[34] But the prince's position in Etienne's poem is more ambiguous. He and the other feudal lords are cut off from their natural allies in the knightly class, their vassals and retainers, by the interposition of the clergy. This arrangement is, of course, not innocent of ideological intent, and Etienne's strategy seems to be nothing short of an attempt to assimilate him into the clerical order. He decries the vanity and ambition of the great lords, which fuel their desire for conquest, and the idleness of their favorite pastimes, tourneying and hunting. These prevent them from carrying out their primary responsibility in lay society, to do justice. Etienne cites the Ecclesiaste to the effect that the king must be pure and chaste, for the people will rush to commit any sin committed by the prince. Dukes and kings must set an example for the knights and burghers, for the *vilains* and the *corteis:*

> Rele et esxanple est dux et reis
> aus chevaliers et aus borzeis,
> et aus vilains et aus corteis—
> lors feiz lor sunt preceiz et leis. (149–52)[35]

[Dukes and kings serve as rule and example / to the knights and the burghers / and to the villeins and those at court—/ their deeds are as precepts and laws to them.]

In this stanza the figure of chiasmus serves to separate the knights from the *corteis,* just as the larger ternary structure in the first half of the poem separates the knights from king and court. The king, Etienne continues, must love Holy Church and its servants, both clergy and monks, above all. If any members of the clergy should dishonor themselves by committing a crime, either great or small, the prince must still honor them, not for themselves but for their Lord. The sins of the king who acts accordingly will be pardoned, and he will be crowned by God. This last formulation is, of course, a standard way of expressing the idea of salvation, but it also serves as a reminder that true kings owe their crowns to God. The reference to the travails of Henry in these stanzas, in which Etienne asserts what he considers to be the proper relationship between king and clergy and which serve as a transition to the section of the poem on the latter, could hardly be more transparent. It is rather doubtful that Henry would have recognized himself in this bloodless king, separated by the clergy from the natural realm of carnality. For like any Christian moralist worth his salt, Etienne is a sworn enemy of carnality, the condemnation of which is a dominant theme of the poem. Even Etienne, though, makes certain concessions to the flesh. He allows that hunting in moderation is good recreation from the cares of court life—perhaps a concession to Henry's well-known passion for the hunt (*LM*, p. 110 n. 54). The tension between the condemnation and grudging recognition of carnality is most pronounced, however, in the passages of the poem that are devoted to sexuality. Let us now, at last, turn to Etienne's sexual politics.

The Most Dangerous Game

The polemical intent of the *Livre des manières* is perhaps most glaring in its representation of women. The exclusion of women was one of the essential, constitutional features of the triadic model. Yet even ecclesiastical writers who used the triadic model realized, at least in some cases, that this was one of its drawbacks. In the early twelfth century, Gilbert of Limerick (d. 1145), for example, expanded on the triadic model by using the image of pyramids inscribed within each other, each pyramid corresponding to a different social structure. Regarding women, Gilbert wrote:

> Those things comprised . . . within the jurisdiction of the Church are to be divided in a threefold way. Understand by those at the top of the pyramid the learned class, and since some of them are married, we have therefore mentioned both men and women. Truly on the left of the pyramid are the plowmen, both men and women. Also, on the right are the warriors, both male and female. Truly it is the position of women neither to speak, plow, nor (certainly) fight; nevertheless, women are married to, *and serve,* those who speak, plow, and fight.

> [Qui autem sub his gradibus intra sinum parochialis Ecclesiae continentur, trifaria dividuntur. Ex quibus superiores in pyramide *oratores* intellige; et quia quidam ex eis conjuagati sunt, ideo viros et feminas nominavimus. Sinistrales vero in pyramide *aratores* sunt, tam

viri quam feminae. Dextrales quoque *bellatores* sunt, viri atque feminae. Nec dico feminarum esse officium orare, arare, aut certe bellare; sed tamen his conjuatae sunt atque subserviunt, qui orant, et arant et pugnant.][36]

This attempt at including women in the triadic model bears the clear enunciation of their social subjugation. Similarly in Etienne, the identification of women as a group can hardly be considered a social promotion, for they are included only to be relegated to the bottom of the social structure.[37] Furthermore, the misogynistic representation of women by Etienne de Fougères is violent to a degree that is striking, even for a medieval text characterized by such exceptional polemical vigor.[38] We will see, however, that he knows how to temper his misogyny when it suits his purposes, as in the case of his pro-marriage stance.[39]

Etienne first turns his wrath against women in the section of the poem devoted to the burghers, where he deftly conflates the economic sin of usury with the sexual sin of adultery.[40] Thus, in speaking of the usurer:

Il cuide aveir chatel ou monte,
mes cil li deffet molt son conte;
encor li fet il meire honte:
sa fame ou sa file li monte.

Et tel I a qui pas n'en peisse
si l'en joüe o sa borzeise—
"Idonc est el" ce dit "corteise,
si el se rit et el s'enveise." (837–844)

[He thinks he'll get his capital back with interest, / but the borrower knows how to undo this reckoning; / he does the usurer even greater shame: / he mounts his wife or daughter. // And then there's the man who doesn't mind / if you take your pleasure with his *bourgeoise*—/ and then he says she's *courtoise* / since she laughs and gives herself to pleasure.]

The burgher thinks that by prostituting his wife he can get out of paying back his debt. But how, Etienne continues, should a man punish his adulterous wife?

Mes face la beivre a la jalle
et la relit bien a l'espalle,
et li atourt tres bien l'estalle,
ne mes qu'el fust fille au rei Charle.

Des qu'el bevra l'aive a la seille
et vestira la povre peille,
donc sera il motl grant merveille
si autrement ne se conseille. (861–68)

[Let him have her drink from the tub / and attach her well at the
shoulder; / and let him get the stable ready for her, / even if she were
the daughter of King Charles. // Once she drinks water from the
bucket / and puts on rags, / it will be a great marvel / if she doesn't
change her ways.]

In short, the woman who fornicates should be treated as a beast—
her husband can try beating her, and if that doesn't work, he can
hand her over to Holy Church (869–872). In this first presentation
of women, they are reduced to the role of prostitutes in a deadly
game that puts the players beyond the pale of Christian society, for,
Etienne says, they and their children will die as pagans and be
buried like dogs.[41] Etienne shows himself to be the foe of any kind
of illicit *jouissance,* whether it is that which is anticipated from "unnatural" economic activity or that which is, as we still say, "taken out
in trade."

These passages set the tone for the section of the poem devoted
to high-born women. Having already dispatched the *bourgeoises,*
who think themselves *courtoises* in their debauchery, and having literally nothing to say about peasant women, Etienne turns his attention to ladies of the court. As already noted, this is the only section
of the poem in which the negative depiction precedes the positive.
The opening stanzas are a diatribe, a sort of anti-text, against
fin'amors in which Etienne uses topoi from the literature of the
court to turn the courtly syndrome on its head. Countesses and
queens, he says, are worse than simple maids because they are the
cause of violent conflict, the *semence,* or seed, of war (977–84).[42]
The rich lady who is pretty will be nothing but trouble for her husband because she will take a social inferior for her lover. Then she

will burn for him but will be sullen and mute in her husband's presence (993–96). Etienne draws on the rich store of misogynistic motifs in classical Roman poetry in his portrait of a lady. His description of how she changes her face for her lover through the artifices of makeup echoes Juvenal's sixth *Satire,* as do several other passages in this section. Etienne refers to actual recipes for cosmetics: sheep's bile mixed with tallow of white dog for eye makeup, quicklime mixed with yellow arsenic for hair removal (1017–24). From these concoctions, it is but a short step to other "female arts" and charges of sorcery. Many a good man, he warns, has been laid in his grave through the application of plasters and the administering of herbal mixtures. The lady will also have recourse to charms uttered over clay and wax figures. Further, she will cause her daughters to abort after they become impregnated through low couplings. Or, as Ovid says in the *Amores,* she may practice abortion on herself, dying in the process and thus committing a double homicide. If her husband tries to prevent her from seeing her lover, she will use an *entremetteuse* to set up a meeting with him in church at a vigil, thus compounding the sin of adultery with that of fornication at a forbidden time and place.[43]

Further on, after his tirade against women who make love with women, Etienne returns to his anti-courtly, pro-marriage strategy in the section on virtuous women:

Si espouse son espous aime,
n'est vers Dé ne vers home en peine;
segurement son non reclaime
et de ses maus a lui se claime.

Fei que je dei sainte Marie!
Nule joie n'est tant garie
con de mari et de marie
—ja la lor joie n'iert tolie. (1165–1172)

[If a wife loves her husband, / she is not guilty before God or any man; / she can call his name out with confidence / and address all her troubles to him. // By the faith I owe Saint Mary! / No joy is so sure / as between husband and wife. / Never will their joy be taken from them.]

In the following quatrain, Etienne goes on to use the word *joie* ('sexual pleasure'), which he has appropriated from courtly literature, twice more, along with the word *aimer* for good measure:

Joie se funt tal con lor semble,
ne lor chaut qui ques treise ensenble.
Dahez ait joie que l'en enble
ou l'en toz jorz de poür trenble! (1173–76)[44]

[They give each other such joy as they see fit, / and they don't care who may find them together. / Cursed be the joy that must be hidden away, / in which one trembles with fear!]

The open celebration of sexual love within marriage is of course a courtly heresy, skillfully deployed against the unsavory secrecy of courtly romance.

This is the context—the general condemnation of carnality and the related deployment of misogyny—in which one must read the highly unusual section in which sex between women is condemned (see appendix). Critics have understandably been perplexed by this passage. Even in a poem of such extraordinary verve, not to say vehemence, it stands out—so much so that Charles-Victor Langlois felt that it had all the hallmarks of an interpolation: unnecessary, shocking, leering . . . hardly the sort of thing one would expect from a bishop![45] And yet, by another logic, the passage is exactly where it belongs. After the long downward spiral—from the secrecy of the courtly romance to the secret arts of women, including the illicit manipulation of sexually charged objects—we reach rock bottom, the place of the abject. From here, the only way to go is up, which is of course where the poem does go: the following stanzas lead us through the description of the "bones fames" and the portrait of the exemplary Countess of Hereford to the culminating Last Judgment and litany.[46] And as Etienne reminds us, the heritage that was lost through a woman was regained by one who took away the "evil of the apple" and now sits above the angels. Jeri Guthrie sees the passage condemning "lesbianism" as separate and central in a tripartite division of the section on women.[47] While the reference to "ces dames" certainly marks a transition, as Guthrie argues, it also forms continuity with what precedes it: Etienne is still dealing with the vices that he attributes to the ladies of the court.[48] But the position of this passage within the poem—the result of the already noted reversal of the pattern that Etienne has followed up to now—makes it a liminal moment, the turning point that marks the threshold between the lowest and the highest, the abject and the holy.

Let us look more closely at the rhetorical strategies that Etienne deploys in his condemnation of female homoeroticism. The opening stanza (273) makes it clear that he is still dealing with sexual sin, but now it is the "sin against nature."[49] This term had a very general—if confused—meaning in medieval texts, close to that of "fornication," and thus covered a variety of sexual offenses.[50] The meaning in Etienne is, however, unambiguous: after the illicit male-female couplings he has just evoked, he now turns to illicit same-sex relations. Among the various injunctions against the "sin against nature," specific references to sex between women were much rarer than references to sex between men, although Etienne may possibly have been familiar with condemnations which sought to broaden what was usually expressed or understood as referring to sexual relations between men to include female-female relations. Thus, in Peter Abelard's *Commentary on Saint Paul's Epistle to the Romans, Book V:* "Against nature, that is, against the order of nature, which created women's genitals for the use of men, and conversely, and not so women could cohabit with women" [Contra naturam, hoc est contra naturae institutionem, quae genitalia feminarum usui virorum praeparavit, et e converso, non ut feminae feminis cohabitarent].[51] But in stanza 274, which has the tone and formulaic structure of a biblical condemnation, the object of Etienne's wrath, expressed through the depiction of a ritualized public drubbing, is gendered male.[52] How do we explain, then, the slippage that occurs after stanza 274, for in the remainder of the passage Etienne concerns himself only with "ces dames"? Further on, there is more gender confusion—this time of the grammatical sort—in stanza 281, with the awkward shift from "un" to "chascune," although the defective meter of lines 1122 and 1123 suggests that this may be due to scribal error or confusion.[53] But we have already seen that Etienne's text contains many such slippages,

silences, and disjunctions, and the limiting of homoerotic relations
to women is one of the more remarkable of these instances, at once
spec(tac)ular (the sexual foibles of "these ladies" are offered as a tit-
illating spectacle for his readers)[54] and obfuscating. That is, by focusing on the ladies, Etienne diverts attention from the issue of
clerical sodomy.[55] The section of the poem devoted to the clergy
makes only one passing reference to sodomy, and it is made in such
a way that no sooner has it been raised than it is quickly laid to rest.
In condemning the keeping of concubines by the clergy, Etienne
laments the fact that archdeacons and deans are easily bribed by
their subordinates, who offer them meals or even a small sum of
money. And then the senior cleric goes away content: "Ceste clerc"
fet il "n'est pas erite / qui tient Horhan et Organite. / Bon est l'os-
tel ou fame habite" (249–50) [This clerk, says he, is no sodomite /
who keeps Horhan and Organite [that is, concubines]. / It's a fine
dwelling where there is a woman].[56]

The following five stanzas mark a radical shift in tone and technique, but generally speaking they continue the above-noted tension between showing and occultation. The tone is, however, ludic
rather than condemnatory, with an accumulation of references to
games and other types of actions, starting with the use of the
generic word *jeu,* a standard euphemism for sexual intercourse.
Subsequently the dominant figure is metaphor, indeed a whole series of metaphors used to represent female-to-female sexual relations. Or so it would seem at first glance. An analysis of this passage,
which fairly bristles with phallic symbols of no great subtlety, shows,
however, that Etienne has made a brilliant rhetorical move.
Metaphor is the figure of displacement par excellence, and Etienne
has (almost) succeeded through the use of phallic metaphors in
evoking but not representing these sexual practices by expressing
them primarily in terms of absence and lack. And what is lacking,
of course, is the phallus. Thus the games and other activities are all
represented as being ridiculous and, more to the point, fruitless or
sterile, as trying to make or get something from a nonsensical approach that can produce only nothing.[57] It should be noted that
Etienne does not generally make abundant use of metaphor. In
those passages that do show a high density of metaphors, he is striv-

ing to achieve a certain effect, as here, and also perhaps signaling a passage's importance. Thus, his treatment of the pope is marked by a series of five metaphors developed in an equal number of stanzas (477–496). Just as those metaphors mark the apex of what for Etienne is the highest order, the accumulation of metaphors around the problem of female homoeroticism marks the nadir of what is doubtless for him the lowest of his social groupings.

Etienne's mockery cannot entirely conceal, of course, his dismay and anxiety at seeing the male's "proper role" being filled by women.[58] To be sure, some of the actions he evokes, such as fishing or weighing, are gender-neutral—that is, they cannot readily be identified as tasks proper to either sex. Nor would they, for that matter, carry such an erotic charge if they were not deployed, as they are, *in serie* and juxtaposed with actions more suggestive of (heterosexual) intercourse, the pestle grinding away in the mortar, for example.[59] Other actions are, of course, gender- (and indeed class-) specific, especially jousting and fencing. Helen Solterer has studied the figure of the female combatant in the cluster of four thirteenth-century texts known as the *Tournoiement des dames,* noting the way they invert the eroticized chivalric tournament in a "world-upside-down," that is, comic or fantasy mode and yet also may figure at another level male anxiety over the reality of female militancy in the context of the crusades.[60] Closer in tone to Etienne's text is the fabliau "Berengier au lonc cul" ("Long-assed Bérenger"), which shows a similar anxiety over the male's place usurped by a wife who, cross-dressing as a knight, vanquishes her low-born husband in a joust, forces him to kiss her ass (which, in his confusion, he takes to be the "longest asshole" he has ever seen) and then confounds him with the spectacle of herself and her lover lying in bed.[61]

While such literary parallels are revealing, the comic or ludic register that Etienne adopts in this passage ultimately draws on images rooted in "popular" or "folkloric" tradition.[62] Such images often make more explicit the nexus of meanings that some of Etienne's metaphors may have called up for his medieval audience. Thus, the cockerel-as-phallus image, in addition to the well-documented associations of this animal with lechery, was also connected with the marginal and subversive figure of the fool, whose fantastic, crested cap might incorporate erect phalluses.[63] Etienne's use of the "poule qui fait le coq" motif might thus have suggested to his audience not only sexual inversion but other confused or problematic opposi- tional fields such as order/disorder, cleanliness/filth, human/animal, wisdom/folly. More to the point, medieval visual culture very often showed the interpenetration or juxtaposition of the profane, in- cluding the erotic and/or obscene, with sacred imagery. This was certainly less incongruous in Etienne's cultural milieu than Langlois was willing to imagine. Among the visual parallels that one can in- voke are the erotic carvings on misericords, the ledge-type seats in choirstalls that could be discreetly folded down, thus allowing the canons or monks to rest during liturgical services. Although the heyday of misericord carving postdates Etienne's poem by several centuries—the form was in full flower in the fifteenth and sixteenth centuries—the themes represented often have earlier textual and vi- sual analogues, especially images in the margins of manuscripts. Of the subject matter of misericords, Dorothy and Henry Kraus have written that it "ranges over the entire gamut of medieval life: work scenes, professional occupations, daily activities, domestic subjects, human relationships, love, sex and pornography, portraiture, humor, recreation, games, music, dancing, animals," and the illustration of proverbs and popular sayings.[64] Among the latter are several exam- ples of literal visualizations of the kind of ridiculous or impossible tasks that Etienne is fond of: "To fill a purse with air," "To shoe a goose," "He shits eggs without shells."[65] In discussing the miseri- cords of Beverly Minster, Malcolm Jones notes a number of exam- ples representing "stereotypes of human folly" that take the form of "World Turned Upside Down" imagery (including the reversal of relations between man and beast, between man and woman, be- tween the social classes) and *adynata* (impossible tasks).[66] Michael Camille theorizes a link between the "relative position of this art" and its "low subject-matter." He argues that "these carvings were lit- erally debased by those [that is, the clergy] 'above' them," resulting in the "censorship of the 'low' realism of these scenes by the portly canons' behinds during the divine service . . . the obliteration of one social group by another."[67] In my view this reading is tenden- tious and unnecessarily reductionist (although it is tempered somewhat in further remarks); however, I would agree with Camille that in misericord imagery, "in the very centre of the sacred space, the marginal world erupts" and that such images, as in Etienne's poem, may bear ideological messages not readily apparent behind their surface of playfulness.

As already noted, the imagery of misericords—which includes in some cases the scatological, the erotic, and even the sodomitic[68]—presents many similarities with the marginal imagery of medieval manuscripts and other artifacts, also a privileged space for representing bodily functions and erotic play.[69] With regard to the denigration of women that Camille reads in the margins (here, of the Bayeux "tapestry") he writes provocatively that

> we are forced to see overlaps and continuities in the cultural practices and spaces that we tend to separate, and to see how revealing are the edges of discourse, which always return to the rules of the center—where women, like peasants, servants and other subjected groups are, in the end, the ones who have to eat shit.[70]

Camille's survey makes it clear, though, that the representations of women in marginal images are extremely varied and, however problematic, they certainly cannot be explained by a single interpretive model—as indeed no single model will allow an adequate interpretation of marginal imagery in general and its relationship to the images and discourses of the "center."[71] There is, however, a certain insistence in the way that women "in the margins" are deployed in—or in relation to—suggestive or overtly erotic imagery, and it is in this regard that they present the greatest similarity with Etienne's "mauvaises femmes." Etienne's "ladies" do participate in the dynamic of the "edge" of which Camille speaks, but they occupy, as I have suggested above, not so much a marginal as a liminal space where different registers of representation are juxtaposed with the aim of subsuming dissonance within a master discourse.[72] I am suggesting that the marginal and the liminal are in fact two different if related cultural functions which at certain critical junctures—the passage under discussion is one of them—are held in extreme tension, marking the site of highly ambivalent cultural negotiations. Etienne's intention may indeed be an attempt to "marginalize" female homoeroticism, but what at first may appear marginal reveals itself to be "necessary" and even integral to the structure, movement, and meaning of his text. It is highly suggestive that the "mauvaise femme" returns to haunt another liminal moment in the text, the evocation of the Last Judgment in the poem's final stanzas. Here, at the poem's outer "edge," where all distinctions but one, as noted above, are swept away, Etienne twice evokes the woman with snakes hanging from her breasts, a familiar figure of the vice of *luxuria* (1302, 1306).[73] Then, in a final, breathtaking volte-face, the evocation of the hideous, leprous figure of lechery gives way to the beginning of the litany with its invocation of God and "Marie, dolce Mere." This and the other examples we have discussed demonstrate how the complicated play of overloaded metaphors in Etienne's attack on female homoeroticism taps into cultural homologies through which he and his society ordered and interpreted their world.

On another level, Etienne's phallic metaphors point, so to speak, very directly at another dangerous game, doubtless too repugnant for him to broach in a more open fashion: the use of dildos in female sexual relations. Etienne would certainly have been familiar with the condemnation in the penitentials of the use of a *machina* or *machinamentum*—it was an aggravating circumstance in cases of otherwise illicit sex—but it is of course impossible to determine from the prescriptive literature how widespread such illicit practices were.[74] It should be noted, though, that while the ever-present but always absent phallus is the dominant image in this passage, other images are more suggestive of female genitalia. The most arresting image among these, not especially phallic at all, is that of two coffins banging together, in which the illicitly used womb becomes a locus of death and damnation.[75]

I have noted that Etienne's text, for whatever reason, makes scant mention of sex between men. One possible explanation for this silence is that he may have seen sex between men as a less threatening form of behavior for the social order than sex between women. For in the former case, it is still a matter to be dealt with "between men." What is unacceptable to Etienne about sex between women is that it removes them from men's control without necessarily placing them under the control of the Church. Like *fin'amors,* female-to-female sex is an alternative that threatens the still precarious position of marriage, promoted by Etienne and the Church as the only sanctioned site of a necessarily procreative sexuality. But most threatening of all is the idea that these ladies apparently do not need men, that they can appropriate the phallus (or not) and find sexual satisfaction with each other.[76] It is especially ironic that despite Etienne's anxious efforts to ridicule these sexual practices, they still manage to emerge as satisfying to the parties involved, and in this one sees the ultimate failure of the strategies of containment he deploys.

What, if anything, we may ask, lies behind the evocation of "these ladies"? It has been said, of course, that there was no social reality that corresponded to the courtly syndrome; similarly, it is impossible to know to what extent the sexual offenses catalogued in the penitentials corresponded to actual behavior. One might conclude that Etienne's condemnation of female homoeroticism is nothing more than textual play, the crusty old bishop having a bit of fun. Such a conclusion, however, neglects the way that Etienne's text, with its skillful manipulation and confusion of the political, the economic, and the sexual, participates in the formation of a persecuting discourse directed against those who are perceived as standing outside the sanctioned forms of (re)production. As such, there is in this text an incipient homophobic discourse, the wellsprings of which are the all-too-familiar topoi of medieval misogyny through which women are first identified with the body and then judged according to the sole criterion of chastity. And while the categorization at work here is one of proscribed sexual practices, as opposed to that of individuals possessed of distinctive "sexualities," in Etienne's poem we can see what Judith Butler terms "the violence of the letter," a violence that is at once material and discursive in that it orders and produces bodies in accord with the category of sex.[77] We see the production of textual bodies that must necessarily precede the real, queer bodies that will be the victims of homophobia. We also see that the discourse of persecution, whether it be misogyny or homophobia or some marriage of the two, as in the *Livre des manières,* is, despite its monolithic aspect, contingent, cobbled together for immediate political ends. As in Etienne's text, it is characterized by dissymmetries, incoherence, and representations that are in fact dissimulations, all of which are so many structural weak points. And such a realization is, as Michel Foucault, Judith Butler, and others have helped us see, the necessary first step in the undoing of the discursive formations through which sexual violence is deployed in our own culture.

Appendix[78]

275 De bel pechié n'est pas merveille,	There's nothing surprising about the "beautiful sin"
des que Nature le conseille,	when nature prompts it,
mes qui de lei pechié s'esveille	but whosoever is awakened by the vile sin
encontre Nature teseille.	is going against nature. 1100
276 Celui deit l'en a chiens hüer,	One must pursue [him] with dogs,
pieres et bastons estrüer;	throw[ing] stones and sticks;
torchons li devreit [l'en] rüer	one should smite him with blows
et con autres gueignons tüer.	and kill him like any other cur. 1104
277 Ces dames ont trové i jeu:	These ladies have made up a game:
o dos trutennes funt un eu,	with two bits of nonsense they make nothing;
sarqueu hurtent contre sarqueu,	they bang coffin against coffin,
sanz focil escoent lor feu.	without a poker stir up their fire. 108
278 Ne joent pas a piquenpance,	They don't play at "poke in the paunch"
a pleins escuz joignent sanz lance.	but join shield to shield without a lance.
N'ont soign de lange en lor balance,	They have no concern for a beam in their scales,
ne en lor mole point de mance.	nor a handle in their mold. 1112
279 Hors d'aigue peschent au torbout	Out of water they fish for turbot
et n'i quierent point de ribot.	and they have no need for a rod.
N'ont sain de pilete en lor pot	They don't bother with a pestle in their mortar
ne en lor branle de pivot.	nor a fulcrum for their see-saw. 1116
280 Dus a dus jostent lor tripout	In twos they do their lowlife jousting
et se meinent plus que le trot;	and they ride to it with all their might;
a l'escremie del jambot	at the game of thigh-fencing
s'entrepaient vilment l'escot.	they pay most basely each other's share 1120

281 Il ne sunt pas totes d'un molle;   They're not all from the same mold:
l'un[e] s'esteit et l'autre crosle,   one lies still and the other grinds away,
l'un[e] fet coc et l'autre polle   one plays the cock and the other the hen,
et chascune meine son rossle.   and each one plays her role.   1124

Notes

* "Lesbian Intertextuality," in *Homosexualities and French Literature: Cultural Contexts/Critical Texts,* ed. George Stambolian and Elaine Marks (Ithaca: Cornell University Press, 1979), p. 361.

1. An earlier version of this essay was presented with a slightly different title at the 28th International Congress on Medieval Studies, held at Western Michigan University in May 1993. I would like to thank the organizer of that session, Ann Matter, and its sponsor, the Society for the Study of Homosexuality in the Middle Ages, for encouraging this work. I would also like to thank the colleagues, students, and friends at the University of Michigan, Ann Arbor, who heard a later version and offered comments and suggestions, especially Catherine Brown and Domna Stanton. I would also like to thank Samuel Rosenberg for his generous help and advice with linguistic matters.

   Etienne's poem, which consists of 1,344 octosyllabic lines divided into 336 monorhyme quatrains, survives in a single manuscript dating from the early thirteenth century, Angers, Bibl. mun., 304 (295). Etienne's is the last text in the manuscript and the only one in the vernacular. All textual citations are by line number with reference to the following edition: Etienne de Fougères, *Le livre des manières,* ed. R. Anthony Lodge, Textes Littéraires Français (Geneva: Droz, 1979), hereafter referred to as *LM.* Lodge's edition, generally well received by the philological community, supersedes the earlier editions by Talbert (1877) and Kremer (1886).

2. Michel J. Raby cites two other cases of supposed "homosexualité féminine": a poem by the *trobairitz* Bieiris de Romans addressed to another woman and the relation of the Amazon myth in Mandeville's *Travels.* The imputation of homosexuality is problematic in both instances and, in any event, in neither is the question of sexual relations broached, as it is in Etienne's poem ("Le péché 'contre nature' dans la littérature médiévale: deux cas," *Romance Quarterly* 44 [1997]: 219–20). See also Michèle Perret, "Travesties et transsexuelles: Yde, Silence, Grisandole, Blanchandine," *Romance Notes* 25 (1985): 328–40, in which cross-dressing results in what Perret terms "homosexualité au second degré" (328).

3. This unreflexive use of the term "lesbianism," which figured in the title of this essay's earlier version, is what has prompted me to replace it with "female homoeroticism." In so doing, I do not wish to suggest, however, that the latter term is unproblematic, nor indeed that the use of "lesbian" cannot be justified in the study of medieval culture, as Jacqueline Murray has done in her "Twice Marginal and Twice Invisible: Lesbians in the Middle Ages," in *Handbook of Medieval Sexuality,* ed. Vern L. Bullough and James A. Brundage (New York: Garland, 1996), pp. 191–222. Sahar Amer's crosscultural study of Etienne's poem in this volume takes Murray's approach. As one might expect, it is the earlier, more conventional scholarship on the *Livre des manières* that makes uncritical use of the term "lesbian," although this is also the case in Jeri S. Guthrie's groundbreaking article ("La femme dans *Le livre des manières:* Surplus économique, surplus érotique," *Romanic Review* 79 [1987]: 251–61, esp. 260–61).

4. Bernadette J. Brooten, *Love Between Women: Early Christian Responses to Female Homoeroticism* (Chicago and London: University of Chicago Press: 1996), p. 18.

5. As quoted in Maria Corti, "Models and Antimodels in Medieval Culture," *New Literary History* 10 (1979): 339.

6. Georges Dumézil, *L'idéologie tripartite des Indo-Européens,* Collection Latomus 31 (Brussels: Latomus, 1958); Georges Duby, *The Three Orders: Feudal Society Imagined,* trans. Arthur Goldhammer (Chicago: University of Chicago Press, 1980; originally published as *Les trois ordres ou l'imaginaire du féodalisme,* 1978), in which Duby devotes a brief discussion to Etienne (pp. 282–85).

7. Duby, *Three Orders,* p. 6.

8. Jean Batany accepts Dumézil's model as a working hypothesis but notes that no society, let alone feudal society, has so simple a structure as to present clearly a triadic structure ("Des 'trois fonctions' aux 'trois états'?" *Annales: Economies, Sociétés, Civilisations* 18 [1963]: 935).

9. Joseph Dane, "The Three Estates and Other Medieval Trinities," *Florilegium* 3 (1981): 283–309.

10. Corti, "Models and Antimodels," 345.

11. Duby, *Three Orders,* pp. 16–18.

12. Claude Carozzi, "Les fondements de la tripartition sociale chez Adalbéron de Laon," *Annales: Economies, Sociétés, Civilisations* 33 (1972): 683–702.

13. Georges Duby, *The Knight, the Lady, and the Priest: The Making of Modern Marriage in Medieval France,* trans. Barbara Bray (New York: Pantheon, 1983; originally published as *Le chevalier, la femme et le prêtre,* 1981), p. 63. For a concise description of the *Decretum* and its

importance, see Pierre Payer, *Sex and the Penitentials: The Development of a Sexual Code 550–1150* (Toronto: University of Toronto Press, 1984), pp. 81–83; for the date of the text's compilation, between 1008 and 1012, p. 186 n. 29.

14. Payer, *Sex and the Penitentials,* p. 82.

15. The burgeoning of homiletic and confessional literature accompanied by the atomization of the estates model is especially pronounced after the promulgation of the canons of the Fourth Lateran Council of 1215, among which was the requirement of annual confession of all Christians who had attained the age of reason. John of Freiburg's *Confessionale,* at the end of the thirteenth century, divides sins according to a breakdown of society into fourteen estates: 1. bishops and prelates; 2. clerks and beneficiaries; 3. parish priests; vicars and confessors; 4. monks; 5. judges; 6. lawyers and attorneys; 7. doctors; 8. holders of the doctorate or the master's degree; 9. princes and other nobles; 10. husbands; 11. merchants and burghers; 12. artisans and workers; 13. peasants; and 14. *laboratores* (Jacques Le Goff, *La civilisation de l'Occident médiéval* [Paris: Flammarion, 1982], p. 243). A German sermon collection from around 1220 numbers twenty-eight estates (Le Goff, p. 241); and as already mentioned, the preaching manual of the Dominican Humbert of Romans (d. 1277), one hundred.

16. Paul Edward Dutton, "*Illustre civitatis et populi exemplum:* Plato's *Timaeus* and the Transmission from Calcidius to the End of the Twelfth Century of a Tripartite Scheme of Society," *Mediaeval Studies* 35 (1983): 88–89.

17. Etienne may have been influenced by the political thinking of John of Salisbury's *Policraticus.* See, in this connection, Etienne's formulation of the theory of the two swords (635–672; n. 635). It is not without interest that immediately after the exposition of the theory of the two swords comes the quatrain in which Etienne articulates the principle of the three orders. Etienne does not, however, use the body as a metaphor for social structure, as do the texts analyzed by Dutton.

18. "Wherever he may go, [the bishop] must preach, / even as he holds his people dear; / he must censure all their vices, / praise the good and denounce the bad" (329–32). All translations from the text are my own.

19. James Brundage points out that Burchard's penitential was much too large and expensive for many churches or even cathedrals to own (James A. Brundage, *Law, Sex, and Christian Society in Medieval Europe* [Chicago and London: University of Chicago Press, 1987],

p. 181), but Duby assumes that Etienne had direct knowledge of the *Decretum* (Georges Duby, *Dames du XIIe siècle, III: Eve et les prêtres* [Paris: Gallimard, 1996], p. 20). Duby describes Etienne's poem as a sermon "sous forme plaisante" (Duby, *Dames,* p. 12). In this regard, it is not without interest that the manuscript in which Etienne's text survives opens with a sermon collection by Hildebert of Lavardin. Keith V. Sinclair has suggested that Etienne's poem, especially in its structure, shows the influence of the bidding prayers that the celebrant of the mass addressed to the faithful in the vernacular ("L'inspiration liturgique du *Livre des manières* d'Etienne de Fougères," *Cahiers de civilisation médiévale* 40 [1997]): 261–66).

20. On Etienne's life see Charles-Victor Langlois, *La vie en France au Moyen Age de la fin du XIIe au milieu du XIVe siècle d'après des moralistes du temps* (1926; reprint, Paris, Geneva: Slatkine, 1984), pp. 1–2; and Lodge, *LM,* pp. 13–22. In the poem's penultimate quatrain (line 1338), Etienne de Fougères is named in language that suggests that he may not himself be the author of the poem. Langlois thus refers to "Etienne ou son adaptateur," but the attribution to Etienne, well defended by Lodge, is commonly accepted.

21. R. W. Eyton, *The Court, Household and Itinerary of Henry II* (Holborn and London, 1878), p. 30, 53. In all, fourteen royal charters have been identified as being in Etienne's hand (T. A. M. Bishop, "A Chancery Scribe: Stephen of Fougères," *Cambridge Historical Journal* 10 [1950–52]: 106–107).

22. B.-A. Pocquet du Haut-Jussé, "Etienne de Fougères," in *Dictionnaire d'histoire et de géographie ecclésiastiques* 15 (Paris: Letouzey et Ane, 1963), col. 1224. Even after becoming bishop, Etienne continued to sign as "Stephanus, Dei gratia Redonensis ecclesie presbiter et regis Anglie capelanus" (Langlois, *La vie en France,* p. 2).

23. Among the works that can be associated with Henry and Aliénor with a greater or lesser degree of certainty and with which Etienne could have had some acquaintance one may include Wace, *Roman de Brut* and *Roman de Rou;* Benoît de Sainte-Maure, *Roman de Troie* and *Estoire des ducs de Normandie;* the *Lais* of Marie de France; and Thomas d'Angleterre, *Roman de Tristan.* To this list may be added the other romances of Antiquity (Etienne refers to the Alexander legend, 112 ff.) and the romances of Chrétien de Troyes, which were certainly well known at the Angevin court.

24. "Ipse enim multa ritmico carmine et prosa jocunde et ad plausus hominum scripserat" (*Chronique de Robert de Torigni,* cited by Lodge, *LM,* p. 15).

25. Claude J. Fourcade suggests that Etienne's regrets refer to "involvement with women in his youth," although his text is in fact silent on this point ("Etienne de Fougères," in *Medieval France: An Encyclopedia* [New York and London: Garland, 1995], p. 326). The conventionality of such regrets in the moral literature of the time is noted by Lodge (*LM,* p. 134 n. 1256).

26. On Marbod's homoerotic verse see John Boswell, *Christianity, Social Tolerance, and Homosexuality: Gay People in Western Europe from the Beginning of the Christian Era to the Fourteenth Century* (Chicago: University of Chicago Press, 1980), pp. 247–49, 370–71. On the influence of Marbod's poem on Etienne's, see Duby, *Dames,* p. 19.

27. Since Etienne invokes Saint Thomas among the martyrs in the litany that closes the poem (1322), the work's composition can be dated with a fair degree of certainty to between 1173, the date of Thomas's canonization, and 1178, the date of Etienne's death.

28. "The bishop must keep a close watch, / he who has the duty of preserving souls; / even on account of death, he must not shrink / from what is right, even if someone would like to pierce him through. / Let him be prepared for martyrdom, / if there is anyone who should want to kill him for God's sake" (285–90); "For this reason he must both think and say / that he is prepared for martyrdom, / without any quarrel or objection, / if there is anyone who should want to kill him for God's sake" (457–60).

29. As with the king, Etienne seeks to subsume the knight into an order controlled by the Church. He allows that a knight can be saved "in his order" (621) if he fulfills all of his obligations to the Church (especially the tithe). Otherwise, one should expel him (*desordenner,* 625) and strip him of his sword and spurs; after all, the knight was "ordained" (*prist l'ordre*) in Church (621–29). As with *ordre,* Etienne plays with the related word *ordené,* applied four times to members of the clergy (317, 321, 607, 645) but also used for knights (590). Cf. Anthony Lodge, "The Literary Interest of the 'Livre des Manières' of Etienne de Fougères," *Romania* 93 (1972): 490.

30. The treatment of nepotism is curious in that after condemning its practice by archdeacons and deans (273–76), he defends it in the case of bishops, who need to surround themselves with people they can trust (361–72).

31. Duby attributes Etienne's strategy of adding praise to the customary blame of women to the influence of Marbod's *Liber decem capitulorum,* in which the "meretrix" (that is, prostitute) precedes the "matrona" (Duby, *Dames,* p. 49). Marbod's poem is available in three

editions: PL 171: 1693 ff.; Marbodi, *Liber decem capitulorum,* ed.
Walther Brust (Heidelberg: Carl Winter, 1947); and Marbodi, *Liber
decem capitulorum,* ed. Rosario Leotta (Rome: Herder, 1984).

32. The allegorical figure of Death does appear in one passage in
which Etienne states: "La Mort a son guichet overt / a qui saignore
et a qui sert" [Death has his gate open / to lord and serf alike]
(119–20).

33. Le Goff, *La civilisation,* p. 241.

34. Duby, *Three Orders,* p. 276.

35. It is tempting to see in "dux et reis" a reference to Henry II himself, who of course held both titles.

36. As quoted in Corti, "Models and Antimodels," 344 (emphasis
added) from Gilbertus Lunicensis, *Liber de statu ecclesiae,* PL 159:997
(emphasis as in Migne).

37. See Roberta L. Krueger, *Women Readers and the Ideology of Gender
in Old French Verse Romance* (Cambridge: Cambridge University
Press, 1993), p. 107: "The placement of noblewomen of all qualities
after men of all classes evidences the fundamental gender division
and hierarchical order of medieval society."

38. Duby notes that in one of the two Latin saint's lives by Etienne,
Saint Firmat burns himself with an ember to overcome the temptation of a girl sent to seduce him (Duby, *Dames,* pp. 11–12; *Vie de
saint Firmat, Acta Sanctorum,* Aprilis III, 336 ff.).

39. R. Howard Bloch makes no mention of Etienne in his work on
medieval misogyny, perhaps because as a champion of marriage,
Etienne does not fit Bloch's representation of misogyny as essentially anti-connubial. See Bloch's *Medieval Misogyny and the Invention of Western Romantic Love* (Chicago: University of Chicago Press,
1991) and his earlier article, "Medieval Misogyny," *Representations*
20 (Fall 1987): 1–24, in which he identifies "the defining rhetorical context of all misogynistic literature, which seeks to dissuade
from marriage." (18).

40. Etienne has already condemned members of the clergy for keeping
concubines ("fole fame," 237–40) and practicing usury (221–24),
and archbishops for borrowing money at interest (413–15).

41. Usurers had to repair their illicit gains in order to receive absolu-
tion; if they did not do so, it fell to their heirs to make restitution.

42. The same charge is made in Marbod, *Liber* III, lines 5–14.

43. For an illuminating discussion of the transformations in the
Church's thinking on sex in consecrated buildings, including important changes in the twelfth century related to a large degree to
the increased importance accorded to the conjugal debt in the

church's teaching on marriage, see Dyan Elliott, "Sex in Holy Places: An Exploration of a Medieval Anxiety," *Journal of Women's History* 6 (1994): 6–34.

44. As Duby notes, Etienne also uses the word *jovent(e)* 'youth' (598, 1059, 1259), which has a similar resonance with the love poetry of the troubadours (Duby, *Dames,* p. 48).

45. Langlois, *La Vie en france,* p. 23 n. 1.

46. Lodge identifies this Countess as "Cécile, veuve du comte Roger de Hereford." According to Lodge, she retained the title Countess of Hereford even after her second and third marriages (*LM,* pp. 17–18; p. 133 n. 1255).

47. Guthrie, "La femme," 254–55.

48. Only the reference to "meinte autre fame petite / qui entre nos encore habite" [many a little woman / who lives yet amongst us] (1131–32) may be taken as possibly referring to women other than high-born.

49. On its use in Augustine, see Mark D. Jordan, *The Invention of Sodomy in Christian Theology* (Chicago: University of Chicago Press, 1997), p. 34. Use of the term seems to have become more widespread in penitential, canonical, and theological texts after the twelfth century.

50. See the appendix on the "Language of the Penitentials" in Payer, *Sex and the Penitentials,* pp. 140–53.

51. As quoted in Louis Crompton, "The Myth of Lesbian Impunity: Capital Laws from 1270 to 1791," *Journal of Homosexuality* 6.1/2 (Winter 1980–81): 14, from Peter Abelard, *Commentarium super S. Pauli epistolam ad Romanos libri quinque,* PL 178: 806.

52. I have rendered OF *torchons* as 'blows', as in the expression *torchon d'espee* 'sword blow' used in the fourteenth-century prose romance *Perceforest* (cited in Frédéric Godefroy, *Dictionnaire de l'ancienne langue française* [1892; repr. Vaduz: Scientific Periodicals; New York: Kraus, 1961] 7: 750), but it may refer to straw or rags twisted into a wad, an object suitable for drubbing an opponent. The word has the latter meaning in the twelfth-century epic poem *Aliscans* with the same verb, *rüer* 'hurl', used by Etienne (Godefroy, 10:778).

53. Lodge emends both lines by making the article feminine.

54. "On croit entendre s'esclaffer [les chevaliers] dans l'auditoire" (Duby, *Dames,* p. 16).

55. See the discussion in Jordan, *Invention of Sodomy* (pp. 29–30, 45–66) of Peter Damian's invention of the term "sodomy" in the *Book of Gomorrah.*

56. The term *erite* is the same word that the evil queen Eufeme uses against the cross-dressed heroine Silence in the romance of that

name when the latter refuses her amorous advances (lines 3935 and 3947). Sarah Roche-Mahdi renders the first occurrence of the word with "queer," the second with "fag"; Regina Psaki uses "homosexual" for both (*Silence, a Thirteenth-Century Romance,* ed. and trans. Sarah Roche-Mahdi [East Lansing: Colleagues Press, 1992]; Heldris de Cornuälle, *Le Roman de Silence,* trans. Regina Psaki [New York and London: Garland, 1991]).

57. This is the meaning, I believe, of the most difficult line (1106), which contains two words not elsewhere attested in Old French, at least not with Etienne's spellings. (Generally speaking, the text's dialect is that of western France and, more specifically, of the southwestern region of *langue d'oïl,* that is, of the Angevin lands from which Etienne hailed.) Samuel Rosenberg has suggested in private correspondence that the first of these words, *trutennes,* shows a variant spelling of O. F. *trudaines,* whose various meanings include 'twaddle, nonsense, incoherent fantasy' or 'trouble, agitation'. Also of interest is the meaning of the related O. F. *trudain* 'impostor'. It is intriguing that in medieval Latin the term *machinamentum* had the same nexus of meanings: 'dildo', and also 'trick, ruse, treachery' (J. F. Niermeyer, *Mediae Latinitatis lexicon minus* [Leiden: Brill, 1997]). The second *hapax, eu,* probably means 'egg', as Lodge suggests in the glossary of his edition. The use here would be the same as in various expressions where "egg" is used to designate something negligible or insignificant, "zilch." For a different interpretation of this difficult line, see the essay in this volume by Sahar Amer.

58. Guthrie ("La femme") likens Etienne's diatribe to a "hysteria" induced by his (frustrated) desire to be himself the "Ideal Woman," that is, possessed of a feminine body, at once pure and sterile (259–61). I can agree with Guthrie's ingenious but rather far-fetched interpretation to the extent that Etienne celebrates "sterility," or at least childlessness, in the person of the Countess of Hereford, all of whose children have died, and that perhaps for this reason sex between women, necessarily non-procreative but clearly unacceptable to him, provokes such a violent reaction. Guthrie cites Etienne's statement to the effect that he is a "tree that gives no fruit" [Ge suis l'arbre qui fruit ne done] (1270) in support of her hypothesis, but this is a forced reading in that he is deploring the *moral* sterility of the life for which he will have to give a reckoning at the Last Judgment. See also Krueger, *Women Readers:* "insofar as she [i.e., the recipient of Etienne's text] occupies the position of the 'other' whose sexuality might tempt or contaminate that of the

speaker, she is a source of the speaker's anxiety about masculinity, about his relationship to that necessary 'otherness'" (160).

59. For the use of the mortar as a metaphor for the vagina in Deschamps and Villon, see Francesca Sautman, "'Des vessies pour des lanternes': Villon, Molinet and the Riddles of Folklore," *Neophilologus* 69 (1985): 174; and in misericord carvings, Malcolm Jones, "Folklore Motifs in Late Medieval Art II: Sexist Satire and Popular Punishments," *Folklore* 101.1 (1990): 72.

60. Helen Solterer, "Figures of Female Militancy in Medieval France," *Signs: Journal of Women in Culture and Society* 16 (1991): 522–49.

61. *Nouveau recueil complet des fabliaux* 4, ed. Willem Noomen and Nico van den Boogaard (Assen: Van Gorcum, 1984), pp. 270–77. See the discussion of gender-role and sexual anxiety in this and other fabliaux in E. Jane Burns, "This Prick Which Is Not One: How Women Talk Back in Old French Fabliaux," in *Feminist Approaches to the Body in Medieval Literature,* ed. Linda Lomperis and Sarah Stanbury (Philadelphia: University of Pennsylvania Press, 1993), pp. 188–212. For a brief but suggestive queer reading of "anomalies of gender" in the fabliaux and other Old French texts, see Peter L. Allen, "Male/Female/Both/Neither: Gender as Floating Signifier in the Literature of Medieval France," *Medieval Feminist Newsletter* 14 (Fall 1992): 12–16.

62. Both terms are problematic in that they impose distinctions (popular versus elite culture, in particular) that are emphatically not those of medieval culture itself. So-called popular culture was in fact more properly a general culture, common to all levels of medieval society.

63. Claude Gaignebet and Jean-Dominique Lajoux, *Art profane et religion populaire au Moyen Age* (Paris: Presses Universitaires de France, 1985), p. 190. For examples of the cockerel's associations with lechery, see Malcolm Jones, "Folklore Motifs in Late Medieval Art Art III: Erotic Animal Imagery," *Folklore* 101.2 (1991): 192–93.

64. Dorothy and Henry Kraus, *The Hidden Word of Misericords* (New York: Braziller, 1975), x. A revised and expanded version of this work appeared as *Le monde caché des miséricordes,* trans. Solange Schnall (Paris: Editions de l'Amateur, 1986). See also, by the same authors, *The Gothic Choirstalls of Spain* (London and New York: Routledge and Kegan Paul, 1986); and Gaignebet and Lajoux, *Art profane,* pp. 192–201.

65. Kraus and Kraus, *Hidden World,* pp. 53–58.

66. Malcolm Jones, "Folklore Motifs in Late Medieval Art I: Proverbial Follies and Impossibilities," *Folklore* 100.2 (1989): 201. For a discussion

of *impossibilia* in François Villon's *Testament,* see Sautman, "'Des vessies pour des lanternes,'" 173.

67. Michael Camille, *Image on the Edge: The Margins of Medieval Art* (Cambridge: Harvard University Press, 1992), pp. 94–95.

68. See, for example, the misericords carved for the priory church of Brou, several which are characterized by what Kraus and Kraus refer to as "anal play" between naked young men and animals or "friendly" monsters (Kraus and Kraus, *Misericords,* pp. 119–122).

69. See Lilian M. C. Randall, *Images in the Margins of Gothic Manuscripts* (Berkeley and Los Angeles: University of California Press, 1966), *passim,* especially the "obscenae" (plates CXI–CXII), including images of anal play involving men and beasts; and Camille, *Image on the Edge,* esp. pp. 99–115.

70. Camille, *Image on the Edge,* p. 127.

71. On the interpretation of marginal imagery, in addition to Camille (especially chap. 1, "Making Margins"), see Jeffrey F. Hamburger's highly critical review of *Image on the Edge* in *Art Bulletin* 75.2 (1993): 319–27; and Lucy Freeman Sandler, "The Study of Marginal Imagery: Past, Present, Future," *Studies in Iconography* 18 (1997): 1–49, especially her conclusions: "Is a single interpretation of marginal imagery possible? As my review demonstrates, the answer is manifestly not, much as partisans of one or another view have insisted" (43).

72. Camille evokes liminality—the state of being "betwixt and between," in Victor Turner's well-known formulation—in the first paragraph of *Image on the Edge* and several times thereafter (most notably just before the passage cited above) but unfortunately he never clearly distinguishes between the marginal and the liminal. For a succinct but thorough presentation of Turner's theory of ritual, see Victor and Edith Turner, "Religious Celebrations," in *Celebration: Studies in Festivity and Ritual,* ed. Victor Turner (Washington: Smithsonian Institution Press, 1982), pp. 200–219. For evaluation and criticism of Turner's theories and influence, see Clifford Geertz, "Blurred Genres: The Refiguration of Social Thought," *American Scholar* 49.2 (1980): 172–73; Caroline Walker Bynum, "Women's Stories, Women's Symbols: A Critique of Victor Turner's Theory of Liminality," *Fragmentation and Redemption: Essays on Gender and the Human Body in Medieval Religion* (New York: Zone, 1991), pp. 27–51; and *Victor Turner and the Construction of Cultural Criticism: Between Literature and Anthropology,* ed. Kathleen M. Ashley (Bloomington: Indiana University Press, 1990).

73. This figure was often part of the program of vices and virtues on church portals, as may be seen on the south portal of Saint-Pierre de Moissac. For an provocative discussion of how the figure of Luxuria may have been perceived by male pilgrims as a site/sign of gender instability, see Daniel Smartt, "Cruising Twelfth-Century Pilgrims," *Journal of Homosexuality* 12 (1994): 35–55.

74. For citations of condemnations of the use of dildos from the penitentials, see Murray, "Twice Marginal," pp. 198–99, and Duby, *Dames,* pp. 28–29. See also Benkov's essay in this volume.

75. See Duby's discussion of the "sins of women" in Burchard and Regino of Prüm: "la femme inquiète en premier lieu les hommes parce qu'elles sont porteuses de mort" (Duby, *Dames,* p. 33).

76. In this regard, it is interesting that Etienne does not use what Christiane Marchello-Nizia and Michèle Perret term the "grande accusation de l'*Enéas,*" that is, that the world would come to an end if homosexuality were to become rampant ("Une utopie homosexualle au quatorzième siècle: l'île sans femmes d'Agriano," *Stanford French Review* 14 [1990]: 240–41). This would suggest that it is not just the "sterility" of homosexual couplings that so disturbs Etienne but the illicit pleasure that they give.

77. Judith Butler, "Contingent Foundations: Feminism and the Question of 'Postmodernism'," *Feminists Theorize the Political,* ed. Judith Butler and Joan W. Scott (New York: Routledge, 1992), p. 17.

78. An earlier attempt at rendering this difficult passage appeared as an appendix in Murray, "Twice Marginal" (see n. 5 above), p. 210. I would like to thank Professor Murray for her support of my work on Etienne.

CHAPTER SEVEN

LESBIAN SEX AND THE MILITARY: FROM THE MEDIEVAL ARABIC TRADITION TO FRENCH LITERATURE

Sahar Amer

> *The inclusion of Arabic terms and images of lesbian sexuality in Etienne de Fougères's account of lesbian sexual practices demonstrates the import of Arabic homoeroticism in the literary construction of lesbian desire and sexuality in medieval France.*

Critics today readily acknowledge the essential role played by medieval Arabic civilization and culture in the transmission to the West of Greek philosophical, scientific, mathematical, astronomical, and medical knowledge. They are, however, much more reluctant to accept the idea that Arabic culture and literature may have also been essential to the formation of Western vernacular literatures, even though it was impossible in the Middle Ages to separate the scientific from the literary. Despite much research in the last two hundred years on the "Oriental period of Western history"[1] that seeks to uncover the Western indebtedness to Semitic civilization in such literary fields as the courtly love tradition, the fables, the fabliaux, or the nouvelles, its findings continue to be largely ignored or occulted, as Maria R. Menocal has amply demonstrated in *The Arabic Role in Medieval Literary History.*[2] Among others, Thomas Glick, Alice Lasater, Dorothee Metlitzki, and Menocal herself, basing their

studies on the theoretical and political work of Edward Said, have
pointed to the orientalist biases that continue to plague most literary critical studies and university curricula and that consequently
prevent the Arabic (and Semitic) theory of origins from taking a
firm hold within the discipline.[3]

To this "myth of Westernness" corresponds another myth, that of
heterosexuality. Susan Schibanoff has noted the same resistance to
the oriental theory of origins in much of the scholarship on medieval Western love and desire.[4] She has accurately observed that
even though critics tend to recognize the indebtedness of Provençal
poets to the Andalusian love tradition in purely formal areas such as
rhyme schemes or meters, they continue to question the troubadours' indebtedness to the Arabic tradition in the actual expression
of desire, mainly because the Arabic love tradition is highly homoerotic. Faced with the explicit verbalization in Arabic medieval
courtly love literature of what Western medieval theologians considered the "unnameable vice" or the "vice against nature," modern
critics have opted for two main interpretive stances. Some have rejected entirely the oriental theory of origins, claiming that Arabic
erotic poetry could not be a forerunner of Western courtly love
since Arabic literature is explicitly characterized by homosexuality,
whereas Western courtly love textuality is much less explicitly so. In
this case, Western homoeroticism is explained away as homosocial
bonding.[5] A second group of critics, seemingly more tolerant of
plurality, accepts the oriental theory of origins only after heterosex-
ualizing the homoerotic dimension of medieval Arabic literature.
They rationalize same-sex love poems as "allegory," "heterosexuality in drag," or "literary clichés." Only then is the Arabic love tradition deemed worthy to be a forerunner of Western courtly
discourses. This type of criticism is perhaps best exemplified by John
Jay Parry who, in the introduction to his 1941 translation of Andreas
Capellanus's *The Art of Courtly Love,* traces the possible literary genealogy of the Latin treatise. After examining its Andalusian equivalent, *The Dove's Neck Ring* by Ibn Hazm, he admits the possible
influence of Ibn Hazm on courtly love, but only after heterosexu-
alizing *The Dove's Neck Ring*'s same-sex lyrics. He writes: "Among
the Arabs, public opinion required that if the beloved was a woman

she must 'for decency's sake,' be spoken of as a man and referred to by masculine pronouns, adjectives, and verbs."[6] Furthermore, Parry speculates, "this alleged Arabic convention of encoding a heterosexual poem as a homosexual poem . . . may account for the troubadour practice of the male poet addressing his lady as his lord (*midons* or *senhor*)."[7] Both of the interpretive stances briefly summarized here demonstrate that accepting or rejecting the multicultural dimension of European literary production leads to the same assumption, the assertion of the heterosexual and Western nature of courtly love. Evidently the proclamation of a Western heterosexual identity represents yet another means of establishing European hierarchies of domination, both cultural and sexual.

If this myth of Western heterosexuality has impeded, since the twelfth century, any clear understanding either of East-West relations in the Middle Ages or of the literary expression of male homosexual desire in medieval French literature,[8] it has completely erased the literary manifestation and literary lineage of lesbian sexuality. Yet today, as Jacqueline Murray has shown, the medieval Western lesbian has been regularly elided in most literary criticism, first under the rubric "homosexual" in mainstream women's history and under the rubric "woman" in studies of medieval homosexuality, which have focused almost exclusively on male homosexuality.[9] I have concluded that in French literature the medieval lesbian has also been elided under the rubric "Western" by literary critics who remain resistant to the Oriental theory of origins. The question that I pose here is therefore twofold: First, where is the medieval lesbian? And second, can the literary expression of lesbian desire and lesbian love in medieval French literature claim an Arabic literary genealogy as male homosexuality can? Thus far, critics, including feminists, scholars in gender studies, and researchers of multiculturalism in the Middle Ages, have excluded altogether the question of the lesbian from the cross-cultural debate on love and desire.

In comparison to the number of extant descriptions of male homosexuality, very few French medieval literary texts treat explicitly either lesbianism or lesbian sexuality.[10] In fact, only three or four main texts form the entire corpus of the French lesbian tradition: the single

courtly love poem we have by trobairitz Bieiris de Roman ("Na
Maria, pretz e fina valors") dating from the first half of the thirteenth
century; the two texts that have preserved the story of *Yde et Olive,*
namely one of the thirteenth-century continuations of the epic poem
Huon de Bordeaux and the late fourteenth-century dramatic adaptation known as the *Miracle de la fille d'un roy;*[11] and finally the earliest
extant description of lesbian love in medieval French literature, that is
the seven stanzas included in *Le livre des manières* written by Etienne
de Fougères, Bishop of Rennes and Chaplain of Henry II Plantagenêt, sometime between 1168 and 1178. It is revealing to note that
these texts, perhaps because of their overt descriptions of lesbianism,
are each preserved in only one manuscript.[12] This might be an indication that they did not enjoy wide circulation in the Middle Ages,
or on the contrary that they were purposely destroyed because of
their popularity. One may consider this a first-level erasure of lesbian
sexuality effected in the Middle Ages. A second-level erasure has been
performed by modern-day scholars who have given minimal critical
attention to these texts. I might point to a third-level erasure of the
cultural meaning of the lesbian in the Middle Ages in the total lack
of scholarship to date addressing the cross-cultural context of the representation of gender and of female sexuality.

Among the rare French texts describing lesbianism, Etienne de
Fougères's depiction of lesbian lovemaking contained in seven stanzas of his *Livre des manières* undoubtedly offers not only the earliest,
but also the most explicit and most detailed account of lesbian sexual practices. In his 1979 edition of this text, Anthony Lodge had
even asserted: "This is the only allusion to sapphism in medieval
French literature."[13] This greatly understudied short poem belongs
to the ambiguous genre called *états du monde,* or estates literature,
which may be defined as a genre that seeks both to justify and to
rectify the actions of the various members of society.[14] *Le livre des
manières* divides society into two main categories (those who belong
to the upper estate or social level, and thus hold power—that is, respectively, the king, the clergy and the knights; then those who
make up the lower estate, and thus lack power, namely the peasants,
the bourgeois and women),[15] and it discusses the bonds and con-
tractual relations that ought to exist between them.

Though placed in Etienne de Fougères's text at the very bottom of the social hierarchy, after the peasants, the category of woman is present, a noteworthy inclusion since women are typically absent from the genre of *états du monde*.[16] It is this inclusion of woman that, to a great extent, contributes to making this text much more secular than other representatives of the genre, which typically remain more moralistic in intent. The section on women in *Le livre des manières* is itself subdivided into three portraits: first, the aristocratic woman, who receives a particularly misogynist description; second, the lesbian; and finally, the "good woman," whose main representative is the Countess of Hereford, to whom the entire poem is dedicated (lines 1205–1224).[17] In this essay I focus on the highly erotic status of the second portrait inserted between the two extremes of the bad and good woman, that of the lesbian.[18]

At first blush, it is evident that Etienne de Fougères attributes to lesbians a phallocentric sexuality in accordance with the common contemporary theological views on female sexuality, just as the authors of the *Yde et Olive* stories do one and two centuries later.[19] In fact, Robert Clark has accurately observed that what paradoxically predominates in de Fougères's poem when he speaks of lesbian sex is "the ever-present but always absent phallus":[20] the absence of any lance, or its multiple synonyms in the text, poker, pointer, handle, rod, pestle, fulcrum. Evidently lesbian sexual acts are understood here in terms of heterosexual relations, which the two women are presumably attempting to replicate.

Etienne de Fougères's description of lesbian sexual acts remains, nevertheless, original—so original, in fact, that both Clark and Murray recently reasserted what Lodge had already pointed out. Murray writes: "The uniqueness of the discussion and the literary devices de Fougères employed to describe female sexuality make this one of the most important medieval descriptions of lesbianism."[21] The most striking images in Etienne's description are undoubtedly the military metaphors used in stanzas 278 and 280: the joining of the two shields in stanza 278 ("join shield to shield without a lance") and the joust in both stanza 278 ("They don't play at jousting") and in stanza 280 ("At the game of thigh-fencing"). If, as mentioned above, the lance (in stanza 278) represents the absent phallus, the shields in the text are evidently a metaphor for female sexual organs. As a consequence, the joust here would represent a highly erotic and explicit scene of lesbian lovemaking. The absence of the lance, combined with the image of two shields rubbing against each other in a sexually charged tournament (stanza 278) thus elaborate a type of sexuality that is inherently idiosyncratic, lesbian, certainly different from and escaping heterosexual normativity. The uniqueness and originality of this military description of lesbian sexuality, especially from the pen of a bishop, has so perplexed critics that Charles-Victor Langlois, in his work on the *états du monde,* even suggested that the seven stanzas on the lesbian may well be "une interpolation postérieure" [a later interpolation].[22] Moreover, Lodge has pointed out that the tone and the vocabulary in the section on the lesbian in Etienne's *Livre des manières* stand in stark contrast to the rest of the work, and that some of the words used in this passage (particularly *trutennes* and *eu* in stanza 277, to which I will return) are of unclear etymology and unattested elsewhere in medieval literature.

Though unique indeed in medieval French literature, Etienne's military description of lesbian sexuality is not uncommon in Arabic homoerotic literature. In fact, the erotic military images used in *Le livre des manières* (the lance, the rubbing of the shields, and the joust in particular) strikingly echo various passages from widely circulated Arabic erotic treatises. These Arabic texts are likely to have been familiar to Etienne, especially since he was living in England under Henry II Plantagenêt's reign, and, I will argue, they may well have been the direct sources for his description of the lesbian. I focus here on two Arabic treatises dating from the tenth and eleventh centuries, thus written earlier than Etienne's *Livre des manières,* and which I believe to constitute the literary and cultural lineage of the French text. These Arabic texts are the late tenth-century *Encyclopedia of Pleasure* (*Jawami' al-lazza*) written by ⁰Abdul Hasan ⁰Ali Ibn Nasr Al-Katib, which is considered to be the earliest example of Arabic homoerotic compilations, and the eleventh-century philological work entitled *The Book of Metonymic Expressions of the Littérateurs and Allusive Phrases of the Eloquent (Al-Muntakhab min kinayat al-udaba' wa isharat al-bulagha')* written by Iraqi religious judge Abul-⁰Abbas Ahmad Ibn Muhammmad Al-Jurjani.[23] These two texts provide us with some of the most crucial insights into the culture of the medieval Arab lesbian, who has been elided in contemporary historical or critical work even more completely than her Western counterpart.[24]

Before I discuss the striking parallels between the French and Arabic literary traditions on lesbian lovemaking, a bit of background on the Arabic erotic tradition is in order. As may be clear from the second title, *The Book of Metonymic Expressions . . . ,* erotic material in the Arabic tradition is not usually confined to a specific genre. Rather, many different manifestations of sexual behavior are given equal treatment in the text. Therefore, sexual expressions as diverse as heterosexuality, homosexuality (both male and female), adultery, prostitution, effeminacy, masturbation, anal intercourse, and bestiality, to cite but a few of the more typical examples of sexualities evoked in Arabic texts, are more or less lumped together under the general category of sexuality or, in Al-Jurjani's case, of language. *The Book of Metonymic Expressions . . . ,* despite its focus on language, thus becomes a particularly rich reservoir of information on homosexuality in the Arabic literary tradition. Focusing on the use of indirect expressions among the *littérateurs,* and in an effort to display his erudition and mastery of the Arabic lexicon, Al-Jurjani quite naturally turns his attention to euphemisms used for sexuality and homosexuality. This technique, prevalent in the Arabic tradition, indicates that homosexuality, in opposition to its contemporary status in the European Middle Ages, was not simply viewed as an anomalous form of sexuality, but rather as one among multiple types of sexuality. It further reveals one of the ways that some of the Arabic material on homosexuality may have been transmitted to the West in the Middle Ages, namely embedded in various rhetorical, poetic, legal, medical, or scientific treatises.

Back to the military metaphors. If, at the end of the twelfth century, the lance, shield, and joust metaphors were still unusual in French erotic writings, they were, on the other hand, quite conventional throughout the Arabic erotic tradition. Central to this study is the fact that in the Arab world, as early as the tenth century, the word "shield" was understood to represent the vulva. For example, in the tenth chapter, "Lesbianism," of his *Encyclopedia of Pleasure,* Al-Katib writes, "Your vulva became like a shield."[25] The penis, not surprisingly, comes to be referred to in Arabic erotic writings as both the "lance" and the "sword."[26] Once this basic eroto-military semantic field was established, the joust (or war or tournament) metaphor logically followed and came naturally to mean lovemaking. These eroto-military metaphors were repeated verbatim from one century to the next, from one writer to the other throughout the entire Arab world.[27]

The military metaphors that we find in Etienne's text and that appear so new and original to modern-day critics can easily be traced to specific lines of any number of Arabic erotic treatises. In fact, they seem to repeat verbatim the Arabic homoerotic tradition. For example, Al-Jurjani writes in *The Book of Metonymic Expressions,* "They [lesbians] manifest a war in which there is no spear-thrusting,/ But only fending off a shield with a shield."[28] Anyone who remains unconvinced of the obvious sexual connotations of the words "war," "spear-thrusting," and "shields" need only compare their usage in this quotation with Al-Katib's *Encyclopedia of Pleasure* from the century before. This work, which was undoubtedly one of Al-Jurajani's sources, presents the metaphoric military words in their literal garb: "What's the good of two vulvas rubbing against each other? / It is the penetration of the penis that is important."[29] Clearly, Al-Jurjani's "spear" and "shield" respectively mean "penis" and "vulva." Similarly, his "fending of a shield with a shield" represents the "rubbing of the vulvas."

Exactly the same metaphors appear again in an early thirteenth-century Arabic text written by a Tunisian author named Shihâb al-Dîn Ahmad al-Tîfâshî (1184–1253) and entitled Nuzhat al-Albâb fîmâ lâ Yûjad fî Kitâb, which may be translated *The Delight of Hearts, or, What One Cannot Find in Any Book*. Although this text is written slightly later than Etienne de Fougères's time (and as such cannot have been his direct source), its importance cannot be underestimated, because it shows the extent to which the military metaphors used to describe lesbian lovemaking had become conventional in the Arabic homoerotic tradition:

They invented a tournament
In which there is no use of lance,

Hitting only with great noise
One shield against the other![30]

Speaking of lesbian lovemaking as the rubbing of shields/vulvas is so embedded in the Arabic homoerotic tradition that it may be considered one of its most identifying trademarks. Even the word for lesbian in Arabic, *sihaq,* evokes this rubbing behavior. The word *sihaq* is a verbal noun of stem III of the root *s-h-q,* meaning 'to rub,'[31] and lesbians are referred to as *sahikat, sahhakat,* or *musahikat,* meaning 'those who engage in rubbing behavior, or who make love in a rubbing fashion.' Thus, when a reader familiar with the Arabic homoerotic metaphoric conventions reads in Etienne de Fougères's *Livre des manières* that women join one another shield against shield, as though in a joust (as we saw in stanzas 278 and 280), she or he cannot fail to recognize the indebtedness of the French text to the Arabic tradition. In the context of medieval *convivencia* and of the multicultural relations between East and West, the parallel in the military metaphors indicates that Etienne de Fougères was undoubtedly familiar with Al-Katib's or Al-Jurjani's works and/or with other similar homoerotic texts. Let us not forget that Etienne de Fougères was chaplain to Henry II Plantagenêt, lived in England, and dedicated his *Livre des manières* to the Countess of Hereford. This in itself was a way of connecting his work with the matter of Araby, since the Cathedral of Hereford is well known to have been a major center for the transmission of Arabic scientific (and literary) learning in the twelfth century.[32] Etienne de Fougères's association of his work with the Cathedral of Hereford is thus an indication that he was familiar with Arabic literary material, including, undoubtedly, its important homoerotic elements.

The striking parallels between Etienne de Fougères's *Livre des manières* and Arabic descriptions of lesbian sexuality do not end here. They are present throughout the seven stanzas that interest me, although they do not come through clearly in the modern English translation. Critics of Etienne de Fougères often comment on the unusual vocabulary used in the section on the lesbian and have gone so far as to doubt Etienne's authorship of these stanzas. However, the vocabulary used to describe the lesbian that sounds

unusual to the Western ear resonates differently for the critic at-
tuned to the multicultural milieu of the twelfth century. All that
appears unusual today in this text seems so only because it belongs
to a different cultural tradition. The eroto-military metaphors are,
as we saw, an example of this phenomenon. Another example occurs on the last line of stanza 277: "Sanz focil escoent lor feu,"
translated as "Without a poker to stir up their fire." The cross-
cultural reading of *Le livre des manières* proposed here would suggest that the translation of "escoent lor feu" by "to stir up their
fire" reduces the tremendous ambiguity of the Old French verb *escoer,* which results in silencing the Arabic literary tradition that
stands evident behind this line. *Escoer* is one of those verbs in Old
French that has multiple significations. It means 'to deliver, to ag-
itate, to preserve, to avoid, to protect' and also 'to cut the tail' or
'to castrate' (and these two last significations, 'to cut the tail' or 'to
castrate,' are the primary meanings of the verb *escoer*). The use of
escoer with "fire" is uncommon; but its association with a "poker"
may explain the selected English translation, for a poker stirs up a
fire, after all. However, I do not believe that this is the only way
one can translate this line. In fact, I would propose that this line
may also mean, "They deliver themselves from their fire without
the use of a poker." This translation is not only linguistically and
grammatically possible, given the Old French verse, but has the
added merit of further illuminating Etienne de Fougères's indebtedness to the Arabic erotic material. For in translating this line the
way I propose, one may see Etienne aligning his French text with
the medical definition of lesbianism as it was known in the medieval Arab world, and as discussed in Al-Katib's *Encyclopedia of
Pleasure:*

> Lesbianism is due to a vapour which, condensed, generates in the labia
> heat and an itch which only dissolve and become cold through fric-
> tion and orgasm. When friction and orgasm take place, the heat turns
> into coldness because the liquid that a woman ejaculates in lesbian in-
> tercourse is cold whereas the same liquid that results from sexual
> union with men is hot. Heat, however, cannot be extinguished by
> heat; rather, it will increase since it needs to be treated by its opposite.
> As coldness is repelled by heat, so heat is also repelled by coldness.[33]

In these lines, Al-Katib explains that lesbianism is a condition whereby heat is generated in the labia and can be reduced only through friction and orgasm with another woman. This is because friction between two vulvas results in the ejaculation of a cold liquid that calms the original heat. The reduction in heat cannot be achieved through intercourse with a man since the man's liquid is hot and, as he writes, "heat . . . cannot be extinguished by heat." Returning to Etienne de Fougères's text, we now recognize that given the context of "sanz focil escoent lor feu" (it is between two sections strongly reminiscent of the Arabic tradition since they both evoke rubbing and include the military metaphors discussed earlier), "escoent lor feu" probably refers to the extinction of fire (and therefore the reaching of orgasm) and not the stirring up of fire that the two women seek to achieve in their union. It is evident here that if one ignores the Arabic homoerotic tradition that clearly appears to be Etienne de Fougères's source in the seven stanzas of *Le livre des manières,* one encounters either (unintended) mistranslations or obscurities in the text. These mistranslations lead to further silencing of the multicultural dimension of medieval society and further eliding of the sisterhood of the Arab and French lesbian in the Middle Ages.

The final example of the parallels between the French and Arabic homoerotic traditions that I will present here has to do with the usage of two words in Etienne's text, *trutennes* and *eu* in stanza 277, for which, as I mentioned earlier, critics have found no clear etymology and that remain unattested elsewhere in medieval literature. I would like to propose that these two words may well be transliterated Arabic terms. That Etienne de Fougères included two Arabic words in his poem would offer undeniable proof of his deep familiarity with Arabic homoerotic literature. I recognize the tremendous problems involved in making a case for transliterations of Arabic terms into romance (in this case Old French), for there can never be hard proof. However, and especially given my analysis of the parallelism in the metaphors used, and given the fact that these words are unattested in French, the hypothesis of Arabic terminology seems to me to be a convincing one. I suggest that the word *trutennes* comes from the Arabic root *t-r-t* (the ending *ennes* is the

grammatical ending for the dual form), which literally means 'fore-
lock' and thus by extension 'mons.' Although the word *t-r-t* is not
used in any of the three Arabic homoerotic treatises cited above, I
have found this word used in another erotic Arabic text that is not
well-known today. Dated to the ninth century, it was written by
Ahmad Ibn Mohammad Ibn Falita and is entitled *Rushd al-labib ila
muíasharat al-habib* [*Preference of Homosexuality over Heterosexuality*].[34]
The word *t-r-t* is used in this work to refer to the mons of the
beloved (both male and female).[35]

The word *eu* in the same line appears to be an onomatopoeia, attested both in Old French and in Arabic, that would reflect the
moaning and panting associated with lovemaking and pleasure as
well as the ultimate fulfillment of desire in orgasm.[36] The line
would thus signify: "In addition to the rubbing of two mons, they
make moaning and gasping sounds." In the Arabic erotic tradition,
these moans were believed to be essential to lesbian lovemaking. In
fact, they were thought to be one of the foundations of lesbian
knowledge and were an integral part of the training of future lesbians. Al-Tîfâshî writes that between lesbians attention was regularly paid to "this music of love that the breath produces as it escapes
the throat and passes through the nostrils."[37] One of the pieces of
advice given by an experienced lesbian mother to her daughter is
precisely about these moans: "Make sure to always accompany the
back and forth movements (rubbing movements) which you know
well with the sweet music of breath you exhale from your nostrils."[38] A bit later in the text, al-Tîfâshî speaks of "wheezing, panting, purring, murmurs, heartbreaking sighs."[39]

The use of these two Arabic words (*trutennes, eu*) in Etienne de
Fougères's poem has not previously been noted. This and the
quasi verbatim rendering of various erotic metaphors that I discussed earlier constitute undeniable proof not only of the availability of Arabic homoerotic literature to the medieval West, but
also of the familiarity of Etienne de Fougères with Arabic lesbian
eroticism. Etienne de Fougères's inclusion of Arabic terms and
images of lesbian sexuality in his poem testifies to the magnitude
of cross-cultural relations between East and West in the Middle
Ages. It also convincingly points to the import of Arabic homo-

eroticism in the literary construction of lesbian desire and sexuality in medieval France.

Equally significant however is the exclusion, on the part of Etienne and other medieval writers, of other Arabic homoerotic elements, for only fragments of texts (and only a few fragments) describing lesbianism have been transmitted from the East to the West. Though they were as available to the West as other scientific, medical, astronomical, mathematical, or literary material, explicit descriptions of homosexuality in general, and of lesbianism in particular, were much less likely to be assimilated into the nascent vernacular literatures of Europe. The medieval Arabic treatises on homosexuality that were undoubtedly available to the West in the Middle Ages (for example, *The Encyclopedia of Pleasure* and *The Book of Metonymic Expressions*), though no less phallocentric than their French counterparts and written from a male (not lesbian) perspective, are by far more detailed, direct, and explicit than that of Etienne de Fougères, or indeed any description of female lesbianism in the French Middle Ages. Thus, even though Etienne de Fougères's description of lesbianism is both original and explicit in the context of the French erotic tradition (there is probably nothing as explicit in French until the eighteenth century with the Marquis de Sade and Restif de la Bretonne), it still cuts a pale figure when compared to any of the Arabic homoerotic treatises. A final example of a description of lesbian sexuality drawn from an Arabic treatise demonstrates how much more explicit and extensive were the descriptions of lesbianism in that culture. I take this example from al-Tîfâshî even though this treatise, as pointed out earlier, was written later than Etienne de Fougères's. Nonetheless, al-Tîfâshî's *The Delight of Hearts* represents an excellent compilation of earlier Arabic writings on homosexuality. Some of the works he cites have been preserved (like *The Encyclopedia of Pleasure* and *The Book of Metonymic Expressions*), whereas others have not survived and are only attested through his extensive references to them. The erotic metaphors that pervade *The Delight of Hearts* form a very useful source of information on the sexual metaphoric conventions in the Arabic world up to the thirteenth century. Etienne de Fougères may well have been familiar with any number of these Arabic texts, which existed in the twelfth century, but have since disappeared. This is what al–Tîfâshî writes:

> The tradition between women in the game of love necessitates that the lover places herself above and the beloved underneath—unless the former is too light or the second too developed: and in this case, the lighter one places herself underneath, and the heavier one on top, because her weight will facilitate the rubbing, and will allow the friction to be more effective. This is how they proceed: the one that must stay underneath lies on her back, stretches out one leg and bends the other while leaning slightly to the side, therefore offering her opening (vagina) wide open: meanwhile, the other lodges her bent leg in her groin, puts the lips of her vagina between the lips that are offered for her, and begins to rub the vagina of her companion in an up-and-down, and down-and-up, movement that jerks the whole body. This operation is dubbed "the saffron massage" because this is precisely how one grinds saffron on the cloth when dyeing it. The operation must focus each time on one lip in particular, the right one, for example, and then the other: the woman will then slightly change position in order to apply better friction to the left lip . . . and she does not stop acting in this manner until her desires and those of her partner are fulfilled. I assure you that it is absolutely useless to try to press the two lips together at the same time, because the area from which pleasure comes would then not be exposed. Finally, let us note that in this game the two partners may be aided by a little willow oil, scented with musk.[40]

Such an explicit and detailed description in Arabic of lesbian sexuality in the Middle Ages certainly stands in stark contrast to the current political climate in Arabo-Islamic countries and explains, partly, the deletion of the Arabo-Muslim lesbian from any contemporary cultural production, critical or otherwise. But it certainly also stands in marked contrast to any description of lesbian sexuality in French literature, at least up to the eighteenth century. At the same time, it is not possible to deny the fact that both the French and the Arabic traditions are written from male and phallocentric points of view, not from a lesbian perspective. Nevertheless, the overall view of homosexuality in the medieval Arabic tradition remains not only much more detailed and explicit, but also more open and positive than the view on same-sex relations in the French tradition.

Certainly, parts of this quotation from al-Tîfâshî evoke some lines of Etienne's description (once again, al-Tîfâshî is not Etienne de Fougères's direct source in these instances, since his treatise was written slightly later than Etienne's. However, there may very well have been intermediary sources known to Etienne that are now lost or not yet edited.). For instance, the uncommon Old French phrase "escremie del jambot" or "thigh-fencing" (stanza 280) seems reminiscent of the insistence on the positioning of the legs in the Arabic erotic treatise. The balancing of the two women in the act of love and their effort to rub only one vulva at a time strongly resonates with the third line of stanza 278, "n'ont soign de lange en lor balance," and with the last line of stanza 280, "s'entrepaient vilment l'escot." The similarity between these lines and the Arabic treatise is, however, once again lost in the translation. I would propose to translate the third line of stanza 278 as "they do not need a tongue in their balancing act," and the last line of stanza 280 as "they go at the game of thigh-fencing one person at a time." These translations would evoke much more explicitly the truly balancing and serial act of lesbian lovemaking described in al-Tîfâshî's text.

Yet, and once again, these parallels are allusive at best. For the most part, and despite their recognized explicitness, the metaphors we find in Etienne de Fougères often remain ambiguous (perhaps intentionally so),[41] and they never match the unsparing details or at times the unabashed and blunt literalness of the Arabic treatises and the Arabic erotic tradition in general. It may be tempting to interpret the relative paucity of direct parallels in the description of lesbianism between medieval Arabic homoeroticism and French literature as a sign of the lack of influence of Arabic literary writings on vernacular literatures of the Middle Ages. However, given the presence of other types of literary, scientific, and cultural influences, it may be more accurate to conclude that despite the access of the West to Arabic homoerotic literature, there has been, because of the subject matter, a process of selective borrowing, or perhaps even at times of outright violent silencing, in the material that was available. Those aspects of love and desire that dealt with male, but even more so, female homosexuality, were more readily rejected, especially from the twelfth century on, with the increasing tendency

toward heteronormativity. Literary devices, metaphors, and images
describing male homosexuality were integrated more readily than
those dealing with lesbianism, even though the latter material was
as available to the Western public as was the former. One might say
that some form of censorship took place at some level, though it is
hard to pinpoint at which one—at the level of the translators, of the
poets themselves, or of the scribes. What is evident, however, is the
erasure of lesbian Arabic homoerotic desire from the Western love
tradition, traceable in so many other ways to various Arabic and Andalusian sources. In a period as preoccupied as was late-twelfth-
century France with the elaboration of regimes of sexual repression,
social order, and heteronormativity, despite the prevalence of descriptions of lesbian love in the Arabic tradition, and despite the assimilation of various aspects of Arabic homoeroticism in Western
descriptions of love, French authors and poets still chose to follow
the lines of heterosexual desire, and phallocentric sexuality more
generally, when speaking of female erotic encounters.

Notes

1. See Maria Rosa Menocal, *The Arabic Role in Medieval Literary His-
   tory, A Forgotten Heritage* (Philadelphia: University of Pennsylvania
   Press, 1987), p. 2.
2. Menocal, *Arabic Role.*
3. Thomas Glick, *Islamic and Christian Spain in the Early Middle Ages*
   (Princeton: Princeton University Press, 1979); Alice Lasater, *Spain
   to England* (Jackson: University of Mississippi Press, 1974);
   Dorothee Melitzki, *The Matter of Araby in Medieval England* (New
   Haven: Yale University Press, 1977); Menocal, *Arabic Role;* Edward
   Said, *Orientalism* (New York: Vintage Books, 1979).
4. Susan Schibanoff, "Mohammed, Courtly Love, and the Myth of
   Western Heterosexuality," *Medieval Feminist Newsletter* 16 (Fall
   1993): 27–32.
5. This is the conclusion of critics such as Georges Duby and Christiane Marchello-Nizia; see Georges Duby, *Mâle Moyen Âge* (Paris:
   Flammarion, 1988), in particular his chapter entitled "A propos de
   l'amour que l'on dit courtois," pp. 74–82; and Christianne
   Marchello-Nizia, "Amour courtois, société masculine et figures du

pouvoir," *Annales: Economies, Sociétés, Civilisations* 36.6 (Nov.-Dec. 1981): 969–82.

6. "Introduction," in Andreas Capellanus, *The Art of Courtly Love,* ed. and trans. John Jay Parry (1941; reprint, New York: W. W. Norton, 1969), p. 10.

7. Cited in Schibanoff, "Mohammed, Courtly Love," 30.

8. John Boswell reached this conclusion in his now-classic *Christianity, Social Tolerance and Christianity: Gay People in Western Europe from the Beginning of the Christian Era to the Fourteenth Century* (Chicago: University of Chicago Press, 1980).

9. Jacqueline Murray, "Twice Marginal and Twice Invisible: Lesbians in the Middle Ages," in *Handbook of Medieval Sexuality,* ed. Vern L. Bullough and James A. Brundage (New York: Garland, 1996), p. 193.

10. In this study I am interested only in explicit descriptions of lesbian sexual behavior, as opposed to what Judith Bennett has dubbed "lesbian-like" in her proposition to study the social history of the lesbian in the Middle Ages by considering the lesbian as a larger category that would include all single women. See Bennett's "Lesbian-Like and the Social History of Lesbianisms" in *Journal of the History of Sexuality* 9.1–2 (January/April 2000): 1–24.

11. On *Yde et Olive,* see the essay by Francesca Sautman in this volume.

12. Bieiris de Roman's poem is preserved only in MS T208 (BnF, fr. 15211). *Yde et Olive* is in Turin, MS 1311, and the *Miracle de la fille d'un roy* in BnF Cange fr. 819–820. The single copy of Etienne de Fougères's *Le livre des manières* is in Angers, Bibl. mun., MS 304 (295).

13. Etienne de Fougères, *Le livre des manières,* ed. R. Anthony Lodge, Textes Littéraires Français (Geneva: Droz, 1979), p. 34 n.12; translation mine. Despite the rarity and obvious importance of this section, which Lodge recognizes, the editor himself ends up undermining the value of these stanzas, as he does not bring up the question of lesbianism in his outline of the text, writing only that in the text "some women go so far as to commit acts against nature" (p. 27; translation mine). All future references to *Le livre des manières* are to Lodge's edition and are indicated directly in the text.

14. Jeri S. Guthrie, "La femme dans *Le livre des manières:* surplus économique, surplus érotique," *Romanic Review* 79 (March 1988): 251.

15. The lines are divided exactly into two parts: lines 1–672 and lines 677–1344.

16. Guthrie points out that this inclusion nonetheless represents an exclusion of women ("La femme," 254).

17. It would be interesting to speculate on the placement of the lesbian in between the other two descriptions of the woman.

18. See the Old French text and the English translation by Robert L. A. Clark included as the appendix to his article in this volume.

19. In *Yde et Olive,* the narrator comments, "N'a membre nul qu'a li puis abiter" [she has no member with which she could possess her] (line 7076).

20. Cited in Murray, "Twice Marginal," p. 205.

21. Murray, "Twice Marginal," p. 204.

22. Cited in Lodge's introduction to Etienne's poem, p. 34. See also Charles-Victor Langlois, *La vie en France au Moyen Age de la fin du XIIe au milieu du XIVe siècle d'après quelques moralistes du temps* (Paris: Hachette, 1908), p. 25. Langlois even suggests that since all of Etienne de Fougères's other writings were in Latin, and given the uncanny nature of these seven stanzas, it is possible that his *Livre des manières* is a translation from a now-lost Latin original by Etienne rather than an original work.

23. ꜥAbdul Hasan ꜥAli Ibn Nasr Al-Katib, *Encyclopedia of Pleasure,* ed. and annotated Salah Addin Khawwam, trans. ꜥAdnan Jarkas and Salan Addin Khawwam (Toronto: Aleppo Publishing, 1977). All future references to this text are to this edition. Al-Qadi Abdul-ꜥAbbas Ahmad Ibn Muhammad Al-Jurjani, *Al-Muntakhab min kinayat al-udaba' wa-isharat al-bulagha'* (Hyderabad, 1983). This is in fact an anonymous abridgment of Al-Jurjani's original work, which has not survived.

24. See the essay by Fedwa Malti-Douglas in this volume.

25. Al-Katib, *Encyclopedia of Pleasure,* p. 191.

26. Al-Katib, *Encyclopedia of Pleasure,* pp. 193 and 73.

27. On this subject see Arie Schippers and John Mattock, "Love and War: A Poem of Ibn Khafajah," *Journal of Arabic Literature* 17 (1986): 50–68.

28. Cited in Everett K. Rowson, "The Categorization of Gender and Sexual Irregularity in Medieval Arabic Vice Lists," in *Body Guards: The Cultural Politics of Gender Ambiguity,* ed. Julia Epstein and Kristina Straub (New York and London: Routledge, 1991), p. 65.

29. Al-Katib, *Encyclopedia of Pleasure,* p. 196.

30. Citations from Ahmad al-Tîfâshî's text are to the French translation by René R. Khawam, *Les Délices des Coeurs ou ce que l'on ne trouve en aucun livre* (Paris: Phébus, 1981; earlier incomplete edition 1977). This passage is on p. 262. An English translation of this work by Winston Leyland and Edward A. Lacey, *The Delight of Hearts, or, What You Will Not Find in Any Book* (San Francisco: Gay Sunshine

Press, 1988), was based on the French translation by Khawam, but only those sections dealing with male homosexuality are included. The chapter on the lesbian that is of interest here therefore does not exist in English. All translations provided here are mine.

31. It is similar in this sense to the Greek etymology; hence the English word "tribadism." See Malti-Douglas's essay in this volume for an analysis based on a different meaning of *sihaq*—'pound' rather than 'rub'.

32. The Cathedral of Hereford is known to have been a major translation center with important library holdings. It is also known to have been the place where Western scholars went back to teach after their trips *Arabum studia*. For example, it was the teaching center of Petrus Alfonsi's astronomical lessons based on Arabic scientific findings in the first quarter of the twelfth century (that same Petrus Alfonsi, author of the *Disciplina Clericalis*, who was responsible for the introduction of a significant amount of Arabic literary material into the West); during the twelfth century, well-known Western scholars of Arabic science such as Walcher of Malvern, Roger of Hereford, and Adelard of Bath received their educations at the Cathedral of Hereford. See Melitzki, *Matter of Araby*, and John Tolan, *Petrus Alfonsi and His Medieval Readers* (Gainesville: University Press of Florida, 1993).

33. Al-Katib, *Encyclopedia of Pleasure*, p. 188.

34. Ibn Falita's treatise (*Preference of Homosexuality over Heterosexuality*) has to date not been edited or translated, with the exception of three chapters (9–11) edited and translated into German by Mohamed Zouher Djabri as a Ph.D. dissertation at the School of Medicine, University Friedrich-Alexander, Nuremberg, 1967. This dissertation is based on two of the many known manuscripts of the work: Paris, BnF Arabe Slane 3051; and Berlin, Ahlwardt 6390. The word *t-r-t* occurs in chapter 9, which is devoted to the subject of lesbianism (Djabri, p. 7).

35. It is certainly also possible that Etienne de Fougères wrote (or intended to write) *srutennes*, not *trutennes*, for the Arabic word *s-r-t* occurs on numerous occasions in all the Arabic homoerotic treatises. This word, which means 'navel,' has a very sexual connotation throughout the Arabic homoerotic tradition. It may well be that there is a scribal error due to non-recognition of a foreign word in the text of *Le livre des manières* as it has been transmitted to us. Such an error would be consistent with a general tendency toward errors on the part of the scribe, a tendency that all editors of this manuscript have recognized.

36. In Ibn Falita's treatise, we find the Arabic word *Hen,* which means 'moaning and gasping' (7). Could the intended French word be *en* instead of *eu?*

37. Al-Tîfâshî *Les Délices des Coeurs,* p. 252.

38. Al-Tîfâshî, *Les Délices des Coeurs,* pp. 252–53.

39. Al-Tîfâshî, *Les Délices des Coeurs,* p. 258.

40. Al-Tîfâshî, *Les Délices des Coeurs,* pp. 251–52.

41. The ambiguity in Etienne de Fougères's text may well have been intended. It would be intentionally obscure, as Ulrike Wiethaus has pointed out for female homoeroticism in medieval Germany (cited in Bennett, "Lesbian-Like," 8). This ambiguity/obscurity may have allowed both the expression and the masking of lesbian sexual practices. In the case of Etienne de Fougères, we would have the expression of sexuality through a medieval French scholar's lens (Robert L. A. Clark's translation) or through the lesbian's perspective and seen through cultural borrowing (my proposed translation).

CHAPTER EIGHT

WHAT CAN THEY POSSIBLY DO TOGETHER?
QUEER EPIC PERFORMANCES IN
TRISTAN DE NANTEUIL

Francesca Canadé Sautman

> *In* Tristan de Nanteuil, *a sex change makes a cross-dressed woman
> into a man. Queering this narrative brings out same-sex desire and
> disruption of the gender order.*

The Man–Woman of French Medieval Literature

The most famous transvestite of the French late Middle Ages,
Joan of Arc, struggling with the constraints of gender-
normative behavior and dress, staked her life on her choice to wear
male clothing. Nevertheless, she was never thought of as anything
other than woman—or maiden.[1] This was not so, however, in the
world of fiction and legend, particularly the *chanson de geste,* in
which women donned male garb for a variety of reasons, most notably to evade pursuit, and thus made every effort to pass as men.[2]
To these we must add the numerous women of hagiography who
fled unwanted marriage and preserved their chastity under male
clothing. Such women were so successful that they could receive
unexpected advances from other women.[3] In another genre, the
lady in the fabliau "Berenger au Long Cul"[4] dresses as a knight in

order to ridicule her weak husband[5] and, in so doing, installs the ambiguity of same-sex contact within normative gender expectations. However, women who actually undergo a sex change and become "biological" men are a much rarer occurrence in medieval French literature.

This motif actually appears in two *chansons de geste* from the first half of the fourteenth century that seem to originate in the same general geographical and cultural area: *Yde et Olive* (*YO*), followed by versions for the theater and later prose narratives, and *Tristan de Nanteuil* (*TdN*). These two texts allow the possibility of affective, marital, and sexual bonds between two women, which are subsequently normalized by the transformation of one into a man and the ensuing procreation of an heir. The complexities of that normalization, the place of desire and pleasure, the nuances in the two women's interactions both before and after the sex change, the underlying assumptions about the body as social vector and the body as sex, and their implications for the embodiment of gender itself provide vivid traces in the history of same-sex love between medieval women, as well as puzzling medieval constructions of gender. Their version of the "man-woman" theme differs greatly from those texts in which the disguise and the behavioral change are a fleeting convenience and are rapidly brought back to female, strictly gendered identity.

These multiple inflections to the presumed stability of the sexed body are most detailed in *TdN*, a text that has been commented on far less than *YO*, which has attracted the attention of gender theorists and queer theorists for the serious challenges it poses to the gender order.[6] Yet *TdN* provides its own challenges, and its precise location in the northern French lands of Hainaut, its connections to the history of Flanders and Picardy, and its parallels with other fictional texts of the time pose an intriguing set of problems with respect to fictional gender instabilities in relation to historical contexts, and the possibility of a queer history. Arguably, its most important tool for category-blurring is not transvestism per se, which has historically been appropriated by many medieval fictional texts, but the slippage from one gender to the other, the uncertainties that continue to shadow the newly minted body. And at the core of such ambiguities lies the fraught relationship between sex (of the body) and gender, which, as was noted in the introduction to this book, has been acutely opened up by Judith Butler's work, and allows veiled inscriptions of same-sex desire among women in conventional medieval narratives.

Gender instability in these texts is indeed original and to be read against a backdrop of other narrative situations in which women step out of the ordinary boundaries of gender. That such infractions to the gender order are found primarily in the *chanson de geste* is worthy of attention:[7] gender incoherence cannot be considered in one category, even in French medieval literature. Different gender expectations are embedded in different genres: the epic woman is routinely capable of ire, vengefulness, harsh treatment of enemies and inferiors, and violent behavior to achieve desirable ends. None of this behavior seems particularly reprehensible, and none of it is incompatible with portraits of actual noblewomen. Women in the fabliaux act differently, as even aggressive behaviors are primarily characterized by the good use of wit and ruse,[8] and violent treatment of disobedient women lurks frequently in the background.[9] And if one were to consider the literature of books of conduct,[10] again different expectations would be raised, as they are in a complex way by Christine de Pizan much later in her excursus on historically and mythologically noteworthy women. The epic genre has been incorrectly characterized as aristocratic,[11] but it is true that the matter itself consists of the feuds and adventures of the feudal aristocracy. And while narrative treatment of gender cannot be conflated with its actual construction in society, it remains to be seen just what relationship with social reality such narrative situations entertain.

Perceptions of women's behavior as demure and suitably passive cannot be assumed, even in the narrow context of Western Europe, to be eternal and unproblematic. Contemporary views of gender are in a great deal of flux but still have their roots in the particular nineteenth-century bourgeois acculturation of women into a reproductive order.[12] French medieval society between the twelfth and fourteenth centuries did not necessarily follow that model, even if such a model had a place in it. In all their limits, narrative portrayals of aggressive women propose different gender scripts that are not incompatible with the subjection of women, scripts in which women are expected to play active, physically confrontational roles in clearly delineated contexts. One of the most significant examples of women in warfare is provided by the *chanson de geste Anseis de Mes* (*AdM*), which belongs to the vast *Lorrains* cycle that is characterized by family feuds and revenge.[13] These caveats are crucial before one reads and interprets the remarkable sex transformation of both *YO* and *TdN*. It is, for instance, important to distinguish between, on the one hand, adopting male identity every day and attempting to pass, which includes conforming to the warrior ideal (*Silence, YO, TdN*), and, on the other hand, appearing to change temporarily into a man by donning armor and taking to the battlefield (*AdM*), which implies "manly behavior" but no change in the construction of identity if that behavior is warranted by family policy or social crisis. Thus the problems of the man-woman and of the warrior-woman, although related, are not coterminous.

Textual Families: YO and TdN

Both *YO* and *TdN* belong to mini-cycles in which women play important roles; in fact, these are some of the only French epic *cycles* clearly identified with women's names: *Parise la Duchesse* and *Aye d'Avignon*[14] in the "Geste de Nanteuil," for *TdN; Esclarmonde, Clarisse et Florent, Yde et Olive,* for *YO*. Both texts hail from similar linguistic environments[15] and show narrative connections to each other as well as some important differences, such as the incest theme in *YO,* and the form of the bath motif and the role of the deer in *TdN,* which also contains several female warrior figures, positive and negative. In both *YO* and *TdN* the change of sex is brought about as a continuation of borrowed male identity after both female heroes have disguised themselves as male and functioned socially as warriors.

The story of Yde, extant in one fourteenth-century manuscript,[16] reappears in several versions in different literary genres, including a late fourteenth-century miracle play called *Miracle de la fille d'un roy,* also preserved in a single manuscript[17] and in a later English version. *YO*'s *chanson de geste* mini-cycle originates with

Huon de Bordeaux, a narrative distinguished by the importance of magic and the supernatural.[18] Yde's borrowing of male clothing is her own device to escape the incestuous pursuits of her father. This motif squarely connects the romance to an entirely distinct corpus with an extensive folk tradition, represented in medieval French literature by miracle stories and a brief chanson entitled *La Belle Hélène de Constantinople.* In fact, an Italian miracle play concerning "Sancta Uliva" makes the link with hagiography explicit while transferring it to the other woman, Olive.[19] An important tool for unpacking the multiple layers of meaning in this sex-change motif is provided by the study of this folk tradition. Folklorists such as Catherine Velay-Vallantin and others[20] have shown that the legend is a variant of the general type known in folk tale typology as the story of the "girl with cut hands":[21] girl cuts off her hands to repulse her father's incestuous advances and flees her family.[22] Philippe de Beaumanoir's thirteenth-century romance *La Manekine* is one of its earliest examples. In modern folk tale versions, the amputated hands are a mutilation performed by a cruel and spiteful parent or in-law; eventually the girl miraculously retrieves her hands in most French versions, when her infant child is dropped in a stream and she leans forward to save him.[23] A wide range of texts reproduce this story, raising important questions about the ability of a specific narrative cluster to impact upon a large audience and to provide a distinct reading of gender over a long period of time. They underscore the cultural importance these motifs might have had in authorizing certain types of gender scripts that were viable and writable in the fourteenth century, yet strangely unsettling of contemporary gender norms. Strictly Freudian interpretations of the *Manekine* romance have been proposed, whereby the daughter entertains repressed incestuous desire for the father, the Manekine's amputated hand becomes an "all-purpose phallus," and the mutilated daughter is the phallic woman who represents the phallus itself.[24] In a critical reading of this interpretation, Robert L. A. Clark has suggested instead a "structuralist approach," in which the notion of "category as a construct [is] constantly under the threat of indeterminacy and collapse," and that category crisis is understood through the tool of transvestism.[25] Motifs of the "girl with cut hands" type are recognizable in *YO,* and also in *TdN,* where Blanchandin (formerly Blanchandine) has his arm lopped off in battle, signaling again the importance of motif clustering and migrations in the task of situating and interpreting medieval texts.[26]

However, far from being mutilated or constrained by passive, resigned behavior, the epic Yde is combative and peculiarly effective for one who seemed to have been raised in silks and in women's chambers. Although "feminine denominations" are used for her in combat scenes, these are probably not a clearly comical device, as has been claimed.[27] There is no evidence of comic intent in the narrative of Yde's tribulations and violent confrontations with various villains; rather, it suggests danger and terror.[28] Such passages can in fact be interpreted as extolling the class basis of violence, and, to this paradigm one might oppose the more subversive violence of figures like the Comtesse de Ponthieu[29] or the Judith figure.[30] Women who fight for their honor are praised throughout the *chanson de geste;* women who turn violence against husbands or other legitimate figures of authority are much more problematic, and so is the link among female status, gendered roles, and acceptable levels of violence. Furthermore, these scenes in *YO* carefully create tension by juxtaposing feminine and frankly masculine denotations that effectively prepare the terrain for Yde's sex and gender passing, and the he-she's amorous impact on Olive.

This group of texts invites a closer look at their unraveling of gender definitions and at the particular position of biological and anatomical sexual markers in the disembodiment of gender. In this context, one of the most useful formulations of gender is to be found in Kathleen Biddick's essay "Genders, Bodies, Borders: Technologies of the Visible." Biddick proposes "gender as a theory of borders that enables us to talk about the historical construction and maintenance of sexual boundaries. . . . Theories of gender, therefore, need to be histories simultaneously of corporeal interiority and exteriority: sex, flesh, body, race, nature, discourse, and culture."[31] These histories are peculiarly inscribed on Yde's fictional body, with its passage from a stereotypically beautiful fifteen-year-old girl with lithe hands[32] to a strong, tall warrior who nevertheless remains linguistically coded as female, from a woman praying on her knees, about to be burned at the stake with her *wife,* to an "homme carné" [a man in the flesh, made flesh].[33]

Tristan de Nanteuil is the last chanson in the "Geste de Nanteuil;" written down in the first half of the fourteenth century, it is a seemingly endless adventure narrative that has generated commentary since the 1930s.[34] Little was said about *TdN* between A. H. Krappe's essay in 1935 and Keith Val Sinclair's edition of the text in 1971. This edition was followed by a separate analysis of the text and its sources in 1983. Sinclair's commentary, however, contributed nothing very new to the understanding of this disconcerting text, although he claimed to have devised an original method. He merely discussed the Indian origins question, called attention to several traditional narrative themes in the text (Man Tried by Fate, Cowardly Knight, Change of Sex, Handless Maiden, Hermit Saint), and stressed similarity with and difference from *YO* and the *Estoire de Merlin.* Sinclair saw this as a series of "narrative substitutions" and "intercultural adjustments between East and West," between the Gujerati tale quoted by Krappe and *TdN,* made not by the *trouvère,* but "already effected in his source material."[35]

In spite of its enormous size, *TdN* contains sufficient local geographical detail to be situated regionally. Keith Val Sinclair pointed out that the murder of Gui provides such an indication.[36] Several localities in the forest were associated with murders in medieval writing, and the author of *TdN* would have been "familiar with accounts of murder in the Forest of Mormal. Indeed, his choice of venue was very appropriate for the times. It would certainly have been recognized and appreciated by readers or listeners in the entourage of the counts of Hainaut in the first half of the 14th century."[37] The *trouvère* records a belief about the place of Gui's murder: "seigneurs, en la forest est la place Guyon/Ains puis qu'i fust occis, n'y crut haie ne buisson" (vss. 19548–59 and 19560–61); [my lords, in the forest is the place of Guy/Never since he was murdered there has bush or hedge grown there]. According to Sinclair, this forest was situated near the Belgian border, in the département of the North, within a diamond-shaped territory, with Bavaisis at the northeast, Berlaimont on the east, Landrecies on the south, the old Chaussée Brunehaut on the northwest, and Le Quesnoy to the west. The forest belonged to the domain of the counts of Hainaut, as confirmed by the 1303 will of Jean of Avesnes.[38] The language of *TdN* is another clue. By careful comparison of its linguistic characteristics with other texts of the period, Sinclair identified many of these traits as found exclusively or predominantly in the fourteenth-century chanson *Baudouin de Sebourc* (*BdS*), which can be located with great precision in the immediate region of Valenciennes; other linguistic characteristics of *TdN* Sinclair found in the work of Jean Froissart, an Hennuyer, and he identified forms with distinct Walloon and even Valenciennes traits.[39] Medieval Picard covered a large area surrounded by Flemish, the Walloon dialect, the Champenois of Brie, the speech of Ile-de-France, and Norman. A Germanic *adstratum* was combined with local forms through maritime commercial contacts, and the position of Picard increased because of the commercial expansion of the coast and because the dukes of Burgundy used it as the language of chancellery in their lands of northern France, Belgium, and southern Holland.[40] Nanteuil was in fact a Picard name and place, with powerful lords established in Nanteuil-le-Haudouin from the eleventh century on, producing a known *trouvère,* Philippe, lord of Nanteuil.[41] Picard was disproportionally present in medieval French literature, but the linguistic particularities of the texts studied here point to strong regional associations and linguistic networks. Because of such linguistic and toponymic detail, *Tristan de Nanteuil* and *Baudouin* (a text filled with gender discoherence, mostly with respect to men)[42] can thus be identified as originating in the same region, French Hainaut, particularly around Valenciennes, and were written down roughly at the same time.[43]

There are also parallels between aspects of both *YO* and *TdN* and an earlier text, the thirteenth-century *Roman de Silence.*[44] *Silence* involves no actual sex change, but in all three texts[45] there is a forceful interrogation of the boundaries of gender and its embodiment in a clearly sexed corporal site, and insistent allusions to same-sex desire among women, albeit women who appear to ignore the sex of the other.[46] A significant detail may be the mutilation motif, as Silence cuts off the rebel count's hand, but there are other puzzling twists and turns. *Silence* was initially located in the marches of Brittany, in the area now known as Mayenne, around Laval, and thus, loosely integrated into a Celto-French orbit.[47] Yet this identification is not certain, since *Silence* remains written in Picard and shows an interest in the toponymy of England, historically a land with close political connections to the medieval Boulonnais.[48] Picard was generally an important literary vector in medieval France, but it is noteworthy that for Thorpe the particular form of Picard used in *Silence* was localized along the Tournai-Mons-Douai axis,[49] geographically close to the region that produced *TdN*.

Second, it seems curiously coincidental that while *Silence* explores at length the modulations of male to female and back through naming—the contrast between the names Silence and Silentius—this motif is not typical of other French medieval romances involving women disguised as men[50]—except, that is, *YO* and *TdN*. *YO* also resolves the passage from female to male by slight linguistic inflection, the female Yde [Ydée], notably another abstract name, becoming the male Ydés. And the heroine in *TdN*, named Blanchandine, becomes Blanchandin, a change that elicits a certain amount of wordplay at the time of the transformation. Her name belongs to the stock of fictional exoticized names used in the *chanson de geste*. Linguistically it follows the pattern of adjectives like *marbrin*, fm. *marberine*, or the name Yvorine, a feminization of the masculine Saracen name Yvorin. Blanchandin thus has two connotations: semantically, generic lightness; and by association, Saracen origins. The absence of the letter "r" cannot conceal its kinship to Blancandrin, the treacherous counselor of King Marsile in the *Song of Roland*,[51] or the tendency for names ending in "in" to belong to evil or monstrous figures (Harpin, Amauguin), confirming the name's incription in categories of ambiguity.[52]

Finally, there is one more intriguing piece to this puzzle. *Silence* is, by all accounts, the work of an unknown writer by the name of Heldris of Cornoualle. However, Lambert of Ardres, the thirteenth-century chronicler of the powerful counts of Guînes and Ardres in the general Boulonnais region, attributes the authorship of an otherwise undefined "Roman de Silence" to a *clerc* of that region, Maitre Gauthier de Sillart.[53] Although none of these elements can be considered conclusive evidence of direct links between *Silence* and the *chansons de geste YO* and *TdN,* they do suggest that we are faced here with a very special group of texts that stand in greater proximity to each other both geographically and narratively than to other French texts of the period. And this raises the problem of whether this type of narrative was in some way grounded in the particular regional culture and history of northern France in the thirteenth and fourteenth centuries.

Desire, Sex, and the Body in TdN

In concentrating on *Tristan de Nanteuil,* I address the ways that its views of gender roles, greatly informed by the folk tradition, produce numerous complications rather than the monolithic thinking often ascribed to folk imagination in cultures predicated on the subjection of women. Desire can act as a strategy to subvert old meanings and heteronormative plots, and this narrative can be interrogated to uncover any space, however minimal, for identifying erotic attraction between women. The narrative's many twists and turns in staging discrepant gendered interactions allow an understanding of the technologies of gender, with a view to considering women not solely in comparison/opposition to males but in relation to each other, as Teresa de Lauretis judiciously advocated.[54]

The sex change episode in *TdN* follows a pattern only superficially similar to that of *YO.* In brief, Blanchandine, masquerading as a man to prevent her Saracen relatives from recognizing her, becomes the object of a Saracen princess's relentless passion. Under duress the disguised Blanchandine is married to the princess but cannot "perform" the expected marital duties, or to be more precise, she cannot produce a penis, the expected—and apparently solely permitted—instrument of that bliss. Panicked, faced with a revealing public bathtub and under penalty of death, she prays to God for help and is given the option of transforming herself fully into a man.[55] This episode, as we shall see, is more remarkable for what is left out than for what is included. As fiction, it provides intriguing perspectives on the availability of gender scripts. As a folklore text, it demands attention to details of the sex change that have been oddly ignored, although there is a distinct ritual meaning to the transformation scene, with its links to symbolic mutilations.[56] In effect, the Aarne-Thompson classification of folk tale types regrouped various narrative elements, or motifs, to form type 514, rather loosely labeled "The Shift of Sex," which is summarized as follows: "the sister becomes a soldier in place of her brother. Marries the daughter of the king [K1837, K1322]. She is driven away and rescued by her companions. The change of sex in the ogress' house [D11]. Marriage with the princess [L161]."[57] These somewhat mismatched motifs—most do not occur in any single tale— add another piece to this already ample puzzle: many clusters around the same-sex change are centered in Spain and Italy, which is consonant with the mention of Aragon, Castille, and Barcelona in *YO* and the use of the southern name Olive.[58]

Blanchandine, just about to be exposed publicly through the bath prepared for her, is saved by a huge deer who invades the palace where her bath is waiting, knocks everything down, and draws the court in pursuit. Blanchandine joins the chase, loses the others, and, penetrating deeply into a thicket filled with thorns that tear her flesh and pierce her foot, hears a voice from Heaven offering her the choice to live as a woman or become a man, but she must first sacrifice the deer.[59] The deer, a locus of complex symbolic articulations, is highly meaningful in this passage and throughout *TdN*. He is the horned one who, marked visibly as male, is at the same time the spurious, questionable male, subject to cuckolding jokes; as one who sheds horns, is linked to snakes, and always needs water, he is connected to renewal, rebirth, and regeneration.[60] In *TdN*, the animal already occupies a transgendered position at the very beginning, since a she-deer—not a doe, but a giant female deer with antlers—feeds the infant hero and then protects him and his lover, Blanchandine, by massacring with her deadly antlers all those who approach them.[61]

The deer is thus a crucial actor in *TdN*, not merely a borrowing from *YO*, since early in the text it appears as an avatar of the Wild Ones—wild man and wild woman—who protects the protagonists.[62] Later in the narrative, Blanchandine loses an arm in battle, a loss that only her son, Saint Gilles, can repair.[63] This motif is directly reminiscent of the Manekine story, but it is even closer to the *Belle Hélène de Constantinople,* in which the severed hand of the heroine is carried around his neck by her son, Brice/Bras [arm], and put back by him. However, some question remains as to whether Blanchandine's transformation is complete: the initial "lack" may rather be reproduced in the missing peripheral member, since in folklore terms, at least, the leap from peripheral wound to sexual wound is a small one indeed.

Ostensibly the wound is a representation of male castration, and that meaning is certainly germane to the whole narrative's underpinnings. But the connections made by the folk tradition add further complications by reinscribing the feminine in an apparently male sign. In the agonistic experiences of women who flee contact with men and seek defacement, mutilations treat the feminine as a site for discursive remappings and rewritings, while also freeing women from male contact. This is the case of the virgin martyr Wilgefortis, who grows a beard to escape marriage and is crucified by an irate father.[64] Since the beard is the most obvious sign and the essential gender marker, not only of maleness but of virility and of virile potency, and women pray to Wilgefortis to free themselves from cumbersome husbands, her story is very liminally heteronormative. As I have argued previously, Wilgefortis and other Virgo Fortis types appropriate male sexual and physical strength prerogatives precisely at a calendar moment when men are thought to be weak and women insatiable, during the Dog Days or Canicula. At this time, women's peripheral bleeding from feet, arms, and hands sheds, unlike menstrual blood, the "terrible blood" of sexual inversion.[65] The second half of Blanchandine's story, her mutilation, is thus another aspect of this appropriation, one that seriously complicates the apparent completeness of the sex change from female to male. The thorns, the abundant bleeding, the piercing of the foot before the final change, are all significant markers of the feminine incorporated, but not obliterated, into the sex change.

The sex-change episode in *TdN* has, not surprisingly, received superficial treatment from traditionalists. Keith Val Sinclair's commentary, so carefully built on knowledge of narrative motifs and their relation to the folk tale tradition, reveals the limitations of a type of folklore study oblivious to gender and sexuality. The disconcerting aspects of this episode are left untouched, its discontinuities ignored, and a reassuring thematic structure based on a string of familiar folklore types and motifs takes over, imposing flatness and completion where there is none. In effect, the genealogies of motifs can be only a tool for interpretation; they cannot tell us how the particular situation was viewed, the complex modulations informing its perception, possibly even contradictory ones (awe, wonder, repulsion, amusement, erotic fantasizing) within a given audience, and even less, whether diverse medieval audiences interpreted these incidents in different ways depending on their own gendered positionality and perhaps even depending on their sexual practices.

Blanchandine is only the second of two women in *TdN* to face battle situations under male guise, for Aye, Tristan's grandmother, fights, while Blanchandine as warrior is ignominiously kept at home over her protests until she has become Blanchandin. Aye (already presumably famous because of previous epics in which she plays a strong role) has masqueraded as the knight Gaudion to escape a man's amorous pursuits and has become so daunting in her new role that she can be captured only by ruse. Her disguise is so successful that she is offered her own daughter-in-law Aiglentine, who does not recognize her, as a sexual prize.[66] The distinction between the two women is noteworthy: Blanchandine is kept from the male-defining activity of war until she actually becomes a man, whereas Aye, who never abandons her female body, is a fearsome warrior whom no one recognizes as a woman. In Aye's case as well, there is some play on the homoerotic potential of Aiglentine's being handed over to her as concubine, whether to underscore the effectiveness of disguise or, less innocently, to play with the "naughtiness" of transgendered situations. Aye's name is changed as well, but unlike Blanchandine—and Silence—it cannot be by mere inflection of the feminine to the masculine form: she becomes Gaudion, a name replete with other sorts of meanings and with the distinctively masculine ending "on." Is this to say that Aye is a fully transgendered person within the still female biological body? The text apparently wrestled with this problem, since in all her aggressive warlike glory, Aye still expresses a "female" gesture: opening her armor and showing her breast to the infant son of Aiglentine, her grandson. For Blanchandine, on the other hand, the only allegedly "female" behavior is her fear of discovery and retribution, but even as a woman, she does not fear battle and is shamed by dishonorable safety. Further, once she has become male she knows no parental gestures other than those of a father.

These women in knight's garb might be mere variants of folklore's woman-as-soldier motif since tale type 504 can feature the final sex change of the heroine.[67] In some of these tales, even though sex changes do not take place, the narrative voice switches from the description of a young girl in male garb to a "he" who ceases to exist only when the final unveiling returns the heroine to the feminine plane of existence. Furthermore, the "fille-soldat" does not always set out to find or protect her lover: in one subtype common in early modern and modern France, she actually seeks him out to challenge him and kill him for his infidelity. Thus, the "fille soldat" theme has not always, even in modern folklore, had a conclusion altogether reassuring to the heterosexual order of gender and sexual relations. The story's nineteenth-century popularity may also relate to another type of narrative on the vengeful violence of women that spread at the end of the century: a seduced young woman shoots or douses with vitriol the man who deceived her; she is then heard and absolved by courts more alarmed by the destruction of the family unit than by women's use of violence.[68] But in the medieval context, the theme of the cross-dressed woman challenges assumptions rather different from our own about women's biophysical and emotional limitations. Most texts in which women cross-dress as warriors imply that physical prowess is well within the scope of what can be expected of women, that their actual bodies experience no difficulty at all in melding into the warrior's craft, and that they are able to function on a par with men in that domain. The "core" of gender that Judith Butler speaks of lies elsewhere, for instance, in the mark, the body tattoo of pregnancy, or, as in Aye's case, in the exposure of the breast. Further, it may well be that women in armor on a battlefield are more of a surprise to the modern mind than we acknowledge. Although such things were certainly not ordinary in medieval France, they were not unheard of, as Megan McLaughlin has suggested, nor were they necessarily taken to be subversive, especially in an adventure narrative.[69]

Remarkable as a cultural attitude is the list of great women featured by Christine de Pizan in her *City of Ladies* (*CL*) This list includes a sizable cohort of women warriors whose presence has been inscribed in fiction as a legitimate theme that raises interesting questions with respect to Christine's construction of gender. Christine's woman warriors may not be that much at odds with the general belief system, in which a figure like Penthesilea loomed large.[70] Helen Solterer analyzed the "Tournoiement des Dames" as a man's dream-vision: warring women who slaughter each other do not galvanize the male narrator's attention because of their military character, but remain, in armor, the object of prurient vision.[71] The reading is astute, but it skirts long overdue questions: how do medieval texts treat rare evidence of violence between women, and was there already an audience for woman-on-woman violence as spectacle? By the Third Crusade and in the Fifth Crusade, some women had been known to engage in operations in the Middle East, although the extent of their military role has been hotly contested,[72] but these controversies remain minor compared to the quasi-routine quality of violence for women in feudal wars. What then is the "Tournoiement" really about? The infraction to gender normativity of women fighting in armor? Or a metaphor of violence between women as a transfer of erotic same-sex engagement? And are men the privileged audience? The homoerotics of medieval violence, discussed in relation to men,[73] have not been applied to representations involving women, presumably because they are rarer but perhaps also because the possibility of such mediated sexuality is not even considered. Yet this possibility is somewhat pertinent to the explosive rapport between Blanchandine and her forceful paramour, Clarinde.

TdN presents the sex-change episode in a way that is particularly interesting precisely because of its many disrupted meanings. The predictable theological reading (woman, an incomplete, imperfect being, lacks that which makes marital intercourse possible, and thus the highest gift to a pious heroine is her sex-change sanctioned by God) is far from the only reading possible. In this narrative a folk and literary tradition with an established genealogy, the theme of the heroine in male disguise becoming the object of another woman's love, takes a very precise turn. From the heavily belabored question: "How will they—could they—do it?" one thus glides imperceptibly over the crucial question, "Why does she pass so well?" Or does she? Does the presumably heterosexual female paramour in these narratives fall precisely for the ambiguous Blanchandine, a *queer* body, and reflect a *queer* desire rather than a desire for a non-performing male? And why do women in disguise, whose height and girth have presumably not changed, attract other women in so many of these transvestite tales, if not by the very androgyny of their cross-dressed bodies? For Michelle Perret, commenting on Ide's appearance as a male, "grant et membru et formé," [tall, well formed and strong of limbs] the answer is: "un dire fausse le regard, la féminité non dite ne peut être vue" [to speak distorts the gaze; unspoken, femininity cannot be seen.][74] But is it exact to say that the femininity of "actual" women is seen *because* it is spoken? The question might be flawed from the onset, overlooking the crucial importance for the visual and the act of seeing of clothing as symbol, as site of representation, and expression of gender and social belonging in medieval texts. In that sense, then, seeing the clothes makes the man or woman, regardless of other body markers: clothing confers on women at least a series of physical qualities that allow them to function as quite creditable male warriors—that is, until matters of heart and bed are involved.

Why then does Blanchandine accept so readily the change offered to her by the angel? Narratively, her acceptance is explained by her despair at Tristan's purported death and by anger that moves her to avenge him, something she can achieve better as a man able to put his enemies to the sword. At the risk of feeding into a rather trite brand of symbolism, one cannot fail to note the parallel "lacks" articulated by sword and member, although women noncombatants do not hesitate to avenge themselves throughout the *chansons de geste,* and non-sex-changed women have been known to pick up a sword once in a while when they are roused to intense anger, as exemplified by Yseut's attempt to execute Tristan in his bath, an attempt chastised for its impropriety. How do these "lacks" then construct the woman Blanchandine as vulnerable, powerless—*impotent,* in fact? If, theologically and socially, the hierarchy of sexual values makes being a man more desirable, we might see many reasons that such a choice should appeal to a medieval woman. Indeed, one is reminded of Christine's cry: "Alas, God, why did You not let me be born in the world as a man, so that all my inclinations would be to serve You better, and so that I would not stray in anything and would be as perfect as a man is said to be?" (*CL* I.1.2), but such rhetoric is absent from this narrative. Thus, in the "off-spaces" or interstices of discourse,[75] persistent questions continue to resonate. Foremost, what makes a text such as *TdN* so obdurately resistant to any solution other than a sex change to the sexual demands made by one woman on another? It is too easy to explain away the formidable silence that erases the mere possibility of sexual contact between women by stating that it could not be conceived of at the time, when there is clear indication that such acts were feared and condemned, as discussed below. Rather, that silence, juxtaposed with the very talkative mode of the sex-changed body and its linguistic and sexual excess, brings the unsaid and the erased out under a glaring spotlight. It is indeed not enough for *TdN* to resolve Blanchandine's lack of performance with a newly sexed body: the new member itself is vaunted, deployed, discursively located as the exclusive proof of acquired manliness; the logistically needed penis has thus become the enshrined phallus.

One also has to ask why Blanchandine, the woman, felt shamed at being publicly reproached for not satisfying another woman sexually (given again the premise that only anatomical conformity to the male sex will do)? Further, how could the newly formed "Blanchandin," who has not shed the memory of his life as Blanchandine, so summarily dispatch his sorrow at finding Tristan alive and his change now theoretically useless, and then rush home to show his stuff to Clarinde? And why did Blanchandine protest being held back from battle by the oversolicitous Clarinde (who, like a true femme, rules the roost with an iron hand) as something shameful ("honte est c'on me tient en cest fermerie" [it is shameful for me to be kept thus locked up])?[76] Attention must be afforded all textual detail pertaining to gendered discourse and behavior in this narrative and not only to the actual sex change, particularly when warfare is linked to sexual conduits (Clarinde "emasculates" the woman who passes as a man by refusing her military prowess, while Blanchandine's female identity "emasculates" the realization of desire). It is noteworthy, for instance, that the He/Blanchandine switches audibly from a meek, threatened female voice to an aggressive male one, the voice of He/Blanchandin, adopting vulgar terms as the sign of his newfound prerogative.

Textual detail in *TdN* implicates the body in much more subversive readings than it does with respect to gendered roles. Passing, in this case, means that this young girl looks, if not like an average virile man, at least like a very androgynous, male-inflected being. This option is confirmed by the text; the hesitations, the slippage from one gendered body to the other even after biological sex has been changed, are brought out in the absurdly dense reaction of a male character. Her brother-in-law Doon first recognizes Blanchandine "herself" in the new man he meets on the road. But when told by his interlocutor that he is mistaken, he is curiously no longer able to retrieve her features and identity as Blanchandine, the woman who passed as a man, in the person of the "new man"—Blanchandin—he is addressing. Ambiguity about gender representation is maintained throughout the episode: the comment "maisement est aidee poulle de la geline" [poorly is the hen helped by the chicken] (13391) is followed by another aviary comparison: [Doon] "Blanchandin a trouvé sautelant con geline" [(Doon) found Blanchandin skipping along like a chicken] (16220). In this curious passage, after the sex transformation, Blanchandin's body language spells relief, but in a blatantly feminized mode. Even more so, this slippage is apparent in the expression of the two women's quandaries over ambiguous appearance, allowing a crucial space, however textually small, to same-sex desire. During Blanchandine's flight, Clarinde laments:[77]

car la beauté de lui le sien coeur enlumine
Ay, dist elle, amis, que vostre beauté fine
M'embrase nuyct et jour d'amoureuse doctrine

Car n'a sy bel de vous jusques a la marine . . .
Adès vise Clarinde se revenir venoit
Blanchandine *la belle que forment desiroit* (my emphasis)

[For the beauty of him so illuminates her heart,
Ah, she says, friend, how your fine beauty
Fires me up night and day with amorous doctrine,
For there is no [man] as handsome as you from here to the sea . . .
And then Clarinde looked to see if Blanchandine was returning
The beautiful [woman/maid] whom she so strongly desired](my emphasis)

Blanchandine's relation to Clarinde is just as ambiguous. First, she refuses to allow a more-than-willing Doon to "stand in" for her at the marriage bed, objecting that as long as Clarinde believes in God (although, in fact, she still is not baptized), "ja ne consentira/Qu'elle soit point deceue, ainçois l'eslongera" ["I will never allow her to be deceived; instead, I will keep her away"]. More ambiguous still seems the following line, which alludes to a religious, not moral, objection to her commerce with Clarinde: "A La loy de Mahon Clarindë espousa/Mais oncques n'y offry, car elle ne daigna" ["According to Mahomet's law she married Clarinde/But never offered (anything) to her, for she deigned not"].[78]

In this narrative, as in other variants of the type, the well-stated predilection of a (very heterosexually defined) woman for an androgynous-looking "creature" raises serious questions about the ways sexual desire could be gendered in medieval cultures. In the interstices of the heterosexual narrative, same-sex modes of desire and affectivity begin to surface and textual details "queer" the *TdN* fiction quite a bit more than mere identification of the obviously unusual sex change: it is no longer possible simply to consider an inadequate woman replaced by a full man as another woman's sexual partner and companion. The importance of paying attention to the discrepancy between the fact of passing for the other sex and the ambivalent readings of that passing by witnesses has been borne out, for instance, by Nancy Partner's discussion of the man disguised as a nun in the monastery of the abbess Richilde.[79]

The heavy-handed insistence on that *one* thing Blanchandine lacks, the *escourgie,* which the newly made man crudely vaunts in front of the whole court ("or sarés que je sçay jouer de l'escourgie/ la lui paroit le membre qu'estoit gros et quarré" [then you will know that I can put my whip to use/and there appeared the member that was big and square]), and his suddenly authorized discourse on the anatomy of sex[80] make public the dirty little secret of male prerogative: that it is located nowhere but in a missing organ, one that can be, by all accounts, quite problematic for its rightful owners and, worse yet, one that a woman could duplicate by unholy means. Again a central question is raised in the reading of *TdN*: "Who speaks? Who is speaking now?" Depending on how one answers that question, Blanchandin's shameless flaunting of the newfound member will appear as either reassuring or parodic, in the sense used by Judith Butler.[81] In this crude, raunchy mode, the flippant exposure of sexual organs, a carnivalesque performance of the properly hidden—costume has not yet evolved to underscore male organs as it would in the next century—serves to mask a more dramatic performance: that of authoritative voice. The question of female authority is posed here as lack, for speaking of sexual organs has been a contested territory that medieval narrative seems to reflect uneasily in the mouths of women.[82] Ultimately, in a certain type of context, a now-axiomatic question can be answered firmly in the negative: no, the subaltern cannot speak—that is, not unless "she" becomes a credible "he." Yet again in this dense narrative, linguistic detail intervenes to unsettle what seemed established. The word used by Blanchandin, *escourgie,* does not in fact denote a "square and rigid member" at all, but the strap of a cat-o'-nine-tails, a lash, a flail. No doubt the term itself had a distinct sexual meaning, as does the whip for a male sexual tool; nevertheless, even if applied to a pliable stick, the word *escourgie* transmits the image of flexibility and sharpness, of slightly unorthodox erotic stimulation, rather than of bluntness and strength.[83]

Thus *TdN,* under its apparent smugness and ineffectual contesting of sex and gender, performs a disruption similar to what Carolyn Dinshaw ascribed to incest narratives in the "Man of Law's tale": while incest doesn't violate patriarchal social organization, incest narratives reveal its violations of its own laws; specifically, "the *Man of Law* tale is absolutely disruptive of masculine prerogative, what the Man of Law mentions first as a tale not to be told, is the tale of feminine incestuous desire."[84]

Examples have been given of early medieval ecclesiastical railings against women who used "certain instruments" ("machinas"), in their fornication, a crime much more serious than ordinary "unnatural" acts.[85] The *Livre des manières* by Etienne de Fougères, written in the late twelfth century, alludes to such practices and to the wicked women who sin against nature. In this passage, the bishop certainly gives the lie to the saying that this sin is too vile to name,[86] and in five stanzas he describes the ladies' passionate intercourse with numerous allusions to the famous lack: they dare to operate without *focil, mance, pilete* or *pirot* [poker, handle, pestle, fulcrum] and engage in frenzied *escremie de jambot* [ham-fencing].[87] Further, the bishop mentions top-bottom roles, describing one woman as lying down and the other moving and shaking, one as a cock, the other as a hen: "l'un s'esteit et l'autre crosle/ l'un[e] fet coc et l'autre pole."

Against this backdrop, then, the sex-change episode in *TdN* takes on particularly ambivalent meanings, with its preposterous affirmation that one woman cannot do anything to another, whether with the help of the *machina* or by "natural" means, that the *jeu* so forcefully required by the lady Clarinde is not only limited to penetration (presumably but not obviously vaginal) but must be accomplished solely with the living male anatomical part itself. These assumptions are predicated on the complete heterosexuality of both women, a predicate that self-destructs, however, because the narrative inscription of androgynous bodies as locus of desire and the carefully constructed passage from female to male are complicated by symbolic patterns of female sexual ambiguity. These presuppositions, these erasures, are considerably enlightened by the concept of "dominant fiction" elaborated by Kaja Silverman.[88]

The repeated claim that nothing can be done until the *membre gros et quarré* enters the scene may appear as anxiety-ridden overcompensation destined to neutralize a complex sexual persona, imbricating male and female several times over. At the same time, it performs a radical occultation of women's body parts and of their potential for providing sexual pleasure other than as passive recipients of penetration. Because of what we do know, it becomes doubtful that the medieval imaginary could be so narrowly cir-cumscribed that other sexual practices were not even conceivable. The dichotomies male/female, aggressive/passive, man/woman, penetrator/penetrated are quite insufficient to frame the hesitations, the modulations, the ambivalences that textual matter can yield, in opposition to the apparent rigidity of the tale-type meaning.

Thus French medieval literature produced a theme, extant in its northern lands at the turn of the fourteenth century, that conveyed a great deal of ambiguity about gender borders and dangerously fa-cilitated the imaginary of same-sex relations. The Aristotelian notion that a woman was an incomplete, deficient male and the Hippo-cratic-Galenic idea that she was a man turned outside in are con-stantly complicated by codas to learned scripts and popular beliefs that reflect the awareness of the at-times-inchoate, at-times-manifest manliness that lurks within women. Anna Comnena could describe the "manliness" to be found in women, using language fitted to de-scribing gladiators and wrestlers that was rooted in the story of the martyrdom of Perpetua.[89] This quality, to be found in exceptional women, stands in complete contrast to *that* which, we are told, no woman can possess, the male organ. But even "that" is not so simple, as the fabliau of the "Gelded woman" [La Dame escoilliée] demon-strates. In Sarah Melhado White's analysis, the mutilation the hus-band performs is fictional, but the woman accepts its reality, her vice (pride residing in *coilles*) being worse than that of men because it is "unnatural."[90] *TdN* mentions no *coilles* at all, except by implication, when both women are referred to as *gelines* ("maisement est aidee poulle de geline"). Yet the belief that women are owners of *coilles* hidden in the body is well established, repeated in the sixteenth cen-tury by Guillaume Bouchet as a given fact, and ingrained in the folk-loric tradition of the obscene innuendo "vos avez escaillié nois" [you have shelled nuts].[91] Miri Rubin discusses an extreme case of her-maphroditism exemplified by a woman of Colmar in 1308–14, who could not have sex with men and, upon being cut open, was found to have a penis and testicles.[92] Such a case emphasizes that women, as a biological sex, could be a troublesome border population, posi-tioned between the fragile male-centered model and hermaphro-ditism and likely to swing illicitly over the great divide.

By charting the life cycle of tale types and clusters of motifs, folklorists are able to provide some evaluation of whether certain texts are subversive or traditional; knowledge of folk tale motifs and types is important also: without it, literary commentators condemn themselves to misunderstand totally texts that are rooted in traditional modes or, at the very least, they use them as tools. In spite of its old reputation as inimical to discussions of sex, folklore can be highly disruptive; indeed, folk tales and other oral narratives constantly reveal society's sexual underbellies, the sexual violence, the coercion and rage, the struggles for power, the acts of mutilation that simmer beneath the polished surface of happy heterosexual couples, families, and communities, incest stories figuring prominently among these.

In this essay, I have proposed an alternative reading of both the *TdN* narrative and folk tradition around the "passing woman" desired by another woman. These traditions may be paradigmatic of societal recognition that such desire is conceivable and writable, and implicitly compromises the established sexual order. Thus the narrative reestablishes some form of that order at its conclusion, so that the danger inherent in female same-sex desire can be contained and neutralized. But in so doing, it cannot avoid lurking in a hazardous border zone, becoming the object of raids in which the very sex of women allows them to relativize the sex of men and leads to reversals and blurring of dominant gender configurations. In this terrain, the heteronorm is relentlessly challenged by queer desire.

Notes

1. Susan Crane, "Clothing and Gender Definition: Joan of Arc," *Journal of Medieval and Early Modern Studies* 26.2, Special Issue: Historical Inquiries/Psychoanalytic Criticism/Gender Studies (Spring 1996): 297–319.

2. See Francesca Canadé Sautman, "L'Epopée taisible"(Ph.D. diss., UCLA, 1978) chap. "La Femme-Homme"; Lewis Thorpe, "Trois guerrières arthuriennes: Maligne, Avenable et Silence," *Bulletin Bibliographique de la Société Internationale Arthurienne* 3 (1951): 104; Lucy A. Paton, "The Story of Grisandole," *PMLA* 22 (1907): 234–76. For a general discussion of options available to disempowered women,

see Joan Ferrante, "Public Postures, Private Maneuvers; Roles Medieval Women Play," in *Women and Power in the Middle Ages,* ed. Mary Erler and Maryanne Kowaleski (Atlanta: University of Georgia Press, 1988): pp. 213–29.

3. John Anson, "Female Transvestite in Early Monasticism," *Viator* 5 (1974): 1–33; Evelyne Patlagean, "L'Histoire de la femme déguisée en moine et l'évolution de la sainteté féminine," *Studi Medievali* 17 (1976): 597–623; Paul E. Szarmach, "St. Euphrosyne: Holy Transvestite," in *Holy Men and Holy Women: Old English Prose Saint's Lives and Their Contexts* (Albany: State University of New York Press, 1996), pp. 353–65; Valerie R. Hotchkiss, *Clothes Make the Man: Female Cross Dressing in Medieval Europe* (New York: Garland, 1996); John Kitchen, *Saint's Lives and the Rhetoric of Gender: Male or Female in Merovingian Hagiography* (New York, Oxford: Oxford University Press, 1998), esp. pp. 101–33; Andrew P. Scheil, "Somatic Ambiguity and Masculine Desire in the Old English Life of Euphrosyne," *Exemplaria* 11.2 (1999): 345–61.

4. "Berenger au Long Cul," ed. Anatole de Montaiglon and Gaston Raynaud, in *Recueil général et complet des fabliaux des XIIIᵉ et XIVᵉ siècles,* 6 vols. (Paris: Librairie des Bibliophiles, 1872–90), 3.

5. See discussion in E. Jane Burns, *Bodytalk: When Women Speak in Old French Literature* (Philadelphia: University of Pennsylvania Press, 1993), pp. 31–48.

6. See Robert L. A. Clark, "A Heroine's Sexual Itinerary: Incest, Transvestism, and Same-Sex Marriage in *Yde et Olive,*" in *Gender Transgressions: Crossing the Normative Barrier in French Medieval Literature,* ed. Karen Taylor (New York: Garland, 1998), pp. 89–105; Diane Watt, "Read My Lips: Clipping and Kyssyng in the Early Sixteenth Century," in *Queerly Phrased: Language, Gender and Sexuality,* ed. Anna Livia and Kira Hall (New York: Oxford University Press, 1998), pp. 167–77; Diane Watt, "Behaving like a Man? Incest, Lesbian Desire, and Gender Play in *Yde et Olive* and its Adaptations," *Comparative Literature* 50.4 (Fall 1998): 265–85.

7. I must disagree with both Joan Ferrante's and Simon Gaunt's characterizations of women's roles in the *chanson de geste.* Ferrante states: "For the most part, women in epic are passive victims of power struggles and wars, ignored when they attempt to participate openly, forced to maneuver behind the scenes" ("Public Postures," p. 216). Simon Gaunt (*Gender and Genre in Medieval French Literature* [Cambridge: Cambridge University Press, 1995], pp. 62–70) argues that women have no place in the ethical system of the *chanson de geste,* even if they are sometimes active. Both readings appear to

me excessively hasty.

8. Burns, *Bodytalk,* pp. 31–70.

9. Sarah Melhado White, "Sexual Language and Human Conflict in Old French Fabliaux," *Comparative Studies in Society and History* 24.1 (1983): 185–210; "escalating horror and brutality," pp. 200–202.

10. Roberta Krueger, "Chascune selon son estat: Women's education and Social Class: The Conduct Books of Christine de Pizan and Anne de France," *Papers on French 17th-Century Literature (PFSCL)* 24.46 (1997): 19–34.

11. In my dissertation, "L'Epopée taisible," I argued for the relationship of the *chanson de geste* to folk culture through both form and content.

12. Robert Nye, *Masculinity and Male Codes of Honor in Modern France* (New York: Oxford University Press, 1993).

13. Herman J. Green, *Anseïs de Metz, according to Ms. N (Bibliothèque de l'Arsenal 3143).* Text Published for the First Time in its Entirety, with an introduction. Paris, 1939. Ph.D. diss., Columbia University, 1940. See my analysis in "L'Epopée taisible."

14. See Thelma Fenster, "The Family Romance of Aye d'Avignon," *Romance Quarterly* 33.1 (February 1986): 11–22.

15. Max Schweigel, *Ueber die Chanson d'Esclarmonde, die Chanson de Clarisse et Florent und die Chanson d'Yde et Olive, drei Fortsetzungen der Chanson von Huon de Bordeaux,* Ausgaben und Abhandlungen no. 83 (Marburg: Elwert, 1889). *YO* covers pp. 152–73. This is the edition referred to in this essay as *YO.* Forms identified are Picard, East Frankish, and Walloon, pp. 31–32; the poet is identified as Picard, pp. 4–12.

16. This is the Turin manuscript, dating from 1311: Turin, Biblioteca Nazionale ed universitaria MS L.11.14, fol. 583v: "ci livres fu escris en l'an de l'incarnation MCCC et XI ou mois de joing" (Edmund Stengel, *Mittheilungen aus französischen Handschriften der Turiner Universitäts-Bibliothek, bereichert durch Auszüge anderer Bibliotheken, besonders der National-Bibliothek zu Paris* [Halle a/s: Lippert; Marburg: Pfeil, 1873], pp. 11–38). It contains the chanson of *Huon de Bordeaux,* followed by several continuations: the *Chanson d'Esclarmonde,* the *Chanson de Clarise et Florent,* the *Chanson d'Yde et Olivier* (*sic*) and the *Chanson de Godin* (Stengel, pp. 11–31). It also contains the *Roman de Sapience* of Herman de Valenciennes and several versions of the Lorrains' saga, all of which are connected to that one region.

17. Cange manuscript (Paris, BnF fr. 819–20) containing forty Marian miracle plays; see Robert L. A. Clark, "'The Miracles de Nostre

Dame par personnages' of the Cange Manuscript and the Socio-cultural Function of Confraternity Drama" (Ph.D. diss., Indiana University, 1994).

18. In fact, Huon *le faé* [the fairy] reappears in the ending of *YO* as a savior of the family, lines 7835–8420.

19. Alessandro d'Ancona, *La Rappresentazione di Sancta Uliva* (Pisa, 1863).

20. Jacques Berlioz, Claude Brémond, and Catherine Velay-Vallantin, *Formes médiévales du conte merveilleux* (Paris: Stock, 1989), pp. 113–21.

21. Tale-Type 706, Aanti Aarne and Stith Thompson [usually abbreviated as Aarne-Thompson], *The Types of the Folk-tale: A Classification and Bibliography* (1961; Helsinki: Academia Scientiarum Fennica, FF Communications no. 184, 1987), pp. 240–41. General type: "The Banished Wife or Maiden," 705–12. Motifs: S322.1.2 Father casts daughter forth when she will not marry him. Q451.1: hands cut off as punishment. T411.1: lecherous father. E782.1: Hands restored. Collections by region: Austrian, Catalan, Czech, Danish, Estonian, Finnish, Flemish, French, German, Greek, Hungarian, Icelandic, Indian, Irish, Italian, Lappisch, Livonian, Lithuanian, Polish, Rumanian, Russian, Scottish, Serbocroatian, Sicilian, Slovenian, Spanish, Swedish, Turkish; also Franco-American, Latin American, and West Indian.

22. For other interpretations, in relation to the story of Salomé and Anastasia, midwives to the Virgin Mary, and Saint Brigit of Kildare, see Donatien Laurent, "Preface," *Philippe de Beaumanoir, Sire de Rémi, La Manekine: roman du XIIIᵉ siècle,* trans. and ed. Christiane Marchello-Nizia (1980; Paris: Stock, 1995).

23. Hélène Bernier, *La Fille aux mains coupées (conte-type 706),* Archives de Folklore (Presses Université Laval, 1971). Historical summary of all written versions, pp. 1–6 and 7–26. Bolte and Polívka counted 186 written variants (Johannes Bolte and Georg Polívka, *Anmerkungen zu den Kinder- und Hausmärchen der Brüder Grimm,* 5 vols. [Hildesheim: Georg Holms, 1963]) and a dissertation was written on the tale (J. Warren Knedler, "The Girl Without Hands," Ph.D. diss., Harvard University, 1937). See also Jean-Louis Picherit, "La Légende du Pape Léon et le conte de la fille à la main coupée," *Neuphilologische Mitteilungen* 84.3 (1983): 297–300; Elie Konigson, "La Fille du roi de Hongrie et le calendrier de la Manekine," in *Arts du spectacle et histoire des idées. Recueil offert à Jean Jacquot,* ed. Jean-Michel Vaccaro (Tours: Centre d'Etudes Supérieures de la Renaissance, 1984), pp. 37–46.

24. Otto Rank, *The Incest Theme in Literature and Legend: Fundamentals of a Psychology of Literary Creation* (1912), trans. Gregory C. Richter (Baltimore: Johns Hopkins University Press, 1992). Thelma Fenster, "Beaumanoir's La Manekine: Kin D(r)ead: Incest, Doubling and Death," *American Imago: Studies in Psychoanalysis and Culture* 39.1 (Spring 1982): 41–58.

25. Robert Clark, "A Heroine's Sexual Itinerary," 103.

26. For an example of such an analysis over a wide range of texts, see Madeleine Jeay, "Sanguine Inscriptions: Mythic and Literary Aspects of a Motif in Chretien de Troyes's *Conte du Graal,*" in *Telling Tales: Medieval Narratives and the Folk Tradition,* ed. Francesca Canadé Sautman, Diana Conchado, and Giuseppe Di Scipio (New York: St. Martin's Press, 1998), pp. 137–54.

27. Michelle Perret, "Travesties et transsexuelles," *Romance Notes* 25.3 (spring 1985): 328–40. From a different perspective, see Jacqueline de Weever, "The Lady, the Knight and the Lover: Androgyny and Integration in the Chanson d'Ide et Olive," *Romanic Review* 82 (Nov. 1991): 371–91. Perret's "Travesties et transsexuelles," while accomplishing the very valuable task of naming the subversions, thus glosses over some other important aspects. For instance, the use of *belle* is not incongruous, as men in chansons de geste are often referred to as *bel et asceme* also.

28. Yde flees for her life after both such encounters; after the first, she is starved and lost, and the second is a very narrow escape indeed; *YO,* lines 6640–6775.

29. Or, in the German tradition, the Kriemhilde of the Nibelungenlied, who is killed as a wretched woman after avenging her husband's death on the unarmed Hagen. For a brief discussion see Ferrante, "Public Postures," pp. 214–15.

30. As Leslie Abend Callahan demonstrates in her essay "Ambiguity and Appropriation: The Story of Judith in Medieval Narrative and Iconographic Traditions," in *Telling Tales,* pp. 79–100.

31. Kathleen Biddick, "Genders, Bodies, Borders: Technologies of the Visible," *Speculum* 68 (1993): 393.

32. *YO,* 6479.

33. *YO,* 7334: "Hui main iert feme or est uns hõ carné," says the angel. The preceding verse, "Dix li envoie e donne par bonté / Tout chou cuns hom a de sumanité," (7230–31) clarifies just what it means to be such an "homme carné." Yde's presentation at the court made this double-sexed identity of her body clear: "Li rois de Rome a Ydain regardé / Mout le vit grant et membru et formé" [the king of Rome looked at Yda/he saw her/him (the pronoun "le" can be

either in O. F.) tall and strong and comely of limb] (lines 6806–6807); then: "Forment estoit grande et fors et formée/Ens v palais est li bele arresté[e]," [she was very tall and strong (the adjective "fors" is now used instead of "membru," which has a clearly masculine denotation) and well formed/in a palace the lovely (girl) went to stay] (lines 6885–86). In the same passage, Yde's disguised identity is underscored by the comment that because of her father, she was "tainte et mascurée" (line 6880), meaning both dyed and masked with darkening substances, and wan and sallow, from hardship.

34. A. H. Krappe on *TdN* in *Romania,* 41 (1935): 55–71; Keith Val Sinclair, ed., *Tristan de Nanteuil,* (Assen: VanGorcum, 1971), and *Tristan de Nanteuil: Thematic Infrastructure and Literary Creation* (Tübingen: Max Niemyer Verlag, 1983), pp. 98–105, 102, 115. See also Keith Val Sinclair, "Proverbial Material in the Late French Epic *Tristan de Nanteuil,*" *Speculum* 38 (1963): 285–94.

35. Sinclair, *Tristan de Nanteuil: Thematic Infrastructure,* pp. 102–103.

36. Keith Val Sinclair, "Murder in the Forest of Mormal and Tristan de Nanteuil," *Romance Notes,* 4.2 (1963): 161–65.

37. Sinclair, "Murder," 162, my translation.

38. Ibid.

39. Keith Val Sinclair, "Notes on the Vocabulary of *Tristan de Nanteuil,*" *Zeitschrift für Romanische Philologie* 78 (1962): 452–63.

40. Robert Louit, "Langues," *Picardie: Cadre naturel, histoire, art, littérature . . . ,* ed. J. Estienne, Y. Brohard, J.-F. Lebond et al. (Condé-sur-Noireau: Christine Bonneton, 1980), pp. 153–69; p. 156.

41. Fabienne Gégou and Jacques Guignet, "Littérature: Moyen Age," *Picardie . . . ,* pp. 172–88; pp. 186–88.

42. Francesca Canadé Sautman, "A Troubled History: Folklore and Competing Texts in *Baudouin de Sebourc,* A Fourteenth-Century Chanson de Geste," in *Telling Tales,* pp. 231–48, and "'Just Like a Woman': Queer History, Womanizing the Body and the Boys in Arnaud's Band," in *Queering the Middle Ages,* ed. Steven F. Kruger and Glenn Burger (Minneapolis: University of Minnesota Press, 2001), pp. 168–89.

43. There are also narrative connections among this group of texts. Once Yde (*YO*) has become carnally male, she engenders a son, Croissant, whose name reappears, albeit under another guise, in *Baudouin de Sebourc.*

44. The story is by now well-enough known to medievalists that a summary should not be needed. It might just be pointed out that Silence grows up reflecting upon her own identity, seeing herself at

once as an imperfect male who fears that she will be incapable of adequate physical prowess when the time of contest comes, and as a woman aware of the lowly status of other women, which she is in no hurry to assume. To test the validity of her borrowed gender identity, she adopts another male disguise, that of a *jongleur,* in an attempt to experience maleness stripped of its military, aggressive nature. Eventually she reverts to the knight-warrior model in which she excels. These hesitations are significant for a history of gender instability in medieval French adventure narratives.

45. The connections among these texts are too many to be fortuitous, and the powerful motif of female cross-dressing and subsequent sex change calls for rereading. The textual groupings can be summarized according to narrative theme as follows:

> *Silence, YO, TdN:* woman in love with woman disguised as man.
> *Silence* and *YO:* father's direct or indirect role in transvestism.
> *YO* and *TdN:* disguised woman changes sex into male.
> *TdN* and *BdS:* lover disguises woman as man to hide her.

46. A wealth of commentary has been generated on *Silence,* some of it going so far as to claim that it expresses lesbian desire and, in many cases, arguing that Silence's final return to the womanly garb and role she eschewed previously and her marriage to the king are disappointingly normative. See the essays collected in *Arthuriana* 7.2 (1997), especially Kathleen Blumreich, "Lesbian Desire in the Old French *Roman de Silence,*" 47–62. Also, among a number of essays deconstructing Silence, see Peter L. Allen, "The Ambiguity of Silence: Gender, Writing, and *Le roman de Silence,*" in *Sign, Sentence, Discourse: Language in Medieval Thought and Literature,* ed. Julian N. Wasserman and Lois Roney (Syracuse: Syracuse University Press, 1989), pp. 98–112; Kate Manson Cooper, "Elle and L: Sexualized Textuality in *Le roman de Silence,*" *Romance Notes* 25 (1985): 341–60; Simon Gaunt, "The Significance of Silence," *Paragraph* 13 (1990): 202–16. In my view, the indictment of the text for failing to affirm lesbian love and permanent gender reversal is thin and overlooks its far-ranging implications for the reexamination of gender, articulated with a certain degree of rhetorical sophistication, which is absent from both *YO* and *TdN.* I would agree with Regina Psaki's assessment (Heldris de Cornualle, *Le Roman de Silence,* trans. and intro. Regina Psaki [New York: Garland, 1991], p. xxxii).

47. Heldris de Cornualle, *Le Roman de Silence: A Thirteenth-Century Arthurian Verse Romance,* ed. Lewis Thorpe (Cambridge: Heffer, 1971), p. 11.

48. Mahaut, daughter of Etienne III of Boulogne and Marguerite of Scotland, became queen of England and, marrying Etienne of Blois, remained countess of Boulogne. Her son, Etienne IV, married Constance, daughter of Louis VI, king of France. Etienne and Mahaut were mainly interested in England and spent little time in Boulogne; their children were raised in England, and both Mahaut and Etienne IV died there. Their youngest son, Guillaume, also ended his days at the English king's court. Their daughter Marie became abbess of Romsey and was the center of long-lasting political turmoil and scandal between 1159 and 1168, when Matthew of Alsace kidnapped her to force a marriage and appropriate Boulogne (Anne-Dominique Kapferer, "Boulogne devient une ville (1113–1339)," in *Histoire de Boulogne-sur-mer,* ed. A. Lottin [Lille: Presses Universitaires de Lille, 1983], pp. 55–86; pp. 58–60). From Cassel and Bouvines, the kings of England were heavily involved in the politics and dynastic disputes of northern France.

49. Heldris de Cornualle, *Le Roman de Silence,* ed. Thorpe, Introduction, p. 16.

50. In *Floovant,* the Saracen Maugalie dons the garb of a soldier; once she is adorned with the requisite costume, her physical appearance changes—"molt bien resanblai home a la grant forchaüre" [she surely resembled a man with a great stride (leg span)], but her name remains the same (*Floovant,* ed. S. Andolf [Uppsala: Almqvist and Wiksells Boktryckeri, 1941], line 1780).

51. André Moisan, *Répertoire des noms propres de lieux et de personnes cités dans les chansons de geste françaises et les oeuvres étrangères,* 5 vols. (Geneva: Droz, 1986), 4:132–33, "Blanchandine sv Blanchandin sv Blancand(r)in, conseiller de Marsile"; 5:iv, "Blancandin, conseiller de Marsile."

52. It is interesting to note that Lambert of Ardres mentions a noblewoman of the north of France who has the puzzling male name Eustache (Lambert d'Ardres, *Chroniques de Guines et d'Ardres par Lambert, curé d'Ardres, 918–1203. Textes latin et français en regard,* ed. De Godefroy de Menilglaise [Paris: Jules Renouard, 1855], pp. 217 and 363). Eustache, daughter of Hugh of Saint-Pol, is betrothed to Arnald of Guisnes, but he later leaves her. The Latin uses a feminized form: Eustochia, Eustacia, but the Middle French translation gives the masculine form Eustache (" . . . fiancha Eusache, fille de Hues Campdavaisne . . .").

53. Lambert d'Ardres, *Chroniques,* p. 175.

54. Teresa de Lauretis, "The Technology of Gender," *Technologies of Gender* (Bloomington: Indiana University Press, 1989), pp. 1–30.

55. *TdN,* lines 16033–204.

56. Francesca Canadé Sautman, *La Religion du Quotidien: Rites et Croyances populaires de la fin du Moyen Age* (Florence: Olschki, 1995), pp. 72–81.

57. Aarne-Thompson, p. 182. Areas: Arabic, Austrian, Danish, Finnish, German, Greek, Irish, Italian, Lithuanian, Norwegian, Polish, Rumanian, Russian, Scottish, Serbocroatian, Slovenian, Spanish, Turkish, Tuscan, Walloon.

58. These mentions do not necessarily make *YO* a "southern" text: there had been commercial and religious links between the Boulonnais and the Mediterranean since 1087, date of the building of the church of Saint Nicholas of Boulogne (Michel Rouche, "L'Age des pirates et des saints (V^e-XIe siècles)," in *Histoire de Boulogne-sur-mer,* p. 48).

59. *TdN,* lines 16170–204.

60. The deer's opposite, the snake, as the feminine: Stith Thompson, *Motif-Index of Folk Literature,* FFC 106–109 (Helsinki, 1932–36), Motif D 513.1, Apollodorus: man looks at snakes copulating and is transformed into a woman; B511.1.2: a snake heals a mutilated maiden with herbs (Rotunda, Novelle italiane).

61. *TdN,* vss. 479–86. The she-deer's original transformation from an ordinary doe (the text uses the feminine neologism *cerve,* or female deer, rather than *biche*) is effected by her accidental ingestion of a bowl of mermaid's milk. She then begins to massacre people (790–93), including the family of the fishermen who had adopted the infant Tristan (801–803). Her ferocity culminates in the killing of a pagan king who was stalking her; after tearing him apart, she devours him (1599–1693): "Il abati le roy et sy le devora, / Mille pieces en fist, celle nuyt en menga. / L'enffes en ot sa part que la best garda" [She killed the king and then devoured him, / In a thousand pieces tore him, ate some that night. / The child the beast was keeping had his share].

62. On the deer and the wild man, see Claude Gaignebet, *Art profane et religion populaire* (Paris: Presses Universitaires de France, 1985).

63. *TdN,* lines 18548–59; 19560–61. Actually, none of this is in the fanciful vernacular vita of the saint: *La Vie de Saint Gilles, poème du XIIe siècle par Guillaume de Berneville,* ed. A. Bos et G. Paris (Paris: Didot, 1880), esp. pp. lxxxii-iii and cxviii-ix. Gilles is himself a profoundly puzzling figure in medieval folklore (see Sautman, *Religion,* pp. 93–94).

64. On the cult of Saint Wilgefortis, see Regina Schweiger Vullers, *Die Heilige am Kreuz: Studien sur weiblichen Gottesbild im späten Mittelalter und in der Barock Zeit* (Bern: Peter Lang, 1997).

65. Sautman, *Religion,* pp. 81–87.

66. *TdN,* lines 1730–2044.

67. At least one tale of that well-known group recorded by Catherine Velay-Vallantin from a Gaspésie teller attests to that motif. See Catherine Velay-Vallantin, *L'Histoire des contes* (Paris: Fayard, 1992), pp. 285–99.

68. Louise-Anne Shapiro, *Breaking the Codes: Female Criminality in Fin-de-Siècle Paris* (Ithaca: Cornell University Press, 1996).

69. Megan McLaughlin, "The Woman Warrior: Gender, Warfare and Society in Medieval Europe," *Women's Studies* 17 (1990): 193–209. McLaughlin's essay makes some interesting points but remains too sketchy and general.

70. For a translation of Christine's poem, see Christine de Pizan, *The Book of the City of Ladies,* trans. Earl Jeffrey Richards (New York: Persea, 1982). Laura Rinaldi Dufresne ("Women Warriors: A Special Case from the Fifteenth Century: 'The City of Ladies,'" *Women's Studies* 23.2 [1994]: 111–31) discusses manuscript illustrations in which the warrior aspect is de-emphasized.

71. Helen Solterer, "Figures of Female Militancy in Medieval France," *Signs* 16 (1991): 522–49. For Solterer, "that the women are made warriors commits them still further to the regime of erotic combat—and without creating space for a female homoerotic" (533, 535).

72. Helen Nicholson, "Women on the Third Crusade," *Journal of Medieval History* 23.4 (December 1997): 335–49.

73. Burns, *Bodytalk,* pp. 164–66, on bonding and exchange in combat.

74. Perret, "Travesties et transsexuelles," p. 333.

75. De Lauretis, *Technologies,* p. 26.

76. *TdN,* line 13671.

77. *TdN,* lines 15897–902.

78. *TdN,* lines 15360–69. In other words, she did not lower herself to touch an unbaptized pagan, but this is a far cry from "she could not do anything to her."

79. Nancy F. Partner, "No Sex, No Gender," *Speculum* 68 (1993): 419–43.

80. *TdN,* lines 16346–47.

81. Judith Butler, *Gender Trouble: Feminism and the Subversion of Identity* (New York: Routledge, 1990), pp. 31–33; 46–48, on Lacan and

masquerade, and p. 138: "The notion of gender parody defended here does not assume that there is an original which such parodic identities imitate. Indeed, the parody is *of* the very notion of an original . . . so gender parody reveals that the original identity after which gender fashions itself is an imitation without an origin."

82. Danielle Régnier-Bohler, "Voix littéraires, voix mystiques," *Histoire des femmes en Occident,* gen. ed. Georges Duby and Michelle Perrot, Vol. 2, *Le Moyen Age,* ed. Christiane Klapisch-Zuber (Paris: Plon, 1991), pp. 443–500; esp. pp. 475–83, "nommer le sexe, dire l'indicible."

83. Godefroy, *Dictionnaire de l'ancien français,* vol. 3, gives *escourgie, escorge, escurge,* 'strap of a whip,' *etriviere* and *escojon,* 'derivative for the virile member,' and *escorge,* 'from the Latin *scutica,* of *escurge,* as in *escorgier, battre a coups d'escourgee,'* and cross-references the term to vol. 1, from BdS, "buleter de son escorjon," *buleter* meaning 'putting flour through a bolter.'

84. Carolyn Dinshaw, "The Law of Man and its Abhomynacions," *Exemplaria,* I.1 (Spring 1989): 117–48; p. 129.

85. E. Ann Matter, "My Sister, My Spouse: Woman-Identified Women in Medieval Christianity," in *Weaving the Visions,* ed. Judith Plaskow and Carol P. Christ (San Francisco: Harper and Row, 1989), pp. 51–62. On the place of "machines" in medieval law, see Edith Benkov in this volume.

86. Jeri S. Guthrie, "La Femme dans *Le Livre des manières:* Surplus économique, surplus érotique," *Romanic Review,* 79 (1987): 251–61. Etienne de Fougères, *Le livre des manières,* ed. A. Lodge (1979), lines 1097–1124. Questions have been raised as to the authenticity of the language in this particular passage, which is indeed somewhat surprising from the pen of a bishop; it is, in fact, very much in tune with the codes and conventions of obscene language, as it is found in the fabliaux and in didactic works. See Robert Clark's discussion of the text in this volume, and for the sources of this language in Arabic texts, see Sahar Amer's essay in this volume.

87. I am using the translations by Robert L. A. Clark in the appendix to his essay, except for the last term, where I keep "ham" rather than "thigh."

88. Kaja Silverman, *Male Subjectivity at the Margins* (New York: Routledge, 1992), pp. 15–52.

89. Vern L. Bullough and Bonnie Bullough, *Cross-Dressing, Sex, and Gender* (Philadelphia: University of Pennsylvania Press, 1993), pp. 66–67.

90. Sarah Melhado White (see above n. 9), "Sexual Language and Human Conflict," p. 202.

91. Sautman, *Religion,* p. 46.

92. Miri Rubin, "The Person in the Form: Medieval Challenges to bodily 'order,'" in *Framing Medieval Bodies,* ed. Miri Rubin and Sarah Kay (Manchester: University of Manchester Press, 1994), pp. 100–122.

CHAPTER NINE

"AT ALL TIMES NEAR":
LOVE BETWEEN WOMEN IN TWO
MEDIEVAL INDIAN DEVOTIONAL TEXTS

Ruth Vanita

> *Some medieval Indian texts, visual and scripted, including the songs*
> *of a woman mystic, represent love between women.*

One of the most important phenomena that developed in medieval India was the rise and spread of Bhakti or devotional mysticism. Arguably rooted in ancient religious practice, these forms of devotion proliferated throughout India from about the fifth century onward, and their multidimensional political, religious, and cultural influences are still very evident in Indian society today. This paper will examine how love between women is centrally built into two canonical texts of fourteenth-century Vaishnava mysticism, one from Maharashtra in western India and the other from Bengal in eastern India.[1]

Same-sex love, although often rendered invisible, disapproved of, and punished, has not been violently persecuted in the Indian public sphere as it has in some other parts of the world. Indian societies have tended to be heterosexist rather than homophobic. One reason could be that various religious traditions from the medieval past still survive in other forms today, and these traditions often make space for different types of ungendering, same-sex community, and the privileging of celibate same-sex love and friendship over heterosexuality.

In most medieval texts, love between women seems to be constructed as a framework that supports the central heteroerotic engagement, whether between human lovers or between devotee and deity. The *sakhi,* or intimate woman friend, is an omnipresent figure in Hindu bridal mysticism—she functions as witness, go-between, and confidante for the heroine, who represents the human spirit yearning for god. The central female figure in the heterosexual romance characteristically addresses her laments of unrequited love or of separation from her divine male lover to her woman friend as often as to her lover himself. This convention is found in secular love poetry as well. The intimate woman friend can also be read as an aspect of the self or as a fellow-seeker; she is close and accessible, in contrast to the divine male lover who is often distant and unavailable. Hence the dialogue with her is like a dialogue with oneself. In the text I analyze here, Mira's speech to the *sakhi* is not nuanced differently from her speech to herself. In medieval miniature paintings that reflect this eroto-mystic aesthetic, the heroine and her friend often look almost exactly alike.

It may be argued then that the woman friend or *sakhi* occupies a psychological space in some ways analogous to the philosophical space occupied by the *sakshi,* 'witness,' which in Hindu philosophy is the real Self that observes the doings of the phenomenal self but does not participate in them. The two are alike and yet unlike, one and yet different—in terms of the classical Vedic trope, one is the bird that eats the fruit while the other is the bird that looks on.

The odd space occupied by the woman friend lends itself to various uses in different texts. That some readers of this space wanted to fill it in, wanted more, is suggested by the popular legend of the life of north India's best-known woman mystic, Mirabai, that developed after her death. This legend tells us more about her ubiquitous but nameless woman friend. The woman, we are told, is her maid-servant and companion, Lalita, who accompanies her from her natal to her marital home and remains with her throughout her life, acting as her amanuensis. Dhruvdas, in his hagiographical account of Mira's life, writes that Mira said, "I will take Lalita with me wherever I go, I have great love for her."[2] The legend concludes with a romantic dual death—when Mira jumps into the sea at Dwarka, Lalita jumps in after her. One interpretation of their togetherness, which is also clearly the basis of the legend, is that Mira was a reincarnation of Krishna's beloved Radha, and Lalita of Radha's closest woman friend who had the same name.

The doctrine of rebirth can be and is used in various ways at different times and places to explain and legitimize intense love between women. In a recent case of two Indian women marrying one another, the Hindu priest who performed the marriage justified it by saying that in a previous birth one of them must have been a man; hence it would be unfair to deny their obviously great love and to separate them in the present birth just because both are women.

In the Sahajiya and Radhapyari cults, female friendship is eroticized in interesting ways.[3] The members of the all-male community in Eastern India that practiced these cults spent their lives dressed as women and took female names, considering themselves reincarnations of Radha's female friends.[4] Their devotional and mystical practice took the form of worshiping Radha and imaginatively reconstructing her life with Krishna. The vicarious participation of the female friend here takes on both a heteroerotic and a homoerotic tinge. Since the participants are all men dressed as women and direct their amorous devotion to a male god, the homoerotic dimensions are in practice male rather than female but are expressed in a community that perceives itself as all-female. Since these supposed women consider themselves reincarnations of Krishna's paramours, the milkmaids of Braja, their status as concubines or co-wives of Radha gives the all-women community a heteroerotic dimension. On the other hand, these devotees express their devotion to Krishna vicariously, through devotion to Radha. This adds a female homoerotic dimension to their devotion.

It is noteworthy that cross-dressing, like the argument from reincarnation or the trope of the sex-change common in Puranic stories as well as in folk tales, suggests that same-sex love can become fully eroticized only when it is expressed as heteroerotic or can be legitimized only when explained as disguised heteroeroticism. These tropes operate most powerfully in the writings of male mystics who address a male god in the terms of bridal mysticism. Numerous devotees in the Vaishnava tradition address Krishna as bridegroom, themselves taking on the role of his consort or of a woman in love with him. Even devotees like Kabir, who take the path of knowledge rather than love, occasionally resort to the trope of bridal mysticism in order to address god. It is a commonplace in Vaishnavism that for the devotional community there is only one male—god, since all the devotees are female in relation to him. This formulation draws on the idea of god as Purusha and nature as Prakriti. It also expresses the devotee's humility—the same mystics who construct themselves as brides of god also call themselves his servants, slaves, or even dogs.[5] The relationship of devotion, even at its most reciprocal, appears to premise difference or the principle of heterogeneity as a prerequisite for union to be desired and to occur.

However, the ubiquitous space of love between women, which is everywhere and nowhere, is capable in some texts of acquiring interesting resonances. In miniature paintings, for instance, the female friend is often present not only when the heroine (most often Radha) is alone and pining for her male lover, but also when the man and woman are together, engaged in sexual play. Sometimes the other female or females act as attendants; sometimes they participate in the love play. But often they occupy a space of their own in the painting and are engaged in their own amorous play with one another. This space is not necessarily marginal in the composition. In one painting on the common theme of Krishna stealing the milkmaids' clothes, while Krishna occupies his mandatory position on a tree to the side of the painting, the central space is occupied by two of the naked women underwater who are clearly engaged in erotic play with one another. In another painting, Krishna feeds his horses, while behind his back, instead of fanning him with the fan she holds for this purpose, his female attendant turns away from him and toward her female companion, at whom she looks yearningly and whose hand she grasps. The fan in her hand is also turned away from Krishna.[6] Many paintings show two women in close interaction with one another, no male being present.

Except where the women's interaction is explicitly sexual, modern commentators almost always title these paintings in a way that downplays the significance of the interaction. We are generally told that the painting shows the heroine recounting to her female friend her pangs at separation from her male lover or that it depicts a female attendant helping the heroine at her toilet. Even with such bland titles, the paintings are often erotically suggestive in themselves. Thus the female friend is a site that has allowed readers, individually or collectively, to construct widely varying interpretations while apparently keeping intact the mandatory heteroerotic devotional framework.

Sakha Bhava, or the mode of devotion expressed as friendship, is a dominant mode in the practice of the Varkari devotional community of western India. Founded in the late thirteenth and early fourteenth centuries by Jnaneshwar and Namdev, this cult still has a large mass following today. The Varkari deity, Sri Vitthal or Vithoba, is identified with Krishna but has a Shiva linga on his head, and would seem to represent a merging of Shaiva and Vaishnava devotional traditions.[7] As distinct from Shringara Bhava, the mode of erotic love in which the devotee approaches god as lover, Sakha Bhava enables the devotee to approach god as friend. This mode allows for greater equality and reciprocity in the relationship since the hierarchies involved in heterosexually constructed gender do not come into play. Sakha Bhava is often complemented in Varkari texts by the tenderness of Vatsalya Bhava, the mode of parental love. The devotees imagine themselves as children and Vithoba as a loving parent, usually a mother, or, conversely, themselves as parents and the deity as an adorable child.[8] This kind of nurturing love is less susceptible to the torturing pangs that are characteristic of Shringara Bhava, devotion expressed in the mode of conjugal love. A devotee's relation to the deity is one of tender and intimate love, often expressed in the image of two mirrors facing one another. As this image implies, perfect devotional love involves the loss of separate identity—it is impossible to tell which mirror reflects which. Significant here is the emphasis on sameness rather than difference.

God as parent of the community of devotees sets up a family that
often conflicts with the reproductive family of everyday life. The
devotee's primary family and ancestry become the chosen one, rather
than the biological or marital one. Ideally, the two fuse when the
devotee's household members all become devotees too, as in the case
of Namdev, but often the tension between worldly family and devotional family is palpable, as in the case of Tukaram, whose verses comically and tragically recount his ongoing battle with his wife, who
violently objects to his neglecting his duties as husband and father.

Women are integrated into the Varkari tradition from its beginnings, and have their own guru lineage just as men do. Their names
are prefixed with the same honorific, *Sant,* as are the men's names.
Janabai, the woman mystic poet whose songs I examine here, is
honored as a Sant by devotees even today, and her songs are very
popular in written as well as oral traditions. Sant Janabai's verses appear in the *Namdev Gatha,* the collection of verses composed by the
fifteen members of the household of Namdev (1270–1350), which
included his wife, mother, sons, and daughters. Her verses are signed
Namyachi Jani or "Jani of Namdev." She was the child of low-caste
Shudra devotees who were apparently compelled by poverty to
abandon her at Vithoba's temple at Pandharpur (in what is now
modern Maharashtra), the center of the Varkari pilgrim cult. The
little girl was taken into Namdev's household in the village of
Gopalpur near Pandharpur and grew up there as the family's maid-
servant.

Janabai's conception of god is, to my knowledge, unique in medieval Indian devotional poetry, insofar as she envisions the relationship between deity and devotee as a relationship between two
women. Male devotees often conceive of Vitthal as a female figure,
Vithai, but this figure appears as a mother. Janabai's Vithai is sometimes a mother but also frequently a woman friend, Vithabai or
Vithalabai. She is fully realized as a woman, the female pronoun
being used to refer to her. Vithabai is described as sharing Janabai's
labor: grinding, pounding, washing clothes, making cowdung cakes,
going to the forest to collect firewood, sweeping, and throwing out
trash: "O wielder of the disc, how shall I repay the debt I owe you?
You have so honored my devotion that when I begin to sweep, you

lift the basket of trash on your head. Jani says, My Vithalabai begins to do even such low work for my sake"(80).[9]

It is a commonplace in traditions of Vaishnava devotion that god appears and participates in the life of the devotee. But Janabai's vision of this participation takes the mirror trope to its logical conclusion by transforming the male deity into a female like herself. The love between deity and devotee is thus constructed as a same-sex love, a love between women. Interestingly, as in the verse quoted above, god is often initially addressed by an epithet that recalls his performances as a male, here as "Chakrapani" or "Wielder of the disc," a conventional although grammatically ungendered appellation of Sri Krishna. This slides effortlessly into the female name "Vithalabai." The fluidity of god's gender in Janabai's verses contributes to the intimate ease of her relationship with her/him, where the most private spaces are shared:

> One day I went to bathe—
> there was not enough cold water to mix with the hot.
> God came running, gave me cool water, saying "Here you are,"
> mixed it with [his] own hands,
> poured it over Jani, over my hair
> —I had not been able to bathe for many days—
> Washed my hair well, saying:
> "Sit still, I'll do it."
> Jani says: Like a mother, god plaited my hair with [her] own hands.
>   (85)

The pronouns translated as "her" or "his" are ungendered in Marathi. The simile in the last line suggests that god is experienced as female or at least that gender becomes unimportant. Women are commonly witnessed plaiting one another's hair in homes and courtyards in India and are often shown doing this in paintings. It is an activity that occurs not only between adult mothers, daughters, and sisters but also between women friends. Bathing together is a scene frequently depicted by painters as a site for same-sex eroticism, as in the painting referred to earlier. Unlike in the mythological scene of Krishna stealing the bathing milkmaids' clothes, god here is experienced not as intruder into the privacy of bathing but

as nurturing caretaker and participant. God here occupies the space
that already exists in several Indian cultural traditions, of the female
friend or attendant who bathes, dresses, and assists at the toilet of the
central female figure in a narrative or painting. God is thus described as helping Janabai to dress and oil her hair:

> Sitting among the basil plants, Jani undoes her hair.
> God takes some butter and oils her hair,
> Says "My Jani has no one" and pours water on her.
> Jani tells everyone, "My friend is bathing me."

Fluids such as water and melted butter metaphorically express the
tenderness, relaxation, and life-giving nature of the relationship.

The particular forms in which god's nurturance expresses itself
are peculiarly female. These are often activities in which even a male
of Janabai's own status would be embarrassed to engage—for instance, picking lice out of a companion's hair:

"Jani was much troubled by lice on her head. Vithabai came running, and with her the other gods too came. They removed the lice
and arranged my hair; now Jani's head is free of impurities" (83).
Here, god is explicitly feminized as Vithabai; in other verses, the
more conventional attributes of Vitthal, such as yellow clothing, are
retained, but the participation in household chores feminizes him
nevertheless:

> I prepare to pound paddy,
> God cleans the mortar.
> Pounding and pounding,
> the lord of Pandhari grew tired,
> began to perspire all over,
> the yellow clothes got soaked.
> Anklets on the feet, bangles on the hands—
> blisters appeared on those hands wielding the pestle.
> Jani said, "Stop now, you've done enough." (87)

Bodily fluids, such as perspiration, and substances or insects nor-
mally seen as impurities, like lice, catalyze this intimacy. Jani and
Vithabai are depicted as sensitive to one another's feelings and desires.
If Vithabai helps and serves Janabai, Janabai too responds to Vithabai's

exhaustion, telling her/him to rest. In her more philosophical verses, Janabai's vision of god as female almost transforms Vitthal into a goddess who is synonymous with the universal spirit, not a consort or subordinate figure: "I eat god, I drink god, I sleep on god, I see god everywhere. I give god, I take god, I deal with god all the time. God is here, god is there, no place is empty of god. Jani says, 'I fill my heart with Vithabai who is both within and without'" (191).

Janabai's most recent translators, Guy Poitevin and Hema Raikar, are at pains to distinguish god as female friend from god as male lover in her verses. While acknowledging that her "relationship with God, shown and lived in the form of a relation of mutual help and intense friendship between two women, is a peculiar trait of Janabai's poetry," they try to separate this from the element of romantic eroticism in her verses, stressing that the god who loves and serves Jani like a wooer is male.[10] But their own citations indicate that no such separation in fact exists—the genders blend and flow into one another: "Jani orders: God comes in all haste to work, makes the house shine, like a Lakshmi." Lakshmi, the consort of Vishnu, is the goddess of household prosperity and is the closest the Hindu pantheon has to a goddess of love. When a daughter is born or a daughter-in-law enters the house as a bride, she is characteristically referred to as Lakshmi, an auspicious bringer of fulfilment and joy. Radiance is connected with Lakshmi, who is welcomed with lighted lamps. In this verse, then, god is envisioned as the Lakshmi of the house, who works to make the house shine.

The one experienced as a female playmate and companion is also the adored one who creates rapture in the human lover: "O Vithabai, come soon. The Bhima and the Chandrabhaga rivers, washing your feet, have become the Ganga. Come with these rivers to my courtyard; play, dance and sing with me. Singing your praise, Namdev's Jani has forgotten all else" (71). The characterization here is romantic and erotic; the woman speaker expresses longing for union and the rapture of love that makes her indifferent to all else. These emotions are addressed to a god conceived of and named as female. The same "Vithabai" who picks the lice from Jani's head occasions the ecstatic emotion that makes Jani call her to come, play, sing, and dance. The waters of the bath have become the waters washing god's feet and are identified with the water of the sacred river. No clear divide exists in Janabai's poetry between friend and lover or among erotic, tender, and companionate emotions. The life lived with god is figured as the shared life of two loving female companions who work as well as play and rest together, who do household chores together as well as tend to one another's bodily needs.

The image of god as mother, common to most mystics in the Varkari tradition, also acquires a peculiar poignancy in Janabai's verse because the conventionally glorified mother-son dyad is displaced by the mother-daughter dyad, and the daughter here is a motherless and lonely woman who was abandoned by her biological parents:

> Why have you become so cruel, Vithai?
> If you forget and leave your child like this, my life will leave me.
> I am your calf and you my mother.
> If you do not come when I call, what will I do?
> Jani says: "I am staying alive with great difficulty—come to meet
>   me now." (59)

Janabai is able to develop this matrix of same-sex love because the tradition within which she operates is open to it. Vithal is frequently envisioned in the Varkari tradition as loving parent of the devotees, equally loving to men and women of different castes, all imaged as equals, brothers and sisters: "My Vithoba has many children—a company of children surrounds him. He has Nivritti sitting on his shoulder, and holds Sopan by the hand. Jnaneshwar walks ahead, and beautiful Muktai behind. Gora the potter is in his lap, and with him are Chokha and Jiva. Banka sits on his back, and Namdev holds his finger. Jani says, "Look at this Gopal who loves his devotees" (30).[11]

Janabai develops the received tradition when she feminizes not only god and the deity-devotee relationship but also the relationship with other devotees, especially older devotees who are in the position of guru. Thus she addresses Jnaneshwar as a female friend, giving him the female name Jnanabai and using the female form of the noun: "My friend [fem.], Jnanabai, my beloved companion [fem.] Jnanabai, O mother doe, give me your affection. I am your child in devotion, love me as the cow loves its calf. Meet with me soon, Jani is tired, waiting so long for your coming" (59). In another verse, she asks Jnaneshwar to be born as her child in the next birth. She also dwells on the immediacy and fully realized nature of god's motherhood: "The bird flies in the four directions in search of food for its nestlings. It flies about in the sky but returns to its nestlings. The eagle flies very high but its heart is on earth below with its children. The monkey swings on the trees but its baby clings to its stomach. So also, our mother Vitthal is at all times near Jani" (89).

The tradition incorporated Janabai's conception of love. As the legend of her life was elaborated, hagiographers recorded miraculous incidents involving god in the form of her female friend Vithabai. Mahipati in his *Bhaktavijaya* [Victory of the Devotees] recounts the legend, originating in Jani's verses, of how Namdev's mother, Gonabai, hearing voices in Jani's hut, grows suspicious and, looking in, sees another woman working along with her. Thinking that Jani has hired this woman to help her and is giving her a share of the grain, she goes with a stick to beat Jani, but the other woman takes the blow on her own head and then introduces herself: "My name is Vithai. I come here early in the morning to help Jani grind." Gonabai is terribly ashamed to realize that she has hit god.[12] The incident is completely in keeping with the tradition of Vishnu the preserver god intervening to save his devotees from persecution and oppression of various kinds. The variation here, of god as female friend, suggests the openness of the tradition to the envisioning of god by individual devotees in forms most appropriate to their own lives and personal needs or desires.

The integration of Shiva's presence at some level into Varkari devotion may function to open the tradition to more eccentric expressions of love, human and divine. Certainly Shiva functions in this manner, as a sanctioning presence for love between women, in another Vaishnava text from eastern India, the *Krittivasa Ramayana*.

There is no way of assigning a definite date to the Bengali poet Krittivasa—some scholars place him in the thirteenth and others in the fifteenth century. The version of the *Ramayana* ascribed to him is an accretive text. It was and is the most popular Bengali version of the *Ramayana*, and additions continued to be made to it until at least the seventeenth century, so that it is now hard to date any portion of the text exactly. Even so, according to some current South Asianist characterizations of the medieval as that which preceded the advent of the British, this text can be considered medieval. It certainly expresses a medieval devotional spirituality.

A feature the *Krittivasa Ramayana* shares with the Varkari cult is its relationship to both Shiva and Vishnu. Krittivasa is said to have been named after Shiva by his grandfather, who at the time of his birth was preparing for a pilgrimage to south India, the center of Shiva worship. Although as a text devoted to Rama, the incarnation of Vishnu, the *Ramayana* is a Vaishnava text, Shiva plays a prominent role in this as in many other versions of the *Ramayana*.

The section I analyze here comes from the beginning of the text, which relates to the ancestry of Rama. Rama is to be born in the lineage of Dilipa, king of Ayodhya. In earlier Puranic versions of the story, as well as in other medieval versions, the childless Dilipa obtained a son named Bhagiratha after he and his wife performed austerities such as worshiping the wish-fulfilling cow, Surabhi. The sage Bhagiratha, the ancestor of Rama, is famed for having succeeded in bringing the river Ganga down to earth from heaven. Three of his forefathers in succession had tried and failed to perform this task. Even today, in many Indian languages, the term *Bhagiratha Prayatna* is the equivalent of a "Herculean task." However, in the *Krittivasa Ramayana,* Dilipa dies childless after his austerities fail to bring down the Ganga or to procure him a son. At this juncture, the gods discuss the worrisome situation—since Vishnu is supposed to be incarnated as Rama in Dilipa's line, how is this to be brought about? Shiva is then dispatched, riding on his bull, to visit the co-wives, now widows, of Dilipa, in Ayodhya. He appears and tells them that by his blessings one of them will have a son. Surprised, they ask how this can be, since they are widows. He then instructs them to have intercourse with one another and adds that since his words cannot be untrue, one of them will definitely become pregnant. The text continues: "The two wives of Dilipa took a bath. The two young women lived together in extreme love. After some days, one of them menstruated. While the two of them were close to one another, knew one another, and enjoyed love play, one of them conceived."[13]

The term that has been translated here as "living together in extreme love" is *sampriti,* literally meaning an abundance or intensity of
love. It may also carry the resonance of the Sanskrit *sam* (together/re-
ciprocal). This is certainly one of the earliest appearances in Indian literature of a term to characterize same-sex love and shows that
modern terms such as *samakami* and *samalaingikta* are not merely post-
Freudian translations of English terms but have an indigenous linguistic ancestry. Michael J. Sweet and Leonard Zwilling have analyzed
ancient Indian medical texts to show that homosexuality was catego-
rized and named as a behavior and also an inclination characterizing
a personality type much before nineteenth-century European sexologists undertook such an enterprise.[14] Foucault's view that the homosexual as a category was the invention of nineteenth-century
sexologists has also been disproved by Bernadette Brooten, who documents the use of "lesbian" by a tenth-century commentator on
women marrying women, and the use of "tribas" and its derivatives
"tribad," "tribadic," and "tribadism" to signify female homoeroticism
from the Roman period until well into the twentieth century.
Among these is an early fifth-century text.[15] Sixteenth-century uses
of terms like tribade and Sapphist have also been attested. It is to be
hoped that the accumulation of such evidence will sooner or later
dislodge the Foucauldian paradigm, which still reigns supreme in lesbian and gay studies and queer theory through the influence of Eve
Sedgwick, David Halperin and others.

Interestingly, the *Krittivasa Ramayana* draws on an ancient medical text, the *Sushruta Samhita,* which states that a child born from
intercourse between two women will be boneless. The Bhagiratha
story is a clear instance of a medieval rereading of an ancient text,
and, more important, this reading occurs in the context of discourse
about same-sex love. Where the *Sushruta Samhita* does not prescribe
a cure for such a child, the *Krittivasa Ramayana* rights the situation.
The child born to Dilipa's two wives is a boneless lump of flesh.
Weeping and fearing social disgrace, they are about to drown him
in the river Sarayu when the sage Vashistha advises them to leave
him on the roadway. As he is lying there, the sage Ashtavakra, who
is crippled (his name means "bent in eight places"), approaches and,
seeing the child from a distance, thinks he is mimicking Ashtavakra's

bent posture to mock him. Ashtavakra says that if the child is mimicking him, he will remain in that posture forever, but if the child is
genuinely crippled he will be healed and become as beautiful as the
god of love. Of course, the child is thereupon cured, and the text
continues: "The sage called the two queens, who took their son and
returned home, delighted. The sage came too and performed all the
sacred rituals. Because he was born of two vulvas (*bhagas*) he was
named Bhagiratha. The great poet Krittivas is a recognized scholar.
In this Adi Kanda he sings of the birth of Bhagiratha."[16]

To the best of my knowledge, this is the only text that recounts
this particular version of Bhagiratha's birth. The text goes on to
describe how the child, studying at Vashistha's ashram, is teased by
a classmate in the course of a quarrel and called a bastard. Upset,
the child does not return home. His worried mother goes in
search of him and finds him sulking in the temple. He questions
her, whereupon she tells him the whole story of his birth, including the etymology of his name. He laughs with joy and de-
cides to set out at once to bring the Ganga down to earth. When
his mother tries to dissuade him, he tells her that although all his
ancestors could not perform this task, he, Bhagiratha, will succeed
in it, as indeed he does.

Thus this medieval retelling of the *Ramayana* makes the offspring
of two women responsible for bringing to earth the sacred river
Ganga, who is central to Hindu practice and in many ways even to
the modern conception of India. As the river Ganga is an autonomous goddess, it is possible that the text provides an explanation through this version for her choosing to come to earth in the
company of this son of two women. The Ganga's connection with
Shiva is well known—she falls through his hair to earth; thus, he
bears her weight on his head. In Janabai's verse, quoted earlier, rivers
that are touched by the feet of Vithabai all become the Ganga—that
is, they achieve ultimate sacredness.

Interestingly, one effect of these texts is in a sense to feminize devotion addressed to a male god by placing it in the context of love
between women. Since the great warrior king Rama, incarnation of
Vishnu, is the descendant of Bhagiratha, the text in effect traces
Rama's origins to two women, more specifically to two vulvas. It

underlines this through its etymology of Bhagiratha's name from *bhaga,* 'vulva.' According to this story, Rama is only nominally Dilipa's descendant; he is actually the descendant of two women. Without the love between these women, Rama could not have been born. The text stresses slippages in patriliny and valorizes the crucial role of women in fostering children.

I have argued elsewhere that dual motherhood is an important component of the privileged condition of many a hero in European mythological traditions and that the love between his two mothers constitutes his emotional ancestry.[17] A similar argument could be made for many Indian heroes whose fathers' multiple wives are all viewed by them as mothers. The *Krittivasa Ramayana* literalizes this situation, making the co-wife not a jealous stepmother but a co-mother. Given Shiva's own interaction with Vishnu and his non-heterosexual creation of sons in Puranic texts, it seems appropriate that he be the one chosen to direct and bless the sexual union of the two women. Once again, he appears as the god of erotic possibility, comically riding up on his bull to set the enterprise in motion. His presence signals sex between women as an auspicious and sanctioned act; their bathing before rather than after they make love also indicates the auspicious nature of the action. Indeed, one is supposed to take a bath before performing an auspicious act, such as worship of a deity, but after an inauspicious act, such as visiting the cremation ground. The *Manusmriti* decrees that a Brahman who has intercourse with another man should take a bath afterwards, thus signaling the need for purification.

In cultures that valorize procreation and legitimize heterosexuality because it can be reproductive, there are at least two possible approaches to homosexuality. One is to condemn it precisely because it is non-procreative. The other is to construct it imaginatively as capable, under special circumstances, of being procreative. This approach has the effect of undoing the possible binary opposition between heterosexuality as reproductive and homosexuality as non-reproductive. While this approach to a certain extent constructs homosexuality in the image of heterosexuality, the texts also acknowledge difference. The Janabai legend does so by showing the female friend as coming from outside the household. She is a secret

entrant into the woman's life and is disapproved of by authority figures in the family. The *Krittivasa Ramayana* does so by its remarkably
imaginative engagement with the experience of a son of two mothers. Like many a child of lesbian mothers today, Bhagiratha is teased
at school but when reassured by his mother acquires confidence in
his own specialness. While Krittivasa, or whoever composed this
text, is unlikely to have come across a child born of sexual intercourse between two women, he could well have come across the biological child of a woman being raised by her with her woman
lover, the nature of the two women's relationship being masked by
their relation within the family as sisters-in-law, co-wives, or co-
widows. There are many such children in India today, and both texts
are also accurate in their placement of love between women in a
domestic space within the patriarchal family.[18] Medieval Muslim
texts also depict love and sexual interaction between women as occurring within the family, unbeknownst to—or even in defiance
of—male relatives.[19]

Like the contemporaneous legend of the god Ayyappa, identified
with Hariharaputra, the son born of Shiva and Vishnu's sexual interaction, the Bhagiratha legend imagines same-sex parenthood; in
so doing, it provides space within the tradition for legitimization of
adoption by those outside heterosexual marriage, and also for co-
parenting of the biological child of one partner by two same-sex
partners. Perhaps this imaginative insouciance will even be scientifically realized if cloning and parthenogenesis one day make it possible for two women partners to have a biological child without the
participation of a male.

Notes

1. Vaishnavism, the worship of the preserver god Vishnu, is perhaps
   the most widespread form of popular devotion in north India.
   Vishnu took nine incarnations (the tenth is yet to come), of which
   the most popular are Rama and Krishna. Devotion to an embodied (*Saguna*) god (such as Vishnu or Shiva) is one path to liberation;
   another path is that of knowledge, meditation on god as disem-
   bodied (*Nirguna*). Embodied gods also take on different forms and
   names in numerous local cults, of which the Varkari cult is one. The

second half of this paper, dealing with the *Krittivasa Ramayana,* is a version of materials that appear in Ruth Vanita and Saleem Kidwai, *Love Between Women, Love Between Men: Readings in Indian Literature* (New York: St. Martin's, 1999).

2. Excerpted in Parshuram Chaturvedi, *Mirabai ki Padavali* (Allahabad: Hindi Sahitya Sammelan, 1983, 17th ed.), p. 233. For the legend of her life, see also Sudershan Chopra, *Mira Parichay Tatha Rachnayen* (Delhi: Hind Pocket Books, 1976) and Nilima Singh, *Mira: Ek Antarang Parichay* (Delhi: Saraswati Vihar, 1982).

3. See Edward C. Dimock, *The Place of the Hidden Moon: Erotic Mysticism in the Vaisnava-Sahajiya Cult of Bengal,* new foreword by Wendy Doniger (Chicago: University of Chicago Press, 1989).

4. The cults have their origin in the movement led by Chaitanya in early sixteenth-century Bengal. See Donna M. Wulff, "Radha: Consort and Conqueror of Krishna," in *Devi: Goddesses of India,* ed. John Stratton Hawley and Donna Marie Wulff (Berkeley: University of California Press, 1996), pp. 109–34.

5. An example is Kabir's couplet: "Kabir says, 'I am Ram's dog, Moti is my name / Ram leads me by a string, I go wherever he takes me'" *(Kabir Granthavali,* ed. Bhagwatswarup Mishra [Agra: Vinod Pustak Mandir, 1986, 6th ed.], p. 61, couplet no. 14). Devotees frequently suffixed the word *das,* 'slave,' to their names, thus Kabirdas, Raidas, Haridas, Tulsidas, Surdas, and so on.

6. The painting of Krishna stealing the milkmaids' clothes is in the National Museum, New Delhi, and is dated to the eighteenth to nineteenth centuries. For a reproduction see Giti Thadani, *Sakhiyani* (London: Cassell, 1996). The second painting is *Krishna Feeding Sweets to his Horses,* nineteenth century, tempera on paper (Herbert F. Johnson Museum of Art, Cornell University, accession number 75.32.3).

7. Shaiva devotion was dominant in southern India and Kashmir; Vaishnava devotion flourished in northern, western and eastern India. Maharashtra, in the southwest, was historically the site for the mingling of southern and northern cultural influences, a rich mix still clearly visible today. See Charlotte Vaudeville, "The Shaiva-Vaishnava Synthesis in Maharashtrian Santism," in *The Sants: Studies in a Devotional Tradition of India,* ed. Karine Schomer and W. H. McLeod (Delhi: Motilal Banarsidass, 1987), pp. 215–28.

8. The most popular legend regarding the origin of the name Vitthal is based on a valorization of filial love. Krishna hears of the great filial devotion of a man called Pundalik and goes to visit him. Pundalik is busy washing his parents' feet and throws a brick for Krishna

to stand on. Krishna stands on it and is so lost in admiration of Pundalik that he forgets to return to heaven. He gets the name Vitthal from *vitha,* 'a brick'. The image of Vitthal in the Pandharpur temple stands on a brick.

9. All translations of Janabai's songs are by Suhasini Pai and myself. The numbering follows *Shri Sakal Sant Gatha,* ed. Kashinath Anant Joshi (Pune, 1967), Vol. I.

10. Guy Poitevin and Hema Raikar, *Stonemill and Bhakti* (Delhi: D.K. Printers, 1996), p. 74. See especially chaps. 3 and 5.

11. Illustrations of this song of Janabai's, showing Vitthal walking along, surrounded by the Sants exactly as she describes, are among the most popular icons of Vitthal even today. The Sants are represented as child-sized adults.

12. *Stories of Indian Saints: Translation of Mahipati's Marathi* by Justin E. Abbott and Narhar R. Godbole (Pune, 1933; rpt. Delhi, 1982) vol. I:351–56.

13. Nandakumar Awasthi, ed. *Krittivasa Ramayana* (Bengali text with Hindi translation) (Lucknow: Bhuvan Vani, 1966), p. 62. This is the text used throughout. Translation into English by Kumkum Roy, modified by Anannya Dasgupta and myself.

14. Leonard Zwilling and Michael J. Sweet, "'Like a City Ablaze': The Third Sex and the Creation of Sexuality in Jain Religious Literature," *Journal of the History of Sexuality* 6.3 (1996): 359–84. See also Sweet and Zwilling, "The First Medicalization: The Taxonomy and Etiology of Queerness in Classical Indian Medicine," *Journal of the History of Sexuality* 3.4 (1993): 590–607.

15. Bernadette Brooten, *Love Between Women: Early Christian Responses to Female Homoeroticism* (Chicago: University of Chicago Press, 1996), p. 22; n 45 p. 22; p. 337; pp. 137–39.

16. Ibid., 63. The formula regarding Krittivasa's greatness would seem to be placed here to counter any possible objections by the reader to the unconventionality of the story.

17. Ruth Vanita, *Sappho and the Virgin Mary: Same-Sex Love and the English Literary Imagination* (New York: Columbia University Press, 1996).

18. Deepa Mehta's film *Fire* (1996) is astute in its representation of the family as the space in which such love can develop.

19. Numerous Urdu poems in the Rekhti genre by male poets such as Ju'rat, Rangin, and Insha were written in the voices of women in the domestic space, discussing their amorous relationships with one another. For translations and commentary, see Ruth Vanita and Saleem Kidwai, *Love Between Women, Love Between Men.*

CHAPTER TEN

LEONOR LÓPEZ DE CÓRDOBA AND THE CONFIGURATION OF FEMALE-FEMALE DESIRE

Gregory S. Hutcheson

By reading Leonor López de Córdoba's autobiographical Memorias *in tandem with chronicle accounts of her tenure in the court of Catalina of Lancaster, we discover the ways in which López's life plays itself out along Rich's lesbian continuum and admits to the possibility of same-sex desire between women.*

Discovering Desire

In one of the more provocative scenes of Fernando de Rojas's *The Tragicomedy of Calisto and Melibea* (1502), the bawd Celestina makes a late-night visit to Areúsa's bedroom in efforts to set up a tryst for the lovesick Pármeno.[1] The dialogue that ensues addresses graphically the matter of female sexuality, both in the banter between the two women and in the implicit sexual foreplay that ends in Celestina's masturbating her young charge:

> CELESTINA. How sweet your bed smells when you move! It's lovely! I always did like the way you do things, your neatness and style. You're a sweet thing. God bless you! What sheets and what a quilt! How white they are! May my old age be as nice! You can see how much I love you if I came to see you at this hour. Let me look you over and take my time about it, I'm so pleased with you.

AREÚSA. Gently, mother! Don't touch me. You'll tickle me and make
me laugh, and when I laugh I hurt worse.

CELESTINA. Where do you hurt, my love? You aren't joking, are you?

AREÚSA. May I drop dead if I'm joking! For the last four hours I've
been sick with the vapors, and they've got up to my breasts and
I hurt so badly I think I'm dying. But I'm not as old as you think!

CELESTINA. Move over and let me explore a bit. For my sins I know
something about that trouble; we all have to go through it.

AREÚSA. It's higher up, over the stomach.

CELESTINA. God and St. Michael bless you, my angel! And how
plump and fresh you are! What breasts! Beautiful! I thought you
were good-looking before, seeing only the surface, but now I can
tell you that in this whole city, so far as I know, there aren't three
such figures as yours! You don't look a day over fifteen! I wish I
were a man and could look at you! (Rojas 85–86)[2]

Celestina demonstrates here both her skills in verbal seduction
(the stuff of *alcahuetería,* medieval Iberia's highly institutionalized art
of matchmaking) and her expertise in woman-centered medicinal
practice. Her treatment for the "vapors" (*mal de madre* in the Spanish) coincides with Galen's recommendation that midwives bring to
orgasm women afflicted with "suffocation of the womb," and gives
evidence for continued recourse to such practice in an age when it
had been all but stricken from the medical record.[3] Despite Celestina's professionalism, however, and even though she pays lip service to the male prerogative both in her turns of phrase ("I wish I
were a man . . .") and her failure to bring Areúsa to orgasm, the
bawd does little to mask her own desires: "Let me look you over and
take my time about it, I'm so pleased with you." Indeed, the episode,
although male-authored and bound up in both ironic intent and the
sexual dogmas of its age, cannot help but admit to a space where female-female desire is entirely conceivable.[4]

I begin with Rojas's *Tragicomedy* precisely because of the ways in
which it challenges the notion that female-female desire was suppressed, invisible, and even nonexistent during the European Middle Ages. The medieval obsession with male homosociality merely
made irrelevant the concern in the (male) written record for anything but male-female (and secondarily male-male) sexuality, fostering what Judith Brown terms an "almost active willingness to

disbelieve" in the possibility of female-female desire.[5] Even in the juridical record, which in so many other ways regulates sexuality, female-female sexual activity rarely comes to the fore. Alfonso el Sabio's thirteenth-century *Siete Partidas,* the law code operative in Spain throughout its Middle Ages, is ruthless in the prescribed punishment for male sodomy among monastics (castration and hanging by the feet until dead),[6] but makes no provisions for punishing female-female sexual activity. And while Gregorio López's sixteenth-century gloss to the *Partidas* would seem to establish gender parity in cases of same-sex sexual activity,[7] those cases actually tried to give every indication that the crime was understood not as a matter of object choice but rather in terms of the threat it posed to the male prerogative.[8]

Since the *Medieval Feminist Newsletter*'s 1992 Gay and Lesbian issue (edited by E. Ann Matter), scholars have been struggling with varied degrees of success to break the patriarchal hold on discourses of desire and to account for the blank spaces where female-female desire should be. What Bernadette Brooten proposes in her groundbreaking survey of antiquity should perhaps be the first step for medievalists as well—the transcending of the male historical record and the understanding of female-female desire as "a subset of cultural constructs of the female, . . . as part of the history of women."[9] So too does Jacqueline Murray urge us to move beyond the "litany of prohibitions and condemnations" that curiously constitute the bulk of Brooten's sources. She engages Adrienne Rich's notion of the "lesbian continuum" as a means to "a more sophisticated examination of human sexuality in the past, an examination . . . that will read from silence and absence, and that, freed from the limitations of genital sexuality, will see medieval women's relationships in their richness, complexity, and diversity."[10]

Ultimately, just as the presence of female masturbation in the *Tragicomedy* serves as a corrective for the obliteration of such practice in contemporary medical treatises, so too does the suggestion of female-female desire intimate the broad-based existence of such desire in an age when it was discursively impossible. Moreover, Celestina's dalliance with Areúsa is not an isolated incident in the text, but rather part of a broad range of "woman-identified experiences" that corresponds readily to Rich's continuum, encompassing not only female-female desire but "the sharing of a rich inner life, the bonding against male tyranny, the giving and receiving of practical and political support."[11] This is most notable in her rhapsodizing about her friendship with the now-deceased Claudina:

> [She] and I were thick as thieves. She taught me whatever I know. We ate together, slept together, and together took our pleasures and did our business. Indoors and out we were like two sisters. I never earned a penny but I shared it with her. If only she had lived I shouldn't have been cheated as I have been. How many good friends does death take from us! For every one it takes after a long life it cuts off a thousand while they're young. If she had lived I shouldn't be friendless and alone. May she rest in peace, for she was a loyal companion and a good friend to me! (Rojas 40)[12]

Throughout the work, Celestina eschews each of the institutions—patriarchal motherhood, economic exploitation, the nuclear family, compulsory heterosexuality[13]—by which women are controlled, emerging as a "woman-identified woman" whose textual presence is so powerful that her name quickly displaces that of the heterosexual couple that constitutes the main intrigue: from the early sixteenth century on, the work would be known only secondarily as *The Tragicomedy of Calisto and Melibea,* and primarily as *La Celestina.*

"The Story of All My Deeds"

In its open-ended constructions of gender identification and sexual object choice, *La Celestina* serves as an ideal primer for learning to read the blanks (as Matter would have it)[14] of woman-identified experience and ultimately female-female desire in medieval Spain. Ample material is to be had not only in the literary canon but also in the far-less-studied historical record—accounts of women who cut against the grain of sociopolitical (and sexual) normativity and so lend themselves to radical rereadings.[15] One such woman is Leonor López de Córdoba, who served as *privada,* or close personal advisor, to the queen-regent Catalina of Lancaster until her fall from grace and exile to Córdoba in or around 1410. She is better known to modern scholarship for her *Memorias,* a brief series of recollections of her childhood and early adulthood that constitutes one of the earliest autobiographies in Spanish letters as well as Spain's first known female-authored text.[16] The *Memorias* in and of themselves provide compelling testimony of female agency in late-medieval Spain, but only by reading them in tandem with historical accounts of a later period at court do we discover the ways in which López's life, like Celestina's, plays itself out along Rich's lesbian continuum and admits to the possibility of same-sex desire between women.

From the historical record we learn that Leonor López was born ca. 1363 in the northern Spanish city of Calatayud. Her father, Martín López de Córdoba, was a close ally of Pedro I and probably for that reason was elected to the mastership of the powerful military order of Calatrava; her mother Sancha Carrillo was niece to the king's father Alfonso XI and had been raised in the royal household. López was still an infant when her mother died and scarcely four when civil strife broke out between Pedro and his bastard brother, Enrique of Trastámara, in 1369. The narrative part of her *Memorias* begins with Pedro's murder at the hands of Enrique in 1369, the retreat of her father and his household to the city of Carmona in southern Spain, and the siege of the city for well over a year by pro-Enrique troops. Martín López finally capitulated in 1371, only to be beheaded by order of the newly crowned Enrique II; his entire household, including his daughter Leonor (who by then had been married to Ruy Gutiérrez de Finestrosa, the son of a well-heeled nobleman who had served as Lord Chamberlain to Pedro), would be imprisoned in the Arsenal in Seville and remain there for almost nine years.

Leonor López recounts in detail the harsh conditions of their imprisonment, as well as the deaths of her brothers and a substantial number of her father's household. When released upon Enrique's death in 1379, López and her husband found themselves destitute and with very little recourse other than the charity of relatives and former allies of the López family then residing in Córdoba. López focuses in the second part of her *Memorias* on her own efforts to regain prestige and financial solvency in the absence of her husband, who had set out to recoup lost holdings. Allying herself with a powerful maternal aunt, María García Carrillo, during the next twenty years she would overcome a series of setbacks, some by rather unconventional means, to amass a small fortune and not a few holdings in real estate.[17]

López's account ends abruptly with the death of her son, a boy of twelve who falls victim to the plague after caring for an ailing Jewish orphan at his mother's behest—this in or around 1400, some time before she enters into the service of Catalina of Lancaster. For her tenure at court, we have to resort to the spotty but highly suggestive references found in the historical record. No mention is made of her arrival, but we can surmise that by 1405 she had already achieved a high degree of intimacy with the queen.[18] The *Crónica del rey don Juan II,* the official account of both Catalina's regency and the reign of her son Juan II, reports: "Although the queen kept company with many other ladies and damsels of great status and lineage, there was one lady, a native of Córdoba by the name of Leonor López, in whom she placed so much trust and whom she loved in such a manner that she did nothing without consulting her."[19] Given that the queen herself cut a powerful figure as co-regent together with her brother-in-law, the *infante* Fernando, during her son's minority, it stands to reason that López's influence over her should have had a profound impact on the course of Castilian politics. The same *Crónica* certainly bears this out, implying what would seem to be an almost deliberate flouting of the (male) political establishment: "And although a decision had been made in the Council comprised of the queen and the *Infante,* the bishops of Sigüenza, Segovia, Palencia and Cuenca, and learned men and knights, if [Leonor López] opposed it, then it was her will that held sway . . . ; and often that which had been decreed on one day would be rescinded on the next, in such a way that the *Infante* could scarce carry out that which his good conscience bid him do."[20]

Such was López's influence that Spanish historian Juan Torres Fontes deems her "the real arbiter of Castile's internal politics for some time."[21] So too does he impute her fall from grace to the *infante* Fernando and goes so far as to call her exile "a veritable *coup d'état.*"[22] However, while the *Crónica del rey don Juan II* does indeed acknowledge the enmity between López and Fernando, it lays more immediate blame on one Inés de Torres, a young noblewoman whose rise at court López herself had orchestrated. Torres, it would seem, replaced López entirely in Catalina's affections; in terms that recall López's own *privanza*, the *Crónica* says: "she held such sway with the queen that all favors were granted by her hand."[23] As for López, Catalina's rancor toward her was so sudden and so complete ("the queen loved [her] greatly, and then despised her because of this same Inés de Torres")[24] that she stooped to almost desperate measures to keep her at bay. On one occasion she sent spies to monitor López's movements and seize both her and her possessions if she showed any signs of approaching;[25] on another, when López did indeed leave Córdoba in hopes of reuniting with the court in Cuenca, the queen "sent word to the *infante* to order [Doña Leonor López] to return to Córdoba as soon as she arrived, asserting that if [she] appeared in her presence, she would have her burned alive. And when Doña Leonor López arrived in Cuenca and learned of the letters the queen had sent to the *infante,* she was distraught to the point of death; and the *infante* consoled her as much as he could and begged her to return to Córdoba."[26] López dabbled little in politics after this final return to Córdoba, dying there sometime after 1412.

The *Crónica del rey don Juan II* gives every indication that López's exile was less a matter of political expediency than it was the fallout of domestic intrigue, ultimately the passage of the queen's favor from one woman to another. Here we have a patently female-centered history (one that even a male-authored historical account could not entirely suppress), and yet it gives way to our compulsion to understand historical process as bound up in male hierarchical structures. López's fall from grace is seldom read within the context of her relationship to the queen (the intensity of which is evidenced both by Catalina's utter dependency on López and by the extremes of passion each reaches in the aftermath of López's exile), but rather as a consequence of her conflictive relationship with a decidedly male political infrastructure. In modern renditions of the tale, blame seems invariably to be deflected from the queen (or Inés de Torres) to Fernando[27] or the Trastámaran courtiers.[28] And buried deep within the discarded woman-centered history is the possibility of female-female desire.

Clara Estow was perhaps the first to challenge the scholarly status quo by foregrounding Catalina in her own telling of the tale and, what is more, drawing the conclusion that López and the queen "enjoyed a relationship that defied accepted limits of convention (and possibly propriety)."[29] Although she implies lesbianism here, she does so perhaps a bit too hastily, based solely on the conviction that rampant anti-López sentiment had of necessity to be rooted in something more compelling than López's "lack of scrupulosity."[30] Furthermore, her reading, despite its daring, continues to privilege the role of male hierarchy by focusing on López less as the enactor of her own history than as the object of male scrutiny. Ronald Surtz takes more definitive steps towards constructing a woman-centered history: Catalina, he determines, was the focus of "a group of strong and capable women," including López and Inés de Torres, and her rule "was characterized by what one might anachronistically call a sense of sisterhood."[31] While he falls short of eroticizing Catalina's and López's relationship, he does invite a reading that breaks the patriarchal hold on history and reveals yet another instance of what Rich would call woman identification and what queer theory now terms female homosociality.

This is precisely the shift Brooten proposes in *Love Between Women*—a privileging of the history of women and woman identification to serve as a vital first step in our historicizing of female-female desire. Surprisingly, we find precedent for it in López herself: in her *Memorias* she boldly confronts the conventions by which she is compelled to make sense of her life. Initially, however, she enacts a rote subscription to these same conventions. Through her opening remarks—part notarial formulation, part stock piety—she positions herself first and foremost as a daughter bound by filial loyalty, second as the passive recipient of mercy from above:

> Therefore, may all who see this testament know how I, Doña Leonor López de Córdoba, daughter of my lord, Grand Master Don Martín López de Córdoba and Doña Sancha Carrillo, may God grant them eternal glory, swear by this sign && that I worship, that all that is written here is true, for I saw it, and it happened to me, and I write it down for the honor and glory of my Lord Jesus Christ and his Mother, the Holy Virgin Mary, who bore him, so that all

creatures in tribulation might be assured that I believe in her mercy and that if they commend themselves wholeheartedly to the Holy Virgin Mary she will console them and succor them as she consoled me. And so that whoever might hear it may know the story of my deeds and the miracles that the Holy Virgin Mary showed me . . .[32]

Occupying a good half of the document is a definitively male history (civil war; her father's last stand at Carmona; the imprisonment of her father's household) to which López serves as little more than witness. Voices speak in this history (her father's retort to the treacherous Bertrand du Guesclin; the high chamberlain's words of solace to the López family; her brother's entreaties to the jailer), but never López's own voice. Men suffer (her brother is loaded with "a chain of seventy links on top of his irons"; her husband is singled out "to be put in the hunger tank"), but never López herself or the sisters and wives who kept company with these men throughout their nine years of imprisonment.

The earmark of this part of the narrative is undeniably male identification as Rich defines it, "the casting of one's social, political, and intellectual allegiance with men."[33] And yet as the male hierarchy falls away from López's account through a remarkable accumulation of deaths (Pedro I, her father, the male members of her father's household), so too does López begin to shed the constraints imposed on her by this same hierarchy. The pivotal moment, tellingly, is her liberation from prison (occasioned by yet another death, that of Enrique II) and her husband's departure: "And thus was my husband lost, and he wandered through the world seven years, a wretched man. And at the end of seven years, while I was in the home of my aunt Doña María García Carrillo, they told my husband that I was doing very well."[34]

The passing of male presence from López's life, rather than disabling her, renders possible, even desirable, her own passing into what Kaminsky and Johnson have termed a "matrifocal family,"[35] a woman-identified social unit whose center is the powerful figure of María García Carrillo. While we have little historical documentation for García Carrillo, López's text suggests that she enjoyed great social and economic independence, enough so that she could dictate with absolute authority the policy and finances of her household. Here, for example, López negotiates with her aunt to open a passageway from the quarters she occupies directly into her aunt's house (this, as she implies, to avoid the public display of her poverty):

> Every night I prayed three hundred Hail Marys on my knees, so that [the Holy Virgin Mary] would put it in my aunt's heart to agree to open a passageway into her dwellings. And two days before my prayers ended, I asked my aunt to allow me to open the passage, so that we would not have to walk through the street, past all the nobility of Córdoba, to get to her table. And her grace responded that she would be happy to do so, and I was greatly consoled. When on the following day I tried to open the passageway, some of her maids had changed her mind, convincing her not to do it; and I was so disconsolate that I lost my patience, and the one who did most to set my aunt against me died in my hands, swallowing her tongue.[36]

In another instance, López prevails upon her aunt to buy for her some lands she had seen in a dream: "And one day, returning with my aunt from mass at the church of San Hipólito, I saw the clerics of San Hipólito dividing up those courtyards where I dreamed the great arch was, and I begged my aunt Doña [María García] Carrillo to be so kind as to buy that place for me, as I had been in her company for seventeen years. She bought and gave them to me with the condition that a chaplaincy be laid upon those houses for the soul of King Alfonso . . ."[37]

García Carrillo's documented largesse attests to "the considerable autonomy of Spanish noblewomen of the fourteenth century"[38] and to the social and economic leverage of a caste of *ricas hembras* (women of the highest nobility) whose intervention in public life anticipates Isabel the Catholic's rapid rise to power at the end of the following century.[39] More striking, however, is López's manifest preference for social and economic allegiance with her aunt, despite her husband's return to Córdoba as many as ten years prior to her acquisition of lands. Sporadic mention is made of him and other male relatives throughout the second half of the *Memorias,* giving every indication that they are present and even active in her aunt's household, and yet they remain utterly inconsequential to López's designs and peripheral to the telling of her tale. Even the building of her estate is construed as a strictly female and highly personal endeavor: "At this time it pleased God that with the help of my aunt and of the labor of my own hands I built in that courtyard two palaces and a garden and another two or three houses for the servants."[40] Until the end of her narrative virtually every negotiation is with a woman (whether with her aunt or, through her incessant novenas, the Virgin Mary), every quarrel with the female members of her aunt's household, every voice that speaks a female voice (this in stark contrast to the first half of the text). Indeed, all of López's desires seem to be bound up in devotion to the Virgin Mary, service to her aunt, and the quest for financial independence.

Despite the conspicuous nature of this shift from male to female identification, few scholars have made note of it.[41] Fewer still are willing to admit to the internal contradictions it occasions—the moments, for example, when motives become blurred or piety yields to pure opportunism. Indeed, most assessments of the *Memorias* continue to fall into a reductionism that privileges the stabilities in the text rather than the instabilities and lends far more credence to how López represents herself than to what she actually says (or indeed, to what she leaves unspoken).[42] In the final analysis, however, any pretense to family honor, piety, or charity gives way to a far more compelling common denominator, the struggle of a female narrative voice to occupy the center of her own story. López implies this in her opening lines when she sets out not only to describe the favors the Virgin Mary has shown her but to tell "the story of my deeds" ("*all* my deeds" in the original—the emphasis is not gratuitous). It is López herself who foregrounds the passing of male presence from her text, López who clears a space for her own subjectivity and discovers in the process the means to give ample expression to the woman-identified experiences that define her life. What we encounter in the *Memorias* is far more significant than simple evidence for woman identification—it is the genesis of a voice empowered to tell the tale.[43]

Privanza and the Sodomitic Text

López embodies both in her text and in her life an "enormous potential counterforce" as Rich would have it,[44] a dynamic that pushes

continually against the confines of male power structures even
though it never manages to break free.[45] By privileging this dynamic in our reading of López—by acknowledging her emergence
as a woman-identified woman and tracing her movement along a
lesbian continuum—we come closer to bridging the gap between
compulsory feminine discourse (always defined by and subject to
phallocratic order) and authentic female subjectivity. What emerges
in López's text is her reliance on the company of women, her tendency toward a female homosociality. Indeed, it is María García
Carrillo and Catalina who constitute the primary relationships of
her life—the sources of her honor and the objects of a political desire at the very least.

    Here we encounter the limitations of Rich's continuum, its com-
placency with a lesbian identity that need only move toward sexual
desire, even if it never fully arrives. Brown calls Rich's continuum
"fundamentally ahistorical in its inclusiveness";[46] more severe critics point to the ways it diffuses identity by "draining sexuality from
lesbians' lives."[47] Discounting Rich's lesbian continuum out of
hand, however, would serve at cross-purposes with the efforts of
medievalists in particular, who, in line with Brooten, strive to reconstruct the space of woman identification as a prelude to the historicizing of female-female desire. But once that space is
constructed, how can we make use of it? How can we inflect it
without compromising its integrity, tease out the presence of female-female desire without crossing the bounds of plausibility?
How, finally, can we give it a voice with which to speak its name?

    The most immediate means of inflection is a privileging not of
the subject herself, but rather of contemporary readings of the subject, ultimately a probing of the anxieties that govern her inscription into the historical record. Curiously, while sources such as the
Crónica del rey don Juan II lay blame on López for "much upheaval
in these realms, and a great dearth of justice,"[48] they do so in gender-neutral terms that forego all the commonplaces of medieval
misogyny. López is cast, rather, in generic terms, as one of a cabal of
"wicked servants" (*malos servidores*) who conspire to stir up discord
between Catalina and Fernando. So too does the cautionary tale of
her fall from grace conclude with platitudes about the nature of the

privanza and the fickleness of the (suddenly male) head that wears the crown: "All of which should serve as a great example to those who hold the *privanza* with kings and overlords; and they should take great care to do always what they ought, and to lend greater importance to the service of their masters than to their own interests. . . . And the condition of men is such that whatever they love in a given moment, in the next moment they despise."[49]

Such assessments expose another of the invisibilities of the Middle Ages—the invisibility of female power, or rather, its discursive impossibility. López is deprived of her agency as a woman, her gender diffused, even erased, her historical specificity flattened as the chronicle pushes to reconcile a woman-centered history with compulsory discourses of (masculine) power. Aristocrat and author Fernán Pérez de Guzmán effects much the same move in his portrayal of López. Although he calls her a "wretched and frivolous woman" (*liviana e pobre muger*), he is compelled less by a glib misogyny than he is by the anxieties of an old aristocracy that found itself being squeezed out by a powerful new class of *parvenus*.[50] Far more threatening than López's gender is her alliance with men who had achieved high rank and great prestige, although "scarcely did they deserve it by reason of their lineage and even less so by reason of their virtue."[51]

It is precisely in this scripting that López enters into kinship with the most notorious of Castile's fifteenth-century *parvenus,* Alvaro de Luna, who would serve as *privado* to Catalina's son Juan II for more than forty years. Luna's career follows much the same course as López's: he springs from relative obscurity to monopolize both the monarch's will and the political process in Castile, invites severe censure from the aristocracy, and ultimately falls victim to the monarch's sudden and decisive change of heart. (Juan II would have Luna beheaded in 1453.) Each accusation launched against López is present as well in accounts of Luna's own tenure as *privado,* indeed, is magnified to the point of obsession in the historical record. Like the "wretched and frivolous" López, the bastard Luna turns his back on his "base and humble origins" to seize the reins of power and dictate "not only the offices, estates and favors the king was empowered to grant, but also ecclesiastic dignities and benefices."[52] If

López is beset by "unbridled avarice," so too is Luna, to such a degree that "like those hydropics who never lose their thirst, he never lost the desire to gain and possess."[53] And if López's fall from grace serves as a cautionary tale for *privados* in general, it is Luna who becomes the archetypal figure of the *privado*-come-to-naught, ground zero for future deliberations on the *privanza* and subject of half a dozen Golden Age plays on the whims of Fortune.[54]

Luna's tale, recounted to a greater or lesser degree in virtually every contemporary historical source, reads as a protracted gloss on the *Crónica del rey don Juan II*'s—or Pérez de Guzmán's—terse assessment of López. But the accounts diverge sharply when it comes to the nature of Juan II's dependency on Luna or the spontaneous move the male narrative makes into the realm of unnatural desire.[55] In a letter addressed to Juan II by a disenfranchised nobility in 1440, Luna is charged primarily with *lèse-majesté* but also with every contiguous crime, including bewitchment of the king and the introduction into the royal court of "the filthiest of all vices, that thing most detestable to both God and nature, which has always been condemned most in Spain, . . . and whose repulsiveness is such that we cannot bring ourselves to name it."[56] Pérez de Guzmán, while certainly more measured in his prose, is equally as provocative in his allusions to the *nefandum*. He notes that he can scarce contain his marvel at the king's "excessive and extraordinary love" for Luna, alleging that not only in political matters but "even in acts of nature he gave himself over to his charge; although he was a young man and well disposed, and the queen his wife was young and beautiful, he would not go to sleep in her chamber if Luna was opposed to it, nor would he pay heed to other women, even though he was by nature quite inclined to do so."[57]

Juan II's "love" for Luna rides always a slippery course between natural and unnatural, between politics-as-usual and perverse desire.[58] Catalina's "love" for López, on the other hand, seems to be inflected exclusively within the sociopolitical contract of its genesis. It is a love whose consequences are decidedly public, predominantly political, never immediately suggestive of spaces beyond the exercise of power. And yet it too smacks of the unnatural, interrupting as it does those natural alliances that should exist between the queen and the illustrious (male) members of her household. This is made clear not only in the chronicle sources already cited but also in Fernando's own testimony, a letter of 1408, in which he alleges that "the queen is of such good will and so well-disposed that [in the absence of Leonor López] she will give of herself wholly in service to the king [her son] and for the good of these realms, and between her and me by the grace of God there will be no more dissension nor discord such as there has been until now."[59]

López's presence in the royal court is ultimately as disruptive as Luna's, as contrary to natural order. And it is certainly this disruptiveness that inhibits normative readings of her relationship to the queen,[60] that politicizes it, exposing it already to sodomitic readings. But it is López's cohabitation with Luna in the same textual space—both the *Crónica del rey don Juan II* and Pérez de Guzmán's *Generaciones y semblanzas*—that invites the wholesale queering of her story. Luna's alleged abuse of the *privanza* and indictment on charges of *lèse-majesté* cannot help but infuse López with all the implications of the charge, inflecting not only the public spaces she inhabits with the queen but also those far more intimate spaces that remain decidedly beyond the capacity of the chroniclers to speak about them. Sodomy, although twice-removed from the female narrative, cannot help but reflect back on the blank slate of female-female desire. Or rather, it adheres opportunistically to the already provocative circumstances of López's acquisition of property, power, and the affections of a queen.

I do not mean to propose the male narrative as an indispensable complement to the female narrative, the only template against which we can hope to fill in the gaps of López's life and begin constructing the spaces of female-female desire. Indeed, it is far less valuable in this sense—in *what* it says and how it coincides with López's tale—than it is in the fact that it *can say* to begin with, in its very capacity to speak about desire. The anxiety it generates, the nervousness with which it deploys discourses of both power and desire not only renders Catalina's love for women as "excessive and extraordinary" as her son's love for Luna. Also, perhaps more significantly, it begins vibrating the vocal cords of López's own text and compels us to listen again to the details of the story she tells, whether her increasing indifference to male agency; her rage at being closed out of

María García Carrillo's household by scheming servants (not unlike Catalina's own paranoid outbursts decades later); or the discord stirred up by her aunt's manifest generosity toward her: "And
her daughters, my cousins, were never favorably disposed toward
me because of the kindness their mother showed me, and from
then on I suffered so much bitterness that it cannot all be written
down."[61]

Most striking here is López's admission that her story "cannot all
be written down"—a rhetorical flourish, perhaps, but one that begins to build closets in her text, suggesting secret spaces about which
words cannot speak but around which they collect in provocative
patterns. These are Sedgwick's closets, silences with a grammar and
an epistemology, an absence of words as textually present as the pro-
lixity of the chroniclers, as bound up in historicity and intertextuality.[62] What remains unspoken in López's *Memorias* (or indeed, in the
chroniclers) is continuously inflected, producing an identity that is
not only expansive but, not unlike Rojas's *Celestina,* actively inclusive of the possibility of same-sex desire.

This identity is bound by its namelessness to linger just beneath
the surface of text and just out of our line of vision; and yet it
seems to emerge the moment we avert our gaze. We need to approach it indirectly perhaps, to cross our eyes and read just beyond
text in efforts to bring into clearer focus that which appears to be
textually absent. What begin to emerge are images far sharper, far
more explicit than those that text itself is capable of representing.
It is a matter neither of a willed revisionism nor rote speculation
but one of a history beyond words, beyond text, yet claiming both
historicity and discursivity in the very strategies by which it has
been rendered discursively impossible. Here is where Leonor
López begins to speak of desire; here is where she evokes untold
spaces, whispers secrets, and finally tells in the fullest sense "the
story of all her deeds."

Notes

1. My sincerest thanks to Reinaldo Ayerbe-Chaux, Emilie Bergmann,
   Anne Cruz, Mark DeHaven, and the editors of this volume for
   their sage remarks on preliminary versions of this essay.

2. Unfortunately, translations to date have been somewhat pedestrian and even conspire at heteronormative readings of this passage in particular. One exception is James Mabbe's 1631 version titled *The Spanish Bawd* and edited most recently by Dorothy Sherman Severin (Wiltshire, Eng.: Aris & Phillips, Ltd., 1987). Mabbe's glosses actually heighten the playfulness and ambiguity of the original text. By way of example, here is part of the same passage with the gloss emphasized: "Sit not up, I pray any longer, but get you to bed, and cover yourself well with clothes, *and sink lower in, so shall you be the sooner warm*. O how like a siren dost thou look! *How fair, how beautiful! O* how sweetly everything smells about thee, when thou *heavest and* turnest thyself in thy bed!" (191). In deference to the original text, however, I have opted here for Lesley Byrd Simpson's more scrupulous translation (Berkeley: University of California Press, 1962).

3. For the suppression of woman-centered medical practice in late-medieval Europe, see Karma Lochrie, "Don't Ask, Don't Tell: Murderous Plots and Medieval Secrets," *Gay and Lesbian Quarterly* 1.4 (1995): 405–17; see also Jacqueline Murray, "Twice Marginal and Twice Invisible: Lesbians in the Middle Ages," in *Handbook of Medieval Sexuality,* ed. Vern L. Bullough and James Brundage (New York: Garland, 1996), p. 101.

4. Dorothy Severin argues that Celestina's lesbianism may be inadvertent here, a byproduct of her calculated effort to arouse Pármeno; see her edition of *La Celestina* (Madrid: Cátedra, 1992), p. 202 n. 25. Such an argument is compromised, however, by the fact that the text makes no point whatsoever of Pármeno's eavesdropping, and this in a work that misses few opportunities to play up the idea of hearing, half-hearing, and mishearing. The text moves, rather, toward Celestina's ownership of the desire expressed in her seduction, toward what Israel Burshatin aptly names "a rare moment of lesbian *jouissance.*" See his "Written on the Body: Slave or Hermaphrodite in 16th-Century Spain," in *Queer Iberia: Sexualities, Cultures, and Crossings from the Middle Ages to the Renaissance,* ed. Josiah Blackmore and Gregory S. Hutcheson (Durham: Duke University Press, 1999), pp. 420–56; see also Mary S. Gossy, *The Untold Story: Women and Theory in Golden Age Texts* (Ann Arbor: University of Michigan Press, 1989), p. 41.

5. *Immodest Acts: The Life of a Lesbian Nun in Renaissance Italy* (Oxford: Oxford University Press, 1986), p. 69.

6. See John Boswell, *Christianity, Social Tolerance, and Homosexuality: Gay People in Western Europe from the Beginning of the Christian Era*

to the Fourteenth Century (Chicago: University of Chicago Press, 1980), p. 288.

7. "Women sinning in this way are punished by burning according to the law of their Catholic Majesties which orders that this crime against nature be punished with such a penalty, especially since the said law is not restricted to men, but refers to any person of whatever condition who has unnatural intercourse" (quoted in Brown, *Immodest Acts*, p. 14).

8. See Brown (*Immodest Acts*, p. 166 n. 5) for the commentary of Antonio López, who recommends the death penalty only in those cases in which "a woman has relations with another woman by means of any material instrument," referring in particular to the case of two nuns who were convicted of "using material instruments" and so burned at the stake. So too does Cristóbal de Chaves observe that "some female prisoners 'made themselves into roosters' by fashioning penises which they tied to themselves." See also Mary Elizabeth Perry, *Crime and Society in Early Modern Seville* (Hanover, NH: University Press of New England, 1980), p. 84. Josiah Blackmore cites a much earlier case, recorded by the fourteenth-century Valencian preacher Francesc Eiximenis, of a woman who, dressed as a man, had not only served as a judicial officer in some unspecified Spanish city but had taken two wives. When found out, she was condemned as a sodomite and hanged by the authorities "with that artifice around her neck with which she had carnally lain with the two women." Such punishment, Blackmore notes, "mirrors that prescribed for men in documents like Alfonso X's *Fuero real* and *Siete partidas:* death together with castration (achieved symbolically here with the artificial penis hung around the neck)." This case demonstrates that in actual practice women were being tried and condemned for sodomy more than a century prior to Gregorio López's glossing of the Alfonsine law codes. See Josiah Blackmore, "The Poets of Sodom," in *Queer Iberia,* pp. 217–18 n. 30.

9. Bernadette Brooten, *Love Between Women: Early Christian Responses to Female Homoeroticism* (Chicago: University of Chicago Press, 1996), p. 25.

10. Murray, "Twice Marginal," p. 208.

11. Adrienne Rich, "Compulsory Heterosexuality and Lesbian Existence," in *The Lesbian and Gay Studies Reader,* ed. Henry Abelove, Michèle Aina Barale, and David M. Halperin (New York: Routledge, 1993), p. 193.

12. Severin once again suggests "lesbianism" as one of the plausible readings (*La Celestina,* p. 142 n. 10). What lends weight to such a reading is the fact that here Celestina speaks candidly, engaging for a brief moment (one of perhaps half a dozen such moments in the text) in discourse that serves no other purpose than that of self-revelation. It bears mentioning that the poignancy of the passage is entirely lost in the English, particularly in the translation of "[Ella] y yo, uña y carne" (literally "[She] and I [were like a] fingernail to the flesh"), a simile employed in Spanish as early as the twelfth-century epic poem, the *Cantar de mío Cid,* to denote the deepest level of (heterosexual) intimacy. On this correlation see Gossy, *The Untold Story,* p. 51.

13. The list is Rich's ("Compulsory Heterosexuality," p. 228), but its application here is only too evident. Notes Gossy, citing Christina Hole: "The main way that Celestina subverts 'the established hierarchy of dominance . . . of . . . man over woman' is through her willingness to encourage sexual intercourse outside matrimony—thus avoiding the legitimizing and controlling power of the church and the economic influence of the patriarchal family" (*The Untold Story,* p. 39).

14. E. Ann Matter, Gay and Lesbian Issue, *Medieval Feminist Newsletter* 13 (Spring 1992): 3.

15. For example, Doña Urraca, daughter to Fernando I, notorious in both history and the ballad tradition for exploiting her sexuality (and her brother Alfonso's affections) in efforts to maximize her own power base; María Fernández Coronel, governess to the sister of Alfonso XI, who ran afoul of the queen-regent María de Molina and was banished for reasons never adequately explained in historical sources; and Isabel the Catholic, whose relentless propagandistic machine capitalized on her half-brother Enrique's alleged sexual inadequacies and so enabled her own performance of masculine power. On Isabel in particular, see Barbara Weissberger, "'¡A tierra, puto!': Alfonso de Palencia's Discourse of Effeminacy," in *Queer Iberia,* pp. 291–324.

16. Alan Deyermond is to be credited with bringing López's *Memorias* to the attention of modern scholarship in his *A Literary History of Spain: The Middle Ages* (London: Ernest Benn and New York: Barnes & Noble, 1971), p. 154. For the first critical edition of the text, see Reinaldo Ayerbe-Chaux, "Las memorias de doña Leonor López de Córdoba," *Journal of Hispanic Philology* 2 (1977): 11–33. The study of López's text has since become a virtual cottage industry. In English, see Alan Deyermond, "Spain's First Women Writers," in *Women in*

Hispanic Literature: Icons and Fallen Idols, ed. Beth Miller (Berkeley: University of California Press, 1983), pp. 27–52; Clara Estow, "Leonor López de Córdoba: Portrait of a Medieval Courtier," *Fifteenth-Century Studies* 5 (1982): 23–46; Amy Suelzer, "The Intersection of Public and Private Life in Leonor López de Córdoba's Autobiography," *Revista Monográfica* 9: 36–46; and Louise Mirrer, *Women, Jews, and Muslims in the Texts of Reconquest Castile* (Ann Arbor: University of Michigan Press, 1996), pp. 139–150. For a more complete bibliography see Ronald Surtz, *Writing Women in Late Medieval and Early Modern Spain: The Mothers of Saint Teresa of Avila* (Philadelphia: University of Pennsylvania Press, 1995), p. 143 n. 6. López's *Memorias* were translated into English by Amy Katz Kaminsky and Elaine Dorough Johnson; see "To Restore Honor and Fortune: 'The Autobiography of Leonor López de Córdoba,'" in *The Female Autograph,* ed. Domna C. Stanton and Jeanine Parisier Plottel, *New York Literary Forum* 12–13 (1984): 77–88. Kaminsky later revised this translation for inclusion in her *Water Lilies / Flores del agua: An Anthology of Spanish Women Writers from the Fifteenth through the Nineteenth Century* (Minneapolis: University of Minnesota Press, 1996), pp. 19–32. This second translation is the one I use throughout this essay.

17. Both Kaminsky and Johnson ("To Restore Honor," p. 79) and Mirrer maintain that López took refuge shortly after her release from prison in a convent in Guadalajara founded by her maternal great-grandparents; Mirrer even speculates that it was here that "Leonor might have received some formal instruction" (*Women, Jews, and Muslims,* p. 143). However, in her *Memorias* López recounts only her intention to enter the order, never its consummation. Indeed, she suggests that it was her husband's return to Córdoba that interrupted her plans (26).

18. Estow speculates that both her husband's blood relationship (albeit distant) to Catalina and the López family's demonstrated loyalty to Pedro (Catalina's maternal grandfather) facilitated López's gaining access to the queen ("Leonor López de Córdoba," 32).

19. *Crónica del rey don Juan II,* in *Biblioteca de autores españoles: Crónicas de los reyes de Castilla,* vol. 68, ed. Cayetano Rosell (Madrid: M. Rivadeneyra, 1875), p. 278. Unless otherwise noted, all translations of primary sources are my own.

20. *Crónica,* p. 278. Chronicler Alvar García de Santa María reads López's influence in a like manner: "And when [the queen] announced what decisions she had made in consultation with her Council, if [Leonor López] were in agreement, that's what would

be done, so great was the love [the queen] felt for her." Cited in
Manuel Serrano y Sanz, "López de Córdoba (Da. Leonor)," in
*Apuntes para una biblioteca de escritoras españolas desde el año 1401
hasta 1833,* vol. 2 (Madrid, 1903), p. 17.

21. Cited in Estow, "Leonor López de Córdoba," 36.
22. A letter addressed by Fernando to the citizens of Murcia in 1408
    certainly does imply that he considered López a force to be reck-
    oned with, both for her undue influence over the queen and for
    her unbridled avarice and ambition: "She [and others] have placed
    enmity between the queen and me in efforts to further their own
    interests and out of their unbridled desire to obtain from the queen
    inordinate riches and boons for themselves and their relatives and
    servants." He baldly recommends that Catalina "remove Leonor
    López from her presence and send her home and no longer keep
    her company." The complete text of this letter may be found in the
    appendix to Juan Torres Fontes, "La regencia de don Fernando de
    Antequera," *Anuario de Estudios Medievales* 1 (1964): 375–429.
23. *Crónica,* p. 372.
24. García de Santa María's rendition is even more provocative: "[the
    queen] was seized with such a loathing for [Leonor López] that it
    was a great marvel; she couldn't even bear to hear her name men-
    tioned" (Serrano y Sanz, "López de Córdoba (Da. Leonor)," p. 18).
25. The complete text of her order can be found in C. García Rey, "La
    famosa priora doña Teresa de Ayala: Su correspondencia íntima con
    los monarcas de su tiempo," *Boletín de la Real Academia de la Histo-
    ria* 96 (1930): 754–55. Here Catalina offers very little justification
    for her actions other than that López "angered" her [*a mí enojo*].
26. *Crónica,* p. 344.
27. Surtz, *Writing Women,* p. 42.
28. Deyermond, "Spain's First Women Writers," 36.
29. Estow, "Leonor López de Córdoba," 37.
30. Ayerbe-Chaux calls Estow's speculation "gratuitous," although this
    also may be too hasty a conclusion. See his "Leonor López de Cór-
    doba y sus ficciones históricas," in *Historias y ficciones: Coloquio sobre
    la literatura del siglo XV,* ed. R. Beltrán et al. (Valencia: Universitat de
    València, 1992), p. 19 n. 8.
31. Surtz, *Writing Women,* p. 42.
32. *Memorias,* p. 21. Scholars are in disagreement as to the authorship
    of this opening, some positing that it was the notary who appended
    it to López's account. Mirrer sees it, however, as a caricature of no-
    tarial style and suggests the much more plausible explanation that

"Leonor herself tried to imitate official language as a means of validating her intervention in the larger, public arena of men's writing" (*Women, Jews, and Muslims,* p. 144).

33. Rich, "Compulsory Heterosexuality," p. 237.

34. *Memorias,* p. 26.

35. Kaminsky and Johnson, "To Restore Honor," 79.

36. *Memorias,* pp. 27–28. That López herself resorted to violence is the least plausible reading here, despite the implications of the text; indeed, Ayerbe-Chaux notes that the original Spanish is far more ambiguous in its wording, leaving open the possibility that the maid died of a seizure ("Ficciones históricas," pp. 20–21). It would be difficult to erase López's accountability, however, particularly given that the maid's "elimination" is entirely consonant with López's designs and would seem to have come about, as she herself suggests, in answer to her prayers.

37. *Memorias,* p. 28. Both the Ayerbe-Chaux edition of the text and the Kaminsky and Johnson translation respect the original manuscript, which reads "Doña Mencía Carrillo," although there is little reason to believe this refers to any but Doña María García. I thank Reinaldo Ayerbe-Chaux for providing me with a photocopy from the original manuscript of the folio in question.

38. Kaminsky and Johnson, "To Restore Honor," 79.

39. For more on the public role of women in medieval Castile, see María Eugenia Lacarra, "Notes on Feminist Analysis of Medieval Spanish Literature and History," *La Corónica* 17.1 (1988–89): 14–22. Notes Lacarra, "since Castilian legislation allowed women of all estates to inherit property and make wills, women had an important role in the economy of the family. This capacity permitted them to administer their possessions in case of widowhood or when they were sole heirs, even if they were married" (17).

40. *Memorias,* p. 29.

41. Exceptions are Kaminsky and Johnson, "To Restore Honor," 79; Mirrer, *Women, Jews, and Muslims,* pp. 146–47.

42. Deyermond calls the work a "piece of devotional exemplary literature—as well as a memoir and a self-justification" ("Spain's First Women Writers," 31); Kaminsky and Johnson read it as an effort on the part of López "to elicit her readers' sympathy and their acknowledgment of the courage, loyalty, honor, and piety she claims for herself and her family" ("To Restore Honor," p. 78); for Ayerbe-Chaux, it is a private examination of conscience ("Ficciones históricas," p. 19). Mirrer is alone in foregrounding López's blatant materialism despite the pieties of her prologue: "Her text tells chiefly of material,

not spiritual, achievement—the prestige of her lineage, the contents of her dowry, and her attainment of such worldly possessions as a home of her own" (*Women, Jews, and Muslims,* p. 149).

43. Mirrer notes: "Leonor's projection in the *Memorias* into the 'female' universe of hagiographical discourse as well as into the public, male discourse of letters and learning is what testifies to the text's roots in a woman-centered and a woman-identified epistemology. . . . [S]he needed primarily a strategy to authorize the telling of her life story, which was otherwise a 'non-story' in terms of medieval Castilian letters (*Women, Jews, and Muslims,* p. 149).

44. Rich, "Compulsive Heterosexuality," p. 234.

45. Mirrer reads López's recourse to an autobiographical mode as "part of a program of resistance—a form developed out of her struggle, as a secular woman, for the interpretive power otherwise denied her" (*Women, Jews, and Muslims,* p. 150). To this we might add her proactive stance both in financial matters within her own household and in political matters while at court. Within a broader program of resistance we might include her adoption of a Jewish boy, an act that was prompted less by charity, argues Kathleen Amanda Curry, than it was by defiance of Trastamaran hegemony; see "Las 'Memorias' de Leonor López de Córdoba" (Ph.D. diss., Georgetown University, 1988). Curry's study reminds us of the need to take into account not only gender in our reading of López's counternormativity, but also her status as daughter of a staunch *perista* (partisan of Pedro)—a status of which she makes us acutely aware throughout the first half of her *Memorias.*

46. Brown, *Lesbian Acts,* p. 172.

47. For an appraisal of the charges launched against Rich, see Martha Vicinus, "'They Wonder to Which Sex I Belong': The Historical Roots of the Modern Lesbian Identity," in *The Lesbian and Gay Studies Reader,* ed. Henry Abelove, Michèle Aina Barale, and David M. Halperin (New York: Routledge, 1993), p. 435.

48. *Crónica,* p. 278.

49. Ibid., p. 344.

50. Fernán Pérez de Guzmán, *Generaciones y semblanzas,* ed. R. B. Tate (London: Tamesis Books Ltd., 1965), p. 34.

51. *Memorias,* 34. Estow implies that there may be some objective truth to this. She points out that López's father gained favor with Pedro (a notoriously populist ruler) for his loyalty and service, not his ancestry; his "meteoric rise coincided with Leonor's birth, allowing her to assert, in somewhat overstated terms, that her lineage was distinguished" ("Leonor López de Córdoba," 26).

52. Pérez de Guzmán, *Generaciones y semblanzas,* p. 40.

53. Ibid., pp. 45–46.

54. See Raymond R. MacCurdy, *The Tragic Fall: Don Alvaro de Luna and Other Favorites in Spanish Golden Age Drama,* North Carolina Studies in Romance Languages and Literatures (Chapel Hill: University of North Carolina Press, 1978). Luna's notoriety would reach as far afield as England, where he is evoked as exemplar of the favorite's fall from grace by English polemicist Michael Geddes in his *Several Tracts Against Popery, Together with the Life of Don Alvaro de Luna* (1715).

55. For a more detailed analysis of the discourse of sodomy as it manifests itself in documentation of Luna, see Gregory S. Hutcheson, "Desperately Seeking Sodom: Queerness in the Chronicles of Alvaro de Luna," in *Queer Iberia,* pp. 222–49.

56. Pedro Carrillo de Huete, *Crónica del halconero de Juan II,* ed. Juan de Mata Carriazo (Madrid: Espasa-Calpe, 1946), p. 331. The text of this letter was incorporated almost in its entirety in the *Crónica del halconero,* at least partially in the *Crónica del rey don Juan II,* making it something of a fixture in the pan-narrative of fifteenth-century Spanish history.

57. Pérez de Guzmán, *Generaciones y semblanzas,* pp. 40–41.

58. For a consideration of the *nefandum* in medieval Europe, see Jacques Chiffoleau, "Dire l'indicible: Remarques sur la catégorie du *nefandum* du XIIe au XVe siècle," *Annales: Economies, Sociétés, Civilisations* 45.2 (March-April 1990): 289–324. Chiffoleau makes a compelling case for reading the *nefandum* as the point of convergence of sodomy and *lèse-majesté,* that space which necessitates efforts "to make the accused speak the unspeakable" and which is obsessively rehearsed in the later Middle Ages "precisely in order to protect the zone of silence and mystery that surrounds legitimate power" (302) [translation my own]. Pérez de Guzmán's text is exemplary in this regard, in that its wonderment—its overwhelming desire to make the subjects speak—derives precisely from a conflation of the king's two bodies and the suggestion that Luna's crimes impinge on both.

59. Cited in Torres Fontes, 427.

60. Readings such as spiritual friendship, which constitutes one of the primary configurations of female-female relationships during the Middle Ages; see E. Ann Matter, "My Sister, My Spouse: Woman-Identified Women in Medieval Christianity," in *Journal of Feminist Studies in Religion* 2.2 (1986): 81–93. So too the familial bond, which, although suggested by letters in which Catalina addresses

López as "mother" (Surtz, *Writing Women,* p. 161 n. 13), is a configuration never adopted by chroniclers.

61. *Memorias,* p. 30. López continues: "And a pestilence came, and my lady departed with her people for Aguilar, and she took me with her, although her daughters thought that was doing too much, because she loved me greatly and thought highly of me." The original Spanish seems more provocative here: "llevóme consigo aunque asaz, para sus hijas, porque su madre me quería mucho, y hacía grande cuenta de mí" (29).

62. Sedgwick defines "closetedness" as "a performance initiated as such by the speech act of a silence—not a particular silence, but a silence that accrues particularity by fits and starts, in relation to the discourse that surrounds and differentially constitutes it." See Eve Kosofsky Sedgwick, *Epistemology of the Closet* (Berkeley: University of California Press, 1990), p. 3.

CHAPTER ELEVEN

"LAUDOMIA FORTEGUERRI LOVES MARGARET OF AUSTRIA"

Konrad Eisenbichler

> *Laudomia Forteguerri's affection for Duchess Margaret of Austria is examined through her five surviving sonnets to Margaret, her contemporaries' comments about it, and the prevailing neoplatonism of the times.*

In his 1541 dialogue *On the Beauty of Women,* the Vallambrosian monk Agnolo Firenzuola unabashedly "outed" two contemporary women—the Sienese beauty and poetess Laudomia Forteguerri and the duchess of Parma and Piacenza Margaret of Austria. Firenzuola did this through the voice of the dialogue's only male character, Celso, who, while trying to expound in lay terms the neoplatonic myth of the androgyne, explained: "Those who were female in both halves, or are descended from those who were, love each other's beauty, some in purity and holiness, as the elegant Laudomia Forteguerra loves the most illustrious Margaret of Austria, some lasciviously, as in ancient times Sappho from Lesbos, and in our own times in Rome the great prostitute Cecilia Venetiana. This type of woman by nature spurns marriage and flees from intimate conversation with us men."[1]

Set in the context of a conversation among one man and four women, this reference by a mid-sixteenth-century writer to love between women is quite intriguing. First, it admits to lesbian love,[2] a concept that medieval and Renaissance thinking on the subject did not generally acknowledge or, if it did, could not conceive outside of traditional phallocentric parameters.[3] Second, it accepts the possibility of both "pure" and "lascivious" lesbian love, thus indicating that it could be both "good" and "bad."[4] Third, it frames the concept of lesbian love within mid-sixteenth-century neoplatonic thought, thus bringing it into the mainstream of the current debate on love. And fourth, it identifies one classical and two contemporary examples of such love, thereby suggesting that it spans time from antiquity to the present. Given these rather unusual suggestions (for their time), it is well worth examining more closely Firenzuola's reference and its context.

The dialogue claims to recount two distinct conversations on the subject of the physical beauty of women held by a young man, Celso, and four women of varied age and marital status.[5] The first part, from which this particular reference is taken, reports the discussion held in a Tuscan garden on a summer afternoon on the idea that beauty is the correct balance of individually beautiful components. The second part reports the follow-up discussion, held some days later at a soirée hosted by one of the four women, when Celso sought to create the ideal beautiful woman by combining the various beautiful parts identified earlier—hair, face, nose, eyes, and so forth. On the whole, this is a completely male-constructed concept of beauty, both because the dialogue is monopolized and directed by Celso, its one and only male participant, and also because the author himself, Firenzuola, is a man. The dialogue is also conceived in strictly male heterosexual terms. Although four of the five participants are women, it is the only man present (a heterosexual in love with one of the young women participating in the discussions) who sets the standards by which beauty in women is to be determined.

That is not to say, however, that some homosexual undertones or elements are not present. As the passage cited above indicates, the Celso/Firenzuola figure acknowledges the existence of lesbian love and accepts it without condemning it outright. Although he qualifies one type of lesbian love as "lascivious," he does not find the entire concept intrinsically evil or abhorrent.

There is also a subtle homoerotic component. In the frame of the dialogue (the afternoon conversation in a garden), the discussion on female beauty is said to have actually started among the women themselves, while they were without male company, and to have been occasioned by their observing, from a distance, the beauty of another woman who was strolling a little further away. There is, therefore, a sensual *frisson* of same-sex voyeurism present in the premise of the dialogue—a *frisson* that is quickly suppressed, not without feelings of guilt, at the arrival of the young man. In fact, as Celso appears the women fall suddenly silent and need to be relentlessly prodded before they reveal the subject of their conversation—another woman's beauty. At this point the same-sex gazing that had occupied the women while they were alone turns heterosexual, for Celso takes control of the conversation, casting his own male gaze upon the four female co-discussants and, in particular, on Selvaggia, the young woman whom he particularly fancies and courts.

Before the dialogue can go straight, however, its queerness must be exposed and exorcised. If this were an allegorical epic poem, we would see how the valiant knight Celso calls out the beast, fights it, and dispatches it. But since this is a dialogue and civil *conversazione,* the endeavor consists instead of an explanation in neoplatonic terms of the origins of same-sex desire, the naming of both ancient and contemporary examples, and their immediate dismissal in favor of a heterosexual discourse on male-constructed ideals of female beauty. The explanation for the existence of same-sex attraction reveals that such desire originates from the same source as its heterosexual counterpart, for both are seen as the natural inclination of two separated halves to reunite. It also points out that people who are attracted to their own sex are numerically in the minority, because the majority of human beings are descendent from beings who, before they were severed in two, were both androgynous and numerically in the majority. This explanation accounts for the much greater number of heterosexuals in contemporary society and possibly explains why Celso/Firenzuola can assume without question the heterosexuality of his entire audience, saying: "The third type, those who were male and female, and who were the majority, are those from whom you are descended, you who have a husband and hold him dear."[6]

What interests us most, however, is not the sidestepping of the lesbian issue but the exposing of two, possibly three, contemporary lesbians. This "naming" is interesting, especially in light of Jacqueline Murray's evidence of an attempt not to name women found guilty of sexual relations with other women.[7] Although the case she cites comes a very different geographic and cultural area (Geneva, Switzerland), it is chronologically near to Firenzuola's time (1568). This "naming" is also noteworthy because in the previous paragraph Celso/Firenzuola pointedly chose not to name contemporary male homosexuals (again a variant from Murray's evidence). He did acknowledge the existence of male-male attraction, saying, "Those who were male in both halves, or are descended from those who were, wishing to return to their original state, seek their other half, which was another male. They thus love and admire each other's beauty." He then drew the same distinction between "virtuous" and "unchaste" love as he would do, a few lines later, with lesbians. However, while he offered three antique examples of men who loved each other "virtuously" (Socrates and Alcibiades, Achilles and Patroclus, Nisus and Euryalus), Celso/Firenzuola refused to name "unchaste" male lovers, either antique or contemporary, calling them "wicked men, more unworthy of any name or fame than that man who, in order to gain fame, set fire to the temple of the Ephesian goddess." Thus, just as Herostratus was condemned to oblivion for having set fire to the temple of Artemis, so too Celso/Firenzuola condemned unchaste male lovers to remain unmentioned and unrecorded—and this in spite of his statement that his female companions were "familiar with some of these [men] even in our own day."[8]

There is no such condemnation for unchaste lesbian lovers. As far as Celso/Firenzuola was concerned, their love was mentionable and their names recordable, so much so that he eagerly recalled Sappho from Lesbos and openly identified a contemporary lesbian, "the great prostitute Cecilia Venetiana."

We have no reliable historical information about Cecilia Venetiana. The 1526 Roman census records two women by this name, but it does not give their occupations, so the connection remains tenuous.[9] The *Ragionamento del Zoppino,* attributed to Francisco Delicado, describes her as "(a Friulian woman), who at the age of twenty was still Jewish; she had herself baptized, took some fool for a husband, ran away from him, and came to Rome with a glutton priest who was sent to the galleys for his virtues; she then took up with a Sienese teller, who put her on her feet."[10] Although reliable historical information on Cecilia is wanting, we may assume that Celso/Firenzuola's reference to her is not devoid of some truth. During his younger years, Firenzuola had moved in the worldly circles of Leonine and Clementine Rome and, as an aspiring man of letters, had come to know a number of courtesans and prostitutes (and contracted syphilis along the way). His Cecilia Venetiana may be based on personal knowledge of a specific woman whom his readers, and especially his circle of male friends, might have recognized. She could also be a composite of various Roman prostitutes and courtesans. Cecilia was certainly not the only prostitute with a female lover. In his "Discours sur les Dames qui font l'amour et leurs maris cocus," Pierre de Bourdeille, Seigneur de Brantôme, personally recalled a courtesan in Rome who had a lesbian relationship with another woman.[11] Speaking later of sexual acts between women, Brantôme added that "courtesans, who still have plenty of men available to them all the time, indulge in this rubbing (*fricarelles*), and seek each other out and love each other, as I have heard it said in Italy and in Spain."[12] On the other hand, the reference to lesbian courtesans and their sexual activities with each other may be nothing more than a male sexual fantasy akin to lesbian pornography for consumption by heterosexual males, and as such it may have little basis in fact. Whatever the case, in Firenzuola's narrative Cecilia Venetiana represents, by virtue of both her "lasciviousness" and her profession, the unsavory—that is, carnal—aspect of lesbian attraction and activity.

While Cecilia Venetiana remains unknown and unsavory, Laudomia Forteguerri and Margaret of Austria are historical women presented as acceptable examples of same-sex female love. Very little is known of the historical Laudomia Forteguerri (1515–1555?). She was born into the Sienese nobility, married twice, both times into two of the most important families of her city (the Colombini before 1535

and the Petrucci in 1544), bore three children, composed a number
of sonnets, and disappeared from the records sometime around 1555.
The Sienese intellectual Alessandro Piccolomini dedicated several of
his works to her and composed Petrarchan poetry in praise of her.
Giuseppe Betussi from Bassano praised her as one of the twelve most
beautiful women in Italy and made her an emblem of "true" fame
(that is, heavenly as opposed to earthly fame). And, to this day, she is
reputed to be one of the three courageous "ladies of Siena" who, during the siege of 1555, organized and led a troupe of 3,000 women in
defense of their city.[13]

Margaret of Austria, duchess of Parma and Piacenza
(1522–1586), was born in Oudenaarde, Flanders, the illegitimate
daughter of the Emperor Charles V and a local Flemish noblewoman, Johanna van der Gheenst. While still very young she was
married first to Duke Alessandro de'Medici of Florence (1536) and
then, shortly after his assassination (1537), to Duke Ottavio Farnese
of Parma and Piacenza (1538). She served her stepbrother King
Philip of Spain twice as governor of the Netherlands (1559–1567,
1580–1583). Eventually she retired to a quiet country life in her
duchy of Penne (in the central Italian region of the Abruzzi), which
she had inherited on the death of her first husband. Unlike Laudomia, she was not renowned for her beauty. She grew heavier with
age, appeared masculine, and developed a light mustache. Her personality apparently matched her appearance—Ludwig Pastor describes her as "that virile character Margaret of Austria."[14]

We do not know when or even if Margaret and Laudomia met.
Archival sources fail to record their encounter or even to provide
documents that would attest to any contact between them. The
only contemporary reference is literary and comes from Alessandro
Piccolomini's preface to the unauthorized publication of a lecture
he delivered in the fall of 1540 at the renowned literary academy of
the Infiammati in Padua.[15] Expounding Forteguerri's sonnet "Hora
ten' vai superbo, hor corri altiero," Alessandro informs his public
that Laudomia met Margaret in 1535 when the emperor's young
daughter was passing through Siena on her way from Rome to Florence to marry Duke Alessandro de'Medici. The two women met
at a *festa* in honor of Margaret, and "as soon as Laudomia saw

Madama, and was seen by her, suddenly with the most ardent flames
of Love each burned for the other, and the most manifest sign of
this was that they went to visit each other many times" [La qual
(Laudomia) come prima uidde Madama, e dà quella fù ueduta al-
tresì, subito di ardentissime fiamme d'Amore, l'una de l'altra si ac-
cese, di che manifestissimo segno fù, che più uolte da poi con
ambasciate si uisitarono].[16] Their relationship, Alessandro adds, was
rekindled three years later, in 1538, when Margaret, now the young
widow of the assassinated Duke Alessandro, passed through Siena on
her return journey from Florence to Rome. To cite Piccolomini
once again: "And when this great Madama passed once again
through Siena, two years ago, on her journey to Rome, they renewed most happily their sweet Loves, and today more than ever,
with notes from one to the other they warmly maintain them" [Et
al passar che fece, questa gran Madama nuouamente per Siena, due
anni sono, ne la sua andata di Roma, felicemente i dolcissimi loro
Amori rinnouarono, & oggi più che mai, con auisi e da questa parte
e da quella caldamente conseruano].[17]

Without a doubt, the terminology Piccolomini used to describe
the affection between the two noble women is very strong—"with
the most ardent flames of Love each burned for the other" or "they
renewed most happily their sweet Loves" may be bland phrases in
standard Petrarchan love poetry, but they are not so when applied to
the affections felt by two flesh-and-blood contemporary women for
each other. As he was making these statements, Piccolomini was also
keen to point out that this love was not something low, vile, and
sexual but rather something high, refined, and spiritual. For this reason, he devoted a significant part of his introduction to a definition
and a discussion of love, pointing out:

> Love is not a low desire, a vile and unbounded urge, as perhaps
> those who denigrate it would think, but the most happy acquisition
> of a virtuous spirit. The aim of the most perfect love . . . consists in
> nothing else but the possession of the virtuous spirit of one's
> beloved, that is, in being loved by her. And that man who loves as
> is appropriate will achieve this end, since, according to Aristotle in
> book VIII of his Ethics, a true lover cannot help but be loved, as also
> Dante says in the 20th canto of Purgatory. Therefore, if a man truly

loves and contemplates his beloved constantly, either from nearby or from afar, it is impossible for him not to live happily, imbibing with his mind's eyes a certain hidden sweetness, that could never be understood by anyone who has not experienced it.[18]

Piccolomini's words are not new to anyone who has studied medieval and Renaissance theories of love, or has read Dante or Petrarch. There are clear echoes not only of Aristotle and Dante, to whom he refers, but also of earlier Italian love poetry, especially the works of Guido Guinizelli (ca. 1235–1276) and the Sweet New Style (*Dolce Stil Nuovo*) poets of the 1290s to the 1320s. What is relatively new, however, is that these theories on love are applied to the affection existing between two sixteenth-century women.

Far from seeing female same-sex attraction as a problem, Piccolomini presents it as proof positive that this is a higher, purer, and more appropriate form of love. As he points out, the love between two women clearly cannot be procreative and therefore must be pure: "Nor, may it please God, is the Love, which I will speak about today with the reverence that is appropriate to it, the same as that love that we have in common with the beasts and leads us and pushes us to procreate. And this I have on several occasions in this locale sought to explain with valid reasons; and today as well, to support my view, I will give you an example of a most ardent Love that exists in our time not between a man and a woman, no, but between two most unique and most divine women."[19]

In other words, given that two women cannot procreate with each other, the love that joins them cannot be, in Piccolomini's view, the same as that animal urge that drives heterosexual couples to copulation and reproduction. Marc'Antonio da Carpi, Piccolomini's publisher, voiced more or less the same idea, pointing out in his editor's preface: "Here one will see most beautiful and above all most honest discussions on Love, nor will these discussions speak of vile and low Love, but of a Love that is rare in our times and marvellous, and [exists] between two great women of our age."[20]

Laudomia Forteguerri's love for Margaret of Austria was expressed in five of her six surviving sonnets.[21] The first to appear in print (1540), and the one on which Alessandro Piccolomini commented at the academy of the Infiammati, was "Hora ten' vai superbo, hor corri altiero" [Now you go proudly, now you run haughtily].

Ora ten' vai superbo, or corri altiero
Pingendo di bei fiori ambe le sponde
Antico Tebro; or ben purgate l'onde
Rendon l'imago a un sol più chiaro, e vero:
　Ora porti lo scettro, ora hai l'impero
Dei piu famosi: or averai tu donde
Verdeggian più che mai liete, e feconde
Le belle rive: or hai l'essere intero,
　Poi ch'egli è teco il vago almo mio sole,
Non or lungi, or vicin, ma sempre appresso;
E bagni il lembo dell'altiera gonna:
　Ch'arte, natura, e 'l ciel, e così vuole
Che 'l tutto può, mostran pur oggi espresso,
Che star ben pote al mondo immortal donna.

　[Now you go proudly, now you run haughtily,
Coloring both your riverbanks with flowers,
Ancient Tiber; now your waves well purified
Yield the image of a clearer, truer sun:
　Now you hold the scepter, now you command
Over more famous {rivers}: now there's reason
For your pretty banks to flourish green, happy
And fruitful more than ever; now you are fulfilled,
　For my noble, graceful sun is now with you,
Not distant now, now near, always besides you;
And you moisten the hem of that stately gown:
　For art, nature, and heaven, and the one who
Can do all want this, they clearly show today
An immortal woman can dwell in this world.]

As we can see, Laudomia's love for Margaret of Austria is articulated along the lines of traditional Italian lyric poetry. The sonnet is addressed to the river Tiber that flows proudly because the poet's "noble, graceful sun" stands by its shores. In keeping with Petrarchan poetry, the poet describes the effect the beloved has on the nature that surrounds her. The images that follow are not unusual: with her mere presence the beloved delights and replenishes all of nature around her and in so doing reveals she is a creature of heaven descended to earth. Dante had said as much when describing Beatrice who, as he put it, "seemed to be someone who had come to earth to show forth a miracle" [e par che sia una cosa venuta / da cielo in terra a miracol mostrare].[22] These are all standard images of sixteenth-century Petrarchism going back not only to Petrarch but also to Dante and the *dolcestilnovisti* poets of the late thirteenth century.

What is unusual, however, is that not only the beloved but the poet as well is a woman, thus turning these simple verses into a poem of affection by a woman for a woman.[23] Admittedly, were it not for the name of the author, the reader would not be able to identify the poet as female—the language is carefully constructed so as to avoid any gender-specific indicators for the poet. This leads the naive reader to assume that the usual male poet is lamenting because his usual female beloved is far away. The knowing reader, on the other hand, is aware that both the lover and the beloved are women and is thus made cognizant of same-sex desire expressed in terms and structures typical of contemporary Petrarchan poetry.

The same conceit of the Tiber's proud and haughty course, the image of the beautiful flowers, the distance of the beloved from the poet, recur in the other published poems by Laudomia Forteguerri. The sonnet "Felice pianta, in ciel tanto gradita" [Happy plant, so appreciated in heaven] reveals that the beloved is "my goddess, the Marguerite of Austria." In fact, editors have printed this sonnet with the indication of its dedicatee as its title.

A Madama Margherita d'Austria

Felice pianta, in ciel tanto gradita,
Ove ogni estremo suo natura pose,
Quando crear tanta beltà dispose,
Dico mia diva d'Austria Margherita.
So ben, che mai di ciel non fe' partita,
Ma per mostrarne le divine cose,
Scolpilla Dio, e di sua man compose
Questa a Lui tanto accetta, e favorita:
S'a noi fu largo Dio di tanto dono,
Di mostrarne la gloria del suo regno,

Non vi sdegnate a me mostrarla in parte.
    Et s'io del petto v'ho lasciato un pegno,
In cambio un vostro ritratto con arte
Mandate appresso, ove i miei occhi sono.

[To Madam Margaret of Austria

    Happy plant, so appreciated in heaven,
Where nature placed all its ultimate {standard}
When it began to create so much beauty,
I mean my goddess, the Marguerite of Austria.
    I know quite well she departed from heaven
Only to show us those things that are divine,
God sculpted her, and with his own hand composed
This woman so welcomed and favored by him.
    If God bestowed upon us such a great gift,
That would show us the glory of his kingdom,
Do not refuse to show her in part to me.
    If I have left you a token of my heart,
In exchange send here to me, where my eyes are,
A portrait of yourself most artfully done.]

The sonnet is addressed to the beloved herself, Margaret of Austria,
described in the opening words with the epithet "Happy plant," a pun
on her name—the marguerite, or daisy. The opening epithet is also a
subtle reference to "Felix Austria." The Emperor Charles V had decreed that his natural daughter be known as Margaret of Austria.
Forteguerri therefore may well have chosen to use the epithet "felix"
as applied to Austria for her own reference to a member of the House
of Austria. The double pun becomes obvious in line four, where the
beloved is called "the Marguerite of Austria." Margaret is a "happy
plant" not only because she is a flower that comes from "felix Austria"
but also because she is a gift from heaven. Using images drawn from
the Sweet New Style poets, Forteguerri again describes Margaret as a
heavenly being descended to earth to grant mortals a glimpse of divine glory. In the concluding tercet, Forteguerri uses a Petrarchan
motif, claiming that she has offered a token of her own heart—that is,
a poem expressing her love for Margaret—and now she asks in return
for a small portrait of the beloved on which to cast her eyes.

The other three sonnets addressed to Margaret are very similar to these in themes and images. The poem "Hor trionfante, & più che mai superba" [Now triumphant and proud as never before] describes how "ancient Rome" glories and how the banks of the Tiber are richly adorned with emeralds and rubies because "all the good that nature and heaven gave us"—that is, Margaret—is with them. If, on the other hand, the beloved were to remove herself from the eternal city and come to the poet in Siena, the flowers and grass of Rome would cease to be cheerful, while the poet and the Arbia (the river that runs next to Siena) would rejoice. In the sonnet "A che il tuo Febo, col mio Sol contende" [Why does your Phoebus contend with my Sun], Forteguerri tells "proud heaven" to hide its sun in the forest or under the sea while her own sun is about, for while the first can be obscured by a little cloud the second shines even brighter when obscured by clouds or fog—a reference to the distance that paradoxically obscures and makes the poet's beloved brighter still. Continuing with the image of the sun, the sonnet "Lasso, che 'l mio bel Sole i santi rai" [Alas, for my beautiful Sun the holy rays] is a lament occasioned by the fact that the beloved's distance prevents her from seeing her lover. The poet thus calls on "cruel Fortune," asking why the lover's body cannot go where the heart goes—that is, to the beloved. In the final tercets the poet asks Fortune to look favorably upon her request and grant her her wish—to be with her beloved. And here the poet makes it absolutely clear that both the beloved and the lover are women:

> Volgi lieta, & benigna homai la fronte
> A Me; che non è impresa gloriosa
> Abbattere una del femineo sesso.
> Odi le mie parole come pronte
> In supplicarti: ne voglio altra cosa,
> Salvo ch'a la mia Dea mi tenga appresso[24]

> [Turn your face now, considerate and happy,
> Towards me; for it is not a glorious deed
> To cut down someone of the feminine sex.
> Listen to my words, how they are ready
> To beseech you; for I want nothing else
> But that my Goddess keep me close to her.]

Though the images are clear, what is not clear is the depth of the emotion behind them or the extent of Laudomia's personal commitment to her affection for Margaret of Austria. While Michelangelo's poetry for the handsome Tommaso Cavalieri reveals his tortured attempts to sublimate the physical attraction he felt for the young man into a neoplatonic ascent to the divine through the admiration of the beloved's beauty,[25] no attempt at such a philosophical rationalization is evident in Laudomia's sonnets. If anything, her laments for the beloved's absence are unfettered declarations of simple affection expressed in thoroughly Petrarchan terms, elegantly calm and possibly playful or even contrived. No deep internal anguish is expressed, no need to resolve an emotional crux, no guilt, no sublimation. Compared to Michelangelo's, her articulation of same-sex love is quite relaxed. This may indicate either a lack of true love for Margaret or a personal balance that allowed her to deal well with her feelings. In short, her poems reveal no tension between desire and discipline, between her love for Margaret and the need to fulfil a social role or abide by society's standards.

Perhaps because of their non-tortured, non-challenging nature, Forteguerri's poems circulated openly and even found their way into anthologies published at that time. Contemporaries did not object to their expression of a same-sex love by a woman for a woman, possibly because such an expression was articulated along well-established poetic lines and voiced sentiments that within the Petrarchan tradition had by now become quite commonplace.

If we contextualize the five poems with what we know of Laudomia's life when she composed them, we find little to further our analysis. Assuming they were penned at the time of or shortly after Margaret's departure for Rome, we can date them to 1538–39. Laudomia was a young married woman then, twenty-three years old, a mother of two daughters, and soon to give birth to a son.[26] She was also starting to appear in the works of contemporary Sienese writers as a charming and intelligent woman who moved easily within the social and intellectual circles of Siena. She was, in other words, well known and well balanced, respected by her female friends and admired by her male contemporaries. There is no indication in any of the sources that her marriage was unhappy.

Such peacefulness was not, however, to be enjoyed by Margaret of Austria. The late 1530s were turbulent years for her. Although we do not know exactly what the fifteen-year-old duchess felt for her first husband, the womanizing twenty-seven-year-old Alessandro de'Medici, we do know that she very much liked Florence and, once widowed, wished to remain there, possibly even as wife to the attractive new eighteen-year-old duke, Cosimo I de'Medici.[27] That, however, was not to be, for her father, the emperor, was keen to use her for his political purposes by marrying her to the pope's thirteen-year-old grandson, Ottavio Farnese (b. 1524). Margaret plainly did not like the young boy or the idea of marrying him. She arrived in Rome on November 3, 1538, dressed in full mourning, and at her wedding the next day she spoke so faintly she could barely be heard. Later she would claim never to have pronounced the fateful "yes."[28] To make her point, for several years after the marriage she refused to consummate the union. On her father's orders she agreed to sleep in the same bed with her young husband, but would not allow him to have sex with her. Her stubborn refusal and her evident dislike for Ottavio were public knowledge. A letter of August 18, 1540, from Cardinal Marcello Cervini (the future Pope Marcellus II), reported: "When last they slept together [Margaret] did not wish to allow a union, saying that His Majesty [the Emperor Charles V, her father] had not asked her to do so, nor had she agreed to do so, but [that she had agreed] only that they should simply sleep together."[29]

This was, of course, fodder for Pasquino, the ancient Roman torso on which contemporary Romans posted their satirical poems. Many of these "Pasquinades" poked fun at Margaret and Ottavio's marital problems and advanced different reasons for Margaret's unwillingness to have sex with her husband, including the suggestions that she was a lesbian and that Ottavio, his father Pier Luigi, and his grandfather Pope Paul III were all incestuous sodomites.[30] Pasquino was on a roll, and the "recalcitrant mule," as the poems posted in his name were wont to call her, provided plenty of inspiration for these tirades against the pope and the Farnese clan.

Eventually Margaret did relent and consent. On June 7, 1543, the historian and biographer Paolo Giovio opened his letter to Nicola

Renzi and Girolamo Angleria with the enthusiastic news: "The hand-some duke Ottavio fucked in Pavia four times for the first time his Madama, and then he came here *ad sanctissimos pedes* [that is, to his grandfather, the pope], and thus he got rid of the bad reputation he had" [Il bel duca Ottavio chiavò in Pavia quatro volte la prima notte la sua Madama e poi è venuto qua *ad sanctissimos pedes,* e così s'è lev-ata la mala opinione qual si avea].[31] This happy union was not a one-time occurrence. The couple clearly had intercourse again for, in August 1545, Margaret finally gave birth to a set of twins, Carlo and Alessandro, named after their maternal grandfather Emperor Charles V and their paternal great-grandfather, Pope Paul III (Alessandro Far-nese). Having fulfilled her dynastic duty, Margaret soon went back to living without—and far away from—her husband, with whom she then maintained a cordial but distant relationship.

A recent scholar, Renato Lefevre, attributes Margaret's obstinacy against marrying Ottavio Farnese and consummating the marriage to her desire to remain in Florence and marry Duke Cosimo.[32] However, Margaret's obstinacy may also have been motivated by her lack of interest in Ottavio or in any husband. Lefevre admits as much when, trying to explain Margaret's apparent lack of interest in sex or in men, he manages to turn reality into a fine excuse for virtue: "Her womanly seriousness is out of the question. After all the noise she raised about her second marriage, not one of the many more or less scandalous rumors, so frequent at that time, touched her person. If anything, one could say the contrary about her: that she was or became prematurely deaf to physical love, that men were of no interest to her as such."[33]

Lefevre is not quite correct. The irrepressible Pasquinades, for one, had quite a lot to say about Margaret's sexual activities and, al-though their lewd comments are not to be taken seriously, the scan-dalous content does indicate a level and quality of criticism that is not to be completely discounted just because it is unpardonably vulgar. But Lefevre does discount it and rises above the mudsling-ing to defend Margaret's reputation as an honorable woman. In his view, her disinterest in sex reveals her disinterest in men, and this, he assumes, is a sign of a woman's honor. Lefevre seems to equate sex and men and disinterest in one with disinterest in the other. I am more inclined, however, to see Margaret's lack of interest in sex with men as a sign of her interest in an alternative, one that contemporary writers would not have been keen (or able) to identify publicly—sex with women.

Although Alessandro Piccolomini claimed and Agnolo Firenzuola repeated that Forteguerri loved Margaret of Austria, to my knowledge no contemporary writer suggested that Margaret herself loved Laudomia or any another woman, or that she had sex with them. None, that is, except for the gossipy Brantôme who, commenting precisely on Firenzuola's text from *On the Beauty of Women,* claimed outright that Margaret used Laudomia for her sexual gratification. In his "Discours sur les Dames qui font l'amour et leurs maris cocus" [Discourse on Ladies who make love and cuckold their husbands], Brantôme paraphrased the passage from Firenzuola (incorrectly, because he had Margaret love Laudomia, and not vice versa) and then added that his friend Louis-Bérenger Du Guast, who was reading the text with him, voiced his disbelief at the alleged purity of that love:

> Là dessus Monsieur de Gua reprit l'auteur, disant que cela estoit faux que cette belle Marguerite aymast cette belle Dame de pur et saint amour; car puisqu'elle l'avoir mise plustot sur elle que sur d'autres qui pouvoyent estre aussi belles et vertueuses qu'elle, il estoit à presumer que c'estoit pour s'en servir en delices, ne plus ne moins comme d'autres; et pour en couvrir sa lasciveté, elle disoit et publioit qu'elle l'aymoit saintement, ainsi que nous en voyons plusieurs ses semplables, qui ombragent leurs amours par pareils mots.
>
> Voilà ce qu'en disoit Monsieur du Gua; et qui en voudra outre plus en discourir là dessus, faire se peut.[34]

[At this point Monsieur Du Guast rebutted the author {Firenzuola} saying that it was false that this Margaret loved that beautiful lady purely and with holy love; because the fact that she had set her love on this, rather than on another woman just as beautiful and virtuous, led one to assume that she did so in order to use her for her pleasures, no more and no less than others; and in order to cover up her own lasciviousness, she said publicly that she loved her in a holy way, just as we see many like her who cover up their lustful loves with such words.

That's what Monsieur Du Guast said; and if anyone wishes to
continue the discussion on this subject, one can do so.]

Through the words of Du Guast, Brantôme cast doubts on the
purity of the affection that bound Margaret and Laudomia, and he
lets it be known that he is prepared to speak further on this point.
His aspersions, however, must not be given too much credence. First
of all, Du Guast's diatribe is most likely an attempt to discredit
Firenzuola's suggestion that women are capable of pure love—that
is, of contemplating beauty spiritually. Although current neoplatonic thinking on the subject accepted that this might be true in
theory (as Firenzuola's use of Aristophanes' myth of the androgyne
from Plato's *Symposium* indicates), it did not actually believe that
such pure love on the part of women was possible in practice. The
Aristotelian discourse that equated men with the spiritual and
women with the corporeal, or men with strength and women with
weakness, was simply too ingrained in the mentality of the times for
people to be able to accept fully the possibility that women were as
capable as men of contemplating beauty. Their innate weakness, a
sixteenth-century Aristotelian would argue, would inevitably lead
them to fall from the spiritual into the corporeal.[35] Du Guast's refusal to accept Firenzuola's statement thus reveals his disbelief that
women can love chastely and spiritually.

There are further hidden agendas in Brantôme's words. For one,
his "Discours" clearly had a point to make—that women can cuckold their husbands even without the assistance of a man. Given
Branôme's premise, Margaret's love for Laudomia had to be presented as a physical, sexual love in order to provide the author with
the evidence he required. Furthermore, his unilateral reversal of the
direction of love (from Laudomia for Margaret to Margaret for Laudomia) and his use of this reversal to suggest an abuse of power on
Margaret's part reveal a rather nonchalant attitude to precision. This,
in turn, raises questions about his intentions. One wonders whether
the French writer may not have been voicing an anti-Spanish or
anti-Hapsburg bias that sought to discredit the House of Austria,
bitter rival of the Valois, by slandering one of its scions. Or perhaps
Brantôme was just envisioning the relationship within a neoplatonic

understanding of sexual roles, one that saw the socially superior partner (the "older man") as the lover and the inferior partner (the "young boy") as the beloved. According to this view, Margaret, the emperor's daughter, had to be the active partner while Laudomia, the Sienese noblewoman, had to be the passive one. In neoplatonism it would be inconceivable for the socially superior person to be the object of desire—though, ironically, this was exactly the case in Petrarchism and in poetic tradition as far back as the troubadours. Last, one should note that the "Discours" was composed at least forty years after the supposed relationship between Laudomia and Margaret was said to have blossomed, and in the intervening time hardly anyone had mentioned it.

In fact, Forteguerri's affection for the emperor's daughter was not common tender among contemporary writers. Although Alessandro Piccolomini and his publisher Marc'Antonio da Carpi made much of it in 1540 and Agnolo Firenzuola reported it in his 1541 dialogue, no other writers even mentioned it. When they did refer to Forteguerri, it was for completely different reasons.

The first to mention Laudomia Forteguerri in one of his works was the Sienese intellectual Marc'Antonio Piccolomini (1505–1579), a cousin of Alessandro. His dialogue, "Whether one is to believe that a woman perfect in all her parts, both physical and spiritual, that one might wish for, is produced by Nature by chance or by design," recounts a conversation between Laudomia Forteguerri and Girolama Carli de' Piccolomini held on November 1, 1537.[36] Although the topic may appear frivolous and innocuous, in reality it gave the discussants the dangerous opportunity of entering into the theological arena.[37] And so, Girolama Piccolomini, while adhering to a neoplatonic affirmation of free will, affirmed the providential aspect of a Nature that is guided towards perfection by the Prime Mover; Laudomia, on the other hand, presented a solidly Aristotelian argument grounded in determinism and firmly supporting predestination. These were dangerous ideas in 1537–38, especially in dogmatically turbulent Siena, home to fervent discussions on theology and to future reformers and heretics such as the Socini brothers, Bernardino Ochino, and Aonio Paleario.

Laudomia's second appearance in literary circles took place the following year, in 1539, when Marc'Antonio's cousin, Alessandro Piccolomini, dedicated to her his absolutely scurrilous dialogue, *La Raffaella, or On the Fair Perfectioning of Ladies.* Under the guise of an old woman teaching a young woman all she knew about men and sex, the thirty-one-year-old Alessandro argued in favor of adultery, saying that young wives, especially if married to older men, should all have secret lovers to keep them sexually satisfied. Forteguerri was thus once again associated with a disreputable text, this time not dogmatically dangerous but sexually risqué.

In 1540, the year following this dialogue, Alessandro dedicated to Laudomia a compendium of astronomical information, *De la sfera del mondo.* Its dedicatory letter paints the twenty-five-year-old mother of three in a much more respectable and honorable light. It also gives us detail about Laudomia's interests and activities that is well worth examining closely for the insight it offers into her personality and interests.

It is August 1539, and Alessandro writes from his villa outside Padua, where he is a student at the university, saying he has heard that the previous springtime Laudomia had spent a sunny afternoon chatting with other noblewomen in her garden in Siena. They had formed a circle in the shade of a laurel tree and had engaged in "beautiful and most learned and philological discourses." Turning eventually to "things divine," they had talked of the beauty and splendor of heavenly bodies, their marvelous order, and other similar matters. At this point Laudomia lamented she had been born a woman, for had she been born a man, she would have dedicated herself "to some precious study and honored science." What most pained her was "that she had not been able to feast her spirit on matters of Astrology, to which she felt inclined more than to any other science." Wishing to alleviate Laudomia's pain and at the same time assist her in learning more about the heavenly bodies, Alessandro gathered astronomical information from a variety of scientific sources and placed it at her disposal in this volume, which, as he explained, he composed in Italian so that she might understand it fully. He then claims he was inspired to do this also by the knowledge that Laudomia was well versed in Dante's *Divine Comedy* and that in the past she had publicly commented on some cantos of the *Paradiso* "so subtly that [he] marvelled at it every time [he] thought of it." A compendium of astronomical information, he suggests, would help her in her study of Dante's *Paradiso*. Piccolomini concludes the letter with the usual praises and salutations, and dates it August 10, 1539, at his villa in Valzanzibio.[38]

Though admittedly still a male writer's construct, the Laudomia depicted in this preface is quite unlike the women of contemporary Italian literature. She is not the Boccaccesque beauty who delights her male and female companions in pleasant gardens by telling them fictional stories. Nor is she Castiglione's courtly lady, who entertains the men of the court by singing or dancing for them, or by asking questions that will allow them to stay up all night expounding their views. Instead, without the help of men around her, Laudomia engages her female companions in discussions on the very nature and physical movement of the heavenly bodies. We note that her interest in the heavens is not at all mythological (that is, in the sense of the stars as echoes of Greco-Roman myths), nor is it astrological (in the sense of the stars as indicators of future events). It is, rather, thoroughly scientific (the nature and movements of the stars). In the same vein, Laudomia's interest in the heavens has nothing to do with the Christian heaven of salvation and beatitude but everything to do with the workings of the physical cosmos—the universe as a mechanical system that can be studied scientifically. Her interest in Dante's epic poem is focused on the *Paradiso*—that is, on the one canticle that is set in the scientifically "real" cosmos of contemporary science. Finally, her lament for having been born a woman is not phrased in the usual terms of subservience to men, but in terms of lack of opportunity as a woman to pursue scientific studies.

In Piccolomini's dedicatory letter, then, Laudomia Forteguerri is at first depicted as the usual beautiful woman, most gentle and most noble, spending a sunny afternoon in a garden in the company of other ladies. Soon, however, this stereotype of Italian narrative and poetic tradition is broken and Laudomia is presented as a self-assured woman with unusual interests and exceptional intellectual abilities. If this is even an approximate portrait of Laudomia Forteguerri, one can appreciate why she would have been depicted by Marc'Antonio Piccolomini as a figure with heterodox views; or why his cousin Alessandro would choose her as the dedicatee of a dialogue that expressed unbridled and unbounded feminine sexuality; or why Agnolo Firenzuola would have seen in her poetry of affection for Margaret of Austria a suitable example of a neoplatonic attraction between two people of the same sex.

Not everybody, however, was impressed by Laudomia. Paolo Giovio thought she was rather fatuous. In a lighthearted letter from Poggibonsi addressed to cardinal Alessandro Farnese (grandson of Pope Paul III and brother of Ottavio Farnese), he lamented that the prelate's retinue had been left idle and without orders while the cardinal himself lingered in Siena "occupied in the cogitations, not to say the deflation of underpants, of the Forteguerri woman" [Noi andaremo a madonna la ventura, poi che V.S. R.ma, occupata nella cogitazione per non dire sgonfiatura di brachesse della Fortiguerra, si scorda di darci avviso della partenza nostra].[39] Given the tone of the letter, his assessment of Laudomia is not necessarily to be taken seriously.

What is to be taken seriously, instead, is the manner in which Laudomia Forteguerri was depicted. The men of her time presented her as a woman outside the norm—dogmatically suspect, sexually liberated, intellectually curious. Her few surviving sonnets reveal instead a culturally well-versed woman who expressed her love for another woman in the calm language and well-worn images of traditional Petrarchan poetry. They also suggest that she was not at all troubled by her same-sex feelings. In fact, she seems emotionally rather well adjusted. In the end, one is left wishing for more information about her and wondering where all her letters to Margaret of Austria could have gone. If they ever existed and were now to be found, these letters would shed enormous light on the nature and depth of the affection that bound two mid-sixteenth-century women.

Appendix

THE SONNETS OF LAUDOMIA FORTEGUERRI

Edited and Translated by Konrad Eisenbichler

A Madama Margherita d'Austria

Felice pianta, in ciel tanto gradita,
Ove ogni estremo suo natura pose,
Quando crear tanta beltà dispose,

Dico mia diva d'Austria Margherita.

So ben che mai di ciel non fe' partita,

Ma per mostrarne le divine cose,
Scolpilla Dio e di sua man compose

Questa a Lui tanto accetta e favorita:

S'a noi fu largo Dio di tanto dono,

Di mostrarne la gloria del suo regno,

Non vi sdegnate a me mostrarla in
     parte.
     E s'io del petto v'ho lasciato un
     pegno,
In cambio un vostro ritratto con arte
Mandate appresso, ove i miei occhi
     sono.

Or trionfante e più che mai superba

Sen va l'antica Roma, che possiede
Tutto 'l ben che natura e il ciel ne
     diede:
Essa in se lo raccoglie e lo riserba.
     Ma s'a me fosse dolce e a te acerba

La mia nimica, che m'ha sotto il piede,
Te lo togliesse e me ne fesse erede,
Più non ti riderian fioretti e l'erba.

To Madam Margaret of Austria

Happy plant, so cherished in heaven,
Where nature placed all its ultimates
When it set out to create so much
     beauty,
I speak of my goddess Marguerite of
     Austria.
     I know well that she departed from
     heaven
Only in order to show us divine things,
God sculpted her and with his own
     hand crafted
This woman so beloved by him and
     favoured:
     If God was so generous to us with his
     gift,
With showing us the glory of his king-
     dom,
Do not disdain to show her somehow
     to me.
     And if I have left you a token of my
     heart,
In return send a portrait of yourself
Skilfully made here to me, where my
     eyes are.

     Triumphant now and more than ever
     proud,
Ancient Rome proceeds along, possessing
All the good Nature and Heaven gave
     us:
She gathers it to herself and keeps it.
     But were my foe, who keeps me
     underfoot,
To be kind to me and bitter to you,
To take it from you and grant it to me,
Your flowers and grass would cease to
     smile for you.

Non sarien piu di smeraldi e rubini
Le ricche sponde del gran Tebro ornate:

Pur l'Arbia s'orneria la fronte e 'l seno.

Più non avresti gli esempi divini:

Ne godresti l'angelica beltate:

Se questo avvien, son pur felice appieno.

Ora ten' vai superbo, or corri altiero

Pingendo di bei fiori ambe le sponde

Antico Tebro; or ben purgate l'onde

Rendon l'imago a un sol più chiaro e vero:
Ora porti lo scettro, ora hai l'impero

Dei più famosi: or averai tu donde

Verdeggian più che mai liete e feconde

Le belle rive: or hai l'essere intero,

Poi ch'egli è teco il vago almo mio sole,
Non or lungi, or vicin, ma sempre appresso;
E bagni il lembo dell'altiera gonna:

Ch'arte, natura, e 'l ciel, e così vuole

Che 'l tutto può, mostran pur oggi espresso
Che star ben pote al mondo immortal donna.

A che il tuo Febo col mio Sol contende,
Superbo ciel, se il primo onor gli ha tolto?

No longer with emeralds and rubies
Would the rich banks of the Tiber be dressed:

For Arbia would have them on her brow and breast.

You would no longer have divine examples,

Nor would angelic beauty then delight you.

Were this to happen, I would be full of joy.

Now you go proudly, now you run haughtily

Colouring both your riverbanks with flowers

Ancient Tiber; now well purged your waves reflect

The image of a brighter and truer sun:

Now you hold the sceptre, now you command

Over more famous ones: now you have what makes

Your beautiful banks more verdantly happy

And fecund; now you are completely fulfilled,

For my fair and spotless sun is now with you,

Not distant now, nor near, but always next to you;

And you flow past the hem of that noble gown:

For art, nature and heaven wish it, and He

Who can do all—today they clearly show that

An immortal woman can dwell in this world.

Why does your Phoebus contest with my sun,

Proud heaven, if it has stolen its first glory?

Torni fra selve o stia nel mar sepolto
Mentre con più bei raggi il mio risplende.
  Picciola nube tua gran luce offende;

E poca nebbia oscura il suo bel volto:
Il mio fra nubi (ahi lassa) e nebbie av-
  volto
Più gran chiarezza e maggior lume rende.
  Quando il tuo porta fuor de l'onde il
  giorno,
Se non squarciasse il vel, che l'aria
  adombra,
Non faria di sua vista il mondo adorno.

  Il mio non toglie il vel né l'aria
  sgombra;
Ma somigliando a se ciò c'ha d'intorno

Fiammeggiar fa le nubi e splender
  l'ombra.

  Lasso, che 'l mio bel Sole i santi rai
Ver me non volgerà: dunque debb'io
Viver senza il mio ben? Non piaccia a
  Dio
Che senza questo io viva in terra mai.

  Ahi fortuna crudel, perché non fai

Che vada il corpo dove va il cor mio?
Perché mi tieni in questo stato rio

Senza speme d'uscire unqua di guai?

  Volgi lieta e benigna omai la fronte

A me; ché non è impresa gloriosa
Abbattere una del femineo sesso.

  Odi le mie parole come pronte
In supplicarti: né voglio altra cosa,
Salvo ch'a la mia Dea mi tenga ap-
  presso.

Let it go back in the woods or stay buried
In the sea while mine shines bright
  with finer rays.
  A little cloud can injure your great
  light,
A little fog obscures its lovely face,
But mine, in clouds (alas) and wrapped
  in fogs,
Shines with more brightness and with
  greater light.
  When yours brings forth the day out
  from the waves,
Unless it tear the veil that dims the air

It does not grace the world with its appearance.
  Mine does not part the veil or clear
  the air,
But, turning what surrounds it to its
  image,
It makes the clouds burn bright and
  darkness shine.

  Alas, for my beautiful Sun will not turn
Its holy rays towards me: must I therefore
Live without my treasure? May it not
  please God
That I should ever live on earth with-
  out it.
  Ah, cruel fortune, why do you not
  arrange it
For my body to go where my heart goes?
Why do you keep me in this wretched
  state
With no hope ever that my woes will
  end?
  Turn, at last, happy and benign, your
  face
Towards me; for it is not a glorious deed
To cut down someone of the feminine
  sex.
  Listen to my words, how they are ready
To beseech you; for I want nothing else
But that you keep me close to my God-
  dess.

Alla Signora Alda Torella Lunata.

Il maggior don che Dio e la natura

Donasse a noi mortal per abbellire
Il mondo e farlo d'ogni ben gioire
É de la signora Alda la fattura.
    Chi può veder l'angelica figura,
Beato essere in tutto può ben dire:
Chi può le saggie sue parole udire,
Null'altro mai che Lei sentir procura.
    Deh perché a me non è tanto concesso
Da la mia sorte ria, dal fier destino,
Ch'io veder possa l'angelico volto?
    Non sia che vuole, io pur nel petto impresso
Porto per relation quel suo divino

Aspetto: e questo mai non mi sia tolto.

To the Signora Alda Torella Lunata

The greatest gift that God and Nature gave
To us on earth to beautify the world
And let us find delight in what is good
Is the shape and form of Signora Alda.
    Whoever her angelic figure sees
Can truly say he has been richly blessed;
Whoever her judicious words can hear,
Seeks nothing else but to listen to her.
    Alas, why am I not allowed this much
By cruel destiny, by my evil fate,
That I may look on this angelic face?
    It will not let me, yet in my heart I hold
Her divine appearance as described to me:
And this will never be taken from me.

Notes

1. Agnolo Firenzuola, *On the Beauty of Women,* trans. Konrad Eisenbichler and Jacqueline Murray (Philadelphia: University of Pennsylvania Press, 1992), p. 17. Written in 1541, the dialogue was published posthumously in 1548. The platonic myth of the androgyne is expressed by Aristophanes in Plato's *Symposium,* 189b–193a.

2. I use the term "lesbian" as a convenient short form to indicate those women whose primary emotional and/or sexual focus was placed on other women, without at all implying that the construction of same-sex desire has remained unchanged through time.

3. See Jacqueline Murray "Twice Marginal and Twice Invisible: Lesbians in the Middle Ages," in *Handbook of Medieval Sexuality,* ed. Vern L. Bullough and James A. Brundage (New York: Garland, 1996), pp. 191–222 and, idem, "Agnolo Firenzuola on Female Sexuality and Women's Equality," *Sixteenth Century Journal* 22:2 (1991): 208–209.

4. Dante made a similar distinction when he placed some homosexuals in hell (*Inf.* XVI) and others in purgatory (*Purg.* XXVI), thus indicating that same-sex male attraction was not *per se* damnable.

5. For a fuller discussion and a bibliography, see Firenzuola, *On the Beauty of Women,* pp. xiii-xlvii; Murray, "Agnolo Firenzuola," 199–213.

6. Firenzuola, *On the Beauty of Women,* p. 17.

7. Murray, "Twice Marginal," p. 203.

8. Firenzuola, *On the Beauty of Women,* pp. 16–17.

9. *Descriptio Urbis: The Roman Census of 1527,* ed. Egmont Lee (Rome: Bulzoni, 1985), entries no. 2262 and 3325.

10. Francisco Delicato, attrib., *Ragionamento del Zoppino fatto frate, e Lodovico, puttaniere, dove contiensi la vita e genealogia di tutte le Cortigiane di Roma* (Milan: Longanesi & C., 1969), p. 44. Unless otherwise indicated, all translations in this article are mine.

11. Brantôme, *Recueil des Dames, poésies et tombeaux,* ed. Etienne Vaucheret (Paris: Gallimard, 1991), p. 362.

12. Brantôme, *Recueil des Dames,* p. 364. As Jacqueline Murray points out, "The association of courtesans with lesbian sexual preference can be traced to Antiquity." She gives several references for this association in her "Agnolo Firenzuola," 210 n. 42.

13. For Alessandro Piccolomini's poetry, see his *Cento sonetti,* ed. Giordano Ziletti (Rome: V. Valgrisi, 1549). For Giuseppe Betussi, see his *Le imagini del tempio della Signora Giovanna Aragona* (In Fiorenza: Lorenzo Torrentino, 1556), pp. 75–80. For Forteguerri's actions before and during the siege, see Marco Guazzo, *Cronica di M. Marco Guazzo* (In Venetia: Appresso Francesco Bindoni, 1553), fol. 443v; Blaise De Monluc, *Commentaires,* ed. Paul Courteault (Paris: Librairie Alphonse Picard et fils, 1913), pp. 106–107; and Florindo Cerreta, *Alessandro Piccolomini letterato e filosofo senese del Cinquecento* (Siena: Accademia Senese degli Intronati, 1960), p. 31 n. 18. I am currently preparing a monograph study on Laudomia Forteguerri tentatively titled *Constructions of a Woman. Laudomia Forteguerri (1515–1555),* in which I will provide more extensive biographical information on Forteguerri and examine how various writers, scholars, and artists from the 1530s to the present have depicted her.

14. Ludwig Pastor, *The History of the Popes from the Close of the Middle Ages* (London: Routledge and Kegan Paul, 1950), 12:52. For physical descriptions of Margaret, see S. A. Van Lennep, *Les années italiennes de Marguerite d'Autriche, duchesse de Parma* (Geneva: Editions Labor et Fides, [1952]), p. 30; *Giornata di studi margaritiani,* ed. Paolo Brezzi (Penne: Cassa Rurale ed Artigiana di Castiglione Messer Raimondo, 1989),pp. 17–18.

15. *Lettura del S. Alessandro Piccolomini Infiammato fatta nell'Accademia degli Infiammati, M.D.XXXXI* (Bologna: Bartholomeo Bonardo e

Marc'Antonio da Carpi, 1541). Forteguerri's sonnet was published again in *Rime diverse di molti eccellentiss. auttori nuovamente raccolte,* ed. Lodovico Domenichi (Vinetia: Appresso Gabriel Giolito di Ferrarii, 1546), p. 246 and in its 1549 reedition, and then in *Rime diverse d'alcune nobilissime, et virtuosissime donne,* ed. Lodovico Domenichi (Lucca: Per Vincenzo Busdragho, 1559), p. 102, this time with five other poems by Forteguerri (102–104). These same six poems were later included in *Rime di cinquanta illustri poetesse,* ed. Antonio Bulifon (In Napoli: Presso Antonio Bulifon, 1695), pp. 94–96 and in *Sonetti di Madonna Laudomia Forteguerri Poetessa senese del secolo XVI,* ed. Alessandro Lisini (Siena: Sordomuti, 1901), pp. 17–20.

16. Piccolomini, *Lettura,* unnumb. page.
17. Piccolomini, *Lettura,* unnumb. page. I have been unable to locate any of the "notes" that Piccolomini claims the two women exchanged.
18. Piccolomini, *Lettura,* unnumb. page.
19. Piccolomini, *Lettura,* unnumb. page.
20. Piccolomini, *Lettura,* unnumb. page.
21. The sixth sonnet is written to and in praise of Alda Torella Lunata from Pavia, herself also a poet. It is a simple poem of admiration and is not particularly noteworthy for our discussion. Betussi presented Lunata in his *Le imagini del tempio della Signora Giovanna Aragona,* pp. 63–66, as the emblem of chastity. Three of Lunata's poems appeared in *Rime diverse d'alcune nobilissime, et virtuosissime donne,* pp. 236–37.
22. Lines 7–8 of the sonnet "Tanto gentile e tanto onesta pare" in Dante, *Vita nuova,* ed. Luigi Pietrobono (Florence: G. C. Sansoni, 1968), p. 97.
23. Although there is an earlier example of this in France in the poetry of the woman troubadour Bieiris de Romans, I am not aware of similar cases in Italy.
24. *Rime diverse d'alcune nobilissime, et virtuosissime donne,* p. 104. The previous sonnets are on pp. 102–104.
25. Konrad Eisenbichler, "The Religious Poetry of Michelangelo: The Mystical Sublimation," *Renaissance and Reformation* 23.1 (1987): 123–36; reprinted in *Michelangelo: Selected Scholarship in English,* ed. William E. Wallace (New York: Garland, 1995), 5:123–36.
26. Olimpia Antonia (1535), Antonia Maria (1537), and Alessandro (1539); Archivio di Stato di Siena, Biccherna 1135 (olim 1035), ff. 348v, 379v, 419r.
27. Van Lennep, *Les années italiennes de Marguerite d'Autriche,* pp. 66–67; Pastor, *History of the Popes,* 11:324.

28. Pastor, *History of the Popes,* 11:325.

29. Vatican Archives, Fondo Borghese, ser. I, 36 f. 119v, letter of August 18, 1540, cited in van Lennep, *Les années italiennes de Marguerite d'Autriche,* p. 145 n. 34. See also Renato Lefevre, "La figura di Margarita d'Austria duchessa di Parma e Piacenza," *Aurea Parma* 52:3 (1968): 161–62; Pastor, *History of the Popes,* 11:325–26.

30. *Pasquinate romane del Cinquecento,* ed. Valerio Marucci et al., 2 vols. (Rome: Salerno Editrice, 1983), especially poems 439, 443, 448, 449, 450, 451, 463, 471, 476, 481, 491, 496, 507, 511, 514, 515, 527, 539, 541, 546, and 613.

31. Paolo Giovio, *Lettere,* ed. Giuseppe Guido Ferrero (Rome: Istituto Poligrafico dello Stato, 1956), 1:312. Others claimed the consummation took place earlier, some in 1539, others 1540; see Pastor, *History of the Popes,* 3:326 n. 2.

32. Lefevre, "La figura di Margarita d'Austria," 161.

33. Ibid., 164. This is not, however, what the scurrilous Pasquino was saying at the time; see note 30 above for references to the Pasquinades touching on Margaret's sex life.

34. Brantôme, *Recueil des Dames,* pp. 369–70.

35. For a discussion of this point with reference to Firenzuola's words and for further references on this topic, see Murray, "Agnolo Firenzuola," pp. 203–207.

36. The work was first published as an appendix in Rita Belladonna, "Gli Intronati, le donne, Aonio Paleario e Agostino Museo in un dialogo inedito di Marcantonio Piccolomini il Sodo Intronato (1538)," *Bullettino senese di storia patria* 99 (1992): 59–90.

37. Ibid., 53.

38. Alessandro Piccolomini, *De la sfera del mondo. Libri quattro . . . De le stelle fisse. Libro uno* (Venice: Al Segno del Pozzo, 1540), unnumbered pages.

39. Giovio, *Lettere,* 1:268. The letter is dated September 4, 1541. The sentence is quite hermetic and clearly rich both in sexual innuendoes and vulgar humor.

INDEX

This index combines concepts and proper names. The latter include scholars whose work is discussed in the text or that focuses on gender and sexuality. For full references to the vast body of work in women's studies and medieval studies, please refer to individual essays.

239, 240, 246, 278; hand, 203–204, 206,
210; head, 17; labia, 129–31, 188–89,
192; mouth 17, 218; penis, 59, 129–32,
185–86, 215, 218–19; testicles, 110, 220;
thigh, 129–31, 183, 193; tongue, 193;
tooth, 41n.60; vagina, 192; vulva, 30,
46n.100, 130–131, 185–186, 189, 193,
245, 246–247; womb, 67, 252.
Bonnet, Marie-Jo, 11, 38n.31, 117n.4,
119n.15
Boswell, John, 6, 20, 25, 43n.75, 44n.87, 63,
77n.45, 78n.61, 79n.63, n.67, 118n.6,
145, 119n.13, 120n.25, 121n.38,
171n.26, 195n.8, 267n.6
Bouchet, Guillaume, 220
Boudhiba, Abdelwahab, 137n.4
Brahman (and purity), 247
Brantôme, 11, 25, 118n.5, 281, 292–93
bride, 236, of Christ, 86, 95, 96, 97
bridegroom, 236; Christ as bridegroom,
85–87, 91, 95, 97
Brooten, Bernadette, 11, 38n.30, 41n.57,
43n.77, 76n.41, 105, 119n.14, n.15,
144–145, 168n.4, 245, 250n.15, n.16,
253, 258, 262, 268n.9
Brown, Judith, 25, 58, 60, 76n.41, 77n.48,
117n.4, 118n.5, 252, 267n.5, 273n.46
Brundage, James, 38n.37, 75n.38, 76n.41,
107, 118n.6, 119nn.19–21, 120n.22,
n.23, n.27, 168n.3, 169n.19, 195n.9,
267n.3, 301n.3
Bullough, Vern L., 75n.38, 76n.41, 118n.6,
n.9, 119n.12, 120n.30, 168n.3, 195n.9,
267n.3; and Bonnie Bullough, 231n.89,
301n.3
Burchard of Worms, 119n.16, 169n.19,
Decretum 147, 148, 149; *Corrector et
medicus,* 147–148
Burger, Glenn, 38n.28, 226n.42
Burns, E. J., 14, 36n.20. 39n.43, 42n.66,
175n.61, 222n.5, 223n.8, 230n.73
Burshatin, Israël, 2, 34n.1, 267n.4
Butler, Judith, 1–16, 18, 34, 41n.53, n.64,
47n.109, 166, 177n.77, 201, 212, 218,
230n.81
Byzantium, 88

Cadden, Joan, 8, 36n.19, 42n.66, 68,
81n.83, 82n.84, 111, 112, 121n.41
Caesarius of Arles, *Testamentum,* 90
Camille, Michael, 34n.2, 162–163, 176n.67,
nn.70–72
Campbell, Mary Anne, 83n.94
Carlini, Benedetta, 25, 102
Carozzi, Claude 147, 168n.12
Carrillo, Doña María García, 259–61

Castle, Terry, 87, 98n.5
Catalina of Lancaster (queen-regent),
254–266
Cathars, 108, 120n.29
Cecilia Venetiana, 277, 280–281
Celestina, 251–253, 266, 269n.12
celibacy, 14
Chansons de geste, 24, 44n.86, 199–232
passim
Chauncey, George, Jr., 5, 35n.8
Chebel, Malek, 137n.4, 138n.8
Chiffoleau, Jacques, 274n.58
Christ, 18, 29–30, 62, 65–67, 93, 04, 95, 97,
152; feminization of, 46n.100, 64–65,
67, 258. *See also* wound
Christine de Pizan, 31, 38n.28, 201, 213,
215; *City of Ladies,* 213
Church, 14, 32, 53, 55, 102, 103, 149, 151,
152, 153, 156, 165, 172n.43; Eastern 10;
Ecclesia, 65–66, 68
Cicero, *De amicitia,* 63, 64
Cino de Pistoia, 110
Cistercians, 63, 78n.56, 147
Clark, Robert L. A, 119n.18, 183, 196n.18,
198n.41, 203, 222n.6, 223n.17, 225n.25,
231n.86, n.87, 143–78
Classical period, 6, 11, 20, 64, 115, 157, 278
Clement of Alexandria, 16
Cloke, Gillian, 80n.74
closet/s, 76n.39, 266
Clover, Carol J., 36n.21
Cohen, Jeffrey Jerome, 39n.37
Comnena Anna, 220
confessor's manuals, 56–58, 59, 75n.36
constructionism 5–6, 102–103, 145, 200,
201, 203, 213, 235, 237, 253
Corti, Maria 146, 148, 168n.5, n.10,
172n.36
Court Cases, 102, 112–114, 115, 280
Cranach, Lucas, the Elder, *ill.,* 32–34
Crane, Susan, 37n.24, 221n.1
Crompton, Louis, 43n.80, 101–102, 112,
117n.1, n.2, 119n.17, 120n.37, 173n.51
cross-dressing 8, 19, 19, 36n.18, 80n.74,
117n.4, 161, 167n.2, 203, 211–212, 214,
217, 228n.50, 235, 268n.8

dance, 2–3
Dante Alighieri, 283, 284, 286, 296,
301n.4
daughter and mother, metaphor, 29, 51, 52,
61–62, 78n.56, 92, 94, 97, 203, 239, 242,
258, 266. *See also* mother
Dekker, Rudolf M. and Lotte C. van de
Pol, 122n.52
De Lauretis, Teresa, 208, 229n.54, 230n.75